Secular Muslim Feminism

Secular Muslim Feminism

An Alternative Voice in the War of Ideas

Hind Elhinnawy

I.B. TAURIS
LONDON • NEW YORK • OXFORD • NEW DELHI • SYDNEY

I.B. TAURIS
Bloomsbury Publishing Plc
50 Bedford Square, London, WC1B 3DP, UK
1385 Broadway, New York, NY 10018, USA
29 Earlsfort Terrace, Dublin 2, Ireland

BLOOMSBURY, I.B. TAURIS and the I.B. Tauris logo are trademarks of
Bloomsbury Publishing Plc

First published in Great Britain 2025

Copyright © Hind Elhinnawy, 2025

Hind Elhinnawy has asserted her rights under the Copyright, Designs and Patents Act, 1988, to be identified as Author of this work.

For legal purposes the Acknowledgments on pp. xx–xxi constitute an extension of this copyright page.

Cover design: Adriana Brioso

All rights reserved. No part of this publication may be reproduced or transmitted in any form or by any means, electronic or mechanical, including photocopying, recording, or any information storage or retrieval system, without prior permission in writing from the publishers.

Bloomsbury Publishing Plc does not have any control over, or responsibility for, any third-party websites referred to or in this book. All internet addresses given in this book were correct at the time of going to press. The author and publisher regret any inconvenience caused if addresses have changed or sites have ceased to exist, but can accept no responsibility for any such changes.

A catalogue record for this book is available from the British Library.

Library of Congress Control Number: 2024943994

ISBN: HB: 978-0-7556-4930-3
PB: 978-0-7556-4934-1
ePDF: 978-0-7556-4931-0
eBook: 978-0-7556-4932-7

Typeset by Newgen KnowledgeWorks Pvt. Ltd., Chennai, India
Printed and bound in Great Britain

To find out more about our authors and books visit www.bloomsbury.com
and sign up for our newsletters.

For Leena,
My love, my life, and the light in my eyes

Contents

Preface	ix
Acknowledgments	xx
Note on Text/Transliteration	xxii
List of Abbreviations	xxiii

1. **Introduction** — 1
   - Situating Secular Muslim Feminism — 2
   - Unpacking "Secular"–"Muslim"–"Feminism" — 7
   - The Power and Pitfalls of Terminology — 11
   - Navigating Methodological Challenges — 15
   - The Organizing of the Book — 18

2. **Demystifying Secular Muslim Feminism** — 21
   - Don't Label Me! — 22
   - Which "Muslim Woman"? — 26
   - Which "Feminism"? — 29
   - And Whose "Islam"? — 35
   - A "Secular" Champion of Religious Freedom — 38
   - Challenging Multiple Fronts — 43
   - Emerging Counternarratives? — 47

3. **Islam, Feminism, and Secular Resistance** — 49
   - Early Feminist Consciousness — 51
   - Muslim Women's Scholarship — 54
   - Muslim Women's Activism — 60
   - Between the Religious and the Secular — 74

4. **The Politics of "Saving" the Muslim Women** — 77
   - Orientalism Then and Now — 78
   - Orientalism, Gender, and Empire — 81
   - In the Crossfires of Change — 85
   - The Unresolved Legacies of Colonialism — 89

	Mapping Feminist Responses	94
	Navigating the Path Ahead	98
5.	Beyond Resistance versus Subservience	103
	Theorizing "Agency"	105
	"Piety" and the "Agency" Turn	107
	The Limits of Pietist "Agency"	112
	Beyond Faith and Agency	118
6.	Islam, Secularism, and the Woman's Question	123
	Secularism in a Post-secular Age	125
	Secularism Confronts Islam	130
	The "Muslim" Woman's Question	133
	Secularism in the Muslim World	139
	Beyond Western Conceptualizations	143
	Reimagining Secularism	148
7.	Can the Secular Muslim Feminist Speak?	151
	Silenced Voices in Their Homelands	153
	Dismissed by the International Community	158
	The "Native Informant" Conundrum	160
	The Impasse of Apologism	163
	The Limits of Relativism (and) Universalism	167
	Solidarity across Difference Is Possible!	172

Concluding Remarks	179
Notes	185
Glossary	219
Index	255

Preface

Locating My Voice, Deconstructing the Narrative

As academics, we are often expected "to write ourselves out of the story we are telling."[1] Living by this expectation, on many occasions, I felt the urge to edit myself out (write myself out) of this preface to avoid any critical evaluations of its contents. But the more I thought about it, the more it made sense to include it. I see immense value in articulating the position that I take as an academic and a scholar, a position that shapes not only this work but also the myriad scholarly discussions I have engaged in and anticipate engaging in in the future. I am Egyptian, born and raised solely in Egypt, except for a few years of childhood spent in London with my Egyptian parents. Even though my roots are deeply entrenched in the sands of Egypt, I find myself most at ease using English within my home's privacy and in the public sphere. I identify as an atheist, but I regard Islam as my culture.[2] As a scholar and academic born and raised in a Middle Eastern Muslim country, now living and working in a western country, speaking and writing about 'Muslim' women, a subject charged with misinterpretations and complex nuances, I am placed at the intersection of multiple cultural narratives. This often leads to paradoxical situations where my critique of certain behaviors and legal frameworks in Muslim-majority countries becomes subject to misrepresentation by western media. Moreover, my work, often seen by my community as being excessively driven by western ideals, casts me as a traitor in their eyes.

This extended preface not only situates my ideological and personal positioning, which may cast me as a "native informant" similar to those I am writing about, but it also rejects the prevailing discourse of homogeneity within the Muslim world. This rejection is a crucial aspect of my work, as it challenges the oversimplified and monolithic portrayals of 'Muslim' women. I believe that feminist ideologies should recognize how personal beliefs, histories, and emotions are interwoven into the fabric of knowledge creation. Rather than writing ourselves out of our scholarship, I advocate for integrating our personal narratives within our academic work. This approach helps dismantle the simplistic portrayal of the so-called authentic third world woman. It enriches the discourse with a voice that is often marginalized, unacknowledged, or, at times, deliberately unheard. Such an account enhances a more refined, truly decolonized feminist politics that is anti-racist at its core. This narrative thread is further developed as I chart my journey—from my initial defiance against misogyny, sexism, and gender discrimination to my political activism and, eventually, my entry into the academic world. It aims to shed light on how my work may be read and interpreted by varying audiences, especially since moving from a Middle Eastern country to Britain.

My becoming a feminist and activist encapsulates a deeply personal story that echoes the narratives highlighted in this book and hinges on what Deniz Kandiyoti terms "patriarchal bargain."[3] This concept refers to women's strategies to achieve greater autonomy within patriarchal constraints. My upbringing in Egypt was marred by frequent clashes with my parents, extended family, friends, and broader society, all centered around what I saw as an excessive fixation on the female body. There were moments when I felt as if women were merely vessels for male pleasure and reproduction. In the views of some, women are the instigators of temptation and the primary carriers of sin. And even when both genders partake in "sinful" acts, it typically falls upon women to endure the worst of societal blame. It is for this reason that some religious extremists ardently enforce the covering of women's bodies, heads, and occasionally faces as if the Muslim world is free of sins except those related to women. This is not to say that I do not see the commodification of women's bodies happening in the west, albeit in different ways. My parents were liberal. They were also political activists, intellectuals, and researchers. But the pressures inflicted upon them by society's traditions and the troubles they faced, from harassment to political prison,[4] were far fiercer than their grit to raise their children "differently." Despite their efforts that swung from standing firm against these pressures at times and giving in at other times, they failed to bring up "docile," "obedient" children. My brother and I ultimately embodied their rebellious spirit, challenging the same dictates they intermittently tried to shield us from.

In the early 1990s, during my time in high school and university, Egypt faced numerous political challenges that hindered the expected shift toward democracy. My involvement in student-led nationalist protests during these years marked the awakening of my political consciousness. These demonstrations demanded freedom of speech and the end of authoritarian rule. Later, movements like Kifaya (Enough) and "April 6" emerged in response to the regime's policies and ineffectiveness in creating job opportunities for young people.[5] These early experiences of activism, although not directly connected to gender inequality—a topic that feminists had broached since the 1920s yet never became a mainstream national issue—had a profound, empowering impact on me. I felt free; I was able to challenge oppression and exclusion in the face of my extended family as well as the wider society.

In recent decades, Egypt witnessed a further marginalization of gender equality issues, which are often deemed nonessential in a society grappling with poverty and corruption. The political turmoil of the 1990s and early 2000s, coupled with increasing confrontations with Islamists over the application of sharia (Islamic law), led the Mubarak regime to implement more conservative laws toward women and reduce support for their political representation. The issue, which during the 1950s nationalist independence project was framed as a conflict between the "traditional" and the "western," has transformed into a struggle between the "Islamic" and the so-called "anti-Islamic." As Islamist forces gained influence within the contemporary Egyptian state, secular liberal women like myself faced growing vilification. Women's contemporary activism in Egypt was primarily linked to the battle over marriage, divorce, and issues such as contraception and female genital mutilation. My battle, along with other self-proclaimed "secular" feminists, was more associated with personal autonomy and freedom of choice, matters that were not prioritized within the nationalist agenda and were often deemed "radical" by both fundamentalists and some feminists who aligned with either nationalists or Islamists.[6] Some feminist colleagues advised me to compromise to address more pressing concerns, suggesting that I "choose my battles," as the battle I was fighting was "surely a lost cause." As a result of my constant refusal to compromise, I was labeled "western," "infidel," "loose," "reckless," and sometimes even "Islamophobic" by colleagues, neighbors, extended family, and society at large.

Fresh out of graduation in 2001, I embarked on a yearlong adventure through Europe. My heart brimmed with new ideas and a longing for freedom, especially around sexuality and LGBTQ+ rights.[7] Back in Egypt, my "progressive" views clashed with the more conservative social norms, causing further friction with friends and family. These ideas worried my mother and disturbed many of my friends. Undeterred, I plunged into the world of women's and human rights, challenging the status quo and advocating for freedom of choice, even as my calls were met with disapproval, deemed "unacceptable" by traditions and "religion." In 2004, my life took a dramatic turn. An unplanned pregnancy, met with denial from my ex-partner, threw me into an unending cycle of legal battles and public scrutiny. I fiercely fought for my child's rights, all while facing societal pressure to justify my "disgraceful" act of becoming a mother outside of marriage. In Egypt, where a man's reputation remains untarnished even if he fathers a child out of wedlock, I faced a harsh reality. With no marriage contract, only my ex-partner could register my child's birth.[8]

Empowered by my family's unwavering support, I boldly entered the public arena, fiercely advocating for my daughter's rights.[9] My actions, challenging deeply ingrained sharia laws, Middle Eastern women's rights, and personal status laws, sent shockwaves across the region.[10] The fire of my struggle ignited a national debate, shattering countless taboos and generating a regional and international media frenzy. In those years of relentless pursuit, I became a symbol of courage, the woman defying the societal code of silence surrounding sexuality.[11] My victories in every court case I brought forth set legal precedents that ultimately led to the reformation of paternity laws in Egypt.[12] Yet, the public's disapproval persisted even after my legal triumphs. Daring to speak against traditions and sharia earned me labels like "western," "infidel," "promiscuous," and "anti-Muslim" from colleagues, neighbors, the public, and even my extended family. The impact of these personal experiences was so profound. I discovered the relationship between the liberation of women and the liberation of the country from a corrupt regime and a rising Islamist ideology. As eloquently stated by the late Nawal El Saadawi, a prominent Egyptian feminist and staunch supporter of my activism, "I understood the connection between sex, politics, economics, history, religion, and morality."[13]

Driven by a burning desire for change, I made a life-altering decision to abandon my career as an interior architect and dedicate myself to combating gender discrimination in all its forms. It was a matter of life or death for me, a fight for justice that consumed me entirely. I enrolled at the American University in Cairo, pursuing a master's in Gender and Women Studies. My passion fueled my involvement with various NGOs,[14] leading me to present my pursuits at conferences across the Middle East through blogs, opinion articles,[15] and televised debates, engaging in open discourse, even against religious and legal figures demonizing me on screen.[16] My unwavering commitment transformed me into a serious and recognized advocate for women's rights in Muslim countries. Seeking global support, I traveled to Europe, meeting with leading human rights organizations such as Amnesty International, Human Rights Watch, and Women Living Under Muslim Laws. These leading discussions highlighted the adversities faced by Middle Eastern women within the family court systems. Until 2010, I endured vicious attacks from Muslim clerics on television programs, including Souad Salih[17] and Safwat Hegazy,[18] among others, who accused me of spreading immorality and sin, demanding my exclusion from public appearances. However, their attempts to silence me only strengthened my tenacity to continue fighting for equality and justice.

During my MA project, I conducted a qualitative content analysis of two religious programs on Egyptian television. Watching religious clerics belittle women and portray them as mere shadows of men, confined to the roles of wife and mother, filled me with a profound sense of dismay. In one of the programs I studied, called *Amma Yatasa'aloun* (What are they questioning?), Abdalla Samak, a Muslim cleric known for frequent TV appearances, asserted that "an uneducated man would be preferred as a witness in court over a highly educated woman" (May 5, 2007). Khaled Abdalla, another cleric, responded to a female swimming champion, who, despite wearing a full veil except for her face, hands, and feet, said that "Muslim women are better suited for roles like teaching or nursing, rather than excelling in sports" (August 1, 2007). He argued women shouldn't aspire to be champions as this wouldn't contribute anything to Islam and should focus on staying home to care for their children. One particularly astonishing moment in that program was when he explained that the veil worn by Muslim women is intended to shield them from the gaze of Muslim men. He went as far as to describe that a western woman dressed in a manner typical for her culture, walking in an Islamic nation, would be viewed as a "whore" inviting sexual assault (August 1, 2007).

In recent decades, the rise of religious content on television in Egypt and other Muslim countries has been influenced by various factors. The emergence of ultraconservative Salafi satellite TV stations in Egypt has contributed to the spread of puritanical perspectives. This trend has been further fueled by the declining efficacy and legitimacy of the state, leading to a deadlock that has allowed Islamists to expand their presence in civil society. The development of mass education and mass media has also played a role, with new forms of communication and state interest in religious instruction transforming the Islamic tradition. This surge in religious programming has presented a new, simplified version of Islam to the masses, often bypassing traditional scholarly certification by muftis; a new genre of Islam for mass consumption, so to speak, "Islam for all," easy, quick, simple, and "modern." While the opinions expressed by these television preachers may not hold official religious authority, they have gained considerable influence among viewers. This shift toward a more conservative interpretation of Islam presents a stark contrast to the Egypt of the 1950s and 1960s, which embraced liberty, artistic expression, and respect for women. The condemnation of art as haram (sinful) and the victim-blaming discourse surrounding women's attire are troubling developments that threaten the secular ideals of many individuals. The slogan "Islam is the Solution," while presented as a unifying force, often suppresses cultural and ideological diversity.[19] The slogan carries significant implications for secular liberties, as it reflects a belief in the importance of Islamic principles and governance as the answer to societal challenges, which results in marginalizing or excluding individuals of different faiths or those who adhere to secular beliefs, potentially limiting their rights and freedoms in a society governed by Islamic principles. The slogan's implications on secular liberties also extend to issues of gender equality and LGBTQ+ rights.

I completed my master's degree in 2010 with a personal concern in mind. In a country like Egypt, with the declining quality of public education coupled with the growing popularity of satellite television, there is potential for television viewers to seek out educational material on satellite television. That raises the question of whether the content provided by Islamic media will continue to occupy high popularity among viewers or whether future generations will discover alternatives to address their sexual, social, and ideological concerns. The events of the Arab Spring in 2011, the rise of Islamic rule in Egypt and Tunisia in 2012, the emergence of ISIS in 2013, and the declaration of the Caliphate in 2014 further intensified my desire to understand the evolving landscape of the contemporary Islamic discourse and its influence on the masses. While I initially envisioned a new beginning following the Arab Spring, with dreams of initiating women's empowerment initiatives, the reality proved far more complex. The continued marginalization of women in the political process, from the humiliating "virginity tests" to the exclusion of women from the constitution drafting committee, painted a disheartening picture.[20] Despite the challenges, I remained dedicated to working with women's groups.[21] However, the lack of emphasis on women's rights among many activists and the overall deterioration of women's status in postrevolutionary Egypt presented significant obstacles to the work of feminist activists.

In the aftermath of the Arab Spring, disillusioned by the unfulfilled promises of the revolution, along with witnessing disturbing images of individuals associating terrorism with Islam, such as terrorists fleeing to Syria, engaging in violence, and justifying their actions under the guise of religion, and observing cases like Shamima Begum, a young woman who left the UK at fifteen to join ISIS, I felt compelled to undertake further research. This led me on a doctoral journey that initially focused on exploring the involvement of western-born women in Islamist organizations, a topic that both intrigued and deeply troubled me. I grappled with understanding the reasons driving their participation in such extremist activities, particularly their apparent voluntary choice to abandon what I perceived as a more "liberal" way of life. But as Rahel Wasserfall powerfully articulates, I asked myself, "How do I represent a group of people with whom I had a strong conflict, whom I disliked, and from whom I felt alienated?"[22] Betraying my values in pursuit of academic inquiry seemed an untenable path. I also recognized the precarious position of myself and other "Third world" women residing in the west when critiquing cultural practices within our traditions. As argued by Shāhnaz Khan, such critiques risk reinforcing western stereotypes and perpetuating a narrative of "otherness." Critiquing Zina (adultery) laws in Pakistan, she writes:

> We are silenced … by a fear of being accused of betrayal by members of our communities. In addition, we are also aware that criticism of Third world cultures often serves to further demonize and stereotype Third world peoples, reinforcing a view that, as Gayatri Spivak reminds us, seeks to free brown women from brown men. Similarly, being located in Canada and wanting to write about Zina laws in Pakistan, I need to find a way out of what appears to be a no-win situation. For I am aware that conventional Canadian readings of my work on Zina laws might evoke images of "the other woman."[23]

Having recently relocated to Britain with aspirations to critically examine fundamentalist Islam, I became acutely aware of the potential for my work to be appropriated to reinforce this harmful narrative, providing "another reason [to westerners] to bomb us out of existence and into obedience."[24] Motivated to challenge simplistic representations and provide a nuanced understanding of Muslim women's agency and resistance, I shifted my research focus to an inquiry into secular Muslim feminist activism. This shift was driven by a recognition of the need to counter the prevalent anti-Muslim rhetoric and to illuminate the voices of Muslim women actively challenging radical Islamism and violent extremism. The rise of anti-Muslim discourse in the wake of Brexit and the heightened focus on "terror" attacks in Europe have further underscored my desire to examine the perspectives of secular Muslim activists. Their efforts to confront religious fundamentalism and advocate for social justice offer a vital counterpoint to the dominant narratives that often equate Islam with extremism. As a researcher who shares certain commonalities with these women, such as a commitment to social justice and a critical stance toward religious fundamentalism, I can engage with their perspectives on a deeper level. I also acknowledge our significant differences, particularly in understanding the term "secular" and our respective experiences of being born and raised in different cultural contexts. This "partial" shared positionality allows me to navigate the complexities of representation and "otherness" with sensitivity and nuance. By acknowledging shared experiences and the points of divergence, I strive to produce intellectually rigorous and socially responsible scholarship. Through a commitment to critical self-reflection, engagement with diverse viewpoints, and nuanced analysis of power dynamics, I strive to move beyond simplistic stereotypes and foster an inclusive space where every voice is valued and honored.

Even as I shifted focus in my research, I encountered ongoing contradictions and obstacles. On the one hand, I am driven by a desire to understand and amplify the voices of Muslim women who are actively challenging fundamentalism and advocating for social justice. On the other hand, I am acutely aware of the risks associated with being perceived as a "native informant," particularly given my privileged background and the potential for my work to be misconstrued as aligning with western agendas. As identified by Shāhnaz Khan, "native informants" may be (or probably are) seen as aligning with the west in their desire to liberate the "unprivileged" Muslim woman from her "barbaric" culture.[25] She recognizes three native informants: the Muslim women "victims" narrating their own stories, the Muslim women "over there" battling the system to help those "victims," and the Muslim woman "over here," like herself and myself, who produce an account of these women mainly for the western audience. A fourth native informant, she adds, is the reader who ties their interpretation of such accounts to their own historical and socioeconomical context of resistance to dominant perspectives about women, the third world, and Islam. In my case, the added layer of studying Muslim women who seek to "save" the less-privileged Muslim woman further complicates my positionality. I recognize that this shared desire for social change may be perceived as elitism or paternalism.

Like other western countries, the politics of location in Britain "helps determine my position as a native informant in the West."[26] For example, when I argue against the recent Taliban takeover of Afghanistan[27] or condemn the death of Mahsa Amini in Iranian police custody on September 16, 2022,[28] I am accused by both Islamic fundamentalists and certain leftists in the west of being a "mouthpiece," and a "sell-out" who supports western imperialism fostering the idea that war can both free Muslim women from their oppressive menfolk and liberate the west from Islamic terrorism. As a third world feminist and a postcolonial subject, I resonate deeply with Shāhnaz Khan's words: "I am ambivalently positioned. I am invited to speak as the victim and a subject who reproduces the voice of alterity. I am damned if I do and damned if I do not."[29] My positionality presents an ongoing challenge in my efforts to represent

Muslim women's lives with authenticity and nuance. The tendency to portray them either as victims, often shaped by western orientalist narratives, or as agents, an argument championed by postcolonial feminist scholars, limits our understanding of their complex realities. Creating new modalities for reading and interpreting narratives about Muslim women is critical. It requires a concerted effort to unravel the representational practices that shape our access to knowledge and limit our understanding. By developing counternarratives that challenge simplistic binaries and promote critical engagement, we can move toward a more holistic representation of Muslim women's experiences. This shift involves a conscious effort to deconstruct both the victim-centered militaristic tropes as well as the uncritical celebration of the fully empowered Muslim woman and, instead, prioritize critical practices that dismantle these binary constructs and acknowledge the multifaceted dimensions of Muslim women's lives.

While holding immense potential for positive change, secular Muslim feminism risks being co-opted by dominant narratives that reinforce harmful stereotypes, read as an endorsement of the "white savior" position that justifies oppressive policies, both domestically and internationally. As the west appropriates the native informant's script, the narrative becomes distorted, serving to portray western women as inherently superior to their counterparts in the global south. This comparison hinders genuine feminist collaboration and solidarity, perpetuating a hierarchical power dynamic that undermines the agency and lived experiences of women in diverse cultural contexts. Further complicating this dynamic is my positionality as a privileged, educated Egyptian woman who has relocated to the west. Within Egyptian feminist circles, I am often seen as an outsider, disconnected from the realities of less-privileged women. Conversely, in western circles, my arguments against western interventions in the Middle East mark me as "not one of them," reinforcing the "othering" narrative. My position as a non-white, non-male individual further complicates my ability to navigate these complex cultural and political landscapes. Perhaps the answer lies in acknowledging such tensions as being productive. As a researcher, I choose to place the narratives of the women whose stories, aspirations, experiences, ideas, and challenges are discussed in this book at the center of analysis, recognizing that this centrality can be unsettling as these voices have been largely criticized by postcolonial and anti-racist feminist scholarship for "speaking the 'unpleasant truth'—male violence in immigrant societies, the misogyny of fundamentalist Muslim regimes, and the subjugation of women in the name of 'tradition.'"[30] These voices deserve to be heard and understood in their own right, beyond the confines of theoretical frameworks that may not fully encapsulate their lived realities. While recognizing the valid concerns raised by postcolonial and anti-racist feminist scholarship regarding the potential for essentializing or reproducing oppressive narratives, I believe that centering the voices of these women offers a crucial opportunity to understand their perspectives and complexities. Here, as well as in all my writing, I choose to take the path of self-reflexivity as I travel through these "contested" spaces. I strengthen the research process by striving for transparency in my methodology and by acknowledging the limitations of my research. To understand the configuration of the stories narrated to me, written in various publications, and spoken in multiple contexts—what they emphasize, what they omit, what they may exaggerate—I am sensitive to my interests, as well as to the purposes the narrators bring.

While narratives have been celebrated as a powerful tool for marginalized groups to assert their voices and challenge dominant accounts, it is crucial to acknowledge the complexities and potential pitfalls associated with their use. Kiran Grewal, for example, asks, "What is to be done about those who make highly instrumental use of the identity of the 'vulnerable, disempowered woman'?"[31] Part of the problem with the celebration of "narratives," especially in terms of representation, is that they raise the question of whether all people want to be represented in that way or if this representation is drafted in a way that may be counterproductive. As Kiran Grewal argues, narratives can be read or written in ways that justify other forms of oppression or reinforce dominant discourses. It is certainly important to recognize the problematic history of orientalist and neo-imperialist narratives that have often portrayed Muslim women as victims or objects of rescue. But to blame orientalism and neo-imperialism is to overlook the complex interrelationships between racialized, gendered, sexualized, and (neo)colonial structures of disadvantage and discrimination. The women whose works and challenges are discussed here may not always provide easy solutions. Still, their narratives offer valuable insights into the lived experiences of Muslim women navigating complex social, political, and cultural landscapes. Their stories highlight the need for an anti-racist, feminist agenda that addresses the complex forms of oppression they face. It is also essential to recognize that narratives are not monolithic or static but are constantly evolving. Ultimately, the goal is to create a space where diverse narratives can be shared, analyzed, and debated in a respectful and constructive manner. In order not to fall into the same trap of silencing a different and challenging voice, I make clear here that my interest in secular Muslim feminism, as I call it, reflects my broader motive to support feminist voices that may have been "deliberately" unheard by some. By examining the narratives of Muslim feminists with whom we might disagree, I have sought to appreciate the complexity of living and telling about being a secular Muslim feminist. As a feminist scholar and activist, I am compelled to support and understand the intricacy of such discursive resistance and promote the circulation of these alternative visions and voices. By acknowledging that stories and experiences are embedded in a larger social and political context that challenges their very existence, I make a conscious decision to emphasize the complexities rather than what may seem contradictory. While some may choose to explore different perspectives, it is in this particular moment, where voices calling for this specific standpoint struggle to exist, that I find it most appropriate to amplify their voices. This is not to say that other voices do not deserve to be heard or that their perspectives are less valuable. Instead, it is to acknowledge the unique challenges faced by those whose voices have been hardly examined within research and academic circles and to prioritize their voices to create a space for genuine dialogue and understanding. In this spirit, I invite you to engage with the narratives presented in this book, to read with an open mind and a critical eye, and to embrace the complexity and richness of human experience. It is through such engagement that we can break down barriers, build bridges of understanding, and work toward a more empathetic and harmonious world.

Acknowledgments

This book is the culmination of the long and winding journey narrated in its preface, an anthology of diverse voices and perspectives that have enriched and shaped my understanding of the world. With a heart bursting with gratitude, I acknowledge the profound impact of those who have supported and inspired me along the way. To my former PhD supervisors, Caroline Chatwin and Simon Cottee, my deepest gratitude for your guidance, mentorship, and belief in my work. Your insightful feedback, rigorous questioning, and unwavering support have been invaluable in shaping this book. You have challenged me to think critically and instilled in me a deep respect for the power of scholarship to illuminate the complexities of human experience and contribute to positive social change. To my external examiner, Kiran Grewal, thank you for your insightful feedback and thought-provoking questions. Your engagement with my work has helped me refine and strengthen my arguments, ensuring this book reaches its full potential. Your dedication to amplifying marginalized voices has been a source of inspiration to me.

To my feminist friends here, Trude Sandberg, Marian Duggan, Silvia Gomes, Leah Cleghorn, and May Elshamy, your ongoing support has been a vital source of inspiration and motivation. Your invaluable insights, encouragement, and shared passion for gender equality have shaped my perspective and invigorated my commitment to feminist scholarship. Your friendship and collective wisdom have illuminated my path, and I am deeply grateful for the solidarity and empowerment we have nurtured together. Thank you for being my allies, comrades, and confidantes on this transformative journey. To my best friends and yoga fellows, Sara Baldan, Fatima Garcia Raposo, and Alba Lázaro Obispo, thank you for walking this turbulent yet rewarding path with me. Your support, shared passion for yoga, and deep understanding of the transformative power of movement have been an anchor of strength and joy throughout this process. Our countless hours on the mat have provided a haven of peace and rejuvenation amidst the long hours of research and writing. Your presence in my life is a gift I cherish deeply. To my dearest friends back home, Ruby Fouad and Gaby Dib, thank you for believing in me, even when I doubted myself. Your constant encouragement and willingness to listen to my struggles and triumphs have provided comfort and reassurance. Distance may have separated us physically, but our bond remains strong, a testament to the enduring power of true friendship.

To my family, Mom, Salwa Abdelbaky, Dad, Hamdy Elhinnawy, and my dear brother, Mazin Elhinnawy, words cannot express my gratitude for your love, support, and belief in me. You have been my rock, source of strength, and champion throughout my life. Your sacrifices, encouragement, and faith in my dreams have made this journey possible. I am eternally grateful for the gift of your presence in my life. To my partner, Steven, my soulmate, companion, and biggest fan, thank you for your love, support, and patience. You have been my anchor in the storm, my voice of reason amidst the chaos, and my partner in crime on this journey of life. Your belief in me, willingness to listen to my endless ramblings, and constant encouragement have been a source of strength beyond measure. And foremost, to my daughter, Leena Alfishawy, my sunshine, my joy, and my most incredible creation, thank you for being you. Your laughter, love, and light are the greatest gifts of all. You have taught me the true meaning of unconditional love, the power of joy, and the transformative nature of motherhood. You are my inspiration, my muse, and the reason I strive to make this world a better place.

To all of you, my heartfelt thank you. This book would not be possible without your invaluable support. You are the wind beneath my wings, the fire in my belly, and the light that guides my way. To every one of you, I am eternally grateful.

Note on Text/Transliteration

In this book, Arabic terms are generally transliterated according to the system based on the list of the ALA-LC (American Library Association—Library of Congress) rules. The long vowels transliterated ū, ī, and ā, respectively. The final *alif, wāw, and yā'* are respectively transliterated ā, ū, and ī. *Hamza* is transliterated ', and 'a for initial *alif hamza*. Names of people are transliterated the way they themselves write it (e.g., al-Ali, An-Naim), whereas toponyms and ethnic names are given in their English most common form (e.g., Cairo, Tehran, etc). Place names whose occurrence in English is scarce or non-existing are partially transliterated, using "al-" (e.g., al-Azhar). Arabic words that have become frequent in English are usually not transliterated (e.g., Islam, sharia, sheikh, qadi, jihad).

Additionally, in this book, I prefer to use certain words in lower case (e.g., west, western, third world, orientalism, black, etc) to deemphasize the sensationalization that largely accompanies the use of these words. Exceptions are when they refer to a geographical location (e.g., Western Europe, the Middle East, the Orient, etc), and where they appear in a quote by another scholar.

Abbreviations

AKP	The Justice and Development Party in Turkey, in Turkish *Adalet ve Kalkınma Partisi*, abbreviated officially as AK Party in English
AWID	The Association for Women's Rights in Development, formerly the Association for Women in Development
BBC	British Broadcasting Corporation
CEMB	Council of ex-Muslims in Britain
CEWLA	Center for Egyptian Women's Legal Assistance
CPS	Personal Status Code (largely used in Arab countries)
CVE	Countering Violent Extremism
FLN	*Front de Libération Nationale* (National Liberation Front) Algeria
ISIS	Islamic State of Iraq and Syria
LGBTQ+	Lesbian, gay, bisexual, transgender, intersex, queer/questioning, asexual and many other terms (such as nonbinary and pansexual)
MENA	Middle East and North Africa
NGO	Non-governmental Organization
PhD	Philosophy Doctorate
PKK	Kurdistan Workers' Party
TFN	Transnational Feminist Networks
UNFT	National Union of Tunisian Women
WAF	Women against Fundamentalism (UK)
WAF	Women's Action Forum (Pakistan)
WLUML	Women Living under Muslim Laws
WOT	War on Terror

1

Introduction

With influence reaching every society around the globe, there is no doubt that feminism is the largest and broadest social movement in human history. Yet, despite its unifying aim of achieving equal rights and freedom of choice for all women, it has manifested in a wide array of expressions shaped by the diverse contexts, concerns, and conditions of women's lives. This inherent adaptability, I believe, is a defining strength that allows the movement to resonate across sociopolitical and cultural landscapes without compromising its core value. In the Muslim world, since its inception, feminism has grappled with a complex landscape shaped by sociopolitical transformations and the so-called clash of civilizations. Early feminist movements in the Muslim world were influenced by various factors, including the struggle for independence from colonial powers, the rise of modern nation-states, and the reinterpretation of Islamic texts concerning women's rights. In the 1990s, intellectual discussions around women's roles in Islam surged, driven by the emergence of religious fundamentalist movements that questioned the relevance of concepts like "secularism" and "feminism." Consequently, a rift has emerged between secular and Islamic expressions of feminism, with "Islamic feminism," an approach that seeks to reinterpret religious texts to promote gender equality, gaining significant traction in recent years.

Despite a century of "homegrown" feminist activism and unwavering demands for gender equality within Muslim societies, "secular Muslim feminism" remains shrouded in uncertainty and misunderstanding. This approach to gender equality, grounded in universal human rights principles, faces criticism from various factions. Islamists question its legitimacy, westerners suspect its authenticity, and even feminists within Muslim communities hold doubts. Some accuse it of imposing western ideologies, marginalizing religiously motivated activists, and falling prey to western political agendas. To address this, it is crucial to reassess secularism and feminism in light of their historical contexts and limitations. This book delves into the heart of this contested concept, dissecting the nuances of secular Muslim feminism and its potential to reconcile divergent perspectives within the feminist movement in Muslim contexts. Through an in-depth analysis of the historical, sociopolitical, and cultural contexts that have shaped this contested brand of feminism, this book uncovers its complexities, challenges, and possibilities. Drawing on personal observations from over two decades of feminist activism and interactions with various organizations in the Middle East and Europe to address the complex issue of Muslim women's emancipation and the diverse interpretations it incites, this book unapologetically challenges prevailing narratives. Through its chapters, the book scrutinizes the overly simplistic portrayals of Muslim women, critiquing the instrumentalization of women's emancipation by both western and Islamist agendas. It questions the uncritical glorification of religious agency by postcolonial and Islamic feminists, recognizing how this can inadvertently reinforce patriarchal and conservative ideologies. It also addresses and critiques the narrative of the victimized Muslim woman perpetuated by western media and politics. Furthermore, it condemns the hijacking of the secular Muslim feminist movement by the far right to advance anti-Muslim sentiments under the guise of advocating for women's rights. By revisiting foundational ideologies of secular and Islamic feminism, considering the intricate web of factors affecting the status of Muslim women and the broader sociopolitical landscape, Secular Muslim Feminism proposes a reevaluation of the relationship between religion and gender equality within diverse cultural frameworks. It emphasizes individual freedom of religion and shared societal concerns like political representation, education, and employment while acknowledging the cultural complexity that transcends religious and secular divides. It shows how the imagined delineating lines and boundaries between these concepts are fluid and translucent.

Situating Secular Muslim Feminism

In 2012, Egyptian journalist and feminist Mona Eltahawy wrote an article for Foreign Policy magazine entitled "Why Do They Hate Us?" Referring to the "Arab Springs," Eltahawy claims that "political revolutions will not succeed unless they are accompanied by revolutions of thought—social, sexual, and cultural." Her work, which appears to reaffirm prevalent stereotypes concerning Islam and misogyny, places her among the increasing ranks of "native informants" whose personal testimonies of oppression and subjugation under Islam may have potentially fueled support for military interventions in Muslim countries over the last few decades. Similar works by others, also labeled as "native-informants" like Azar Nafisi's *Reading Lolita in Tehran*, Irshad Manji's *Faith without Fear*, Nouni Darwish's *Now They Call Me Infidel*, Karima Benoune's *Your Fatwa Doesn't Apply*, Wafaa Sultan's *A God Who Hates* and many more, have been rebuffed by postcolonial feminist academics like Lila Abu-Lughod, Leila Ahmed and Saba Mahmood, who argues that such writings help fabricate "consent" for the wars against Muslim countries, by reinforcing the view that Muslim women are victims in need of saving. Similarly, Hamid Dabashi, an Iranian American scholar,[1] has denounced their work, labeling them "native informants" whose role has facilitated "indigenized orientalism" at the expense of anti-imperial feminist politics. Critiquing Azar Nafisi's work in an article for the Egyptian al-Ahram Weekly, he writes:

> Through the instrumentality of English literature, recycled and articulated by an "Oriental" woman who deliberately casts herself as a contemporary Scheherazade, [Reading Lolita in Tehran] seeks to provoke the darkest corners of the Euro-American Oriental fantasies and thus neutralize competing sites of cultural resistance to the US imperial designs both at home and abroad, while ipso facto denigrating the long and noble struggle of women all over the colonized world to ascertain their rights against both domestic patriarchy and colonial domination.[2]

While Dabashi rightly points out the issue of misrepresentation, his critique of Azar Nafisi's work falls short due to its generalizations, lack of evidence, and conspiratorial tone. Instead of engaging with the text in a nuanced way, acknowledging its potential limitations while also recognizing its strengths, Dabashi resorts to broad accusations and inflammatory language. This is just a glimpse into the struggles and challenges faced by secular Muslim feminists, thinkers, and writers. Their perspectives are often misconstrued as either simply mimicking western ideals or betraying their own cultural and religious identities. They face relentless criticism and hostility from both religious extremists and some within their own communities, who accuse them of undermining religious values and traditions. Their voices are often excluded from mainstream discourse, and their contributions to social change are minimized or ignored. In some cases, they face threats, harassment, and even physical violence for their outspoken views and activism.

The context of the current global and geopolitical landscape marked by the "War on Terror" has given rise to competing imaginaries—western imperialist and feminist, orientalist, postcolonial feminist, anti-colonial, and Islamic—creating a "terrain of knowledge production upon which the lives, histories, and subjectivities of Muslim women are discursively constituted, debated, claimed and consumed" through various forms of representation.[3] The formal establishment of ISIS in 2013 further exacerbated the stereotyping of Islam in western discourse, associating it with instability, violence, and terrorism. This has imposed a double burden on Muslim women, subjecting them to both racialized and gendered politics that dictate how their bodies and identities are narrated, defined, and regulated. Consequently, the discourse surrounding Muslim women's liberation often gets entangled within the complexities of ideological extremism, Islamic fundamentalism, racism, and Islamophobia. In their struggle against these oppressive arrangements, both secular and Islamic feminists have been negotiating and contesting the various meanings imposed upon them. The current absence of a unified feminist framework among Muslim women, operating from both secular and religious paradigms, presents a challenge. Secular feminists have forged transnational alliances with global anti-racist feminist and anti-fundamentalist movements but remain ideologically distinct from faith-centered Muslim women who ground their resistance in religious reform.[4] Rebecca Durand and Myk Zeitlin eloquently articulate these conflicts by posing the following questions:

> How do we challenge reactionary ideas when expressed within minority communities without giving firepower to racists? How do we fight racism without constructing monolithic ideas of communities? How do we recognize the role of religious institutions in providing material support in times of a shrinking state, and a sense of solace and belonging, while still allowing for criticism of their domination of struggles within communities?[5]

These questions are not new, nor are they impossible to address, but at the moment, they seem hardly up for debate. They highlight the complex and multifaceted considerations faced by secular Muslim feminists in navigating issues of regressive ideologies, racism, community diversity, and the role of religious institutions in advocating for gender equality and social justice. Secular Muslim feminists address these questions by acknowledging the complexity of identities while promoting progressive values and solidarity. They emphasize individual experiences, complexities, and intersections of race, gender, religion, and culture. However, while recognizing the valuable social services and support networks that religious institutions may offer, they also maintain a critical stance toward their potential domination of community struggles. They advocate for an approach that allows for constructive criticism of religious institutions' power dynamics and potentially oppressive practices while also acknowledging the positive aspects they bring to individuals in need. Despite their significant contributions, postcolonial and western feminists and scholars opted to focus more on publicly pious women. The former portrays them as "agents" of their own choices, while the latter describes them as victims of their "backward" societies.[6] The overemphasis on "Islamic feminism" as the central protagonist within the scholarly landscape of Muslim feminism has inadvertently silenced the voices of diverse Muslim feminist figures. This uncritical focus has created a monolithic image that fails to capture the rich diversity of Muslim feminists, encompassing secularists, feminists, the religiously devout, and many others. As a result, the voices of secular Muslim feminists have been drowned out, their unique perspectives obscured.

While the academic backdrop has historically privileged the study of Islamic feminist movements, recent scholarship has begun to shed light on the significant contributions of secular Muslim feminists. Nadje al-Ali's ground-breaking 2000 work, *Secularism, Gender, and the State*, is a pioneering example. Amid a scholarly focus on Islamic movements, al-Ali's anthropological study delves into secular women's movements in Egypt. She challenges the prevailing narrative that dismissed their role in shaping the gendered political discourse, arguing that scholars had inadvertently "muted" their voices. Following al-Ali's book, a handful of scholars have explored secular feminism in Muslim societies, but merely within the context of broader projects. However, a comprehensive study dedicated solely to this topic, mirroring the depth and scope of al-Ali's work, remained elusive until Afia Zia's 2018 book *Faith and Feminism in Pakistan*, which focuses on working-class women's movements in Pakistan, was published. Zia critiques the post-9/11 intellectual climate that positioned secular feminism as a western imposition, ignoring its pre-9/11 presence in Pakistan and the successes it achieved. As Zia notes, the growing body of literature on "Islamic feminism" scolds secular feminists in these contexts for being pro "western." Zia offers a critical defense of secular feminism, providing examples of its successes in Pakistan.

In "Reclaiming the Voice of the 'Third world Woman,'" Kiran Grewal argues for a critical engagement with diverse voices, even those we may find disagreeable. She highlights the transformative potential of acknowledging women who do not conform to the essentialized and overly celebratory image of the "authentic Third world woman." In *Women against Fundamentalism*, Sukhwant Dhaliwal uses political narratives to reveal the contradictory pressures faced by women who oppose religious fundamentalism but do not fit the stereotypical image of a "Muslim" woman. *Women against Fundamentalism*, a collection of nineteen autobiographical narratives by WAF members, celebrates this unique form of feminism that challenges both fundamentalism and racism while acknowledging its challenges. In her book, Afia Zia explains that most literature on the so-called "Muslim Woman Question", in effect, avoids or downplays the role of religious militancy and conservatism and its growing violation of all secular spaces and expressions in Muslim contexts. Similarly, the celebratory discourses constructed around Muslim women's resistance that do not rethink the limits of such "agency" undermines the resilience and continuity of the secular struggle among Muslim women and the desire for secular space in such contexts. This book emerges as a part and an extension of these burgeoning efforts to recover the value and viability of the work and writings of what I call "secular Muslim feminists," a heterogeneous group that does not necessarily self-identify as secular. Despite their differing standpoints, they all recognize the centrality of secularism to protecting women's rights against the threat of religious fundamentalism. They do not oppose religion as such but emphasize the crucial role of secular spaces in ensuring equality for individuals of all faiths and of none.

Notable secular Muslim feminists, such as Homa Arjomand, Taslima Nasrin, Irshad Manji, Chahla Chafiq, Maryam Namazie, Shadi Sadr, Nawal El Saadawi, and many others, have emerged as powerful voices challenging religious fundamentalism, questioning existing gender norms and contesting inequalities within their societies. These women, representing diverse backgrounds and perspectives, have sparked meaningful conversations and inspired action for social change. Homa Arjomand, founder of the campaign against sharia courts in Canada, has challenged the imposition of religious law on personal matters, advocating for secular legal systems that uphold individual rights and equality. Taslima Nasrin, a Bangladeshi-Swedish feminist writer, has faced persecution for her outspoken criticism of religious oppression and advocacy for women's rights. Her influential writings have given voice to the experiences of marginalized women and challenged societal norms. Irshad Manji, author of *The Trouble with Islam Today*, has stirred controversy with her critiques of conservative interpretations of Islam and her calls for reform within the Muslim community. Her provocative views have sparked debate and encouraged critical reflection on religious doctrines.[7] Chahla Chafiq, an Iranian leftist feminist, has dedicated her life to fighting for social justice and human rights. Her activism has challenged oppressive regimes and advocated for the empowerment of marginalized groups, including women and minorities. Maryam Namazie, a

British–Iranian secularist and human rights activist, has been a vocal critic of religious extremism and advocate for gender equality. Her work has focused on challenging discriminatory practices and promoting secularism as a foundation for a just and equitable society. Shadi Sadr, an Iranian lawyer and human rights advocate, has fought tirelessly for women's rights and legal reforms in Iran. Her work has challenged discriminatory laws and practices, advocating for equality and justice for all citizens. The late Nawal El Saadawi, an Egyptian feminist writer and activist, has been a leading voice for women's rights and social justice in the Arab world. Her groundbreaking writings have challenged patriarchal norms and sparked meaningful conversations about gender equality, sexuality, and freedom of expression. These women, alongside many other Muslim feminists worldwide, represent a diverse and vibrant group whose contributions have been instrumental in raising awareness of critical issues, inspiring action for change, and shaping the global discourse on feminism, religion, and human rights.

Unpacking "Secular"–"Muslim"–"Feminism"

It is essential to distinguish between my focus on "secular Muslim feminism" and the broader concept of the secularization of Islam. While the French state's attempts to transform Islam into a state-sanctioned "French Islam" exemplify secularization efforts, my work specifically explores the lived experiences and perspectives of secular Muslim feminists who navigate their identities within a complex sociopolitical landscape. While acknowledging the historical and ongoing debates surrounding secularization, my primary focus is not on the transformation of religious institutions or practices. Instead, I aim to center the voices of those who contribute to secular Muslim feminism. The consequences of secularization policies, such as the French model, which often alienate diverse Muslim communities and exacerbate tensions, further highlight the need for nuanced approaches that respect individual agency and cultural identities. By focusing on "secularity," I seek to engage with the complexities of navigating faith, culture, and gender within a globalized world, recognizing the diversity of experiences and perspectives within this movement. Secularization, in contrast, seeks to define and produce a "good Muslim," one who is committed to a "secular Islam" that poses no challenge to the State's ideological, political, social, and economic hegemony.

Amna Akbar and Rupal Oza locate secular-oriented Muslim feminists broadly within two domains: the neo-orientalist and the "liberal," which they narrow down to two groups. The first includes women who denounce "militant Islam" and call for efforts to reform Islam and to police fellow Muslims.[8] This group is usually labeled as the "good Muslim,"[9] who positions herself as a liberal-modern standing against an illiberal and anti-modern one. The second draws on global human rights and secular frames, whom they label as "secular Muslims." These women's history of engagement with women's human rights and nongovernmental organizations (NGOs) and their commitments to "secular" politics distinguishes them from the "good Muslim" position, supported and celebrated by western politics. Their work, which at times criticized state policies, carried several objectives:

> highlighting the resurgence of fundamentalism in all religions and lobbying for a secular state; demanding women's rights over their own bodies and control over their own lives; opposing institutionalized Christian privilege; and resisting ethnic minority parity demands for religious accommodation, such as demands to extend rather than abolish the blasphemy law (and later legislation on incitement to religious hatred) and to extend rather than abolish state-funded religious schools.[10]

The difference between these women and the ones labeled "good Muslims," according to Akbar and Oza, is that they do not mobilize a gendered-victimized "insider" status to provide credible access into the deep world of the Muslim psyche; they do not articulate the violence targeted at Islam as legitimate and necessary, and they do not associate all that is liberal and just with the "west." The discursive linking of women's empowerment to anti-terrorism and the downplaying of the significance of other, nonreligious dimensions of identity has trafficked secular feminist discourses into the "good Muslim/bad Muslim" dichotomy, which relies on deeply essentialist constructions of culture and people and endorses the dangerous "us versus them" dichotomy of the "War on Terror." I choose not to make this rigid separation in this book, recognizing that individuals may hold nuanced and evolving positions on faith, culture, and gender equality. It must be noted here that the rise of far-right organizations across Europe, characterized by extreme nationalism and a strong anti-Muslim sentiment, coupled with the growing prevalence of identity politics, further complicates the landscape for understanding and classifying the work of secular Muslim feminists. The political shifts witnessed with the election of Donald Trump in the United States, Brexit in the UK, and the rise of populist parties across the globe highlight the increasing influence of these trends.

The National Secular Society in the UK defines secularism as a political idea concerned with the best way to govern religiously pluralist societies. The model of secularism they advocate for defends the civil liberties of all, regardless of personal beliefs. The principles of secularism as they state include (a) equality, so that religious beliefs or lack of do not put people at an advantage or a disadvantage; (b) freedom to practice one's religion or belief, or change it or not have one, without harming others; and (c) the separation of religious institutions from state institutions and a public sphere where religion may participate, but not dominate. Broadly speaking, secular Muslim feminists agree with this definition, despite that not all of them self-identify as secular for many distinct reasons that I will explain later. They may differ in particular standpoints, but they all agree that secularism is central to the protection against the rise of religious fundamentalism in all religions. Nadje al-Ali explains her use of "secular," referring to the acceptance of the separation between religion and politics without denoting anti-religious positions. In her 1988 *Women, Islamists and the State*, Azza Karam argues:

> Secular feminists firmly believe in grounding their discourse outside the realm of any religion, whether Muslim or Christian, and placing it instead within the international human rights discourse ... To them, religion is respected as a private matter for each individual, but it is totally rejected as a basis from which to formulate any agenda on women's emancipation. By so doing, they avoid being caught up in interminable debates on the position of women with religion.[11]

In the general sense, these definitions resonate with the meaning of secularism I allude to in this book. However, I venture beyond a fixed definition of secularism, delving into its multifaceted nature and exploring its diverse meanings and articulations across different contexts and historical eras. I investigate the various ways in which feminist movements across the globe have articulated secularism. I also explore the potential of secularism to promote gender equality and social justice while acknowledging the challenges and limitations it may face in specific contexts. By engaging with these varied perspectives and interpretations, I aim to develop a nuanced understanding of secularism beyond simplistic descriptions, recognizing its complex and evolving nature.

While acknowledging the diversity within the term "Muslim," which encompasses individuals with varying levels of religious observance, political ideologies, and cultural backgrounds, in this book, I primarily use the term

Muslim in a cultural sense, recognizing that Islam, beyond its religious tenets, has profoundly shaped cultural expressions, social norms, and historical experiences of individuals and communities across the globe. By using "Muslim" in a cultural context, I aim to capture the shared heritage, values, and practices that bind together diverse communities, transcending narrow definitions based solely on religious adherence or political affiliation. This perspective acknowledges the richness and complexity of Muslim identities, encompassing individuals who may or may not subscribe to the tenets of Islam as a religion, recognizing that their lived realities are shaped not only by religious beliefs but also by cultural norms, social contexts, and historical experiences. "Secular Muslim Feminism" is not intended to imply that all individuals who identify as such or draw on secular foundations in their battle for gender equality are religiously affiliated or unaffiliated. Instead, it recognizes that their feminist activism arises from a shared cultural identity, regardless of religious beliefs or practices.

The current debates on feminism, gender, and women's rights in Islam are ideologically charged, reflecting the historical context of broader civilizational dialogues between the Muslim world and the west. Many Muslims view contemporary western feminism as reinforcing reductionist views of Islam as a sexist religion. Azza Karam explains:

> The term "feminism" ... in post-colonial Arab Muslim societies is tainted, impure, and heavily impregnated with stereotypes. Some of these stereotypes are that feminism basically stands for the enmity between men and women, as well as a call for immorality in the form of sexual promiscuity for women ... some religious personalities ... have associated feminism with colonialist strategies to undermine the indigenous social and religious culture.[12]

In response to the inaccurate western stereotyping of Muslim women, Muslim scholars have unfortunately become equally reductionist in romanticizing Muslim women's agency. This makes it harder to identify and address the realities of gender injustice in these parts of the world. Moreover, the limits of international feminism became apparent with the "failure of Western feminists to confront imperialism and its negative implications for democracy and its feminist ideals."[13] Dominant strands of western feminism have been subject to extensive critique from many non-western feminist movements articulating some of the central problems with second-wave feminism well onto the second half of the twentieth century. Here, I follow Sa'diyya Shaikh in her broad understanding of feminism as the critical awareness of the structural marginalization of women in society and the engagement in activities directed at transforming gender power relations within society. My understanding of feminism recognizes its multifaceted nature, encompassing various approaches and aiming at the shared goal of achieving equal rights and empowerment for all genders. It acknowledges the historical evolution of the term "feminism" and the diverse perspectives within the movement, embracing inclusivity and acknowledging the need to address intersectional oppressions. While acknowledging challenges and ongoing debates, I see value in using the term as a tool for transformative change. This understanding is informed by the works of various scholars and activists, as well as my subjective experiences and observations.

Ultimately, "Secular Muslim Feminism" aims to capture the complex interplay between faith, culture, and feminism. It acknowledges and embraces the diverse perspectives and experiences of women of Muslim background, fostering a more comprehensive understanding of their contributions to the global struggle for gender equality. "Secular Muslim Feminism" recognizes the shared heritage, values, and traditions that shape our cultural identity while at the same time opening the space for critical questioning on patriarchal interpretations within faith structures as well as in the social sphere. "Secular" in this context signifies a neutral space, free from religious control or influence. This allows for the inclusion of diverse voices, including those who ground their advocacy for gender justice in religious principles. Therefore, the term becomes a welcoming umbrella for those who draw inspiration from secular principles and those who navigate a fluid space between faith and secularism. In a nutshell, the term "Secular Muslim Feminism" goes beyond mere labeling. It represents a transformative force within the global feminist landscape, reflecting the diverse voices, experiences, and perspectives of individuals dedicated to challenging gender inequality and promoting social justice within the context of their rich cultural heritage, regardless of their religious affiliation.

The Power and Pitfalls of Terminology

In my academic pursuits, I have come to recognize the term "secular" as the most appropriate descriptor for Muslim women activists, feminists, and thinkers who advocate for gender equality by drawing on human rights and secular frames rather than relying solely on Islamic scriptures as the exclusive framework for political advocacy. This choice stems from a critical examination of the various labels involved in reshaping Islamic discourse, each laden with its own preconceptions and restrictions. Terms like "Islamic reformation," "liberal

Islam," "progressive Islam," "critical Islam," "Islamic modernism," and "moderate Islam" are frequently used classifications. However, they often fall short of encapsulating contemporary Muslim perspectives' intricate and evolving landscape.

The term "Islamic reformation," while evoking parallels to the European Renaissance, risks overlooking the unique historical, cultural, and intellectual contexts shaping Muslim reform movements. The term's origins can be traced back to the nineteenth century, when western scholars, influenced by Enlightenment ideals, began drawing comparisons between European modernity and potential reforms within Islam. Figures like Ernest Renan[14] and Ignaz Goldziher[15] suggested an "Islamic reformation" to address the stagnation and decline within Islamic societies. In the twentieth century, Muslim intellectuals themselves began engaging with the concept of Islamic reformation. Prominent thinkers like Muhammad Abduh[16] and Rashid Rida[17] called for reinterpreting Islamic teachings in light of modern challenges, emphasizing reason, individual interpretation, and social justice. Opponents argue that the term uncritically adopts western frameworks and overlooks the unique historical, cultural, and intellectual contexts of Muslim societies, which predate western models.[18] The term is deeply associated with the Protestant Reformation in Christianity, which evokes colonial undertones, reflecting historical attempts by colonial powers to impose cultural, religious, and political changes on Muslim-majority regions under the guise of modernization or reform. As such, it may fail to capture the breadth of perspectives, debates, and initiatives aimed at evolving Islamic thought and practice. In response to these critiques, scholars have proposed alternative terms such as "Islamic renewal," which may imply a return to an idealized past, and "Islamic modernism," very similar to "Islamic reformation," which may convey the idea of conforming Islam to western modernity.

The term "liberal Islam" has a complex history that has evolved over time in response to changing sociopolitical contexts and intellectual debates within the Muslim world. Although the precise origins of the term are difficult to pinpoint, the concept of liberal interpretations of Islam can be traced back to Islamic reform movements in the nineteenth and twentieth centuries. Liberal Islam has resurfaced prominently in academic and public discourse since at least the time of the Islamic Revolution in Iran, if not earlier. Works by Muslim liberals, like Bassam Tibi's 2013 book *The Sharia State* and Tariq Ramadan's 2012 book *The Arab Awakening*, may present apparent contradictions as they attempt to synthesize, adapt to, or critique western liberalism yet remain entrenched in its language. In his book, Tibi advocates for the "engagement without empowerment" of Islamists, an obviously contradictory approach. Tariq Ramadan shares Tibi's assumptions about Islam's compatibility with western liberalism, offering platitudes about freedom, democracy, and civil society yet lacking depth and originality. His work represents semiotic Muslim politics where branding overshadows policy details. Both books offer biased and superficial analyses of the Arab Spring, driven by personal agendas and cultural baggage. Their promotion of abstracted liberalism that acculturates both Islam and the west raises concerns about their understanding of the complexities involved in the region's transformation. The theoretical premise of liberal Islam, which argues that Islam is the necessary foundation for human rights in the Muslim world, may be misguided and risks reifying the notion that Islam monopolizes the Muslim public sphere rather than leaving space for normative diversity.

The term "progressive" was appropriated by several activists and scholars from various parts of the Muslim world in the late 1990s.[19] It has constructed a new paradigm after liberal Islam. Omid Safi's concept of progressive Islam materialized after considering terms such as "reform," "liberal," and "critical." He understands "progressive" as an umbrella term "an invitation to those who want an open and safe space to undertake a rigorous, honest, potentially difficult engagement with tradition, yet remain hopeful that conversation will lead to further action."[20] Progressives see themselves as both a continuation and a radical departure from the tradition of liberalism in Muslim countries.[21] In their view, liberal Muslims uncritically identify with modernity and avoid the critique of imperialism and colonialism both historically and in contemporary forms. In truth, progressive Islam is remarkably similar to liberal Islam, but Safi tries to present it in a different light. The book highlights the need for "reforming" Islam through the notion of *Ijtihād*, which, they argue, "alone" can bring forth its inherent dynamism. However, I would say that the very idea of "progressive" Muslims raises questions about the actual progressiveness of "progressive Islam" and the extent to which individualization within the faith translates to the liberalization of Islamic dogmas. The journal "Critical Muslim," launched by Ziauddin Sardar in early 2011, is, as Sardar states, "an attempt to provide space for the critical spirit of Islam." To make it clear, critical Muslim scholars disagree amongst themselves about means and ends, just as Islamists do. Undoubtedly, the developments within critical Islam express a willingness to engage in an open-ended dialogue. Still, the question is whether critical Islam can actually enter into productive conversations with critical thinkers from different faiths. Can critical Islam win the contention against scholars who argue for literal readings of the sources and Islamists who want the modern state to impose divine law?

Since 9/11, the focus of several scholars and thinkers has turned more squarely on Islam in the west and the campaigning for a "moderate" versus "radical" Islam. New speakers have appeared to join them, including figures like Hamza Yusuf, an American Muslim convert, in the United States; Tim Winter, an academic, theologian, and Islamic scholar, in the United Kingdom; celebrity figures like Ed Husain, a former British Hizb ut-Tahrir member turned Senior Fellow at the Council on Foreign Relations in the UK, and Maajid Nawaz, also a former British Hizb ut-Tahrir and founder of the Quilliam Foundation in the UK. These figures aim to counter violent extremism by asserting Islam's compatibility with liberal western secular ideals, which, instead of unifying, have fractured Muslim identities. The focus on Muslim liberalism, thus, risks suppressing more profound and potentially transformative Islamic thought. However, the intellectual authority of liberal Islam and its domination of the space within which "radical" Islam is contested has put limits on any alternative, nonviolent visions of Islamic thought and practice that challenge the liberal state. This has been, in no small measure, a consequence of the western states' role in the construction of the so-called moderate Islam and the immense resources invested into the counter-extremism agenda, which has helped commodify it. The qualifier of "moderate" suggests that there is something innately violent about Islam, leading to the false conclusion that a small group of "moderates" is standing in opposition to a large crowd of violent, ISIS-supporting radicals.

This is not to say that the label "secular Muslim" comes without critique. There is ongoing debate about the precise definition of a "secular Muslim." For many Muslims, "secularism" remains a loaded term, "equated to everything from mild eccentricity to an unnatural act of blasphemy."[22] Even those who are not at the far end of rejecting the term could still misinterpret it as implying a complete separation between faith and daily life. But being a "secular Muslim" does not denote an opposition to worship, but rather an opposition to political Islam. Secular Muslims encompass a diverse range of individuals with varying interpretations of Islam and secularism. The term helps recognize the agency of individuals to choose their own path within Islam while encouraging engagement with other perspectives. It offers a framework for navigating the complex relationship between faith and modernity, potentially leading to positive social and political reforms. Therefore, unlike "cultural Islam," which is merely a term to express a sense of identity, "secular Islam," despite being an individual choice, is clearly a political position. But unlike Islamists, there is little danger that secular Muslims are pursuing an agenda to undermine liberal democracy. Secular Muslim feminism does not advocate violence yet supports religious toleration. Therefore, acknowledging and amplifying this voice can play a crucial role in bridging the gap between opposing narratives and paving the way for progress in Muslim women's rights.

Navigating Methodological Challenges

A discussion on methods and methodology is crucial here, given that the complexities marking feminist debates about theory, activism, politics, personal experiences, and academia are still intensively felt. Whereas notions of difference have long constituted important issues for feminist theory, politics, and practice, "the overriding preoccupation with sexism have far too often resulted in feminists ignoring differences of race, class, ethnicity, age (dis)ability, sexuality and nationality."[23] These variances have long been critical aspects of feminist theory, politics, and practice. Consequently, some feminist researchers have endeavored to analyze and critique western depictions of the "rest" and address issues concerning gender, race, ethnicity, and class, among others. Patricia Hill Collins suggests that we can truly understand women's lived experiences only by exploring the complex matrix of difference. Kimberlé Crenshaw coins the term "intersectionality" to speak to the multiple social forces, identities, and ideological instruments through which power and disadvantage are expressed and legitimized. Similarly, feminist postmodernists, poststructuralists, and postcolonialists highlight the variations of women's lives and identities, bringing "the other" into research while deconstructing oppositional categories of man versus woman, black versus white, the west versus the rest, and so on.

While postcolonial feminism has contributed to feminist theorizing through concepts such as "othering" and the silencing of third world women's voices, a new discourse, namely, transnational feminism, may have helped us better "understand new global realities resulting from migrations and the creation of transnational communities."[24] Perhaps the best example of this new discourse is Chandra Mohanty's revisiting of her seminal article "Under Western Eyes," in which she notes that while her earlier focus was on distinctions, she now chooses to focus on anti-capitalist transnational feminist methodologies to develop a universalism that speaks to improve all individual lives. Relying on a "feminist solidarity" model that reveals what she calls the "common differences," she argues that it helps us recognize not only the differences but also the commonalities and the development of mutual consideration and understanding despite differing perspectives and experiences. The popularization of transnational feminisms in feminist or women's and gender studies has coincided with a commitment to address the disparities of globalization. Yet, it would be incorrect to suggest that the term has the same salience in the Global South and the global North. Similar to all other feminisms, transnational has emerged out of specific historical moments. Viewed this way, it is essential to be aware of the limits of its use. While it is not within the scope of this book to dive into the theoretical contestations of transnational feminism, I argue that starting with the diverse experiences of women as the initial point for knowledge production while consciously including contextual elements in the analysis and acknowledging its limitations is a crucial step to forming a solidarity within feminism that does not erase the lived experiences of different, marginalized, or contested groups. I engage with feminist transnational approaches to explore the experiences, knowledge, and perspectives of a particular group of feminists largely ignored by mainstream western feminist scholars and scholars of social movements alike. I emphasize the importance of individual narratives and reject overarching narratives and discourse studies that often misrepresent the distribution of power in society. I assert that there is no singular "woman's voice" and, specifically, no uniform "Muslim woman's voice." As a researcher committed to reflexivity, I advocate employing a transnational framework as a dynamic tool through which practical applications can gain relevance and shape within specific locales, moments, and conflicts. I aim to enhance this research process through an ongoing self-reflexive critique of my methodologies, prioritizing this continual assessment over finding definitive conclusions or closures.

It is important to note that the activism and efforts of secular Muslim feminists globally, while extensively documented, remain largely under-theorized. This documentation includes a wealth of case studies, detailed records of meetings, political statements, positions, and debates. These documents vividly illustrate the diversity and evolution of ideological perspectives and the resolutions and alliances that have characterized these movements. However, much of this valuable material remains untranscribed, creating a gap in written literature that could provide historical insights and counterpoints to the criticisms often directed at women's movements in these contexts. It is equally important to understand that secular Muslim feminists worldwide do not represent a monolithic movement. Indeed, some do not even identify with the label "secular," a term I seek to reclaim and clarify from those who view it as contradictory within the context of Islam. To explore the various strands of secular thought influencing Muslim feminist politics, I have drawn on personal observations from fifteen years as a feminist activist. Additionally, I have analyzed NGO publications and engaged in direct discussions with founders and leaders of organizations such as Women Living Under Muslim Laws (WLUML), Inspire UK, and Brigade de Mere in France. Autobiographies and monographs penned by secular Muslim feminists over the past few decades have also been instrumental in this analysis. Moreover, while this book does not aim to empirically prove how organized Islamist groups may have hindered the rights of Muslim women, evidence supporting this perspective is referenced through the writings, talks, and interviews with the feminists featured in this work.

A persistent methodological challenge in feminist scholarship is the question of representation. While all ethical models contribute to "ethical knowing," the feminist model draws upon a reflexive approach that "moves beyond a model of reasoning and rationality and enables the acknowledgment of feelings and emotions."[25] What is at stake here is that, as researchers, our role in interpreting, representing, and authoring our subjects' views, standpoints, actions, and experiences places us in a position of significant authority over the knowledge produced through the research process. Representation in ethnography is intricately tied to power dynamics and can inadvertently foster imperialist tendencies, potentially skewing the portrayal of research subjects' knowledge, experiences, and ideologies. Gayatri Spivak argues that many researchers end up producing the same dominant forms of knowing they aimed to dismantle. In addressing this dilemma, Lorraine Nencel suggests that reflexivity should be practiced in a context-specific manner tailored to the particularities of the research setting. Given the backlash that secular Muslim feminists often encounter due to their work and ideologies, I must avoid exacerbating their challenges by misrepresenting or misinterpreting their narratives. Consequently, my writing strives to provide a space for these feminists to represent themselves on their own terms. Rather than imposing my interpretations, I aim to offer insights into their everyday lives and ideologies. In this capacity, my role as an interpreter has partly involved creating a "bricolage" of these experiences, piecing together a mosaic that respects and reflects their diverse perspectives.

My passage in coming to this inquiry, which started as a self-narrative in the preface, is an integral part of the mapping of this book. The elements of investigation were drawn from my own life experiences that presented and sustained my passion and interest in providing a counternarrative to predominant narratives about "Muslim women." In light of the post-positivist turn in the social sciences, and while the positivist paradigm has focused on the objectivity, validity, and generalizability of social research, others, like feminists, constructionists, and postmodernists, have sought to make a fundamental break from this setting and develop approaches that assure the quality and trustworthiness of their research. In reference to John Creswell and Dana Miller's measures for establishing validity, I hope I have provided a description that is sufficiently "thick" as to give the reader a feel for the settings in which this data was collected and that my commitment to reflexive practice has made transparent my positionality.

The Organizing of the Book

Chapter II of this book explores how secular Muslim feminist thinkers and activists position themselves within broader cultural traditions and contemporary debates. The chapter aims to define the perspectives of secular Muslim feminists who articulate a Muslim "cultural" identity while affirming their commitment to secularism and human rights. It delves into their complex narratives as they respond to oversimplified and polarized mainstream representations, challenging the constraints imposed by rigid categories. The narratives revolve around several topics: their understanding of feminism, their relationship with Islam, their views on secularism and its relevance to Islam, and their critiques of cultural relativism and Islamophobia.

Chapter III situates the activism of secular Muslim feminists within broader historical and political contexts. It reviews critical debates and strategies that have shaped feminist movements in Muslim societies since the early twentieth century, highlighting the ongoing presence and impact of secular feminist thought. It also delves into the complexities of "secular feminism" and "Islamic feminism" in the context of Muslim societies, exploring the arguments for and against each approach. It highlights the importance of acknowledging the diversity of voices within both secular and Islamic feminist movements and the emergence of newer perspectives that have the potential to bridge ideological divides and foster inclusive dialogue. The chapter aims to illustrate that feminism, particularly secular feminism, has always had a presence in Muslim contexts, albeit often overlooked or disregarded. It seeks to highlight the potentially harmful consequences of exclusively advocating for women's rights within a religious framework.

Chapter IV examines the political context by tracing the interplay of race, gender, and religion in historical imperial conquests and colonization. It reveals how the legacies of these colonial encounters have influenced the positioning of Muslims, particularly Muslim women, over the past fifty years in narratives related to war, violence, and empire building. Using "gendered orientalism" as a framework, the chapter also addresses the gendered dimensions of the global "War on Terror." Furthermore, the chapter explores the rise of fundamentalist movements within Muslim societies and the surge of right-wing ideologies in the west, both employing the same trope of "saving Muslim women" from their "misogynist, terrorist" men as a justification for military interventions. This analysis argues that Muslim women become entangled within these competing forces, constrained by the "savior" narratives that limit their public image and agency.

In Chapter V, the discussion shifts to the works on Muslim women's pietist agency that emerged in the 1980s as a counter to the savior narrative, contributing to the post-secular turn that has been encouraged in academia by what has become known as "Islamic feminism," which is distinct from the modernist and secular feminists discussed in Chapter III. The chapter discusses the implications of such theorizations and the application of what Saba Mahmood terms "docile agency" for Muslim contexts, and the challenges they pose for secular "Muslim" feminist activism both within Muslim contexts and beyond, not only by alienating them but also by attempting to wipe out their contributions to the feminist movement in Muslim contexts.

Chapter VI delves into the evolution of the concept of secularism over the past two centuries. It starts by exploring how secularism has traditionally been associated with western norms and values, seen as dramatically contrasting with Islam. This perception has led to the characterization of modern Europe as a secular realm that treats Muslims as abstract citizens and a distinct minority group. The chapter further delves into the complexities and controversies surrounding secularism in Islamic political thought, influenced by historical factors like colonialism and interference from the west and the ambiguities inherent in the concept itself. Adopting a feminist lens, the chapter challenges the historical record of secular states in upholding women's rights, revealing instances where gender equality was not prioritized. Additionally, it examines the global perspective on secularism, discussing the challenges and opportunities it presents in facilitating choice, ethics, and coexistence beyond western contexts. I argue that a new critical engagement with secularism as a normative principle in democratic, multicultural societies may help bridge common ground amidst politically diverse orientations.

The final chapter (Chapter VII) begins with a summary of the overlooked secular feminist movements in Muslim nations to explore how these voices are often misconstrued as either simply mimicking western ideals or betraying their own cultural and religious identities. It then critically analyzes the often-limited methods and strategies of the so-called progressive forces in Europe—western feminists and sections of the left—who are wary of supporting anyone who opposes Islamist ideologists, bending to both the pressure from fundamentalists and the guilty feelings inherited from the colonial past. The chapter further explores the challenges faced by secular Muslim feminists due to critiques from Islamic and postcolonial feminist scholarship that question the appropriateness of a "secular" framework, branding them as compromised, biased, culturally insensitive, imperialist, and "native informants." In closing, the chapter discusses the ways in which diverse forms of feminist organizing can accommodate differences and absorb conflict while allowing for the solidarity necessary for collective action.

Drawing the attention back to the core objective of this book—questioning the notion of an inherent, fixed definition of secularism and challenging the stereotypical orientalist depictions of Muslim women as victims, as well as the fabricated image of an overly empowered "authentic" Muslim woman by postcolonial feminists—the concluding remarks make the case for promoting and enhancing the creation of spaces that enable secular and political expressions for Muslim women's progress in various contexts, while also emphasizing the importance of fostering solidarity and collaboration among diverse Muslim feminists as a means of cultivating a robust social movement strengthened by, rather than diminished, by diversity and disagreement.

2

Demystifying Secular Muslim Feminism

On her website, the self-proclaimed human rights campaigner Yasmine Mohammed states that her mission is to champion "the rights of women living within Muslim majority countries, as well as those who struggle under religious fundamentalism."[1] Mohammed founded Free Hearts Free Minds, an organization that supports "freethinkers" within Muslim-majority countries. In her book *Unveiled*, she recounts her experiences growing up in a "fundamentalist Islamic" household, aiming to shed light "on the religious trauma that so many women still today are unable to discuss."[2] She critiques both Islam and the left, which she accuses of inadvertently enabling radical Islam in the fight against Islamophobia, by labeling all critique of Islamic practices as prejudiced, which stifles necessary internal reform and silences voices advocating for human rights. Mohammed is the founder of the hashtag campaign #NoHijabDay celebrated on the first of February,[3] to raise awareness about girls and women who wish to remove their *hijab* but cannot or who have faced consequences after doing so. One of Mohammed's most impactful projects is the podcast *Forgotten Feminists*, where she interviews women from what she calls "restrictive" religious backgrounds who have survived and overcome their hardships. In my view, the significance of this podcast is that it brings to light the stories and struggles of many ordinary Muslim women whose names we will not recognize and whose voices might go otherwise unheard. "The media wrote nothing about us," Masih Alinejad, an Iranian journalist and political activist, tells IranWire. Masoumeh (Masih) Alinejad, born in 1976 in a village in a northern province in Iran, continues:

> I was thinking that a lot of people pay the price in villages and provincial towns and the media never talks about them. So, I decided to leave the provinces and go to Tehran. I did not want to belong to a small student group that the government could suppress without paying a price. And it did suppress us. But if I worked for newspapers, I could criticize more loudly. When I joined reformist newspapers,

I could criticize those in power from close up. I went to Tehran and decided that I wanted to become a journalist.[4]

By joining reformist newspapers in the capital, Alinejad aimed to confront those in power more directly and effectively, although the price she paid remained high. Following the disputed 2009 presidential elections in Iran, while the government denied any violence against demonstrators, she documented and published the names of fifty-seven protestors who were killed. After the election, the government initiated an extensive crackdown on freedom of speech, arresting many journalists and prompting her to leave Iran for the UK. Despite her relocation, the Iranian regime and its affiliated media continued to smear and attack her. In May 2014, Alinejad launched her Facebook page, "My Stealthy Freedom"; Alinejad's movement, marked by her sharing of photos without a headscarf and her call for Iranian women to do the same, has garnered significant international attention. Her stance, while not anti-*hijab*, advocates for personal choice. Alinejad has emerged as a symbol of resistance for Iranian women who face severe consequences, including physical harm and death, for choosing to remove their compulsory headscarves.

This chapter examines feminists like Mohammed and Alinejad despite the apparent difference in the ways they position themselves. I refer to these feminists as "secular Muslim," "secular," and "Muslim" throughout this book. It explores their perspectives, focusing on the ways they position themselves within broader traditions and debates. Drawing on various interviews and documentary materials, including public talks, online blogs, books, and autobiographies, the chapter explores themes related to feminism, secularism, religion, and the War on Terror. The reflections and insights presented in this chapter do not easily fit into dominant political or academic narratives about Muslim women, which are often simplistic and polarized, failing to capture their nuanced and multifaceted experiences. These perspectives and positions cut across traditional boundaries and defy easy labels, highlighting the complex interplay between feminism, secularism, religion, and sociopolitical contexts and underscoring the diversity and power of their thought and advocacy.

Don't Label Me!

"Labels keep us all in our assigned places. At root, that's why we are divided!"[5] Irshad Manji, founder of the Moral Courage Project at the University of

Southern California, addresses this passage in her book *Don't Label Me*, which begins with an imaginative dialogue with her deceased dog, "Lily." Manji posits that the resurgence of white nationalist sentiment in the United States signifies a backlash against diversity and multiculturalism. She argues that labeling erodes the unifying potential of diversity, distinguishing between what she terms "Factory-style diversity"[6] and "honest diversity."[7] Factory-style diversity objectifies individuals by reducing them to their labels, while honest diversity celebrates varied opinions, ideas, and personalities, transcending people "beyond prefabricated labels."[8] Manji outlines a three-step approach to achieving genuine diversity: rejecting the false certainty of labels, breaking away from the confines of identity politics, and releasing the need for constant validation. She advocates cultivating "internal pluralism," which she defines as the recognition and acceptance of the multiple identities that each individual possesses.

Manji's personal story has significantly shaped her advocacy work, particularly in her call for a reformation of Islam. She has openly discussed her experiences growing up within her faith, facing challenges and conflicts within her community, and her journey toward advocating for a more inclusive and tolerant interpretation of Islam. Through personal anecdotes and life experiences, Manji illustrates the contemporary link between diversity and identity politics. Much like other feminists covered in this book, Manji adamantly rejects being labeled, highlighting the freedom that comes with transcending the constraints of labels. Like other secular Muslim feminists, she advocates for a more inclusive approach to diversity that celebrates individual differences and fosters genuine dialogue across diverse perspectives. In fact, she seems to carry intersectionality to its natural conclusion, recognizing the intersecting web of human identities and viewing the individual as the ultimate minority. Intersectionality, which emerged as a response to the limitations of traditional identity politics, recognizes that individuals hold multiple identities that intersect in complex ways, shaping their experiences of oppression and privilege. We are all different, and each is unique enough, making aligning with one defined identity practically challenging.

Secular Muslim feminists and activists face a significant challenge as they navigate the realms of both battling religious fundamentalism and combating the rise of the extreme right. As they demand the reform of discriminatory laws and practices, they are accused by members of their communities "of being Westernized elites, anti-Islam, anti-sharia, people who have deviated from our faith."[9] Simultaneously, with the rise of right-wing populism in Europe along with "nationalist sentiment and xenophobia" and hysteria over the rights of "poor Muslim women," the voices of these women become more dubious.[10] With identity politics becoming ever more prevalent and powerful, further confusion is added in regard to ways in which the works of these feminists can be read. In a sense, these feminists who embrace secular ideologies view their identities as fluid, a blend of ethnic cultures, Islam, western values, and personal contexts. Unlike those who emphasize a visible Muslim identity through attire like the headscarf, for example, these women reconstruct their upbringing based on ideals of liberty, tolerance, freedom, and democracy while critiquing certain religious practices without denouncing Islam itself. They see themselves as representing a genre of "Muslim" women committed to the feminist goals of challenging patriarchy and transforming the oppressive ideological and material conditions that sustain the subordination of all women. These narratives represent an intersection with broader themes such as the "War on Terror," religious fundamentalism, right-wing politics, and individual agency reflected in their interpretations and reappropriations of culturally available discourses. With the rise of identity politics, it is not surprising that these feminists refuse to align with any of the dominant groups on the global sociopolitical scene. Recognizing that identity politics often leads to exclusion rather than inclusion, Maryam Namazie writes:

> The not-so-funny thing about identity politics is that while it claims that each particular "group" has a singular identity (as if that were even possible), the identity is so restrictive that it keeps out many more people than it allows in. In fact, that's the whole point. If you want in, you have to make sure you look the part and follow the rules. If you terrorise a Primary school in Birmingham to prevent lessons saying that being gay is OK, if you defend Sharia courts despite their promotion of violence against women, or legitimise apostates being shunned and killed, then you will automatically pass the Muslimness authenticity test! Not so much if you are a gay Muslim, or an ex-Muslim, or a feminist who doesn't want to wear the hijab or fast during Ramadan, or a secularist who is opposed to Sharia law.[11]

As a Muslim feminist myself, burdened by various labels that fail to reflect my true identity, I resonate with the feminists discussed in this book. The discrepancy between what is discursively constructed about who we are and what is historically and materially experienced by ourselves seems to be a shared struggle. Like all women of the world, Muslim women are not a homogeneous group, and their emancipation should not be used to divert attention from the patriarchal systems that oppress all women, whose emancipation is far from a given. The question of who gets to define what constitutes legitimate exercises of power and who gets to define what constitutes a legitimate voice are interconnected. Secular Muslim feminists argue that secular voices from minority communities should not be seen as less legitimate than religious voices from those same communities.[12] They critique the notion that religious voices automatically represent the entire community, emphasizing that the diverse perspectives within minority groups deserve equal recognition and participation. However, opposing discourses often attempt to marginalize these voices, marking them as "Islamophobes," "imperialists," and "native informants." This makes it harder to shift focus and create space for alternative visions that highlight the complexity of and redefine the lives of Muslim women. That said, I am well aware that introducing yet another label, "secular Muslim feminism," might seem contradictory. But abandoning identities altogether presents its challenges. Proponents of group identity argue that abandoning such labels leads to the isolation and fragmentation of individuals, rendering them "atomistic" rather than genuinely autonomous.[13] Take, for example, how transgender writer Julia Serano puts it:

> I would "love" to stop talking about being transgender. It would be absolutely wonderful to live in a world where I didn't have to constantly consider that aspect of my person. But you know what? I don't have the privilege of not thinking about it, because there are shit-tons of people out there who hate me, harass me, and who wish to criminalize and silence me *because* I'm transgender.[14]

Serano's perspective underscores the importance of group identities in fostering solidarity and collective action. Group identities provide a sense of belonging and shared experiences, which can be crucial for marginalized individuals navigating societal structures. However, it is equally vital to avoid rigid categorizations that can restrict individual autonomy and expression. Political identities are not inherent; they arise when societies use categories like race, gender, and class to create unequal access to rights and resources. Ironically, only those group identities that restrict access to power gain prominence. This occurs in the process of contesting or protecting the exclusions that define these groups. Often, the narcissism of small differences obscures the far greater commonalities and mutual interdependencies among us. An awareness of the complexity and multiplicity of individual identities can facilitate the formation of political coalitions across otherwise insurmountable divides of animosity and suspicion. In this sense, the intersectionality movement becomes essential to address such concerns. The pursuit of democratic justice is an ongoing aspiration, acknowledging that our understanding and implementation of human rights evolve over time. True justice is an ideal we continually strive for, not a finite goal we can fully achieve. However, we can actively address the most severe injustices in our society by focusing on human rights and responsibilities. This book serves as a "miner's canary," warning of the harms of deeply rooted power structures that threaten the strength of liberal democracies.[15] Nevertheless, it is crucial to avoid suppressing our differences in the pursuit of inclusivity. While building broad coalitions, we must engage in open and honest dialogue that allows a deeper understanding of our various perspectives and experiences. Identity politics, as Audre Lorde argues, may be an essential entry point into a world deeply defined by racism, gender inequality, and hatred, but used on its own is not enough. We must look for connections that bring us together, to help us understand the oppressions we all face, and to build bridges to each other's struggles without glossing over our differences. "Secular Muslim feminism" aims to strike this balance between acknowledging the significance of group identities and promoting individual agency within those identities. While critical of the exclusive nature of some identity-based movements, it recognizes the importance of solidarity and collective action in challenging harmful stereotypes.

Which "Muslim Woman"?

Women have long been a symbol of the Muslim world. Unsurprisingly, in the decades following 9/11, debates about Muslim women have attracted even greater interest. Now, *hijab*, polygamy, forced marriages, female genital mutilation, and the sexual victimization of young Muslim women continue to receive excessive attention from western media. The figure of a victimized and manipulated Muslim woman continues to appear in conversations about Muslim societies and their integration within western societies. At the same time, when scholars like Marnia Lazreg, Sa'diyya Shaikh, Jasmin Zine, Sadia Abbas, Asma Barlas, Afiya Zia and others decry the status of Muslim women in Muslim societies, they are seen as "western apologists" who fuel Islamophobia and opportunistically employ the political conflicts between the West and Islam for their personal gain.[16] These very feminists are precisely accused of portraying *all* Muslim women as victims of their own cultures, reinforcing the view that Muslim women need saving and, in turn, fueling the narrative of the War on Terror. But which Muslim women? Sa'diyya Shaikh writes:

There are also some Muslim women who have internalized the patriarchal dimension of their heritage and become its proponents, while at the other end of the continuum, there are those who have exited the religious tradition as a response to experiences of patriarchal realities ... The realities of gender dynamics in Islam are a complex and polymorphous as the realities of women in other religious, social, and political contexts.[17]

Here, Sa'diyya Shaikh emphasizes that Muslim women's experiences are as diverse as those of women in any other context. Yet, views such as those narrated by Shadi Sadr in *Crime and Impunity*, Shirin Ebadi in *Iran Awakening*, Masih Alinejad in *The Wind in My Hair*, and many more are interpreted by postcolonial feminists as accounts that validate the assumptions of the orientalist writer, that of Islam being a cause of their abuse. In this sense, they argue that if such accounts are accepted as legitimate, the orientalist can no longer be accused of misrepresenting the voice of Muslim women since they say the same things that Muslim women say about their lives under the subjugation of Islam. What do we do then when these feminists' portrayal of Muslim societies helps confirm the image of Muslim women as victims of their backward cultures? How do we address the concerns of feminist scholars who highlight the challenges faced by Muslim women while simultaneously resisting the appropriation of their narratives by orientalist discourses? Accepting feminist critiques as valid could inadvertently bolster orientalist arguments, reinforcing the image of Muslim women as victims of their own cultures. But neither does using the rhetoric of "agency" and "resistance" is helping. It reinforces "systems of inequality and dominance that are the root of oppression experienced by women."[18] In fact, by emphasizing the voice of the "Third world woman" as an "antidote to paternalistic white feminism," as Kiran Grewal puts it, we fall into the trap of celebrating authenticity.[19]

To navigate this, we must distinguish between genuine feminist critiques and orientalist misinterpretations. Feminist scholars aim to empower Muslim women by shedding light on the systemic inequalities and injustices they face. In contrast, orientalist discourses often exploit these critiques to perpetuate prejudiced and essentialist views of Muslim women and their societies. It is crucial to avoid falling into the trap of either accepting all feminist critiques as valid or dismissing them as tools of orientalism. Instead, we must engage in critical analysis, recognizing the valuable insights offered by feminist scholars while remaining vigilant against the appropriation of their narratives for harmful purposes. The narratives recounted in the autobiographies and books written by secular Muslim feminists are personal stories that display rich historical and cultural details. Instead of searching for a singular, monolithic image of a Muslim woman, they acknowledge the rich diversity of individual narratives that shape their lives. Each woman's story is a unique blend of personal experiences and the political realities of their society, weaving together a distinct path that defies simplistic generalizations. By attentively listening to the voices of these women and charting the intricacies of their life stories, we uncover a world far more complex than linear narratives that seek to impose a unifying narrative on their diverse experiences.

In the UK, Sara Khan, a prominent British human rights activist, author, and the founder of Inspire, an organization that focuses on women's rights and challenging extremism within Muslim communities, has frequently condemned the government for neglecting the involvement of Muslim women in policy decisions, challenging the prevalent misconception that all Pakistani women are docile and passive, a far cry from the actual diversity within the community. Khan has received backlash from conservative Muslim groups who view her organization, Inspire, as aligning with governmental agendas promoting a "westernized" version of Islam. Her stance on counter-extremism measures and her engagement with government bodies have led to political opposition and scrutiny from various quarters who question the efficacy and impact of her initiatives. Her outspoken views on women's rights and challenging orthodox interpretations of Islam have caused internal divisions within Muslim communities, with some factions viewing her as divisive or as not representing their interests accurately.[20] Mona Eltahawy echoes Khan's sentiment by cautioning against using the emancipation of Muslim women as a distraction from the pervasive patriarchal systems that oppress women globally, irrespective of their Muslim or western backgrounds. She writes:

> I implore allies in this part of the world to pay more attention to women's rights and refuse to allow cultural relativism to justify horrendous violations of women's rights. This is very different from calling on anyone to "rescue us" ... I expose misogyny in my part of the world to connect the feminist struggle in the Middle East and North Africa to the global one. Misogyny has not been completely wiped out anywhere.[21]

Eltahawy's statement highlights the crucial role of allies in upholding women's rights globally. It emphasizes the importance of refusing to let cultural relativism justify violations of women's rights while explicitly rejecting the "rescue" narrative. Instead, she focuses on connecting the feminist struggles across regions, recognizing shared experiences of misogyny, and advocating for collective action. On World Day for Cultural Diversity and Dialogue, Mariz Tadros, a professor of politics and development, argues that the global threat we must confront is not only the protection of cultural and religious minorities but "the very possibility of mixing and matching our culture, heritage, and beliefs as we want to live and experience them."[22] This resonates deeply with my own understanding of Muslim women who cannot be confined to simplistic binaries. As Tadros, my professor during my MA, emphasizes, our identities are far more complex, shaped by the broader political context, where those who don't fit the image of the "authentic" Muslim woman are finding it hard to be anything else in the public imaginary. It is crucial to remember that Muslim women, like all women across the globe, are incredibly diverse. Their identities are shaped by a multitude of factors beyond their religious affiliation. They are daughters, mothers, professionals, artists, activists, and so much more. Therefore, any analysis of the complexities surrounding Muslim women must consider the broader political landscape and its impact on their lives.

Which "Feminism"?

> Among those unwilling to compromise on the Islamic imperative for gender justice, there are some who define themselves as feminists, while there are others who do not sit comfortably with such an identification.[23]

Saʿdiyya Shaikh's quote above suggests that within the Islamic community, some individuals are committed to upholding gender justice but may have different approaches to how they define themselves in relation to this cause. Some may identify as feminists; others may share similar beliefs but do not feel wholly aligned with the feminist categorization. Despite the clear focus on questioning and challenging male domination within Muslim societies by the Muslim feminists discussed in this book, not all choose to identify as feminists. In her Journal article "Is Feminism Relevant to Arab Women?" Nawar al-Hassan Golley argues that feminism as an ideology is an indigenous product of the region's unique political and socioeconomic dynamics. Despite this argument, the ongoing debate in the western world on the relevance of feminism to Muslim women continues to question the compatibility of women's status and rights with the principles of Islamic sharia.[24] Nevertheless, while data indicates that around 1,500 women are killed annually in the United States by intimate partners, similar crimes in Muslim nations are labeled as "honor killings." Using this example, Rafia Zakaria argues that by labeling crimes against women of color as "cultural," we fail to address the broader issue of male control and violence against women. This creates a divisive category of "other" that hinders progress toward equal rights for *all* women. In the first few pages of her book *Against White Feminism*, she argues that an individual's race does not define white feminism, but by their refusal "to consider the role that whiteness and the racial privilege attached to it have played ... in universalizing white feminist concerns, agendas, and beliefs as being those of all feminists."[25] Echoed by Jamia Wilson in *This Book is Feminist*, Zakaria emphasizes that no single voice can fully define feminism and its possibilities.[26] While some critics view western feminist approaches as perpetuating reductionist views of Islam linked to colonial strategies that marginalize Indigenous cultures, others scrutinize "liberal" strands of western feminism for perpetuating stereotypes that justify harmful practices such as FGM and forced veiling. Critics argue that under the guise of protecting the sentiments of religious minorities, western liberal feminists often deflect discussions on religiously motivated abuses. While they are busy protecting the feelings of religious hardliners, as Khadija Khan writes in a blog post, "they neglect the safety and human rights of many other Muslims."[27] Seeing western liberal feminists aligning with such demands rather than prioritizing the broader human rights concerns within Muslim communities disheartens many secular Muslim feminists.

In the last few decades, the concept of intersectionality, which recognizes that multiple grounds of discrimination and oppression shape different realities, has grown out of black and postcolonial feminist theories. This shift has moved the focus from solely western women to a broader spectrum of perspectives. Liberation movements for minorities addressing issues of race and class have prompted discussions on the limitations of western feminism, which has often overlooked the intricate challenges faced by non-western women. Third world and transnational feminisms have emerged in response to the oversimplified analyses of gender oppression by white feminists. While both movements advocate for historically contextualized analyses of third world women's experiences and emphasize the importance of respecting their agency and voices, they have diverged in their approaches, with transnational feminism concentrating on global dynamics and third world feminism prioritizing local and national contexts. And despite the emergence of these new approaches to feminism, a full-fledged dialogue between mainstream western feminism and various minority-led feminisms remains elusive. This makes it difficult for many feminists to fully align with feminism without either adopting additional descriptors like third world, postcolonial, southern, Muslim, transnational, or casting off the feminist label altogether.

In the Muslim world, as mentioned in the introduction, two Muslim feminist paradigms emerged: Islamic feminism, which have gained currency since the 1990s and have become the label for a new brand of feminist scholarship and activism associated with Islam, and secular feminism advocating for universal rights. Feminists like Afiya Zia, Leila Mouri, Ibtissam Bouachrine, Sa'diyya Shaikh, and others critique Islamic feminism, which some view as an alternative to western feminism, for being burdened with contentious meanings and implications. They argue that it has become so entangled in local and global political struggles that it has lost its utility for descriptive or analytical purposes. According to Margot Badran, this category of feminism, which emerged in the 1980s through the efforts of diasporic feminist academics living in the West, differed from the rise of secular feminism in the Arab and Muslim world in the early decades of the twentieth century that took the form of social movement activism. Instead, it made its mark on the global scene primarily as a form of "discourse."[28] This argument is particularly important because, as Afiya Zia explains, this discourse has caused a rift among feminists in Muslim contexts regarding the value and application of gendered politics based on faith. Zia further notes that this division has complicated the way feminist identities within Islamic contexts are "viewed and interpreted by 'Western eyes.'"[29] Many, if not all, secular Muslim feminists argue that the concept of "Islamic" feminism is inherently flawed and self-contradictory. Mahnaz Afkhami, an Iranian Muslim Human Rights activist, writes:

> Our difference with Islamic feminists is that we don't try to fit feminism in the Qur'ān. We say that women have certain inalienable rights. The epistemology of Islam is contrary to women's right ... I call myself a Muslim and a feminist. I am not an Islamic feminist—that's a contradiction in terms.[30]

By identifying as both a Muslim and a feminist yet rejecting the label of Islamic feminist, Afkhami highlights the perceived tensions between her faith and the pursuit of gender equality. Similar ideas are expressed by Mona Eltahawy, who boldly voices her views on the compatibility of her religious identity and her feminist principles. In one of her public talks, she declares, "I am a Muslim, and I am a feminist," expressing profound outrage at both the Muslim Brotherhood for attempting to shape her Muslim identity and misogynist men for trying to define her feminism. This encapsulates a broader debate within feminist discourse about whether religious frameworks can adequately support the goals of feminism or if they perpetuate gender inequalities.

By critiquing hegemonic forms of feminism, secular Muslim feminists assert their understanding of gender equality within their unique contexts and environments. Some reject being confined to a singular feminist narrative and emphasize that while they strive to empower women, they are committed to distancing themselves from certain problematic philosophies. As a Muslim woman who is passionate about the rights of all women yet dissociates with western feminist discourses, Sara Khan expresses disappointment in how western feminism sometimes undermines the rights of Muslim women, whether in their choice to identify as Muslim or otherwise. She continues to tell me, "I have seen feminists describe Islam as 'a misogynistic faith' and 'illogical superstition,' which can only be described as patronizing and insulting to Muslim feminists across the world who are actively campaigning for the rights of women." From within secular Muslim feminism, there is a call to shift the ongoing debate between universalism and cultural relativism, arguing that the challenges faced by Muslim women should be understood within the specific context of their experiences. Yasmine Mohammed, for example, argues that liberal feminism has failed women and girls by turning a blind eye to the atrocities committed by Islamists against their women and girls. At the same time, many secular Muslim feminists challenge the stereotypical belief that Muslim immigrants are incapable of adapting to western norms of gender equality. They insist that Muslim women, like women of all backgrounds, must be understood within their unique historical, social, and ideological frameworks. This is compounded by the current challenging gendered dynamics in the Muslim world, where Islamic feminists advocate for the protection of women within the Islamic faith. In contrast, secular feminists call for the separation of religion from civil society and the State. In countries like Pakistan and Egypt, for example, the entanglement of secularism and feminism among middle-class Muslim women further complicates the matter, highlighting the intricate dynamics at play for secular Muslim feminists seeking to carve out their identities within the larger feminist discourse.

For instance, consider the ongoing discussions surrounding the Muslim woman's headscarf. While the term *"hijab"* literally translates to "barrier" or "curtain," conceptually, it encompasses a range of different forms of covering Muslim women adopt, ranging from headscarves to loose clothing to a full veil. Half a century ago, *hijab* served as a visible marker of ethnic identity, and more recently, especially after the Islamic resurgence of the 1980s, it has served as a marker of "Muslim identity." The current emergence of overt Islamophobia as a result of the 9/11 attacks and the subsequent "War on Terror" served to intensify the fixation on Muslim women's bodies. Within the current charged controversies—*L'affaire du Foulard* (the Headscarf Affair) in France, the headscarf controversy in Turkey[31], the *niqāb* ban in some European countries,[32] and more—the veil is constructed as a signifier of the pervasive "Islamic threat." According to 2010 and 2011 polls in the UK, most Britons favor a *hijab* ban.[33] Foreign Secretary Jack Straw's statement in October 2006 that women had to remove the *niqāb* when visiting his "advice surgery" resonated with many in the majority society.[34] In America, veiling now evokes "the oppressed woman in *burqa* living under the Taliban rule in Afghanistan."[35] And despite the official separation of state and religion affirmed by the US Constitution, there are documented disputes over headscarves and "mounting discrimination against women who wear them."[36] In France, the controversy focused on the inability of certain immigrants to "melt" into French society.[37] In fact, the controversy and its ripples rendered Islam one of the main roadblocks to the successful integration of postcolonial immigrants in France.[38] In several other European countries, the adherence to *hijab* has led to political arguments and proposals for a legal (partial or full) ban in some or all circumstances. Other countries have already passed laws banning the wearing of the face veil; Belgium, in 2011; the Netherlands, in 2012; Bulgaria, in 2016; Austria, in 2017; Denmark, in 2018; and they are debating similar legislation.

Faith-based and secular-oriented Muslim feminists often collide over such politically charged issues. Many secular feminists, like Nawal El Saadawi, Chahdortt Djavann, and others, view *hijab* as an undeniable example of religious fundamentalism and patriarchal oppression and largely dismiss the views of Muslim women who choose to wear it. And some faith-based feminists, like Sahar Amer, Fadwa El Guindi, Sherine Hafez, and Saba Mahmood, view it not only as an inviolable religious tradition but also as a sign of "agency," "modesty," and "resistance." Between these two poles, Muslim feminists like Leila Ahmed and Amina Wadud do not consider *hijab* to be a religious requirement yet support the civil liberties of Muslim women in Europe who are denied the choice to adopt this style of dress in schools and other public institutions. While they support these liberties, they do not necessarily view this support as an endorsement of patriarchy and fundamentalism. Secular Muslim feminists discussed here do not all agree on a specific position regarding whether *hijab* is empowering or constraining. While some adamantly see the veil as a symbol of societal discrimination against women, others go as far as advocating for its complete ban. Fadela Amara, a secular

French Muslim feminist and the former president of the association *Ni Putes Ni Soumises* (Neither Whores nor Submissives) supports the French dominant line of argument calling for a complete banning of the headscarf. Similarly, Mariam Namazie proposes a ban at least on wearing the face cover, which she describes as "no different from living in a 'mobile prison,' a tomb or a rubbish bag."[39] A more moderate view, Masih Alinejad advocates for women's right to choose whether to wear *hijab* or not, rejecting the idea of a mandatory ban. Sara Khan, while opposing a ban on *hijab*, questions its status as a religious necessity and criticizes the media's fixation on the topic, attributing it to an Islamist resurgence. In an article for *The Guardian*, she makes no attempt to hide her frustration as she criticizes the prevailing media portrayals of Muslim women, particularly concerning *hijab*. She writes:

> As France finds itself in the grip of emergency law brought about by the numerous Islamist-inspired terror attacks that have plagued the country in recent times, you would think the authorities would have more pressing concerns on their mind than the burkini, which as many have pointed out is really not dissimilar to a wetsuit.[40]

Responding to those who see *hijab* as a marker of unquestionable agency, Chahla Chafiq argues that choosing to wear the veil is not akin to selecting lipstick—it is a much more complicated decision. Similar to Amina Wadud and Leila Ahmed's views, Chafiq argues that the concept of *hijab* did not originate in early Islam but emerged later, serving as a symbol of the gendered division and hierarchization of roles prescribed by sharia law. While acknowledging that some young women opt to wear *hijab*, Chafiq emphasizes that "it is precisely the sexual dimension of the female body that this choice exacerbates," she argues.[41] Chahdortt Djavann further challenges the notion that the veil is always a matter of personal choice, writing, "fascism, anti-semitism, racism may all be based on personal choices, but that should not make those choices respectable."[42] Echoing this sentiment, Mona Eltahawy criticizes the lack of substantial debate around issues that infringe upon women's rights, which opens the door for both the political right and the Muslim right to capitalize on the situation. In an article, she writes: "Those of us who really care about women's rights should talk about the dangers in equating piety with the disappearance of women."[43]

The intention is not to strip women of their freedom of choice by outlawing *hijab* but to probe whether this so-called choice is genuinely made by the woman herself. The notion that the Muslim way of life cannot be consistent or compatible with western modernity overlooks the diversity in attire traditions embraced by Muslims worldwide, where, for example, women in Saudi Arabia dress very differently from women in Southeast Asia or North Africa. Even within the same country, dress traditions may vary. In Egypt, for example, women in the coastal north dress very differently from women in the south of the country and the Nubian area. Similarly, *hijab*, as a headscarf, can be combined with western dress forms and worn fashionably, piously, playfully, or creatively. However, for secular Muslim feminists, issues like *hijab* cannot be divorced from broader debates portraying Islam as a monolithic religion or secularism as a western concept irreconcilable with Islam. The controversies surrounding *hijab* highlight the complexity of women's choices within diverse cultural and religious contexts, challenging the notion of a monolithic feminist perspective. By grappling with issues like *hijab*, secular Muslim feminists confront more profound questions around religious freedoms, cultural diversity, and women's agency, which transcend traditional feminist paradigms and call for a more nuanced and inclusive approach to feminist discourse.

And Whose "Islam"?

We are all well aware and probably used to "cultural Judaism," as expressed in music, comedy, and the intellectual heritage. Now, among the children and grandchildren of immigrants from Muslim-majority countries, there are many whose upbringing has been influenced by Islam but who do not really practice or even believe in the faith. Their experience of mosques is limited to weddings, funerals, and *Eid*. But unlike "cultural Jew," the term "cultural Muslim" is not widely recognized. Even proponents use it unsurely. Mohsin Zaidi, author of *A Dutiful Boy: A Memoir of a Gay Muslim's Journey to Acceptance*, states in an interview, "I describe myself as culturally Muslim, which is something that doesn't have a particular meaning, I guess."[44] Generally speaking, the "cultural Muslim" is a member of the Muslim community who is nonpracticing but retains an attachment to elements of Islamic culture.[45] It refers to the ordinary, everyday secularized Muslim who might even be engaged in a private and personal manner with their religion but rather apolitical.[46] The qualifier "cultural," used by Muslims themselves, seems to indicate awareness that the conscious choice of calling oneself a cultural Muslim dissociates them from anti-Muslim sentiment.[47]

In the west, recent research has shown a decline in church attendance, with traditional theories of secularization being challenged. This decline has been linked to the rise of "cultural Christianity," where religion is used to identify with national traditions or ethnic heritage rather than faith. The decrease in church attendance has also been associated with increased diversity in attitudes toward moral issues such as abortion, divorce, and euthanasia. These findings collectively suggest a shift toward cultural Christianity and a decline in traditional religious practice in western societies. Despite this, the term "cultural Muslim" is not widely accepted in western societies because Islam is often perceived as "exceptional," resistant to secularization due to its role in law and governance, a viewpoint held by both Muslims and non-Muslims. Mainstream academic literature and media use the words "Islam" or "Muslim" unvaryingly, implying consistency and homogeneity. The reality, however, is that none of the prevailing assumptions stand up to scrutiny. Similar to all religions, Islam encompasses a spectrum of interpretations based on diverse ideological perspectives, schools of law, sects, ethnicities, and even genders. Contrary to popular notions, secular principles are not incompatible or foreign to Islam. The widespread belief that secularism has no place in Islamic traditions, elaborated further in subsequent chapters, is more reflective of a stereotype than a factual understanding. And the widespread assumption that all Muslims or religious minorities are deeply devout is significantly inaccurate. Likewise, the notion that strong religious adherence necessarily equates to a preference for social policies shaped by religion, be it among "practicing" Christians, Muslims, or adherents of other faiths, is essentially a myth. Research conducted by Southall Black Sisters, for example, shows that even women who are observant of Islam display a desire to traverse different religious spaces for their social and emotional lives and secular spaces for their activism and advice.[48]

Some of the feminists discussed in this book make explicit reference to Islam as a vital part of their identity but assert that their understanding of it is unique to them and does not necessarily reflect any mainstream representation of Islam. Sara Khan, for instance, challenges the idea of a single unified image of a "Muslim." During one of our interviews, she reflects on the concept of the "authentic" or "good" Muslim, dismissing it as a fictional construct. Drawing a parallel with Christianity, she asserts that similar to the diversity within Christian identity, Islam, too, defies any singular portrayal. She emphasizes the multifaceted, unpredictable nature of the Muslim community, underscoring its complexity and diversity beyond a simplistic label like "the Muslim community." In her words, she tells me:

> I do not think there is one monolithic Islam. I believe there are many Islams. There are patriarchal interpretations of the religion and there are egalitarian

interpretations of it. You can argue Islam is a religion of peace, and you can also argue it is a religion of violence ... I think that is the thing with religion. I do not think it is unique to Islam; it is the way all religions are. And if you can have a dominant interpretation of Islam that is egalitarian and advocates for human rights as contextualized for the 21st century ... that should be the way forward.

Khan identifies herself as a Muslim, a "progressive Muslim" who supports human rights and refuses fundamentalist interpretations of Islam. She underscores the diverse interpretations of sharia and challenges the notion that being Muslim necessitates outward symbols like head coverings. In her book, despite describing herself as an atheist, Irshad Manji states that she voluntarily identifies as Muslim because she believes "in Islam's original principles" of which is "the unity of God's vast creation."[49] Maryam Namazie explains that the Council of Ex-Muslims uses the term ex-Muslim rather than atheist, not because they want to create yet another false identity that divides and excludes but to reiterate that religion is a personal matter and a private affair. The council asserts that the pursuit of universal rights and values is a universal human endeavor, not merely a western concept. "To make 'Muslim' the most important characteristic is part of the attempt to Islamicise people and relegate them to the political Islamic movement," Namazie argues.[50] Many of the feminists discussed here do not denounce all religious customs in their personal lives; however, they resist the imposition of such practices by what they call "fundamental" Muslims. Figures like Irshad Manji, Mona Eltahawy, Sara Khan, and Noni Darwish see their religious observance as linked more to cultural traditions and background. For example, the act of fasting during Ramadan is perceived by Sara Khan as a way of engaging in a collective activity, describing Ramadan, *Jum'ah* (Friday prayer), Bairam, and so on as "cultural events" rather than religious practices. Some stress that the observance of Muslim festivities like *Eid* and religious events is primarily a cultural expression rather than purely religious. Comparable to "secular Jews" who associate with Jewish identity based on culture rather than faith, many Muslims view Islam as a cultural facet of their identity rather than solely a religious affiliation. Insisting on a singular, "traditional" image of a Muslim hinders individuals from expressing their unique interpretations of the faith and their personal experiences as Muslims.

In an article for "The Conversation," Milad Milani outlines the concept of a "cultural Muslim," referring to an individual in the Muslim community who, while not actively practicing, maintains a connection to aspects of Islamic culture.[51] Highlighting the rich cultural heritage of the Muslim world, spanning from Spain in the West to Pakistan in the East, Islamic cultures exhibit diversity and distinctiveness. Milani argues that the designation of a "cultural Muslim" not only reflects the cultural variance inherent in Islam but also signifies a disengagement from its religious establishment, similar to cultural Christianity and cultural Judaism. This category, as described by Milani, encapsulates everyday secularized Muslims who maintain a private and personal relationship with their religion, devoid of political associations. As he explains, the cultural Muslim represents an important part of the west's dialogue between religion and secularity. So despite criticism and pushback not only from the west but from the Muslim community, as Kia Abdulla, a British Muslim novelist based in London, describes, "to say you're a cultural Muslim cherry-picks the best of both worlds, I'm told; you avail yourself of the food, music, culture (and, yes, column inches too) without putting the work in."[52] To reject our claim to Muslimness, she continues, "divests us of the customs and traditions that have coloured our lives so deeply."[53]

A "Secular" Champion of Religious Freedom

Differences aside, secular Muslims stand together in opposing Islamic fundamentalism, the application of sharia laws, and the imposition of dress codes. They all agree that religion and politics should remain separate, yet do not see a conflict in identifying as both Muslim and secular. They firmly believe that religion should not constitute the only source of values and axis of orientation in people's lives. Some address religious observance as a "private" feature of everyday life, while others see it as merely a "cultural" aspect. Tehmina Kazi, the former director of British Muslims for Secular Democracy, an organization that aims to raise awareness of the benefits of democracy and its contribution to a shared vision of citizenship, explains to *Faith in Feminism* her understanding of the term "secularism":

> Put simply ... an approach to Islam that believes faith and government are two separate spheres; that the political leadership should not be religious, but secular and democratic. ... On a personal level, one can be a secular Muslim and still pray five times a day, sport a headscarf or beard, and fast during Ramadan, or any combination of the above. What sets secular Muslims apart is their unyielding commitment to equality and universal human rights, even when these may conflict with certain traditions that purport to be religiously inspired.[54]

Kazi's view of being a secular Muslim, allowing for the coexistence of religious practices while upholding a solid dedication to principles of equality and universal human rights, demonstrates a commitment to challenging traditions that may contradict these fundamental values. However, it is important to recognize that secular Muslim feminists who speak from a location that embraces multiculturalism, such as the UK, may have differing perspectives on "secularism" compared to those from regions that adhere to concepts like *laïcité*, such as France. It is crucial to point out that the different conceptions around the role of religion in different contexts contribute to the different ideologies and narratives of those I call "secular" Muslim feminists. Historically, France has allowed access to French citizenship, but only for immigrants who have been willing to assimilate by speaking the language and accepting the French concepts of *laïcité*. *Laïcité* in France advocates for a strict separation of religion and state, striving for a secular public sphere devoid of religious influence and upholding state neutrality in religious matters. This concept, deeply rooted in French history since the Revolution, often results in restrictions on religious symbols in public spaces to maintain a secular environment. This has made it difficult for women like Chahla Chafiq and Chahdortt Djavann to refuse the French secular model, leading to their firm opposition to any display of religion in the public sphere. On the other hand, British secularism takes a comparatively more flexible stance, accommodating a diverse array of religious beliefs within public life. While also endorsing the separation of religion and state, the UK's approach is influenced by the historical presence of the Church of England and operates within a framework of multiculturalism, aiming to respect the plurality of religious practices and beliefs in society. This has made it easier for women like Sara Khan, Gita Sahgal, and Pragna Patel to articulate an acceptance of Islam as entwined in their identity and activism. Yet, a clear similarity between both was the argument that Islam is not monolithic. This recognition counters fundamentalist assertions aiming to enforce a singular interpretation of the religion. Just as diversity exists among Christians, Buddhists, and Hindus, a myriad of beliefs and customs also thrive within the Muslim community.

At the far end of the spectrum, Ayaan Hirsi Ali, born in Somalia and known as a prominent advocate of secularism, is depicted by Angel Rabasa and colleagues as a "well-known public representative of the values of secularism and the universality of civic freedom, rule of law, and women's and human rights beyond multiculturalist relativism."[55] In her defense of secularism, Ayaan Hirsi Ali takes an extremely radical stance that openly criticizes Islam as a backward, violent, and misogynistic religion and argues that Muslim immigrants are culturally unsuited to life in the west. Similarly, the Iranian-born French writer Chahdortt Djavann considers Islam incompatible with philosophical pluralism.

Taslima Nasrin, a Bangladeshi-Swedish physician, feminist, secular humanist, and activist, argues that reform necessitates Muslims to replace religious laws with civil laws, fully separating Mosque and State.[56] A less radical approach is advocated by Canadian-Iranian Homa Arjomand, who focuses her criticisms on fundamentalist Islam as the "aggressive" faction of Political Islam.[57] Unlike Hirsi Ali, Arjomand scrutinizes not only Islamist movements but also conservative nationalist and Christian ideals that oppose gay marriage and abortion and defend capital punishment. She views secularism as a driving force that "obtains all progressive values for everyone."[58] Others like Irshad Manji, Mona Eltahawy, and Mariam Namazie endorse free speech, advocate for the separation of religion and State, and uphold the belief that religion should remain a personal choice.

On the one hand, some base their understanding on the French *laïcité*, which gradually spread throughout Western Europe, where secularism is invoked as a precondition of democracy, especially in defense of the rights of women, children, and sexual minorities. This necessitates the need to safeguard people's freedom "from" religion. On the other hand, those who believe in multicultural politics, at least in theory, allow the freedom "to" assert religious beliefs and make demands for religious recognition. The understanding of the term "freedom" in the French constitution casts it as a simple issue of liberation from constraints. This is paradoxical because the commitment to the Republican values and misunderstandings of what "freedom" entails, as Kiran Grewal explains, "may not serve the desired purpose" because "republican myths of freedom, equality, and solidarity have historically been used as a means of justifying incredible state violence both within the Hexagon and throughout France's colonial empire."[59]

On another note, despite their agreements on many fronts, the feminists discussed in this book consistently assert their resistance to being confined within a specific agenda. They strive to integrate into an open, liberal society. Some embrace Islam as a religion; some view it more as a cultural identity; others believe in the importance of reinterpreting religious texts; while still, others see no merit in operating within religious frameworks. Scholarly literature on secular Muslims often notes that they reference civil laws and human rights conventions rather than sharia as their guiding principles. This definition appears to resonate with many secular feminists. Nonetheless, it is a definition that might gloss over the heterogeneity of understandings and manifestations of secularism. As Nadje al-Ali argues it "also fails to analyse the continuum between religious and secular beliefs and practices in women's everyday lives."[60] Among westerners, there is a common argument postulating a natural and inherent link between

Christianity and secularism, understood as the separation of church and state.[61] In Muslim contexts, however, the interpretation of secularism is intertwined with a complex history of nationalism and modernism in relation to colonial and postcolonial experiences, often centered around nationalist centralizing governments. With the rise of political Islam, "secularism" was given a new meaning by its proponents, who perceive it as "un-Islamic," "anti-Islamic" and "non-Islamic," putting secular Muslims on guard. Some western scholars accused them of "attempting to create a community where there isn't any."[62] As I have already presented, each of the feminists discussed in this book holds a "secular" perspective that reflects her own political struggles and daily life. The distinctions between being secular and being Muslim are not clearly delineated in the ideologies and narratives of most of them. What remains clear, however, is that they find no contradiction between these identities. Sara Khan, for example, clearly challenges the misconception that being both Muslim and secular is contradictory. She frames secularism as a principle that ensures freedom of religious expression, highlighting that many secular Muslims do exist, even if they don't openly identify as such. She tells me:

> There is a very common perception that ... being Muslim, or being of faith and being secular is almost like a contradiction, it is like an oxymoron; you cannot be both ... And I just think that is ludicrous actually ... there are a lot of secularist Muslims out there who do not openly say it ... I think it is just a misnomer. It is what the fundamentalists want us to believe, the literalists want us to believe, the puritanical want us to believe! I do not see why you can't be somebody who is a Muslim, who chooses to be a Muslim, who feels Islam as part of their identity and fundamentally believe in a secular outlook, belief in the separation of politics, State and the Mosque, or state and the Church ... I suppose a lot of people do not understand that the core of secularism is about giving people the right to practice their religion, it is not about favoring one religion over the other.

The trouble with concepts like "secularism" is that we often assume we understand them fully. We may define them in various ways and adopt different political or moral stances, but they seem instinctively clear to us. To describe the secular perspective as merely "non-religious" overlooks the profound impact of feminists like the ones discussed in this book, who, although not engaged in theological debates, center their activism within a standpoint that is concerned with the cultural and political effect that religions exert upon social acts. Their position is neither of a cultural relativist nor of an apologist. This argument is supported by Homi Bhabha, who counters claims that secularism is an alien concept for minority communities.[63] He advocates for the normative importance of secularism as a means to enable and protect the evolution of religions over time and the diverse forms of religious practices that arise with the movement of populations within and across countries. Drawing on a version of secularism shaped by the historical and cultural experiences of migration, diaspora, and resettlement that define today's multicultural minority existence, he conceptualizes what he calls "subaltern secularism." This form of secularism emerges from the limitations of "liberal" secularism. It remains committed to supporting communities and individuals excluded from the egalitarian and tolerant values of liberal individualism.[64] Drawing on Gita Sahgal's work on the experiences of Asian women organizing in Britain, he uses the notion of "the subaltern" to describe oppressed minority groups who challenge the authority of those with hegemonic power. He argues that women of religious minority groups "are caught in the crossfire of a multifaith, multicultural society, where, invariably, the shots are called by the male members of the community who become the recognizable representatives of the 'community' in the public sphere."[65] Therefore, they do not have the choice and freedom upon which liberal notions of secularism are based, but, as Gita Sahgal argues, they need secular spaces to ensure choice and ethics of coexistence.[66]

Secular Muslim feminists demand such "secular" spaces: spaces that consider their particular historical and cultural experiences that define their very existence, spaces that allow them the freedom of choice that is not presupposed or prescribed, spaces that can be shared with "others," and "from which solidarity is not simply based on similarity, but on the recognition of difference."[67] In this context, "secularism" advocates for the separation of religion and state while ensuring equal respect for everyone's human rights so that no individual is advantaged or disadvantaged based on their beliefs. Secular Muslim feminists are committed to grounding their discourse outside the realm of any specific religion, whether it be Muslim, Christian, or any other. As Azza Karam states, "They do not 'waste their time' attempting to harmonise religious discourses with the concept and declarations pertinent to human rights."[68] By so doing, most of them avoid being caught up in interminable debates on the position of women within religion. Their position is not Islamophobic; it is secular and anti-fundamentalist, yet, given the heated nature around such issues, it seems convenient for some to nurture the misperceptions.

Challenging Multiple Fronts

Similar to the views of postcolonial feminists, secular Muslim feminists see that as primary targets of Islamic fundamentalism, women are being instrumentalized as the guardians of identity in both Islamist and postcolonial nationalist movements. They point out that recent movements like ISIS are fixated on controlling all aspects of women's lives and bodies, "imposing a strict dress code and a regime of gender segregation and ensuring women's subjugation to men in the private and public domains."[69] But it is not only violent extremism that concerns them. Sara Khan expresses greater apprehension concerning nonviolent extremism, highlighting the influence of "the preachers with hundreds of thousands of followers, who denounce violence, yet share the same puritanical ideology."[70] She critiques multiculturalism for its perceived leniency toward Islamism. Others also argue that decades of leniency toward Islamism in Europe have significantly strengthened its position.[71] Khan references the case of the controversial guidelines set by Universities UK in 2013. These guidelines permitted the optional segregation of men and women during events like lectures on Islam by guest speakers, citing religious teachings as grounds for the practice and arguing that it did not constitute gender discrimination.[72] Following campaigns spearheaded by organizations like Southall Black Sisters and Inspire, the guidelines were withdrawn with the involvement of David Cameron. In an article for the *Independent*, Khan argues:

> Let me spell it out for Universities UK, segregation results in "less favourable treatment." It enables the unequal distribution of power between men and women, resulting in gender-based discrimination and inequality ... Segregation perpetuates discriminatory social norms and practices, shaping male attitudes about women and restricting the decisions and choices of women. By allowing gender segregation, Universities UK is complicit in the gender inequality being perpetuated by ISOCs whose advice will only make it easier for them to treat socially unequal groups, in this case, women, even more unequally ... But also, rather astonishingly, Universities UK delves into trying to tell us what constitutes Muslim religious belief implying that those opposed to segregation must be people from outside of the Islamic faith, not recognizing that often it is Muslims themselves who oppose gender segregation.[73]

In an interview for *Vogue*, she proclaims, "We made a mistake with multiculturalism ... even Germaine Greer defended FGM as cultural relativism."[74] Khan emphasizes the importance of not compromising on cultural sensitivities that perpetuate harmful practices such as FGM, advocating for interventions to uphold gender equality and human rights. As a British woman of Pakistani origin, she tells me, "I find the argument of not wanting to offend cultural sensitivities offensive in and of itself." Khan's views align with feminists like Mariam Namazie and Pragna Patel, among others, who support the diversity inherent in the multicultural approach yet reject multiculturalism as a political philosophy and policy for submitting to the demands of faith-based communities. They believe this "has aggravated hostility between minority communities and between Muslim communities and the majority British society" and facilitated "the rise of Islamic radicalism and in discriminating against women."[75] Not only in the UK but, as Marieme Hélie-Lucas argues, there also seems to be a global trend of addressing social and political issues with religious solutions. This trend is increasingly promoted and sometimes initiated by various governmental bodies. Currently, across Europe, it is apparent that governments often turn to religious figures to address challenges within immigrant communities. Regrettably, it is usually fundamentalist groups that have the resources, both in terms of human power and finances, to respond to such requests. These groups, with the approval of authorities, play a significant role in influencing and controlling young people of migrant backgrounds.

The issue with cultural relativism lies in its tendency to essentialize culture and religion, thus equating any criticism of a specific cultural or religious aspect with an attack on the entirety. Consequently, secular Muslim feminists are united in questioning both Islamic fundamentalism and cultural relativism, recognizing the symbiotic relationship between the two. Chahla Chafiq challenges those who prefer to defer discussions on Muslim women's rights to Muslims out of fear of being labeled "Islamophobic." She raises concerns about what would happen if the imposition of the veil was not solely dictated by Islamic law but mirrored in other religious doctrines. She illustrates how cultural relativism leaves individuals like herself, with Islamic heritage, bearing the burden of navigating such debates. She criticizes the concept of Islamophobia, arguing that it reinforces identity-based ideologies amid the rise of ideological and religious movements. She replaces the term with "anti-Muslim racism" and explains:

> Indeed, anti-Muslim racism refers to a vision that stigmatizes Muslims as inferior beings and justifies their rejection, while the concept of Islamophobia serves to prevent any critical approach to the Islamic religion, as well as any fight against Islamism (hence the aberrant accusation made against Caroline Fourest and

Charlie Hebdo's journalists of being Islamophobic). The instrumentalization of this term also encourages the creation of similar concepts. Last year, Christian fundamentalist activists who prevented performances of Roméo Castellucci's play on the concept of the Son of God's face at the Théâtre du Châtelet raised the flag of the fight against Christianophobia.[76]

In this quote, Chafiq warns against the instrumentalization of terms like Islamophobia, which could hinder legitimate discussions about Islam and its various facets. As a result, she argues that individuals who resist the dictates imposed by ideological and religious groups are often the ones who suffer. She illustrates this point by referring to the events in Egypt and Tunisia in 2010, where calls for freedom and justice were eventually overshadowed by Islamist influences, demonstrating the perils of prioritizing religious identity over individual rights. She cites Iran in 1979, where women's rights were curtailed, freedoms restricted, and censorship enforced in the name of respecting sharia law. Chafiq further discusses the 1988 mass executions in Iran, where many young Muslim political prisoners were hanged on vague charges in the name of protecting Islam. These experiences serve as a cautionary tale, according to Chafiq, highlighting "the dangers of visions that present Islam as the source of a global and globalizing Muslim identity and tend to justify Islamist violence against disrespect for Islam as clashes of civilization."[77]

By conflating criticism of specific cultural or religious practices within Islam with an attack on Islam as a whole, those advocating for cultural relativism may inadvertently label those voicing critiques as Islamophobic, thus stifling necessary discussions and hindering progress toward addressing gender inequality or human rights violations within Muslim communities.[78] Secular Muslim feminists challenging fundamentalist interpretations of Islam argue that the concept of Islamophobia provides a weapon for Islamists to silence any form of critique against Islam. In an article for the National Secular Society, Nova Daban argues that the term has been used to shield Islam from criticism, which risks "creating a blasphemy code inimical to free speech and a secular liberal democracy."[79] Secular Muslim feminists encounter such challenges precisely because of their critique of specific practices within Muslim societies. They are frequently accused of Islamophobia and are often met with hostility and threats for speaking out against religious norms. For example, CAGE, a London-based advocacy organization that claims to empower communities impacted by the War on Terror, labels the involvement of Southall Black Sisters and Inspire in the gender segregation mentioned above case as "Islamophobic" and aligned with the "Prevent"[80] agenda. In another instance, the Council of Ex-Muslims of Britain, represented by Mariam Namazie, went through an eight-month investigation by Pride in London. This investigation was initiated after accusations of Islamophobia were leveled against the Council by the East London Mosque[81] and Mend,[82] a not-for-profit organization aiming to empower and engage British Muslims in local communities to participate more actively in British media and politics. Mariam Namazie herself faced barring from Warwick University,[83] harassment by Islamic Society students at Goldsmiths, and the cancellation of her speech at Trinity College over similar allegations.[84] As it stands, the concern is that such actions of abuse, harassment, and bullying, as Pragna Patel asserts, are now "conveniently ignored by the police and prosecutorial services precisely because the dominant understanding of 'Islamophobia' as defined by fundamentalists and conservatives precludes this."[85] It is crucial to bear in mind, as previously discussed, that fundamentalist Muslim leaders are often the ones who spearhead unchallenged accusations of "Islamophobia" because "they are the dominant voice and have the power to define the term within the various Muslim populations in the UK."[86] Attempts to tackle racism and hate crime must, therefore, be cautious not to stifle freedom of expression inadvertently. Alas, in a climate of religious intolerance in all religions, it would be easy to give in to demands for the persecution of those deemed to have offended religion out of apprehension of being branded as "Islamophobic."

To wrap up, the intricate challenges encountered by secular Muslim feminists in navigating gender equality, religious ideologies, and societal norms within Muslim communities underscores a heightened sense of urgency among secular Muslim feminists to advocate for gender equality, challenge oppressive cultural and religious norms, and combat misrepresentations. Moreover, the difficulty lies in ensuring that advocating for the appreciation and respect of diverse cultural practices does not result in conflating legitimate critiques of particular cultural aspects within Islam with accusations of "Islamophobia." By confronting these challenges head-on, secular Muslim feminists are paving the way for nuanced discussions on feminism, secularism, and human rights, ultimately striving to create more inclusive societies where diverse perspectives are valued and individuals of all backgrounds can thrive. Their endeavors, which go beyond individual struggles, are sparking critical conversations and mobilizing action to address systemic inequalities and promote social change.

Emerging Counternarratives?

The feminists explored in this chapter share a unified commitment to advocating for women's rights, contesting religious and cultural norms, and challenging leaderships that claim to represent them. They do not oppose religion per se but emphasize the essential role of secular spaces in fostering equality for individuals regardless of their religious affiliations. But because some see notions like feminism and secularism as western impositions that belittle and marginalize not only religions but also local cultural and moral values, their viability is debated. In navigating intricate identities, these feminists confront not just a singular dominant narrative but a multitude of conflicting ones that constrict their freedom of choice and hinder the possibility of individualized narratives. Despite the challenges, these feminists seem to be in the process of finding means to provide more liberatory and contextualized alternatives to the dominant binary narratives that separate the "backward third world Woman" and the "liberated modern western woman." Their struggle to express and articulate their perspectives underscores an essential aspect of their narrative—their refusal to conform to a particular position.

While we might not be free to tell any story, it is crucial to recognize that we are still the authors of our narrative.[87] We are all constrained by the stories in circulation at any given time, but we use them not as readymade scripts but as frameworks that help us construct our own. In telling their stories, these feminists choose among the plots and subplots of different narratives to construct a story that works for them. In this sense, the difficulty they express in articulating a particular position within available discourses reveals their attempts at constructing their own narrative, which builds on existing ones, like feminism, yet does not fully agree with any particular subcategory. These seemingly contradictory narratives should not be seen as untrue but rather as a reflection of the various and multilayered explanations for using such narratives and their constraints in telling them. While bound by prevalent narratives, secular Muslim feminists actively construct their own stories by weaving together different plots and subplots, creating a narrative framework unique to their experiences.

The deliberate choice to adopt a subject position independent of dominant frameworks signifies these feminists' adeptness at leveraging existing political opportunities and constraints, resisting, negotiating, and tailoring them to achieve their desired identities. Whereas some envision multicultural and tolerant societies achievable through current policies, others critique the status quo by juxtaposing unapplied utopias. Some are more experienced narrators than others. Drawing on Francesca Polletta's notion of "narrative performance," proscribed by the social context in which narrators give their accounts, I argue that secular Muslim feminists are both influenced by prevailing discourses and engaged in challenging and reshaping those discourses through counternarratives. As Polletta articulates, "cultural constraints … reflect the institutional rules of the game that those wanting to effect change must play."[88] Utilizing counternarratives in this ongoing process of challenging and reshaping current discourses aims to broaden boundaries, shift focus, and carve out space for alternative perspectives that capture the complexity and redefine their lives and those marginalized and unheard in society.

3

Islam, Feminism, and Secular Resistance

During its relatively short existence, the contemporary women's movement in the west has made considerable progress in developing theories on women's issues and producing studies of the past and present of western societies' gender issues. However, very little is known to the western world about women's experiences in the non-western world and even less about the degree to which western notions of feminism correspond to non-western experiences, self-perceptions, and political aspirations. Whether or not they label their actions as "feminist," women of the world employ various strategies to achieve their objectives under different political systems. In India, for example, working-class women actively resist their oppression by taking to the streets, while educated women do their best to support them; in Russia, the feminists are intellectual dissidents, many of whom have been forced into exile; and in South America, women played a leading role in the struggle against their dictatorships. Despite that, in many countries, authority tends to be centralized within male-dominated structures in both western and non-western contexts; women have always found a way or another to get involved in the decisions that affect their lives.

Throughout the second wave of feminism, the idea of "global sisterhood" underpinned by the belief that western feminist ideology could be universally applicable has alienated women in other parts of the world who have distinct perspectives on women's rights rooted in their individual experiences and struggles. Women in non-western cultures have struggled against sexism, class, caste, religion, and ethnic biases. The impacts of colonialism and neocolonialism have added further layers of complexity to their lives. This chapter outlines vital discussions and strategies that have shaped feminist perspectives in Muslim societies since the beginning of the century, aiming to trace the persisting feminist awareness among Muslim women. Until recently, these voices remained largely unheard, their stories untold, and their contributions unacknowledged within the broader academic discourse. However, the past half-century has witnessed a remarkable surge in research dedicated to exploring the diverse experiences of Muslim women. The chapter then traces the evolution of Muslim feminist scholarship through three distinct waves, each reflecting Muslim women's evolving challenges and aspirations. The first wave, emerging in the early twentieth century, focused on the patriarchal barriers encountered by early feminists and their efforts to advocate for women's rights within a changing social landscape. This scholarship, often classified as modernist or secular feminist, provided valuable insights into the challenges faced by women seeking equality and empowerment. However, the emergence of Islamic feminism in the 1980s offered an alternative perspective rooted in the belief that feminist principles could be reconciled with Islamic teachings. Both approaches have faced critiques, with concerns raised about potential western biases in secular feminism and the limitations of Islamic feminism in addressing patriarchal interpretations within religious texts.

The chapter delves into the complexities of "secular feminism" and "Islamic feminism" in the context of Muslim societies, exploring the arguments for and against each approach. Islamic feminism, while seeking to reconcile feminist principles with Islamic teachings, faces critiques for potentially reinforcing traditional patriarchal structures and limiting the scope of advocacy. Secular feminism, on the other hand, is criticized for its potential western bias and neglect of the cultural and religious contexts within which Muslim women live. The chapter argues that these dichotomies are overly simplistic, failing to capture the diversity of Muslim women's experiences. It highlights the importance of acknowledging the array of voices within both secular and Islamic feminist movements and the emergence of newer perspectives that bridge ideological divides and foster inclusive dialogue. The chapter seeks to emphasize that feminism, particularly secular feminism, has not been absent in Muslim contexts but instead ignored and dismissed. It points to the contributions of early Muslim feminists who challenged societal norms and advocated for women's rights, often within secular frameworks. This is to emphasize the potential risks of exclusively pursuing women's rights from within a religious paradigm, arguing that it may inadvertently reinforce patriarchal structures and limit the scope of advocacy. Instead, it advocates for a multifaceted approach that embraces diversity, acknowledges the complexities of Muslim women's experiences, and prioritizes the pursuit of universal human rights and equality for all.

Early Feminist Consciousness

The emergence of feminism in the Global South occurred concurrently with the west. The feminist movements in India and Egypt during the early twentieth century were instrumental in sparking broader feminist movements in those regions. These movements were shaped by unique historical and sociopolitical contexts, leading to distinct variations in their strategies. Other developments of political struggles in countries in the Middle East, North Africa, and Southeast Asia show parallels in experiences and apparent differences in the strategy of women's movements based on their different historical and sociopolitical backgrounds. In India, the movement focused on suffrage, education, and legal inequities in family laws, with subsequent waves addressing violence against women and transnational issues. In Egypt and most of the Middle East, the women's movement has been influenced by the state's ambiguous role, the growth of civil society, and the increasing influence of Islamist constituencies. In Southeast Asia, the relationship between women's movements and counter movements, particularly Islamist movements, has been a key factor. Nationalism and the push to end western colonialism in the late 1800s played a significant role in sparking dissent among women. During this period, women's movements was said to be primarily involved by academics and members of the ruling elite, occasionally including men, wherein women's rights at the time was as a symbol of modernity, progress, and democracy. A notable challenge faced by early women's movements in the Muslim world, similar to the west, was the limited involvement of ordinary women. Consequently, these upper-class organizations were not perceived as representative of the interests of many women.

The concept of feminism has also led to considerable confusion in several Muslim countries. While questioning and contesting male dominance within Muslim societies has been a central theme for over a century, not all women activists in Islamic regions identified themselves as "feminists." The wariness toward "feminism" among many Muslim women seems to stem from two primary issues. The first issue revolves around the perception that early feminism in Muslim-majority societies was heavily influenced by western feminism, leading some to view it as a foreign concept. The second issue pertains to a broader criticism of western feminism, suggesting that it has often overlooked women's movements outside the west and assumed a universal sameness in women's experiences globally. This perspective implies a Eurocentric bias in which the pursuit of gender equality is believed to be solely a western concern, dismissing the struggles and activism in non-western societies as mere imitations of western models. Some even claim that several western feminists have gone to the extent of characterizing Muslim women's lives as "being so different from theirs that they cannot possibly develop any kind of feminism."[1]

The earliest works demonstrating feminist consciousness in the Muslim world were predominantly expressed in women activists' novels, memoirs, and autobiographies. This mode of activism contrasted with that of western counterparts like Harriet Tubman,[2] as in traditional Muslim societies, women's writing served as the only permissible form of activism during the early nineteenth century. Even this avenue was sometimes limited, leading women to use pseudonyms when publishing their works. Writing served as the initial platform for women to articulate their concerns and advocate for change within the Muslim world. For instance, the writings of Muslim women in Iran symbolized an emblematic unveiling, representing a public assertion of self that relied on both the act of writing and the content within.[3] The same could be said for most Muslim women then, but the specifics varied. Zaynab Fawwāz (1860–1914), a Lebanese poet, novelist, and historian known for her writings on notable women, stood out from other nineteenth-century female authors as she hailed from a modest, uneducated *Shiite* background. According to Marilyn Booth, Fawwāz likely relocated to Egypt around 1870, serving as domestic help for a wealthy household. By the 1890s, in her forties, she started to garner recognition for her essays published in Egyptian newspapers. In 1887, the Turkish-Egyptian writer Aisha Al-Taymuriyya (1840–1902) published a fictional tale titled *The Yield of Facts in Words and Acts*. In her preface, the autobiographical narrative blended into the story, merging into her fiction. Marilyn Booth describes her as follows:

> Aisha ... hints at women's oral storytelling as the earliest source of her writing but sets off this women's culture against her thirst for formal knowledge and the resistance of her mother ... Aisha secludes herself, not because that is what females do, but in order to write. In order to defy the expectations represented in her mother's embroidery tools. For this Muslim woman 120 years ago, writing was an act that expressed triumph over difficult circumstances, as well as an opportunity to "speak," to encourage other women, and men, to seek their chosen destinies—and to encourage their daughters' education.[4]

By the end of the nineteenth century, forms of activism beyond writing began to surface among Muslim women. One notable figure is feminist activist Rokeya Sakhawat Hossain (1880–1932), born in the Bengal region and renowned as Begum Rokeya. Highlighting issues such as women's education, male dominance, patriarchy, and the *purdah* system prevalent in particular South Asian and Hindu communities, Hossain was a vocal advocate for change. She established a girls' school and an NGO named *Anjuman-e-Khawatin-e-Islam* (Islamic Women's Association). Despite facing challenges and criticism, she actively campaigned door-to-door, encouraging parents to send their daughters to school, continuing her efforts until her passing.[5] Critiquing existing norms, she humorously addresses this practice in the Bengal Women's Educational Conference, writing:

> Although Islam has successfully prevented the physical killing of baby girls, Muslims have been glibly and frantically wrecking the mind, intellect, and judgment of their daughters till the present day. Many consider it a mark of honor to keep their daughters ignorant and deprive them of knowledge and understanding of the world by cooping them up within the four walls of the house.[6]

Hossain's critique emphasizes the detrimental impact of confining daughters to the domestic sphere, limiting their access to education and a broader understanding of the world. It underscores the need for reform in attitudes toward women's education and empowerment within these communities. Despite the need for social and political action, autobiographies persisted as a significant testament to women's collective efforts for some time. An illustrative instance is "Harem Years" by Huda Sharaawi (1879–1924), a prominent Egyptian activist. The book was translated and introduced by Margot Badran in 1986. Within its pages, Shaarawi reflects on her upbringing and early adulthood within the confines of an affluent Egyptian household. Recounting her marriage at thirteen, she also describes how her subsequent separation from her husband provided an opportunity for an extended formal education and an unexpected taste of independence. This newfound independence enabled her to engage in writing as a form of activism. As the early twentieth century approached, an increase in contributions to newspapers by women activists became more evident. Among the key trailblazers was Malak Hifni Nassef, who regularly published in *Al-Jarida* (the newspaper), linked to the liberal secularist "the Umma political party" using the pseudonym Bahithat Al-Badiya (Seeker of the Desert).[7] Leila Ahmed describes Nassef as a prolific lecturer and writer whose clear and insightful vision positions her as a prominent intellectual within the feminist movement of the era's initial decades.[8] In the Arab Muslim world during this period, other educated Muslim women such as Seiza Nabarawy and Mai Ziade launched their magazines, focusing on women's status and national resilience and showcasing the biographies of renowned feminists and women activists worldwide to attract female readership. These publications extended beyond Egypt and the Levant, reaching Muslim diaspora communities. These writings tell a great deal about "the woman question" as it evolved and how it relates to social and political issues.

Booth notes that "these biographies do not simply present women's lives. They present themselves rhetorically as activist texts, disciplinary texts that seek, in their language, to guide the reader through a rhetoric of exemplarity."[9] As a result of this literary activism, girls' education and the discourse on modernization surfaced. Girls' education was controversial because it involved girls leaving home. In other words, it required visibility and voice. In conclusion, it becomes evident that through various forms of elusive activism, including writing, newspaper contributions, and educational advocacy, women laid the groundwork for challenging societal norms and advancing the rights and status of women. These pioneers not only brought attention to gender equality issues but also paved the way for future generations of Muslim women to continue the struggle for empowerment, education, and societal change.

Muslim Women's Scholarship

Three Waves of Influence

Until the latter decades of the twentieth century, the question of women's status and roles in Muslim societies remained largely overlooked within academic discourse. The scholarly examination of women's activism and participation in political movements and collective action is relatively new, with its initial wave emerging about five decades ago. This surge in research was driven by two primary factors: the global rise of women's movements in the 1970s and the transition from colonial rule to nationalism in the mid-twentieth century, which heightened the focus on enhancing women's positions in many Muslim nations. Initially pioneered by diasporic researchers and intellectuals in the United States and Europe, this women-centric scholarship quickly expanded across the Muslim world within a decade. By the late 1980s, the influence of this scholarship had significantly broadened, ultimately captivating a wide range of scholars and disciplines globally by the 1990s.[10]

The first wave of this scholarship examined women's participation in national liberation and nation-building in the Muslim world and engaged with the state and its gender policies to push for greater gender equality.[11] Despite arguments in various writings on nationalist movements suggesting that women's involvement and leadership predominantly stemmed from middle- and upper-class backgrounds, this scholarship contradicted such assertions. Partha Chatterjee, for instance, contended that in India, one should not solely seek evidence of women's independent quest for equality and liberation within public political institutions, "for unlike the women's movement in 19th- and 20th-century Europe, the battle for the new idea of womanhood in the era of nationalism was waged in the home."[12] This knowledge is derived from various sources such as autobiographies, family accounts, religious writings, literature, theatre, songs, paintings, and more. Within the domestic realm, women engaged in activities like spinning, weaving, organizing, and teaching classes for fellow women, contributing to nationalist movements through writing articles, poems, and propaganda and offering refuge and support to nationalist figures evading colonial surveillance.[13] In essence, this scholarly wave aimed not only to uncover women's diverse roles but also to unveil the often overlooked narratives of women articulating their identities and sharing their multiple experiences as women, feminists, Muslims, and citizens within Muslim societies.

By the 1980s, Muslim feminists and activists across various postcolonial Muslim nations started to distance themselves from the state, establishing independent groups dedicated to advocating for and advancing women's rights. This shift was in response to both the elitist nationalists and the colonial version of the emblematic Muslim woman, powerless and dependent. Within this movement, Muslim feminists presented a counternarrative of "power and authority,"[14] highlighting the active engagement of the marginalized segments of society, the "subaltern masses," and their efforts in challenging colonial rule and reshaping the narratives of Muslim women's lives in the face of both nationalist and colonial impositions that had previously disregarded their contributions.[15] This literature carried an activist undertone, particularly in response to the influence of religious revivalism gaining ground in predominantly Muslim societies. This body of work mirrored the aspirations of Muslim women who actively pursued legal reforms to enhance their status and rights. A key focus of this "corrective" scholarship, as termed by Afia Zia, was to contest the notion that Islam alone dictates the status of Muslim women; instead, it emphasized the influence of distinct historical and socioeconomic contexts in shaping the experiences of Muslim women.

Currently, Muslim feminists' perspectives vary from conservative to secular, as well as what Jasmin Zine describes as "critically faith-based," among others.

Not only differences in ideologies but also the global divisions between North and South, and West versus "the rest," contribute to further rifts. Muslim feminists and women activists operating from western spheres, who have the capacity to write, mobilize, and resist, often benefit from a sociopolitical and economic context that places them in privileged positions. This sometimes creates a perception that they may be perceived as betraying those fighting for change at grassroots levels. Recognizing these distinctions, Muslim women activists and scholars found themselves navigating a new path. This third wave of Muslim women's feminism, activism, and scholarship is marked by the proliferation of transnational connections among women advocating for progress and emphasizing that Muslim women are immensely diverse but are not as distinctive among women as was formerly assumed.

In politics, "they share with other women the experience of marginalization, and, increasingly, the determination to mobilize against it."[16] Women Living Under Muslim Laws (WLUML), established by Algerian French secular feminist Marieme Hélie-Lucas, aimed to unite Muslim and non-Muslim women living outside their home countries to support their causes, marked the inception of what later evolved into a vast network of Muslim feminists worldwide. Similarly, *Musawah* (equality), a group self-identifying as the "global movement for equality and justice in the Muslim family," advocates for implementing laws that uphold gender equality worldwide. Launched in February 2009 in Kuala Lumpur, Malaysia, during a global meeting attended by over 250 individuals from 47 countries, *Musawah* has evolved into a global network of Muslim feminists.

Two Interpretive Poles

As I have mentioned briefly, in the early 1980s, a significant shift occurred as Muslim feminists in various postcolonial Muslim nations distanced themselves from the state, forming independent groups. This wave saw the emergence of two primary interpretive frameworks or "paradigms" largely referred to as "secular feminism" and "Islamic feminism," each engaging with the traditional patriarchal Islamic narrative. The contrast between these two scholarly discourses lies in their foundational principles, research methodologies, and resulting implications. While "secular feminism" traces back to the late nineteenth century and integrates multiple perspectives like secular nationalist, Islamic modernist,[17] humanitarian or human rights, and democratic ideals, "Islamic feminism" emerged much later in the late twentieth century, grounding itself in a singular religious narrative centered around the Qur'ān. Islamic feminism tends to be viewed as a "paradox" or a contradiction in terms, while "those who conflate it with western feminism see secular feminism as problematic in Islamic states."[18]

Within these paradigms, critiques of western feminism emerged, spurred on by postcolonial scholarship that prompted feminists like Chandra Talpade Mohanty, Uma Narayan, Inderpal Grewal, and Caren Kaplan to broaden their assessments from postcolonial and modernist concepts of liberation to western feminism.[19] This shift is apparent in the ongoing dialogues concerning secular versus traditional, universal versus culturally specific, western versus non-western ideologies, and so on. With the resurgence of political Islam, many secular feminists and activists in Muslim regions have been accused of aligning with "western imperialism" by incorporating foreign ideologies and practices perceived as incompatible with Islamic traditions. In light of these charges, "Islamic feminism" saw itself as the sole avenue for reform within Muslim-majority nations, which led to "a lack of balance in most of the affirmative accounts of Muslim women's activism."[20] By emphasizing Islam as the indispensable factor in women's lives and identities and as the "only" viable alternative to western feminism, the possibility of hearing different voices in diverse cultural and political settings becomes constrained. As a result, voices advocating against sharia authority are often marginalized, inadequately documented, and insufficiently acknowledged. In certain instances, secular women activists have even faced persecution, resulting in imprisonment.

The Contemporary Scholarship

In the past two decades, influences from postmodernism, third world feminism, and insights from women on the margins have contributed to the evolution of diverse interpretations and expressions of feminism. This ongoing process has reshaped feminist perspectives to encompass various women's unique realities and experiences. Nancy Naples underscores the importance of addressing the practical obstacles women face when organizing across the intersections of race, class, and gender. She emphasizes the necessity for fresh definitions, categories, and analytical tools that encompass the multitude of ways women promote societal transformation. While initially highlighting the disparities between western feminism and third world feminist approaches, Chandra Talpade Mohanty later advocates for an anti-capitalist transnational feminist movement, emphasizing the importance of cross-national feminist solidarity and collective resistance against global capitalism.[21] Miriam Cooke refers to this notion as participating in a realm of "multiple critique," where postcolonial individuals construct a counter-discourse that simultaneously challenges local and global adversaries. Sa'diyyah Shaikh emphasizes the need for Muslim individuals with feminist commitments to navigate the delicate balance between critiquing sexist interpretations of Islam and patriarchal norms within their religious communities while simultaneously challenging neocolonial feminist discourses on Islam.[22] By integrating three primary areas of study—globalization, non-governmental organizations and global social movements, and women's movements and organizations—Valentine Moghadam provides a thorough examination of how global trends such as the feminization of poverty, labor, and women's rights, alongside subregional collaborations, militarization, the surge of religious extremism, and middle-class women's access to information technologies, have influenced the emergence and activities of major Transnational Feminist Networks (TFNs) in recent decades.

By bringing together assessments of Islamic fundamentalism and neoliberal capitalism as pivotal elements of globalization that have evoked transnational feminist reactions, she introduces a fresh perspective on topics traditionally discussed independently. Inspired by the "cultural turn," she underscores the importance of networks for women, whether through intimate personal connections leading to formal groups and organizations or more expansive transnational entities.[23] Notwithstanding, she provides little insight into how TFNs maintain and build solidarities in the face of class, racial, and gender disparities.

Within the latter works, two issues continue to generate tension. On the one hand, the increasing focus on examining globalization, neoliberalism, and social justice has propelled the rise and expansion of transnational feminism. On the other, ongoing debates over issues like voice, authority, representation, and diversely located women have continued to widen the divide among feminists globally involved in examining and theorizing the complexities of women's experiences. In efforts to bridge the gaps within Muslim feminist discourse and activism, Jasmin Zine advocates for a "critical faith-based" approach, which entails exploring how religious and spiritual affiliations can serve as sites of oppression, intertwined with broader forms of oppression relating to race, class, gender, ethnicity, sexuality, and colonialism. It involves recognizing that religion has been historically exploited and misused at times.[24] Striving to deconstruct and confront the intertwined systems of oppression and combat the entrenched "hierarchies of racialized and class-based dominance that uphold social distinctions and inequities,"[25] this approach, she argues, enables the examination of these interconnected systems as they intersect in the real-life encounters of different groups. In other words, the shared struggles against neo-imperialism and radical religious puritanism should serve as unifying factors among Muslim women of distinct backgrounds and orientations. Maliha Chishti also proposes fostering a more collaborative environment through a "strategic-integrative approach," emphasizing the importance of cultivating a unified understanding of the diverse challenges, oppressions, and injustices experienced by different Muslim women. This approach calls for forming strategic solidarities at local and transnational levels to establish a foundation for political resistance. This strategy allows for divergent perspectives while establishing shared platforms for social activism and political analysis by avoiding the oversimplification of Muslim women's beliefs and religious affiliations. A vital aspect of this initiative involves acknowledging the limitations of various proposals and recognizing both the shared and conflicting frameworks that arise from these often divergent and contradictory sources.

Despite these possibilities, Muslim women's organizing has yet to capitalize on opportunities to fully forge such transnational connections. The complexities of addressing issues related to women of color and Muslim women, especially when faced with stereotypes and oversimplified narratives, make the undertaking more challenging. To forge such transnational networks, a nuanced understanding of the historical context is crucial for a comprehensive analysis of gender, race, and religion in society. It is crucial to represent these issues accurately and critically, advocating for the deconstruction of stereotypes and misrepresentations associated with feminism and Islam. I recommend incorporating diverse perspectives, including art and fiction, to provide a more holistic view of these complex topics. Additionally, the advent of social media and the internet has revolutionized the landscape of transnational feminism, enabling feminists from diverse geographies and cultures to connect, collaborate, and build stronger solidarity. This interconnectedness is facilitating the exchange of ideas, experiences, and strategies, paving the way for more effective advocacy and collective action. Social media platforms provide a unique space for feminist communities to bridge geographic boundaries. They allow feminists across the globe to engage in dialogue, share their perspectives, and learn from each other's struggles and victories. The internet and social media have emerged as powerful tools for amplifying the voices of marginalized women, evident in the #WomenLifeFreedom, reaching every corner of the globe resulting in an unprecedented support from the international community. Through online campaigns, hashtags, and digital storytelling, Iranian women have raised awareness about critical issues, challenged oppressive narratives, and held authorities accountable. Thus, while acknowledging the diversity within the feminist movement, social media and the internet provide opportunities for building solidarities across differences. By fostering dialogue, recognizing commonalities, and celebrating diverse perspectives, feminists can build bridges across geographical, cultural, and ideological boundaries, strengthening the movement's collective voice and impact. In an increasingly interconnected world, social media and the internet have become indispensable tools for advancing transnational feminism. They provide a platform for feminists across the globe to connect, collaborate, and challenge the structures and ideologies that perpetuate gender inequality. Through online networks, digital activism, and collective action, transnational feminist movements have already started building bridges across borders and identities.

Muslim Women's Activism

The nineteenth century could well be named the era of women because heated discussions about women's rights and women's potential and capabilities became commonplace worldwide. In the western world, feminist consciousness began to take root during and after the French Revolution, leading to increased vocalization of feminist ideals in countries like England, France, and Germany by the century's close. By the mid-nineteenth century, the "woman question" had become a central issue for Russian reformers and anarchists and was criticized by social reformers in India. In the late nineteenth century, educated women in the Ottoman Empire, Egypt, and Iran started to voice their concerns against various gender injustices. As noted earlier, women's magazines significantly influenced these movements, largely arising as resistance against imperialism and foreign control on one front and challenging oppressive local authorities along with traditional patriarchal and religious systems on the other front. Within these contexts, the "woman question" notably gained traction in the early twentieth century. Despite their limited presence in formal political arenas, Muslim women have actively engaged in widespread activism since the early 1900s.

The degree to which the state supported women's quests for gender equality varied across different countries. Turkey, for instance, pursued swift modernization and cultural transformation by following secular frameworks.[26] Consequently, legal changes and alterations in women's public presence became intrinsically linked to establishing a secular government.[27] Turkish thinkers deliberated on women's liberation and empowerment through improved education and equitable civil liberties. With the establishment of the Republic of Turkey by the Kemalists in 1923, women were instrumental in the nation's modernization and secularization endeavors. The "new modern Turkish woman" was created, and women's emancipation was co-opted by the state. Nonetheless, not all women reaped the rewards of this initial feminist wave. The Kemalists primarily targeted urban, ethnic Turkish, middle- and upper-class women for their efforts. Egypt and Iran embraced national unification through cultural and educational advancements, advocating for national language enhancement and incorporating western democratic ideals while maintaining Islam as the state's official religion. In these recently independent nations, discussions regarding women's rights initially involved male reformers, but women's perspectives have also been documented. The feminist movement in Egypt began by intertwining women's concerns with the secular nationalist and anti-colonial movements prevailing at the period. However, the rapport between early feminists and male nationalists was anything but harmonious. Even though they succeeded in establishing a presence for women in the public domain, the enactment of secular legislation never came to fruition. The shortcomings of postrevolutionary Egypt in ensuring gender equality, notably seen through the exclusion of women's voting rights in the 1923 constitution, taught Egyptian women that attaining gender equality required more than the patronage of male elites. Over the last century in Iran, women have demonstrated advancements in education, scientific pursuits, literary and artistic achievements, economic contributions, and social and political engagement.[28] However, gender equality has remained elusive, particularly within the family structure. Even amidst the swift modernization efforts during the Pahlavi era (1930s to 1970s), personal status and family laws continued to be strictly based on sharia. Following the Islamic Revolution of 1979, the legal framework deepened gender disparities, undoing progressive reforms from the Pahlavi period. While the revolution initially offered women opportunities for political involvement, the establishment of the Islamic Republic quickly marginalized women under religious pretexts.

Among the first gender-conscious women were Tahereh Qurrat-ol 'Ayne (mid-1800s Iran), Nazira Zin al-Din (1920s Lebanon), and Fatima Aliya Hanim (late 1800s Turkey).[29] These activist, feminist voices challenged the patriarchal interpretations of the Qur'ān and critiqued the male-dominated interpretations of the *Hadīth*. They opposed the veil, advocated against sex segregation, and condemned gender-based restrictions imposed on Muslim women, each doing so in distinctive manners. Notably, Huda Shaarawi drew significant inspiration from western feminism in her pursuits. Her act of unveiling alongside her associate, Seiza Nabarawi, at a Cairo railway station upon returning from an international feminist conference established her as a pioneer not only within her nation but also across the region.[30] In contrast, Malak Hifni Nassif (1886–1918), an Egyptian feminist, Islamic modernist, reformer, and author, advocated for equality within the context of Islam.[31] Despite their seemingly conflicting nature, modernist or secularist and traditionalist or Islamist ideologies have mutually influenced each other, enriching the political and social spheres.[32] Different shades of these two ideological approaches remained the primary foundations guiding Muslim feminists/activists until the 1980s when the term "Islamic feminism" emerged. During that period, none of these endeavors were carried out under the label of what would eventually be coined "Islamic feminism." At that time, there was no pressing need to highlight or emphasize the "Islamic" character of such activities.[33]

The landscape transformed significantly from the 1950s onward due to nationalist projects, evolving economic dynamics, the escalating significance of oil resources, swift population expansion, and notable shifts in migration patterns from rural to urban areas and between nations, ensuing in rapid urbanization. These advancements contributed to the increased presence of women in public spheres, employed in various roles such as shops, factories, and social services.[34] At this juncture, the progress achieved by feminists did not threaten the ruling elite; instead, it potentially facilitated the development of a more sustainable and modern society by aligning women with the state's developmental objectives. Paradoxically, despite their significant contributions to the struggle for independence in many countries, women often fell short of attaining the rights they had envisioned. Women actively participated in nationalist movements in various countries—India during the 1905, 1909, and 1930 struggles; Iran during the democratic revolution of 1906 and 1911; Morocco from 1935 onward; and Egypt, Turkey, and Iran since the 1919 nationalist uprisings. Many revolutionary women from the third world emerged during this period, yet regrettably, their courageous endeavors have largely been relegated to the sidelines within historical accounts. Once independence was secured, the reinstatement of traditional norms of patriarchy, misogyny, and dominance took precedence. This starkly contrasts with the ideals of freedom and equality championed by individuals and collectives during independence movements, underlining the stark dissonance between the quests for liberation and the passive endorsement of conventional female roles.

Following the onset of the Iranian revolution in 1979, according to Nayereh Tohidi, Iranian women engaged in disseminating news, circulating flyers, participating in street demonstrations, and some even joined guerrilla movements. Tohidi illustrates how these young women found themselves navigating between dual ideologies: the traditional, emphasizing familial and religious norms, and the modern, aligning with the "imported" westernized culture promoted by the Shāh's regime. As fundamentalist Islam gained traction across much of the Muslim world, even in "secular" Turkey, women emerged as the primary demographic facing the most pressing challenges. This scenario unfolded across nations where fundamentalist ideologies seized governmental control: in Pakistan under Zia al-Haq, in Sudan, Iran, and Turkey with the hegemony of the AKP, along with Algeria, where women found themselves caught between the *Front Islamique du Salut* (Islamic Salvation Front) and the Algerian state's oppressive tactics. Even in Afghanistan, where the pervasive impact of war and the population's day-to-day struggles for survival continue to dominate, fundamentalist ideologies have taken center stage. Within this context, and much to the dismay of the fundamentalists, Muslim women continued to emerge as a political force. According to Haideh Moghissi, the discourse surrounding feminism, feminist objectives, and their alignment with Islam has remained central in the agendas of Islamic states and movements across the region.[35] She further elaborates:

> The lslamists' manipulative use of gender issues and feminist concepts has led to confusion for many secular intellectuals, including feminists, who have placed debate over "Islamic feminism" on the agenda, some embracing it with enthusiasm, others rejecting it with passion ... But the relevance of this question extends beyond Iran. This debate situates ideological struggle on ground where the fundamentalists have determined the basic frame of reference; a terrain which is at odds with the needs, interests and the familiar vocabulary of secular feminist academics, researchers and activists both within and outside Islamic societies.[36]

In Iran, as Tohidi argues, the Iranian authorities of the newly founded Islamic State have "usually accused and blamed Iranian feminists and any quest for women's emancipation as an exogenous idea ... accused of promoting sexual license to penetrate the *dar al-Islam* (the house of Islam) and the traditional family and thereby destroying the internal moral fabric of the entire society."[37] While it was not directly colonized, Iran faced significant challenges, notably with the nationalization of oil under Mossadegh. This led to his overthrow by British and American forces, which held substantial control over Iran's oil reserves. Consequently, women activists advocating for equal rights frequently found themselves in a defensive position, balancing the pursuit of national independence alongside the aspirations for individual rights and universal values like equality, human rights, freedom of choice, and democracy. In Pakistan, the initial significant wave of feminist activism surfaced during the 1980s in response to General Zia-ul-Haq's contentious introduction of the *Hudood* Ordinances in 1979. This new legislation amended sections of the British-era Pakistan Penal Code, introducing novel criminal provisions related to adultery and fornication, along with severe penalties of whipping, amputation, and stoning to death. As the Islamist movement gained traction in the comparatively more liberal political atmosphere of the 1990s, religious women increasingly participated in and assumed prominent roles within the Islamist movement, impacting politics and public life. The rise of the new, Islamic-rooted feminism has since redefined the feminist agenda, leading to debates on women's rights within the religious framework.

According to Manal Omar, women activists from Malaysia to Egypt and South Africa to Iran began incorporating the term "Islamic feminism" in their discourse on women's matters, establishing a movement within the broader Muslim *ummah*. This has led to a polarization of the feminist movement, with the potential for a new, radicalized, religiopolitical feminism to dominate the political future within those regions. On one hand, religious women perceived secular feminism as a vehicle for reimposing western standards upon them. On the other hand, they also recognized the necessity to challenge the conservative gender ideologies endorsed by the Islamist movement. While feminists in the Middle East grappled with concerns of potentially betraying their heritage in scrutinizing the Islamist movement, religious women in Turkey encountered their unique internal dilemmas. The perception of Islamist women as opposing the status quo contrasts with the image of Kemalist and Atatürkist women, seen as aligned with western values, pro-state, secular-nationalistic, and advocates for gender equality. The discrepancy in Turkey, where religion and the headscarf were marginalized despite the predominant Muslim identity among citizens and many women choosing to cover their heads, is noteworthy. Yet, while religious individuals faced oppression under Kemalist rule, the AKP's ascension in 2002, led by Tayyip Erdogan, has transformed Turkey into a post-Kemalist nation, placing greater emphasis on Islam in the public sphere. This shift has resulted in biases against secular Turkish citizens in employment opportunities and promotions, particularly disadvantaging women who opt not to wear the headscarf.

In Iran, despite significant strides, unlike Turkey, the Islamic feminist movement failed to garner widespread support among Iranian women. Meanwhile, thousands of secular women endured execution, torture, and sexual assault in prisons. Despite limited avenues for protest, women have showcased individual and collective resistance through various means. Conceptualized as a "women's non-movement," Asef Bayat explains that because large-scale collective efforts may not be feasible in authoritarian settings, the mere presence of women in the public sphere and their daily acts of defiance persevere to sustain the impact of women's activism. The strength of these practices lies precisely in their ordinariness.[38] In Egypt, despite some gains, the Nasser government shut down the Egyptian Feminist Union along with all independent organizations, transforming gender equality activism into "State Feminism." Additionally, the regime suppressed religiously affiliated political movements and parties, leading to a reactionary religious resurgence that divided the women's movement into secular and Islamic ideological camps. However, this did not inhibit Egyptian women from organizing and advocating for their objectives; instead, it prompted a shift in their focus and strategies. While Islamist forces remain a formidable presence in the modern Egyptian state, both secular and Islamic camps play crucial roles in debating women's issues and influencing broader political discussions. These ideological divisions have enabled feminism to resonate with women across varying ideological spectrums. However, this inclusivity has come at the expense of unity within the feminist movement. To address this, I will outline each type of feminism, examining their respective frameworks, achievements, and the criticisms they face.

As I have presented, the history of women's movements in Muslim societies is brimming with diverse struggles, ideologies, and accomplishments. From the early feminist pioneers challenging traditional norms to the modern bifurcation between secular and Islamic feminism, women across the Muslim world have displayed remarkable resilience and ingenuity in their quest for equality and justice. Despite facing significant obstacles, including patriarchal structures, political repression, and ideological divides, these movements have continuously evolved, adapting to changing sociopolitical landscapes. This ongoing journey underscores the dynamic nature of feminist activism in Muslim societies and highlights the importance of recognizing and valuing the diversity of voices within the movement. To this end, I will examine each type of feminism by exploring their foundational frameworks, accomplishments, and the critique they have faced.

The Limits of Islamic Feminism

Afia Zia describes "Islamic feminism" as a "postmodernist, diasporic scholarly project that ... claims a research interest that includes multiple voices and debates in its endeavor to locate women's rights within an Islamic discourse."[39] Haideh Moghissi notes that the term was initially introduced by diasporic feminist academics and researchers of Muslim background who live and work in the west, many of which were educated in Europe and North America. Their critical perspectives are informed by studies on gender that encompass cultural, postcolonial, and subaltern approaches. However, the term itself is fraught with connotations and contradictions. Some perceive it as an oxymoron, while others view it as an attempt to reconcile religious beliefs with individual liberty and equality values. Margot Badran observes that, unlike the emergence of secular feminism as a social movement, Islamic feminism appeared on the global stage as a discourse—"a trenchant religiously framed discourse of gender equality."[40]

A substantial body of literature has emerged on Islamic feminism, with a range of scholars either advocating for it, rejecting it, or remaining ambivalent. There are two primary positions regarding the effectiveness of Islamic feminism. One perspective, supported by scholars like Fadwa El Guindi, suggests that feminism within an Islamic framework—seen as a means of resisting the spread of western values—is the most culturally relevant and effective strategy for women's movements in Muslim-majority countries. The other position, represented by voices like Haideh Moghissi, opposes the notion that Islam and feminism can coexist, arguing that divine laws, including those of Islam, inherently oppose feminist demands. Ibtissam Bouachrine identifies three strategies utilized by Islamic feminists to pursue their objectives. The first involves the reinterpretation of scriptural texts from a feminist perspective to "recover Islam's egalitarian message," which, as Islamic feminists argue, has been lost in the interpretations of male misogynistic interpretations of the Qur'ān and the *Hadīth*.[41] The second is to make visible and celebrate Muslim women's "agency" and resistance from within Islam and its institutions. The third shifts the focus of critique from Islam to western culture, redirecting attention from Islamic patriarchy and the oppression faced by Muslim women in Muslim-majority societies.

A cornerstone of Islamic feminism is Amina Wadud's *Qur'ān and Woman*. Wadud is an American Muslim philosopher often hailed as a leading figure among Islamic feminists. She questions the responsibility of Islam and specifically explores whether the Qur'ān upholds gender inequity. Wadud's research culminates in a Qur'ānic framework advocating for gender equality within familial and societal realms, contending that patriarchy contradicts Islamic principles and absolves Islam of any blame. In 2005, Wadud sparked controversy by leading Friday prayer for a congregation in the United States, a departure from the norm that reserves the role of leading mixed-gender prayers for male *imams*. Wadud has actively participated in various civil society organizations and movements advocating for gender equality grounded in Islamic principles, including "Sisters in Islam" and "*Musawah* (Equality)." Wadud's ideas gained traction among Muslim women seeking an alternative to the patriarchal interpretations they had inherited, leading to a growing following embracing this reimagined form of Islam. Fatima Mernissi, a Moroccan feminist writer and sociologist, also aims to shift the blame away from religious texts. She delves into the question of why the Arab world exhibits hostility toward women, arguing that Islam itself is not inherently sexist or oppressive. In the preface to the English translation of *The Veil and the Male Elite*, "If women's rights are a problem for some modern Muslim men, it is neither because of the Koran nor the Prophet, nor the Islamic tradition, but simply because those rights conflict with the interests of a male elite."[42] While she refrains from questioning the Qur'ān's validity, she casts doubt on certain *Hadīth* that, in her view, endorses the subjugation of women. She suggests that any bias against women in the Qur'ān stems from misinterpretation by elite Muslim men. She also argues for interpreting the veil as a form of asserting identity in response to western dominance, among other ongoing debates.

By presenting Islamic justifications for a theory of gender equality, these two scholars succeeded in persuading numerous Muslim women readers and activists that the "patriarchal family" contradicts Islamic teachings. While some scholars adopt a similar apologetic stance in their works akin to Wadud and Mernissi, others have chosen to break free from these constraints and move beyond this standpoint. In her subsequent book, *Inside the Gender Jihad*, even Wadud moves away from her earlier apologetics, emphasizing the need to view the Qur'ān not as a static text but "as an utterance or text in process."[43] She openly notes that she has "come to places where how the text says what it says is just plain inadequate, or unacceptable, however much interpretation is enacted upon it."[44] Other scholars moved away altogether from rereading Islamic texts to striving to reform family law through *fiqh* (Islamic jurisprudence). Ziba Mir-Hosseini, an Iranian-born legal anthropologist with expertise in Islamic law, gender, and development, argues that although *fiqh* (Islamic jurisprudence) may have served its purpose in the past, the evolving social landscape necessitates reformation to achieve justice and equality beyond what is achievable through adherence to traditional texts. She sheds light on the persisting conflation between divine sharia and human-devised *fiqh*, arguing that because it is human-devised, it should be open to reform. In her journal article "Muslim Women's Quest for Equality," she calls for "a movement to sever patriarchy from Islamic ideals and sacred texts and to give voice to an ethical and egalitarian vision of Islam," which she believes has the potential to empower Muslim women across various cultural and religious contexts to embrace choices aligned with their beliefs.

On the opposite camp of the debates on Islamic feminism, Valentine Moghadam, an Iranian-born feminist scholar, sociologist, activist, and author, argues that the activities and goals of Islamic feminism are limiting and "compromised."[45] She argues that attempts to utilize Islamic texts in this context hinder the advancement of women's status. In a secular analysis, Haideh Moghissi highlights the loose and inaccurate use of the term, arguing that the advocacy for Islamic feminism fails to foster new possibilities for feminists to engage with diverse perspectives and cultivate innovative ideas and approaches adaptable to various cultural and political settings.[46] She views Islamic feminism as an overly idealized depiction of Islam that detracts from substantial dialogues about the potential of feminist initiatives. Challenging the premise of Islamic feminism, Afia Zia contends that the lack of a solid political foundation relegates Islamic feminism to a purely academic pursuit.[47] In other words, without addressing the tangible needs of individuals living within Muslim-majority countries, Islamic feminism risks being confined to a theoretical exercise primarily relevant to the diaspora community. She asserts:

> In any case, in so far as both Islamism and feminism are political perspectives, Islamic feminism at an international level seems to be attempting to redefine both ... Conservative Muslim commentators often take advantage of the Islamic feminism agenda to reference all the rights that Muslim women are granted in Islam—however, they stop short on agreeing that these are unconditionally equal.[48]

Zia's argument alludes to the selective interpretation of rights for Muslim women within Islamic feminism by conservative Muslim commentators. This points to a fundamental tension within Islamic feminism, where the acknowledgment of granted rights within Islam may not always translate into unconditional equality in practice. This raises questions about the internal debates and evolving nature of Islamic feminist discourse. Nevertheless, a significant share of postcolonial Muslim feminist literature remains unaligned with either side. Some are wary of using the term "Islamic feminism" altogether. Drawing on postcolonial critiques, these feminists shed light on how the narrative of "saving Muslim women" is a construct shaped by colonial power dynamics. They challenge the fixation on the plight of Muslim women and their emancipation from perceived oppressive societies. Notable figures within this realm include Leila Ahmed, Chandra Talpade Mohanty, Deniz Kandiyoti, and Lila Abu-Lughod, who interrogates the accuracy of western portrayals of the "victimized," "abused" Muslim women in need of saving. Abu-Lughod argues that the prevalent western narrative, which she frames as "saving Muslim women from their own cultures," reflects not the realities of these cultures but rather the hegemonic geopolitical structures that assume a "savior" role without a comprehensive understanding of the Muslim women's lived experiences.[49] She emphasizes the importance of understanding Muslim women and women from diverse cultural and religious backgrounds within their unique historical, social, and ideological frameworks. Nawal El Saadawi, a prominent Egyptian secular feminist and a vocal critic of Arab patriarchy, echoes this sentiment by urging western feminists to recognize that breaking free from western influence remains a primary concern in developing nations. El Saadawi stresses the necessity for a deep examination of one's history and cultural context, asserting that "rereading one's history and understanding one's culture is essential for nationalist, socialist and feminist movements to build themselves on a firm base, to discover their roots."[50] In response to western representations of Muslim women as backward and powerless, Nadje al-Ali, a German-Iraqi academic of social anthropology and Middle East studies and feminist activist, notes:

> This strict separation between the "modern, secular and Westernizing voice" on the one hand and the "conservative, anti-Western and Islamic voice" on the other obscures the overlappings, contradictions and complexities of discourses and activism that took place against a background of anti-colonial and anti-imperialist struggle.[51]

In this quote, al-Ali emphasizes the importance of understanding the overlapping and diverse perspectives that influence the experiences and agency of Muslim women. This involves transcending simplistic binary representations and recognizing the complexity inherent in their social, cultural, and political environments. Following the initial rise of Islamic feminism on the global stage, a subsequent generation has ushered in a new wave often referred to as "second wave Islamic feminism" or "Muslim Holistic feminism" by different proponents. As described by Margot Badran, this evolving wave draws upon multiple perspectives, not confined solely to Islamic discourse. In contrast to secular feminists, these Muslim holistic feminists are "communally based," presenting themselves as advocates who are rooted in, represented by, and serving Muslim communities while also maintaining a global perspective.[52] She references the *Musawah* organization to illustrate her point. She contends that unlike early-twentieth-century secular feminism, which historically aimed to advocate for the rights of women regardless of religious affiliation, this modern iteration of Islamic feminism, striving to be viewed as "progressive" and "moderate," seems to be primarily concerned with Muslim women's communal needs. Afia Zia posits that this form of empowerment grounded solely in Islamic principles has inadvertently given rise to a concurrent development known as neo-Islamic political feminism. She states:

> Today, this limited form of political empowerment has captured the imagination of young women in a more symbolic way that sometimes offers moments of political confrontation but mostly follows a route of stealth and accommodation with patriarchy.[53]

Zia's argument points toward a critical concern within Islamic feminism, arguing that the narrow focus of addressing the communal needs of Muslim women within an Islamic framework rather than advocating for broader gender equality principles that transcend religious boundaries risks reinforcing traditional gender roles and power structures within Muslim communities, potentially limiting the scope of advocacy and progressive change. The emergence of neo-Islamic political feminism from this narrowed approach raises questions about the inclusivity and effectiveness of Islamic feminist movements in promoting gender equity for all women, regardless of their religious identities. Within the Iranian context, Shahrzad Mojab contends that Islamic feminism has fallen short as a genuine and locally rooted substitute for secular feminism, ultimately perpetuating a repressive patriarchal system. Additionally, she critiques western feminist theories for their narrow emphasis on legal parity, neglecting to address the oppressive gender dynamics prevalent in non-western communities.[54] Ultimately, the ongoing conversations and critiques of the Islamic feminist discourse reflecting a dynamic quest for gender equity may lead to a realization that collaborating with secular feminists could offer a more nuanced and comprehensive understanding of women's rights and empowerment, encompassing diverse perspectives and advocating for gender equality across a broad spectrum of beliefs and ideologies.

The Disparaging of Secular Feminism

As a result of the insistence of Islamic feminists on exclusively using texts and scriptures for women's emancipation projects, Haideh Moghissi describes "a lack of balance in most of the affirmative accounts of Muslim women's activism."[55] In the last few decades in Muslim-majority countries, as Islamists competed with the state for control over nationalist discourses, women's advocacy groups found themselves caught between various ideological conflicts. The clash between modernization for women's progress and claims of cultural authenticity has stigmatized secular approaches to women's development, seen in some contexts as antithetical to the positive religious focus of Islamic feminism, with it being scornfully referred to as the "negative or westoxified camp."[56] Sceptically, Afia Zia writes:

> Secular scholar-activists are more unqualified in their condemnation of misogyny in the name of Islam. Arguing that defensiveness about women's conditions under Islam lapses into dangerous apologetics. From the point of view of this "negative camp," women's interests are best pursued in secular terms and in the name of combatting universal human rights violations.[57]

After an extensive review of academic literature on secular Muslim women's activism and feminism in Muslim-majority and western nations, I encountered only a limited number of focused pieces. In Nadje al-Ali's monograph *Secularism, Gender and the State*, she seeks to place women's secular activism within the Egyptian context. The book begins by defining "secularism" or "secular activism" as an approach separating religion from politics without carrying any anti-religious implications. Al-Ali argues that while the secular Muslim women activists and feminists she interviewed share similar objectives, their navigation of faith and politics varies across different scenarios; they often adapt the notion of secularism to suit their goals in various circumstances and political environments. In her conclusion, she emphasizes the drawbacks of "essentialism," cautioning against oversimplifying intricate concepts like "feminism" or "Islamism" into uniform categories that hinder opportunities for reform. She argues that "rather than holding on to essentialist conceptualisations of 'culture' and 'identity', a post-colonial analysis with an emphasis on hybridity, dynamics and exchange offers a more constructive approach than claims to authenticity."[58] In their 2015 paper "Can the Secular Iranian Women's Activist Speak?" Leila Mouri and Kristin Soraya Batmanghelichi delve into the intricate dynamics surrounding the activism of secular Iranian women within the context of Iran. One of the central themes explored in the paper is the tension between secular feminist perspectives and the prevailing discourse of Islamic feminism. Secular Iranian women activists often find themselves marginalized and silenced, facing accusations of being anti-Islamic or inauthentic in their advocacy efforts. The paper also addresses the perception of secular Iranian feminists as "native informants," a labeling that undermines the legitimacy of their activism and positions them as traitors to their cultural and national identity. The authors call for a more inclusive and nuanced understanding of feminist activism in Iran, recognizing the diversity of perspectives and approaches within the women's movement and works toward empowering all women, regardless of their religious or ideological affiliations. In their 2017 article "Whither Feminist Alliance? Secular Feminists and Islamist Women in Turkey," Hulya Simga and Gulru Z. Goker argue that the existing polarization between secular feminists and Islamist women in Turkey weakens the collective efforts to address urgent women's problems. To overcome these challenges, they advocate for establishing deliberative platforms where women's civil society organizations, both secular and Islamist, can engage in constructive dialogue away from partisan influences. Very recently, through a series of interviews with Muslim women in Karachi and Islamabad who self-describe as feminist and secular, Amina Jamal draws on transnational feminist practices advocated by scholars such as Inderpal Grewal and Gayatri Spivak to expand the discourse beyond identitarian notions of secular versus religious. She highlights the experiences and perspectives of self-proclaimed secular feminists who lament the oppressive nature of a singularly defined, state-implemented version of Islam in Pakistani society. These feminists advocate for a more inclusive and diverse understanding of religious and cultural traditions, emphasizing the importance of contextualizing secularism within specific societal frameworks. Secular Muslim feminists in Pakistan are depicted as actively engaging in critiquing and resisting the Islamization projects of the 1990s and confronting extremist ideologies through their works. Their efforts contribute to reshaping societal perceptions and promoting alternative narratives that challenge patriarchal and authoritarian systems. Broadly, secular feminists within Muslim contexts examine the interplay between structural and legal elements to address women's challenges. Their approaches range from advocating for reforming Islamic laws and faith-based policies in favor of secular principles and universal equality to advocating for the complete rejection of such laws and a call for strict adherence to international human rights principles. Secular Muslim feminists also advocate for the dismantling of clerical structures and authorities, advocating for their replacement with democratic systems.[59]

The Other Muslims, a volume edited by Turkish-American scholar Zeyno Baran in 2010, features a range of alternative Muslim voices, largely based in Europe. Contributors from various backgrounds delve into discussions shaping the future of Islam and Muslims in western societies. While some address theological matters, others share personal narratives about navigating life as Muslims in predominantly non-Muslim environments. In a dossier edited by Merieme Hélie-Lucas and colleagues for *Women Living under Muslim Laws*, several secular Muslim women worldwide describe their challenges in Europe and America. They recount experiences of being accused of collusion with governments and branded as racist or "Islamophobic" for speaking out against the surge in Muslim fundamentalism, "as if one could not struggle at the same time against both the traditional extreme right and the new fundamentalist extreme right," as stated by Hélie-Lucas in the introduction of the dossier.[60] Mayanthi L. Fernando's 2009 journal article "Exceptional Citizens" traces the integration of secular Muslim women into the public sphere in France, using the term *Musulmane Laïque* (Secular Muslim) to portray her research participants, drawing inspiration from recently formed secular Muslim groups in France. Focusing on Fadela Amara, cofounder of the association *Ni Putes Ni Soumises*, the analysis proposes that while such figures may embody the universal concept of abstract citizenship, the racial and cultural foundations of citizenship impede their ability to surpass their Muslim identity, hindering their full integration into French society. In my PhD thesis in 2019, I examined two organizations, Inspire in Britain and Brigade de Mères (Mother's Brigade) in France, battling Islamic fundamentalism and gender inequality, and five life stories of "secular" Muslim women working alongside them. While these women are widely recognized and celebrated among "elite" circles in the west, they have been largely dismissed by postcolonial feminist scholarship as uncritical mouthpieces for their respective states "anti-ISIS" agenda. Moreover, different factions interpret their activism differently: Islamic fundamentalists view it as western imperialism; postcolonial feminists dismiss them, emphasizing "religious" agency over western secularism; neo-orientalists continue to exoticize them; and some on the left perceive them as Islamophobes. In her 2020 paper "Arab Secular Feminism in Arab and/or Islamic Countries and Europe," María Isabel García Lafuente sheds light on the struggles faced by secular feminists, who combat multiple fronts simultaneously, including misogyny, accusations of aligning with Islamophobic narratives in Europe, and criticisms that their advocacy hinders feminist movements in Arab and Islamic regions. Despite these challenges, these feminists remain steadfast in their beliefs, using writing as a form of liberation and taboo-breaking.

This brief exploration of the perspectives of secular Muslim voices recorded in diverse publications reveals the intricate challenges and obstacles they encounter, illuminating the complexities of identity, religious connections, and citizenship that shape their experiences. The scarcity of research on what I term "secular Muslim feminism" underscores the necessity for in-depth investigations in this domain. The aftermath of 9/11 has provoked a reconsideration of the assumptions regarding liberal politics, secular governance, and the agency of Muslim women, prompting discussions on how interventionist imperialist gender politics impact global secular feminist movements. This requires an urgent call for critical reflection on the intersection of gender, politics, and power dynamics within the contemporary sociopolitical landscape.

Between the Religious and the Secular

The arguments of white feminism have often ignored the distinct realities and struggles of women in other parts of the world. Nawar Al-Hassan Golley states that "it is even argued that western feminists have described Arab women's lives as being so different from theirs that they cannot possibly develop any kind of feminism."[61] This chapter stands as evidence that non-western cultures, including Muslim societies, have a rich history of feminist consciousness and activism, challenging sexism and other biases since the early twentieth century. The chapter showcases examples of early feminist consciousness, highlighting Muslim women's continuous and ongoing efforts to advocate for their rights. It also sheds light on the hijacking of feminist discourse by the Islamic feminist movement, which has unfortunately led to the marginalization of secular feminist voices and inadvertently strengthened Islamist agendas. The recent western focus on Islamic feminism has been swinging between dismissing it as an oxymoron for its attempt to reconcile religious patriarchy with feminist aspirations and praising it as a pathway to a more liberal and reformed Islam. However, this dichotomy masks the complexities of feminist engagement within Muslim societies, where both authoritarian regimes and western liberal forces have often silenced secular resistance. The emergence of ISIS and its break from al-Qaeda in 2014, with its claim of establishing an "Islamic State," has further complicated the landscape of feminist activism.[62] Marieme Hélie-Lucas, a secular feminist from Iran and Algeria, argues that the public acknowledgment of ISIS's war crimes has created a "favorable climate for more openly demanding secular states as a protection from these extreme-right political forces."[63] "We have a better chance now to be heard by progressive forces than in the past," she writes.[64]

The critical point here is not to argue that secular Muslim feminism is the ultimate solution to the challenges facing Muslim women within their societies. Instead, the argument posits that the combination of religious patriarchy with local traditions, supported by those who enable them to flourish, creates significant obstacles for them to serve as sources of liberating or progressive ideologies.[65] A secular resistance, therefore, disrupts this established paradigm and the way it is used. While recognizing the contributions of Muslim feminists and Islamic reformists to the advancement of feminist awareness and women's empowerment in Muslim contexts, there is scant evidence supporting the notion that Islamist politics have led to tangible improvements in the material and symbolic status of women in any Muslim setting. For instance, Afia Zia notes that "given the limited agenda of Islamist women politicians, despite their much-discovered agency and the targeted discrediting of secular feminism in post 9/11 scholarship, the impasse in the progress of women's writes in Pakistan remain suspended between the two limiting narratives of faith-based re-interpretive empowerment and gradual symbolic liberal reform."[66] Meanwhile, since 9/11, considerable international scholarship tends to view all events in Muslim contexts through the single narrow lens of the "War on terror," which I reflect upon in the following chapter.

4

The Politics of "Saving" the Muslim Women

The young Afghan refugee girl, Sharbat Gula, immortalized by Steve McCurry's iconic 1985 photograph, has since become the face of Afghan suffering.[1] Her piercing green eyes captivated the world, making her the perfect symbol for a narrative of western "rescue." This chapter examines how this image and the subsequent efforts to find Sharbat Gula in 2002 were enmeshed within a complex web of power dynamics and colonial legacies. In 2001, the US began its military interventions in Afghanistan in response to the events of 9/11 perpetrated against the United States by al-Qaeda,[2] an Islamist group supported by the Taliban government at the time. In 2002, Cathy Newman wrote an article in National Geographic entitled "A Life Revealed: Her Eyes Have Captivated the World since She Appeared on our Cover in 1985."[3] The article exposes the agelong fascination with "saving" the third world woman. It fosters the idea that war can both free Muslim women from their oppressive men and liberate the west from Islamic terrorism. This was the central narrative used when the administration of US President George W. Bush launched the "War on Terror" and the invasion of Afghanistan, with Laura Bush asserting that the terrorists' central objective was the brutal oppression of women, framing the fight against terrorism as also a battle for the rights and dignity of women, and Tony Blair's government alleging that the campaign was needed, among other things, to "give back a voice" to Afghan women deprived of human rights under the Taliban regime.

While it is undeniable that Afghan women endured horrific injustices under Taliban rule, this chapter argues that their portrayal as helpless victims is deeply problematic. Ironically, this narrative has found common cause on both sides of the political spectrum and has even been a rare example of the language of feminism and colonialism coming together to say essentially the same thing. This chapter maps out the intricate interplay of race, gender, and religion within historical and contemporary imperial practices. By examining the enduring legacies of colonialism, it unveils how Muslims, particularly Muslim women, are positioned within representations of war, violence, and empire-building. Drawing on post-9/11 imagery of Muslim women, the chapter challenges their portrayal as passive, voiceless victims of patriarchal cultures. Instead, it draws on Maryam Khalid's concept of "gendered orientalism" to analyze the racialized and gendered underpinnings of the global "War on Terror," revealing its abundance of gendered narratives. Furthermore, the chapter explores the rise of fundamentalist movements within Muslim societies and the surge of right-wing ideologies in the west, both employing the same trope of "saving Muslim women" from their "misogynist, terrorist" men as a justification for attacking each other. This analysis argues that Muslim women become entangled within these competing forces, constrained by the "savior" narratives that limit their public image and agency.

Orientalism Then and Now

The eighteenth and nineteenth centuries witnessed the rise of "orientalism," a western academic discipline exploring the languages, cultures, and literature of the "Orient"; Turkey, the Arab world, India, and later, China, Japan, and parts of Asia.[4] Within these studies, the "Orient" represented the geographical location and its historical and civilizational narratives.[5] The discipline of orientalism produced work that often found the "Orient" a foreign, exotic, and dangerous place. This has fueled the "West" or the "Occident" (mainly Europe and the United States) to conceptualize itself as distinct and superior, justifying its regional imperialist policies. The terms "Orient" and "Occident" are, therefore, "discursively created identities" that enabled the west to control—and even construct—ideas about the East during the post-Enlightenment era.[6] These ideas were built on binaries like "East" versus "West," representing the divide between civilized and uncivilized, modern and backward, familiar and foreign, colonizer and colonized, and ultimately, "self" and "other." Orientalism, in essence, became a system of representation. It allowed the west to construct an image of the East as its opposite, a distorted reflection—"a sort of surrogate and even underground self"[7]—an alien, backward, barbaric, permeated with mysticism and danger.

Anouar Abdel-Malek's seminal work *L'Orientalisme en Crise* (Orientalism in Crisis) emerged as one of the earliest critiques of orientalist scholarship. Abdel-Malek challenged the orientalist institution, writing from within the French academic landscape, arguing that its studies served colonial agendas.

He highlighted how orientalists ignored valuable contributions from the "Orient," instead perpetuating the myth of their "backwardness" and the need for "western intervention." In the following years, Edward Said's groundbreaking work, *Orientalism*, solidified the foundation of what later developed into the framework of postcolonial theory. Said defines orientalism as "a style of thought based upon an ontological and epistemological distinction made between 'the Orient' [the East] and (most of the time) 'the Occident' [the West]."[8] Opening his book with Karl Marx—"They cannot represent themselves; they must be represented"[9]—Said sets the tone for his critique of the condescending and paternalistic western system of representation and domination. He exposes the inherent link between orientalism and western colonialism, demonstrating how the west constructed the "Orient" as its "other," justifying its imperial ambitions and control. Said's work revolutionized academic scholarship across multiple disciplines, sparking a critical conversation about power, representation, and the legacy of colonialism. His insights continue to shape contemporary discussions on the complex relationship between the west and the "Orient" till the present day.

Orientalism features three symbiotic foundations of "orientalist" studies: the academic discipline and its research; a style of thought that fundamentally differentiates "the Orient" from "the Occident" both in ontology and epistemology; and the institution that manages the Orient "by making statements about it, authorizing views of it, describing it, by teaching it, settling it, ruling over it."[10] The major contribution of Said's work is revealing how the Orient was constructed as the contrasting image of the Occident by "decoding the structures of power and knowledge hidden in texts and discourse" historically employed by colonialism to dominate the Orient.[11] Said's work uncovers the underlying structures of power, knowledge, hegemony, culture, and imperialism historically embedded in colonial contexts and discourses. According to Said, colonialism was deeply rooted in its economic, political, and administrative institutions and, more importantly, in the production of power and knowledge. This is evident in the ways colonial leaders have shaped and disseminated knowledge about the Orient. Thomas Macaulay, the British politician who introduced the English education system to British colonies, once remarked that "a single shelf of a good European library was worth the whole native literature of India and Arabia."[12] Similarly, Lord Cromer, who served as the British controller-general in Egypt in 1879, wrote about the necessity of reforming the "native" Egyptian mind to align with the British-European "type."[13] Said argues that such fictitious images were constructed using "tropes, images, and representations of literature, art, visual media, film, and travel writing, among other aspects of cultural and political appropriation."[14] A primary source of these images was the travel narratives of European men, who depicted "oriental" women as "objects of pity, deprived of liberty," yet simultaneously possessing a "libidinous nature," and whose "licentiousness was endorsed by their husbands and masters."[15] These travel accounts served as "factual narratives upon which numerous artists based their paintings," often centering their work around the allure of "nude odalisques, either lying languidly on a divan or engaged in overtly sexual scenes such as a lone dancer performing for an all-male audience."[16] Such representations make clear the way orientalism operates—by embellishing, essentializing, and exploiting the fabricated differences between the east and the west, it served to legitimize the supposed supremacy of the west over the rest of the world. These depictions continue to permeate our culture, shaping the image of the alien "East" to this day. Throughout the colonial project of orientalism, the "Occident" not only manufactured what it termed the "Orient," but the "Orient" also played a role in defining the "Occident," helping "to shape Europe (or the West) as its contrasting image, idea, personality, and experience."[17] Said conceptualizes orientalism as a "discourse," which he defines as the product of the interaction between power and knowledge.

Colonialism and imperialism did not merely conquer the "Orient" and its territories; they also dominated its land, identity, culture, history, and voice. This discourse was bolstered by "institutions, vocabulary, scholarship, imagery, doctrines, and even colonial bureaucracies and colonial style."[18] Thus, European culture came into existence "by setting itself apart from the Orient"—by defining the "self" through what it is not.[19] Intrinsically, to be "oriental" is to be "orientalized"; to embody whatever image the colonizer deems appropriate, whether that be the "terrorist," the "victim," or the hypersexualized *harem* woman, among others. Thus, despite colonial expansion being a brutal process marked by exploitation, genocide, and suppression, colonialism was framed as "a triumph of the civilized, moral, rational, superior human who altruistically carried the burden of bringing the fruits of reason, modernity, liberty, equality, emancipation, technology, progress, and the rule of law from Europe to other parts of the world."[20] Slavery, for instance, was justified based on the alleged inferiority of Africans as a race.

After the publication of Said's seminal text, the term orientalism entered mainstream discourse, but, in the process, it became diluted—detached from its radical roots. Today, the term evokes images of overcrowded, dusty cities, splendid *saris*, Chinese dragons, and exotic dancers. While these representations are indeed a part of what Said describes as orientalism, his central argument, as previously explained, is that orientalism is not merely an abstract concept but "a relationship of power, of domination."[21] The west's significant investment in constructing and perpetuating orientalism legitimized the brutality of European imperialism in the past and continues to do so today. Orientalism, therefore, reinforces the framework that allowed the west to "govern—and even manufacture—the Orient politically, socially, militarily, ideologically, scientifically, and imaginatively."[22] Consequently, Said's work remains as pertinent today as it was upon its initial release, perhaps even more so, given the ongoing legacies of colonialism—from western capitalism and economic hegemony to the savior narrative—indicating that orientalism has not ceased but instead evolved and adapted. Now, orientalism manifests in a fusion of guises, ranging from nuanced indications of western cultural superiority to overt forms of racism, echoing power dynamics that trace back centuries and persist in influencing our contemporary existence. While the era of direct colonial governance and control by imperial forces has ended, we are confronted with enduring patterns and mechanisms of dominance and economic exploitation, embodying a form of contemporary imperialism often labeled as "neo-colonialism." In modern western societies, ethnic minorities are frequently positioned as the "racialized other." This is evident in portrayals surrounding the Gulf War of 1991, the post-9/11 era stereotyping of Muslims, and notably, the justifications for the "War on Terror" that purported to "rescue" the Muslim woman, such as the Iraq War in 2003 and the intervention in Afghanistan. These instances resuscitate narratives of "us" versus "them," the "civilized" against the "uncivilized," and establish new hierarchies. They also expose the dangerous nature of imperialism and the resistance against it in our supposedly "postcolonial" era.

Orientalism, Gender, and Empire

Said's examination of orientalism has introduced an innovative method for examining how the "Occident" has historically and currently portrayed the "Orient" through discourse. While it has garnered significant acclaim, it has also faced notable criticism. Nevertheless, among other works, precisely "orientalism" is frequently referenced, "(mis)quoted, applied, evaluated, criticized, developed and subverted."[23] I view orientalism as "one" of the tools through which western societies exerted colonial control by shaping the image of the "Oriental." I also recognize and concur with critics of Edward Said, who contend that his work tends to oversimplify distinctions between the "East" and the "West," thus rejecting the hierarchical binary categorizations upon which imperialism thrived.[24] Maryam Khalid argues that Said's work lacks historical intricacies and particularities, leading to an oversight of the diverse range of perspectives in "western" writings about the "East."[25] Although Said himself, in his later works *Orientalism Reconsidered and Culture and Imperialism*, penned in the mid-nineties, moves away from establishing strict dichotomies between the "East" and "West," his detractors have not fully embraced these shifts. Despite the critique, Said's contributions have maintained substantial influence up to the present day. I agree with Nadje al-Ali:

> However vague the actual politics suggested by Said [may be], he provides a useful and creative framework in which liberation politics can be further developed. Moreover, as a theoretical and methodological approach, Culture and Imperialism offers a way out of the impasse of essentialism and reductionism that Said criticized in Orientalism yet had reproduced to some extent himself.[26]

Having acknowledged Said's self-critique, I argue that any thorough examination of colonial discourse necessitates considering alternative perspectives. According to Homi Bhabha, the orientalist discourse continually evolves and adapts to its surrounding contexts. On the one hand, exploring these alternative viewpoints helps dismantle the oversimplified portrayal of the East as monolithic. On the other hand, engaging critically with these perspectives provides exciting avenues for reshaping and reimagining both "orientalism" and "postcolonialism." The current calls, for example, for the "decolonization" of knowledge and the engagement in post-orientalist scholarship by "Indigenous" scholars are serving to disrupt cultural stereotyping, generalizations, and misconceptions perpetuated by earlier scholarships. This is not to suggest that "indigenous" scholars are credible by the sheer fact of being a "local." Some may be far removed from their home societies and cultures, while others are self-reflective and critically engaged owing to a keen sense of responsibility and emotional involvement. One must also acknowledge that the absence of a language barrier allows the "native" scholar to relate to and apprehend nuances that often remain blind spots to researchers struggling with the language. In the context of the Muslim world, these discussions have regrettably given rise to a new "trend" characterized by the portrayal of Islamists as the sole counterpoint to escalating western influence. This, in turn, has revived what al-Ali identifies as "simplistic dichotomies: the Islamist, traditional and authentic on the one hand and modernist, progressive and Western on the other."[27]

An equally important, if not more crucial, concern is the neglect or outright omission of gender and class from some discussions of colonial discourse in Said's work. At the outset of *Orientalism*, Edward Said addresses the problematic feminization of the Orient, highlighting the relationship between French novelist Gustav Flaubert, best known for his 1857 masterpiece *Madame Bovary*, and an Egyptian courtesan. For Flaubert, the Orient signified desire, sensuality, and feminine sexuality, as Said argues. Flaubert embodies the authority to observe and analyze, while the Egyptian courtesan represents the passive subject, voiceless and spoken for. Said argues that these themes are routinely echoed: the Orient as feminized, sexualized, and desired. In this sense, Said's work provides a valuable foundation for rereading *Orientalism* beyond the binary logic of otherness. Some scholars have expanded on this by emphasizing its inherent volatility and instability.[28] Meyda Yegenoglu argues that gender issues in the discourse of orientalism are either overlooked or relegated to a different domain, specifically gender or feminist studies. In her comparative study of French and British orientalism, Lisa Lowe questions whether Said's idea of orientalism oversimplifies the way the Orient is portrayed as the opposite of the Occident. She argues that orientalism encompasses discursive conflicts that generate an "instability of the Orientalist terrain," illustrated in how it intersects with and diverges from other discourses such as gender, race, and class.[29] Her study, thus, opens up the possibility for understanding orientalism in a way that takes into account differences related to race, gender, and religion.

As previously noted, *Orientalism* did touch upon the gendering of western representations of non-westerners, which has consistently been used to further western supremacy. However, it did not question the power dynamics underlying these representations. Nor did it investigate the implications of these portrayals in terms of women's agency or control. Examining the construction and perpetuation of social images of Pakistani women in present-day Britain, Avtar Brah uncovers deep-rooted connections to the historical contexts of colonialism and imperialism.[30] This connection is evident in the diverse representations of Indian women in nineteenth-century British India, which varied from provocative descriptions of sensuality to admiring depictions of spousal loyalty. These historical constructions persist in shaping the social perceptions of Indian and Pakistani women in contemporary Britain until the present day. Similar fascination is exhibited by the French colonialists with the veiled woman of North Africa, associating the veil symbol of "otherness"—with their hidden and unattainable sexuality. French orientalism, known for its relentless investigation and interpretation of the veil as a site of fantasy and a tool for the perpetuation of colonial power dynamics, has played a significant role in shaping the representations of Muslim women. They are often depicted as both objects of desire and oppressed victims, reflecting the intertwined nature of orientalism with class and sexuality. Mohja Kahf explains how the portrayal of the oppressed Muslim or Arab woman gained significance during the nineteenth-century expansion of western empires as they sought to exert control over entire Muslim societies.[31] They portrayed women as "objects of desire, sensual, elusive *harem* girls" while also casting them as regrettably victimized by their patriarchal, misogynistic cultures,[32] which underscores the deep association of orientalism not just with gender but also with class and sexuality.

Contrary to Said's reading of orientalism as an "exclusive male province," postcolonial feminist scholars argue that orientalism was the product not only of western male intellectuals but also of women. The inaccessibility of the Ottoman *harems* to European males helped perpetuate the image of the *harem* as purely sexual. However, female travelers and artists have later provided brief glimpses into the source of such fantasies. However, their accounts often reinforced the western idea of the beautiful, powerless "oriental" woman. In her review of the feminist periodical literature of the nineteenth century, Antoinette Burton reveals how British feminism constructed the image of the helpless Indian womanhood, on which their emancipation in the imperial nation-state relied. She concludes that Victorian and Edwardian feminists not only reproduced the moral discourse of imperialism but also embedded western feminism deeply within it. Barbara Ramusack refers to this as "maternal imperialism." At the same time, Nancy Paxton argues that for these feminists, the choice was limited between being racist and loyal or being disloyal to civilization. Additionally, *harem* women themselves were able to control the depiction of their private spaces to suit their own needs. Thisaranie Herath underscores the cross-cultural exchanges and negotiations involved,[33] while Inbisat Ali and Taimur Ali focus on the agency exercised by Muslim women. All this highlights the complexity of such representations.

Postcolonial feminist scholars have spoken and continue to critique the ways in which women in former western colonies were represented, not only by men but also by women, as oppressed and subjugated victims of their culture, their men, and their faith. They argue that white men (and "their" women) position themselves as saviors aiming to "rescue" and "liberate" these perceived "wretched" populations, particularly women of color. In her book *Gender, Orientalism, and the War on Terror*, Maryam Khalid expounds on the ways in which orientalism rested on tropes, such as "civilization versus barbarism," to advance the representation of the former colonized women as helpless victims whose freedom and liberty were contingent on the European colonial "civilizing mission."[34] In this way, both gender and orientalism as discourses intersect and are reflected through each. As Myriam Khalid argues, knowledge generated in any context is "the product of (and (re)productive of) gendered discourses."[35] Western hegemony, thus, is the product of a system that not only orientalizes the East but also genders it. Chandra Talpade Mohanty argues that western feminism has co-opted and subjugated "the fundamental complexities and conflicts which characterize the lives of women of different classes, religions, cultures, races and castes" in developing countries.[36] The west, thus, uses its values and culture as yardsticks for measuring advancement and modernity. While the western woman is perceived as liberated and modern, the third world woman, often portrayed as a homogeneous category, is perceived as unenlightened and traditional. Miriam Cooke argues that the west realized fundamentally through imperial and colonial reasoning to liberate the "third world woman." She writes:

> To defend our universal civilization, we must rescue the women. To rescue these women, we must attack these men. These women will be rescued not because they are more "ours" than "theirs" but because they will have become more "ours" through the rescue mission. ... In the Islamic context, the negative stereotyping of the religion as inherently misogynist provides ammunition for the attack on the uncivilized brown men.[37]

This quote reflects a problematic perspective that justifies aggression against men in specific contexts under the guise of rescuing women. Additionally, the notion that women become more aligned with a particular group or civilization through such actions raises concerns about instrumentalizing gender equality for political gains. The association of negative stereotypes about an entire religion with misogyny can lead to harmful generalizations and further perpetuate discriminatory attitudes toward specific groups. These issues are further explored in the context of postcolonial Muslim states, where gender dynamics intersect with matters of national identity, resistance, and the legacy of colonialism, shaping ongoing conversations about women's roles amidst the historical influences of capitalism, imperialism, and patriarchy, which will be further elaborated on in the following section.

In the Crossfires of Change

In postcolonial Muslim states across Asia, Africa, and the Middle East, both colonial legacies and patriarchal norms have conferred superior roles upon men and relegated women to subordinate positions. When referring to postcolonialism, I specifically address societies and states that have experienced colonial dominion and the period following independence. This is to underline the persistence of colonial influences even after the formal end of colonial rule. By and large, the history of decolonization in the twentieth century is often seen as a history of "Great Men," like Franz Fanon,[38] Mohandas Gandhi,[39] Kwame Nkrumah,[40] and so on. Postcolonial scholarship has frequently overlooked the significant contributions of women and feminist ideologies within anti-colonial movements. However, feminist analysis of western scholarship concerning the "third world" demonstrates how relationships of power were often inscribed as gendered, using "othering" to produce knowledge that situated women in ex-colonies as inferior and unable to act in the face of oppression. This phenomenon persisted during and after the colonial periods of British and French imperialism, among others. For instance, the British, who had control over India from the 1750s until the 1950s, viewed themselves as agents of enlightenment, particularly for women. But it was through the brutality of acts such as *Sati*, polygamy, female infanticide, purdah, and child marriage that orientalists produced their version of India, "*dichotomizing* the world into 'them' and 'us,' the strange and familiar, thereby emphasizing difference to the extreme."[41] Within this discourse, the goal of civilizing the Indian people was not only justifiable but, as Partha Chatterjee argues, also welcomed.[42] Throughout the era of French colonialism in Algeria, Algerian women were perceived as the "oppressed of the oppressed."[43] Nonetheless, under French rule, advancements in women's rights were notably scarce. By the onset of the war in 1954, Algerian women were excluded entirely from public life. Only 4.5 percent were literate, few had jobs or went to school, and they had no voting rights.[44]

Forging a national identity postcolonial rule was essential to challenging the colonizer's narrative that portrayed the colonized as inferior. However, it presented various challenges. To challenge the domination of the colonizer, the colonized people had to navigate reform within their cultures while preserving and affirming the unique essence of their national identities. In postcolonial Muslim nations, women were often used as symbols of the nation in anti-colonial struggles and the formation of modern nation-states. Deniz Kandiyoti highlights how nationalist language singled out women as emblematic figures of collective identity. In India, for instance, the nationalist project demanded the involvement of women in public activities, which created a dilemma; "how to present a modern image of India through demonstrating the ability of self-rule and how to control women's behaviour."[45] The answers to these questions were the fabric of the debates around social reform in the nineteenth century, not only in India but also in many postcolonial states; questions which continue to have an influence until the present day. Partha Chatterjee asserts that Indian nationalists addressed these debates by utilizing the concept of "difference as a principle of selection," aiming to maintain "the distinction between the social roles of men and women in terms of material and spiritual virtues."[46] In other words, they sought to uphold cultural norms and values to preserve the perceived integrity of the society's moral fabric. This approach helped justify and sustain societal structures that were believed to be essential for maintaining social harmony and stability. Using this principle, nationalism created the image of the "new woman," superior to the western woman, the traditional Indian woman and the common woman; modern, educated yet expected to uphold spiritual purity (feminine virtues). Defined this way, the "new woman" is subjected to a "new patriarchy," which assigns women the complex role of epitomizing a distinctively modern national identity. According to Chatterjee, this nationalist approach to reform and modernization is a project of both emancipation from colonial dominance and emancipation of women. This may explain why earlier generations of educated women initially supported the nationalist idea of the "new woman." While Chatterjee emphasizes creating a modern national culture, Kedar Vishwanathan highlights the appropriation of women in imagining a free India.[47] In postcolonial Egypt, factions within the nationalist discussions perceived women as representations of the nation, incorporating gender-oriented narratives into nationalist agendas. Renata Pepicelli argues:

> While the nationalism of male secular progressives, coming mostly from the upper class, claim for women's advancement that envisioned new societal roles for them as part of national empowerment, the nationalism of conservative men, mainly from the middle class, extolled women's domestic roles as part of their defense of a supposed Islamic cultural authenticity, emphasizing their role as mothers and homemakers (Badran 1995:13) ... Thus, Arab nationalism—like nationalism in other parts of the world—made a strategic and instrumental use of the woman's image.[48]

This quote sheds light on how gender dynamics intertwine with nationalist ideologies, underlining how gender becomes a strategic tool in asserting cultural authenticity and national identity. During anti-colonial struggles, the colonizer also believed that enhancing women's status could undermine independence movements. Consequently, colonizers implemented policies purported to emancipate Muslim women from "ignorance and the crushing weight of patriarchal domination."[49] However, these emancipation initiatives often disadvantaged women in practice, with many nationalists feeling threatened by what they viewed as the colonial reforms' moral intrusions.

As the nationalist revolutions gained momentum, conservatism also escalated as a response to what was perceived as colonial encroachment on their cultural norms. The traditional portrayal of women in postcolonial settings, thus, evolved to embody not only national identity but also a narrative of resistance. For instance, Leila Ahmed argues that the veil symbolized "the dignity and validity of all native customs coming under attack (relating to women) and the need to affirm them as a means of resistance to Western domination."[50] In postcolonial Algeria, while resistance movements recruited a small number of women as fighters, akin to the "new woman" concept among Indian nationalists, they promoted a concept termed "patriotic motherhood." This involved being good wives and mothers who would "preserve traditional moral standards" to mold the next generation of Algerians.[51] Nonetheless, they did not hesitate to use them as propaganda tools for their cause. In response to the French emancipation reforms, nationalist movements in Algeria launched their initiatives, asserting that women's only road to equality lies in fighting for a liberated nation devoid of colonial control. This strategic use of women aimed to transform the war's narrative from radical Arabs terrorizing peaceful Europeans into a depiction of the colonized resisting a brutal oppressor. On the one hand, nationalist movements invited women to participate fully in anti-colonial struggles by referring to them as "national" actors: mothers, educators, workers, and even fighters. On the other hand, they reasserted the limits of culturally acceptable feminine conduct. Nira Yuval-Davis and Floya Anthias assert that women's relation to nationalism had embodied at least five primary forms: (1) as biological reproducers of the nation; (2) as symbols and signifiers of national difference in male discourse; (3) as transmitters and producers of the cultural narratives themselves (mothers, teachers, writers, playwrights, artists); (4) as reproducers of the boundaries of the nation; and (5) as active participants in nationalist movements. Kumari Jayawardena puts it in plain language:

> To foreign and local capitalists and landowners, women were the cheapest source of labor for plantations, agriculture, and industry. To the colonial authorities and missionaries, local women had to be educated to be good (preferably Christian) wives and mothers to the professional and white-collar personnel who were being trained to manage the colonial economy. To the male reformers of the local bourgeoisie, women needed to be adequately Westernized and educated

in order to enhance the modern and "civilized" image of their country and of themselves, and to be a good influence on the next generation; the demand grew for "civilized housewives."[52]

This quote highlights the pervasive exploitation of women, as well as the ways in which colonial authorities and missionaries aimed to cast local women into idealized roles, often with a preference for Christian values, to fulfill the needs of a developing colonial economy. In all intentions and purposes, the appropriation of women's identity for ideological reasons by both nationalist and colonial forces helped prevent women's voices from becoming part of an authentic discourse on the war after independence. And even though British colonizers, for example, urged British women to support the "liberation" of their Indian "sisters," "colonialism actually undermined the feminist cause."[53] As Maryam Khalid argues, "colonialism itself was highly patriarchal and oppressive," which ultimately weakened the fight for women's rights.[54] While women in postcolonial Muslim regions actively engaged in nationalist movements, it is the image of the subordinated woman, oppressed by patriarchy, that is reproduced in many western feminist discourses. In essence, both colonial rulers and their nationalist opponents conspired to project a particular image of women's social and political roles that served their own interests. The question then is not whether patriarchal relations predate capitalism but rather how these social relations have been reshaped within the context of capitalism and imperialism. Avtar Brah argues, "Capitalism, patriarchy and imperialism are not independent albeit interlocking systems—they are part of the same structure. Capitalist social relations are themselves patriarchal and imperialist in form."[55]

The Unresolved Legacies of Colonialism

From the earlier section, it is now apparent that the social realities and lived experiences of Muslim women globally are shaped by a complex interplay of economic, political, and ideological frameworks that impact the interconnected realms of race, class, and gender. These structures are firmly entrenched in colonialism and the longstanding "civilizing" processes linked to it for many centuries. When I speak of Muslim women, I am alluding to a highly diverse group distinguished by their race, ethnicity, religion, and class or social standing. Despite these distinctions, the portrayal of the non-western, subaltern woman— or the "third world Woman"—as Kiran Grewal contends, "continues to provide the foundation for intervention and claims of western superiority often in ways that have changed little since the era of the colonial civilizing mission."[56] In her seminal article "Under Western Eyes," Chandra Talpade Mohanty argues that the perception of third world women as victims rather than active agents has long impacted the positioning of Muslims, particularly Muslim women, in historical and contemporary narratives shaped by the legacies of colonialism and imperialism. Avtar Brah provides some examples:

> When Margaret Thatcher constructs black cultures as an "alien" threat to the "British way of life" or Enoch Powell maintains that although black people are in Britain they cannot be of Britain, one is reminded of Kipling's view that. ' East is East and West is West and never the twain shall meet.'[57]

This quote alludes to historical sentiments of xenophobia and exclusion that have manifested in British political discourse, echoing the discourse of the clash of civilizations. But while in the early postwar years, public discussions were primarily focused on racial and ethnic classifications, the rise of Islamist movements globally resulted in populations previously identified by national origins (e.g., Pakistani, Indian, Bangladeshi in Britain and North African or Arab in France) being collectively labeled as "Muslim" in public discourse and policies. Here, it is worth distinguishing between self-identification and external categorization. The former refers to individuals of Muslim heritage in the west asserting their religious practices within their communities, whereas the latter involves an external labeling imposed by the dominant population. Toward the end of the twentieth century, not only has religion achieved a remarkable resurgence, but particular forms of religious movements, grouped under the umbrella concept of "fundamentalism," seem to have become a "vital force for (and against) social change all over the world and within different religions."[58] Related to these developments is the growth of fundamentalist movements in Muslim-majority societies that engage in complex ideological and political interactions with western influences. This phenomenon has been accompanied by the rise of "emancipatory movements" in the west, often responding to the perceived threat posed by fundamentalist absolutism and authoritarian political projects.[59]

Following the events of 9/11, debates about Islam's compatibility with western values dominated political discourse. In the context of the ensuing War on Terror, these portrayals continued to surface, fueling the self-perception of the West as "the brightest beacon for freedom and opportunity,"[60] as articulated by George W. Bush in his address to the nation on September 11, 2001. This "us" versus "them" narrative effectively revived the legacies of the orientalist discourse, justifying western intervention in the War on Terror. According to Maryam Khalid, considering the presence of irrational violence and misogyny within the Muslim world, the military interventions led by the United States in Afghanistan and Iraq are justified as essential for instilling civilization, democracy, and equality among the oppressed and for managing the barbaric threats. Heidi Safia Mirza argues that in the "patriarchal post-imperial project of gendered and sexualized racialization, the black/othered woman is constructed as a passive, docile victim of archaic traditional" customs and practices and of domineering black or othered men. Nacira Guénif-Souilamas argues that sexism is constructed as the elusive and natural practice of the "uncivilized" men "guilty of causing public disorder and oppressing women."[61] Not only imperialist powers but also far-right groups similarly project their xenophobic and prejudiced views outward by depicting Muslims as the root cause of societal issues. They justify their anti-Muslim sentiments as a required reaction to this alleged danger, positioning themselves as protectors of European values and heritage, evoking the ideological language of the crusades during colonial times.

In western media and political discourse post-9/11, Muslim women have often been portrayed as victims of oppressive traditions and extremist ideologies within their communities, mainly focusing on issues like forced veiling, honor crimes, and lack of agency. A striking image in the War on Terror discourse is of the "veiled oppressed Muslim woman." Indeed, the *burqa* and other forms of veiling have once again faced heightened scrutiny, particularly evident in the debates surrounding *burqa* bans in Europe. In this emotionally charged discourse, the veil has become a symbol of the perceived "Islamic threat" and the menace that this "other" poses to the core ideals of liberal democracies, as well as to "our" civilization, where principles like freedom and gender equality are upheld. The aftermath of 9/11 has seen a significant surge in media coverage focusing on Afghan women, with images of women in *burqas* prominently featured on the covers of mainstream publications like the *New York Times*, *Business Week*, *Newsweek*, and *Time*, accompanied by narratives of their oppression.[62] During his 2002 State of the Union Address, President George W. Bush asserted that the defeat of the Taliban had "freed the women of Afghanistan."[63] Similarly, State Department Spokesman Richard Boucher linked liberation to the removal of the *burqa*, as these liberated Afghan women could now be seen "sometimes even without wearing a *burqa*."[64] Inevitably, it goes without saying that neo-orientalist discourse, fueled by a pervasive global patriarchy, has grown in intensity following the events of 9/11. Within these discussions, women play significant roles and are impacted in various ways. Some are deeply entrenched in the fundamentalist agenda, where women serve as symbolic carriers of "culture." Others are crucial to the narrative of saving Muslim women from their "terrorist," misogynist male savages. Recently, Muslim women have been sometimes linked to security threats, with their veils sometimes portrayed as a potential cover for criminal or terrorist activities. Drawing on the case study of Tashfeen Malik and the 2015 San Bernardino shooting,[65] Constantine Gidaris argues that Malik's terrorist actions challenged prevailing notions of terrorism centered on hegemonic masculinity and heteronormativity. This disruption led to a perception of Malik and other veiled Muslim women as cultural and physical menaces to the nation, prompting calls for their exclusion.[66] This all makes clear the ways in which women face compounded challenges manifested through heightened perceptions of being passive, submissive, and sometimes even labeled "terrorists" themselves. Jasmin Zine explains this as a form of "gendered Islamophobia"—a type of discrimination uniquely directed at Muslim women, rooted in ingrained negative stereotypes that reinforce structures of domination.[67] Zine understands Islamophobia as "a fear of Islam or its adherents, that is translated into individual, ideological and systematic forms of oppression."[68] She describes her personal account portraying the challenges she encounters as a Muslim feminist grappling with the intersecting burdens of discrimination, racialization, Islamophobia, and gender biases, as follows:

> As a Muslim feminist and anti-racist scholar-activist, I maneuver between these polarized spaces dodging racialized and Islamophobic discourses on one battlefront and puritan, fundamentalist narratives on another, held hostage to the contradictory meanings being imposed upon my body and subjectivity from these sites.[69]

Zine's quote eloquently captures the complex positionality of Muslim women straddling diverse realms, highlighting the challenges of evading racialized and Islamophobic discourses on one flank while simultaneously resisting puritanical and fundamentalist narratives on another. This reveals a constant negotiation of identities, as the body and subjectivity become battlegrounds for contested interpretations and conflicting impositions. Feminists have critically assessed these impositions, built upon the perpetuation of orientalist stereotypes, through a multitude of approaches. These include, but are not confined to, challenging the "official" narratives concerning women's rights within the framework of the War on Terror,[70] scrutinizing and contesting depictions of the veil and narratives of "liberation,"[71] and questioning perceived homogeneity among Muslim women.[72] Indeed, the rhetoric surrounding Muslim women is a fundamental narrative of the War on Terror discourses as articulated by media, officials, and liberal feminists in the west, who claim to be concerned for the abuses of rights of the "voiceless" Muslim woman, whereas the reality is that these "concerns" are being used as a pretext to justify interventions. The "standard" image of the deprived and subjugated Muslim woman was once again used as a signifier of the barbarity and anti-modernism of Islam and its repression of women. The issue with this narrative of rescue is that it perpetuates familiar orientalist notions of civilizing missions. Such perspectives further propagate the notion that military interventions can liberate Muslim women from their perceived oppressive societies and aid the west in combating Islamic terrorism. Yet, in instances where women faced aggression from the US-supported Afghan government and local warlords prior to the Taliban's rise, the global community stayed silent. As a result, the struggles of Afghan women were oversimplified as merely a battle against fundamentalism, neglecting vital challenges like poverty, internal displacement, inadequate healthcare, and the ability to fulfill basic necessities. These difficulties were further compounded by the impacts of western military interventions.

This essentialized portrayal of Muslim women as the oppressed "other" has evolved into a crucial instrument in the ideological battle aimed at garnering public support for the War on Terror. Such categorization confines all Muslim women to the same limiting narrative. Within imperialistic frameworks, we have observed Muslim women portrayed in the western imagination as either exotic *harem* figures or voiceless, oppressed victims. In contemporary discussions, encompassing viewpoints from both the far-right and fundamentalist factions, women are represented in several different and important ways. For Islamic fundamentalists, Muslim women are constantly viewed as pivotal symbols of their culture, emphasizing the significance of adhering to "appropriate" conduct and attire reflective of their values. Conversely, the far-right often adopts a narrative of rescue in their condemnations of Islamic fundamentalism. Simultaneously, liberal feminists on the left express apprehensions regarding the infringements on the rights of what they perceive as "voiceless" Muslim women. This convergence of perspectives underscores the complex and multifaceted ways in which Muslim women are positioned and perceived within varying ideological frameworks. In the following section, an exploration of feminist responses to these prevailing narratives will shed light on the diverse and dynamic ways Muslim women and their advocates engage with, challenge, and reshape these entrenched discourses. Through a critical feminist lens, the following discussion will navigate the complexities of identity, agency, and resistance in the face of intersecting forces of patriarchy, colonialism, and Islamophobia.

Mapping Feminist Responses

Against the backdrop of the latter intersecting oppressions, postcolonial, third world, and Muslim feminists have been grappling with the complexities of identity, agency, and resistance in the face of interlocking forces of patriarchy, colonialism, and Islamophobia through various strategies. They have been vocal in challenging the homogenizing and stereotyping of their experiences by the west. They have been highlighting the agency,[73] desire,[74] and personal choice of Muslim women, particularly in their decision to wear *hijab*. They have highlighted the need for Muslim women to challenge hegemonic discourses and engage in activism and resistance. Several postcolonial feminists have explored the role of representation in this context, with some discussing the challenges of representing Muslim women in Islamic religious movements and others emphasizing the dialogical dynamics of representation and identity. They have collectively underscored the importance of recognizing the diversity of Muslim women and the need to move beyond simplistic stereotypes.

The initial discussions among postcolonial feminists saw the emergence of two opposing perspectives. One sought to amplify native voices to challenge colonial narratives, portraying third world women as active agents of their own liberation. Conversely, the second group scrutinized these efforts, highlighting the diversity among colonial subjects. The first camp faced criticism for oversimplifying the experiences of the colonized, while the second was faulted for overlooking collective anti-colonial resistance.[75] As the debate evolved, it transitioned beyond these binary positions toward a quest for more intricate insights into the various ways in which women confront both patriarchal and imperialist representations. Currently, prevailing themes in public discourse in western societies persist in portraying Muslim women as particularly susceptible to patriarchal norms and influence from "terrorist" ideologies. However, an expanding body of literature presents a more nuanced perspective, showcasing women's active political participation and resistance. Postcolonial feminist scholarship has also explored Muslim women's endeavors to assert their right to wear religious garments,[76] scrutinized their roles in political activism,[77] and underscored instances of "agency" within colonial contexts.[78] In challenging western feminist assumptions, postcolonial gender scholarship highlighted and problematized the different social, economic, and political dynamics that influenced and created the contexts in which Muslim women inhabited. It revealed the complexity of the relationship between women as active subjects in their "liberation" and as objects of other broader political projects, rejecting the argument that portrayed Muslim women as passive, subjugated, and so on.

In her article, Lila Abu-Lughod explores how the paradigm of saving Muslim women from what she terms "Islam land" has been particularly heightened in the aftermath of 9/11. She elucidates how political forces, both domestic and global, shape the very existence of Muslim women, determining even their most fundamental circumstances. Within the previously mentioned discourse on Afghanistan, for example, there is a conspicuous focus on cultural norms while neglecting the repercussions of war and militarization on Afghan women's lives. Abu-Lughod unveils the voyeuristic nature of conversations surrounding the veil and honor crimes, questioning the prioritization of discerning the "culture" to scrutinizing the repressive regimes in the region. Equally, she underlines the utilization of these discourses to rationalize xenophobic immigration measures. As a researcher specializing in gender, race, and public policy within the UK setting, I have also been struck by the disparity between the popular "Muslim woman" of the public imagination and the reality of the lives and experiences of Muslim women. It is crucial, however, to acknowledge the pervasive apologetics inherent in maintaining this perspective, a notion that Abu-Lughod is cognizant of, encouraging caution in avoiding inadvertently condoning the oppression faced by certain Muslim women.

In the realm of the UK's counterterrorism strategy, Naaz Rashid examines the ways in which "the Muslim woman" is socially constructed to shed light on the relationship between the ways gender is represented by the state and the ways in which Muslims are racialized in immigrant societies. Examining several initiatives implemented by the UK government, she explores efforts to involve Muslim women in the "War on Terror" agenda through initiatives such as boosting the ambitions of Muslim girls, enhancing religious knowledge among Muslim women, and promoting women's involvement in civic activities within Muslim communities. Her analysis reveals that by discursively linking women's empowerment to counterterrorism efforts and downplaying other essential aspects of identity, these programs reinforce a "civilizationist discourse" that, in reality, undermines the agency of Muslim women instead of empowering them. Simply put, this institutional structure compels Muslim women to adopt a form of "strategic pragmatism," shaping their actions to align with policymakers' simplistic emphasis on Islam as a fundamental aspect of identity.

Consequently, this perpetuates a standardized portrayal of the Muslim woman, further homogenizing perceptions of this diverse demographic. In the European context, Sara Farris writes, "The current convergence between the anti-Islam feminist front and anti-immigration nationalist and neoliberal political agendas in the name of women's rights exposes a radical performative contradiction, whose effects are potentially disastrous for women's struggles in general."[79] Farris highlights the complex interplay between feminism, anti-immigration agendas, and nationalist political movements when framed around women's rights. By merging with political agendas that promote exclusion or discrimination under the guise of protecting women, anti-Islam feminist movements risk undermining the broader goals of women's empowerment and equality. The fusion of these varied ideologies, although purportedly advocating for women's rights, could actually hinder the progress of women's struggles overall and lead to detrimental consequences for gender equality efforts.

These initiatives have been accompanied by increasing support for far-right anti-immigration parties, who often appropriate feminist rhetoric to propagate the narrative that Muslim migrant men pose a significant threat to the safety of western women as well as the autonomy of women within Muslim communities. The convergence of feminist aspirations for female liberation from patriarchal constraints with the racialized characterization of non-white men as sexual menaces and non-white women as oppressed individuals in need of rescue is evident. Read this way, the call for the cultural assimilation of migrant women through economic activity mirrors other politics where minority women, often confined to menial and undervalued work roles in the West (the only work available to them: hotel cleaning, housekeeping, child minding, and caregiving) support European women in reshaping gender norms both in domestic settings and the workplace. By positioning Muslim and other racialized immigrant women as in need of rescue from their patriarchal cultures, "femonationalism" coined by Sara Farris Sara, as discussed in her book *In the Name of Women's Rights: The Rise of Femonationalism*, exposes the exploitation of feminist themes by right-wing nationalist parties, neoliberals, and some feminist theorists and policymakers. This exploitation is used to advance anti-immigration, anti-Muslim, and xenophobic agendas, particularly in France, Italy, and the Netherlands. Farris argues that this practice serves an economic function, as it funnels Muslim and non-western migrant women into low-paying and precarious care work, thereby perpetuating a neoliberal crisis of social reproduction.

Within the Muslim world, women's bodies continue to be controlled, not only by oppressive laws under authoritarian regimes such as Iran, Saudi Arabia, and

Afghanistan but also by the laws denying their freedom to wear headscarves in western democratic societies like France, Germany, and Turkey. In both cases, as Jasmin Zine argues, "the fact that their bodies are made subservient to the decrees of patriarchal state authorities is an anti-feminist move."[80] Both ideological views are limiting to Muslim women's agency, autonomy, and freedom. Caught within these dichotomies, Muslim feminists find themselves grappling with conflicting challenges from external forces as well as within their diverse ideological spectrum. Consequently, this dynamic leads to a constriction in the realm of theorizing for Muslim women.

Both Muslim and non-Muslim feminists have underscored the impact of the global imperialist agenda, which has generated structural disparities between the Northern and Southern hemispheres, fostering conditions of poverty, political turmoil, and discontent among marginalized populations. They have highlighted the interconnectedness of these issues with the emergence of global fundamentalist movements. Ayesha Imam, a Nigerian Muslim advocate and creator of the Baobab organization, presents an examination of the upsurge of Puritanism and religious extremism in Nigeria as a consequence of worldwide economic reorganization.[81] Consequently, the adverse impacts of globalization, neoliberal economic strategies, and imperialism fuel the impetus for the proliferation of radical religious factions, leading to the repression of women and the erosion of women's rights. Likewise, in her analysis of the implementation of the *Hudood* Ordinances in Pakistan, Shāhnaz Khan amalgamates political, economic, and social elements to elucidate the factors that trigger and uphold these religiously governed regulations. In the aftermath of the implementation of the *Hudood* Ordinances, numerous Pakistani women who have been victims of rape but cannot present the mandatory four male witnesses to testify to a nonconsensual act are prosecuted and imprisoned under the *Zina* laws. Khan illustrates how poverty heightens the likelihood of a woman being convicted due to her limited access to legal representation. Muslim feminists argue that these regulations violate and distort the Qur'ānic principles on *Zina* meant to safeguard Muslim women from baseless accusations. These analyses are absent in western mainstream media narratives, which tend to sensationalize the struggles of oppressed Muslim women. Khan describes the images presented in the documentary "Murder in *Purdah*" which depicted the effect of the *Zina* Ordinances and honor killing in Pakistan:

> The juxtaposition of text and images is dominated by a narrative of the rise of Islamic fundamentalism and its connection to erupting violence in Pakistan.

Scenes depict terrifying images of armed male Pakistanis rioting in the streets, burning, shooting, and looting. None of this mayhem in Karachi is shown to be related to the further devaluation of the rupee and the resulting rise in food and fuel prices or to the lack of employment opportunities and growing poverty and degradation connected to globalization.[82]

By focusing predominantly on the narrative of Islamic fundamentalism and armed aggression, journalists often perpetuate stereotypes and create a one-dimensional portrayal of the events. The failure to address underlying economic factors like currency devaluation, rising costs of essentials, unemployment, and increasing poverty indicates a lack of comprehensive reporting on the root causes of unrest. This selective framing not only skews public perception but also overlooks critical aspects contributing to societal challenges, impeding a thorough understanding of the multifaceted issues at play. Muslim feminist voices continue to correct these narrow representations of the social, economic, and political struggles Muslim women endure. Nevertheless, as we endeavor to dismantle patriarchal frameworks within our communities, we frequently approach revealing our apprehensions cautiously due to the pervasive backdrop of racism and Islamophobia that intensify upon such disclosures. When we uncover instances of sexism within our societies, we, as Muslim feminists, become targets of the racism and Islamophobia that perpetuate a homogenized view of women's experiences, once more relegating them to the same old savior narratives.

Navigating the Path Ahead

In her 2007 book, *France and the Maghreb: Performative Encounters*, Mireille Rosello describes "performative encounters" inspired by J. L. Austin's theory of performative enunciation as the interactions that link individuals with a long history of conflict, who manage to disrupt the conditions, practices, and languages that have shaped their relationships. In her perspective, a performative encounter occurs when individuals, presumed to be incompatible, resist being confined to roles that restrict the form and substance of their interactions. Despite the violence embedded in specific shared historical experiences, these adversaries manage to develop a mutual, unspoken language. This form of exchange creates a new subject position that, while not entirely devoid of conflict, effectively disrupts dominant discourses by fostering new forms of expression and dialogue. Rosello provides multiple examples of performative encounters in her book. For instance, in the first chapter, she examines the discourses surrounding the public events of 2003 during "The Year of Algeria in France."[83] She explores how the creators of these discourses worked to liberate themselves from the entrenched patterns of Franco-Algerian relations, promoting a reconsideration of the terms in which encounters between these nations are perceived. Although this ostensibly "amicable" encounter soon descended into conflict, Rosello identifies aspects of the event as illustrative of performative encounters that have the potential to disrupt dominant discourse, challenging observers to rethink the boundaries of national identity, the nature of competition, and more. In another chapter, Rosello examines various works by Assia Djebar, exploring how Djebar reimagines the evolving nature of France-Algeria relations through fiction. One key text Rosello examines is Djebar's short story *Le corps de Félicie* (*The Body of Felicie*), featured in her 1997 collection *Oran, langue morte* (*Oran, Dead Language*). Through the narrative of Félicie, Djebar explores the layered identities that emerge at the intersections of French and Algerian cultures. Félicie's children, bearing both Christian and Muslim names, embody the dual identities that Djebar continually reimagines and rewrites. Rather than presenting a single, cohesive model of mixed identity, Djebar shows how individuals navigate a spectrum of reactions to their diverse cultural elements. For Félicie's children, identity is not a fixed state but a dynamic process constantly reshaped by their personal histories and the cultural meanings attached to their names. Expanding on Djebar's narrative, Rosello introduces the concept of *fréquentage* (cohabitation), suggesting that the nature of France-Algeria relations should not be reduced to simple notions of hybridity. Djebar's stories illustrate that these relationships are characterized by ongoing reinterpretations of a "supposedly original encounter"[84] that is anything but static. The continuous negotiation and redefinition of identity and cultural encounters mark the interactions between characters, moving beyond dualistic frameworks to embrace a fluid and evolving understanding. What makes these encounters "performative" is their capacity to disrupt established narratives and dominant discourses.

In his 1982 journal article, "The Subject of Power," Michel Foucault articulates the idea that power and knowledge are intrinsically linked; each influences and supports the other. For Foucault, power is not just a top-down force exerted by authorities but is pervasive throughout society, shaping and being shaped by knowledge. The nature of subjects—how individuals and groups are understood and categorized—emerges from the interplay of power and knowledge through discursive practices, which are the ways in which topics are discussed and understood within a culture. Earlier discourses of orientalism have constructed the veiled Muslim woman in the western literary imagination as both an object of desire—a sensual, elusive *harem* girl—and simultaneously dismissed her as a backward victim of her misogynistic culture. The idea of "performative encounters," as discussed earlier in relation to Mireille Rosello's work, offers a way for these constructed identities to be challenged and redefined. In a "performative encounter," individuals or groups engage in interactions that challenge and reshape established narratives and power dynamics. For Muslim women, these encounters can serve as opportunities to unsettle and transform the entrenched and often reductive discourses imposed by orientalism. Through these interactions, they can negotiate new meanings and identities, thereby altering how cultural encounters are perceived and understood.

Questions about the nature and articulation of resistance, agency, and voice in colonial settings lie at the heart of postcolonial feminist studies and have caused considerable controversies amongst its most eminent scholars. These analyses reveal how imperialism utilizes gender "as a way to justify the imposition of the 'modernising,' 'liberating' regime of empire."[85] They also argue that between imperialists and nationalists, the third world woman remains caught between competing patriarchal ideologies. Equally significant is their criticism of mainstream western feminism for failing to address racial issues and for utilizing the silenced voice of the third world woman to strengthen itself.[86] Many Muslim women who engaged in anti-colonial struggles did not necessarily identify as feminists. Some adhered to nationalist ideologies advocating for the removal of colonial rule, while others distanced themselves entirely from the nationalist sphere.[87] And in some rare cases, as in the case of South Africa, women's voices altered the shape and ideology of nationalism itself, with women playing a significant role that greatly influenced the trajectory of a reformed South Africa. Today postcolonial feminist movements on a global scale grapple not only with the intricacies of postcolonial nation-states but also with the complexities of globalization. Now Muslim feminists are engaging with and resisting the coexistent factors of imperial, nationalist, as well as fundamentalist domination. In the era of imperialist and capitalist expansion, the woman's question, thus, takes on new complexities; as capitalism transformed societal structures and led to the formation of new classes, women within these groups revisited traditional inquiries within a fresh context. This intricate, uneven, and contradictory web of discussions, institutional realms, and landscapes underscores the necessity for a refined understanding of Muslim women's engagement and activism. By placing Muslim women's experiences within a historical context, we gain insight into their nuanced position amidst the intersecting facets of class and religion in today's world. Such a reading holds particular significance when considering race, culture, and multicultural understandings, encouraging a shift away from oversimplified binary views. Lately, many feminists have advocated for fresh perspectives in how we approach feminism, urging a move away from generalizing Muslim women as a homogeneous group irrespective of varying factors like class, religion, or ethnicity. Engaging with the complex realities of transnational Muslim feminists requires a nuanced understanding of their relationship to various contexts, particularly in light of the ongoing struggle against new manifestations of colonialism. The politics of representation within the "War on Terror" often obscures the reality that numerous, interconnected forms of "terror" require our attention. Challenging colonial narratives through a transnational feminist lens becomes crucial in this fight. It is by listening to different voices and acknowledging their existence that we can achieve this. It is by understanding how our identities are complex and overlapping; thus, as mentioned earlier, they cannot be labeled. Even the very label I am proposing should be thought of as a political positioning, not a fixed identity that can be framed within yet another box.

5

Beyond Resistance versus Subservience

In response to the conceptualizations of religious agency that some feminist scholars have been overly celebrating in the last few decades in pursuit of dismantling the savior narrative, Afia Zia questions whether secular politics aims and sensibilities are impossible or undesirable for Muslims and Islamic states. She wonders whether Muslim women should be exempted from feminist attempts at liberation from patriarchy as practiced in the present time.[1] The immediate context for these questions is Zia's discomfort with the emergence of what she calls post-secularist scholarship. This trend has emerged in the aftermath of the 9/11 attacks and the subsequent War on Terror. Broadly speaking, the term "post-secular," which will be explored in more detail in the next chapter, signifies a renewed interest in religion's social, political, and cultural influence. It acknowledges the necessity of engaging with religious groups and perspectives politically and socially. Zia's discomfort with post-secularism stems from her concern that it risks perpetuating stereotypes and prejudices, especially in the representation of Muslim women. These concerns manifest in several ways: representing Islam as a monolithic entity with fixed beliefs and practices, ignoring the diversity of thought and experience within Muslim communities, portraying Muslims as fundamentally different from other religious groups or as a homogeneous "Other," overemphasizing the political aspects of religion, and conflating secularism with western values and practices, ignoring its diverse interpretations and implementations across different contexts. Zia's discomfort also extends to the way post-secularism conceptualizes religious agency, warning against romanticizing it. She cites the Taliban's oppression of women in Northern Pakistan as a cautionary tale. Zia's questions suggest that her discomfort with the post-secularist scholarship is mainly focused on the implications for Muslim women undermining their agency to seek liberation from outside an Islamic framework.

The post-secularist Muslim feminist scholarship, often theorized in the works of diasporic scholars in western universities, emphasizes the concept of Muslim women's "pietist agency." This concept, framed by a strong critique of Islamophobia and western imperialism, theorizes agency as a form of religious devotion and obedience, sometimes overlooking the power dynamics and political consequences of such agency. Critics of this scholarship, including Afiya Zia, argue that it targets secular feminists, portraying them as collaborators with western imperialism by criticizing Islamist politics. Central to Zia's critique is its influence on the work of Saba Mahmood's theorization of "pietist women" in Egypt's mosque movement on this scholarship. Zia critiques this scholarship for neglecting the political implications of religious agency and focusing solely on interiority and noncontentious forms of expression within religious practices. Following the 9/11 attacks, a surge of scholarship emerged, challenging the dominant discourse of the "War on Terror" and its fixation on gender and sexuality, particularly the narrative of "saving Muslim women." This scholarship critiqued the imperialist framing of specific western feminist demands, which were perceived as complicit with US imperialism. The rallying cry "Do Muslim women really need saving?" challenged this narrative, highlighting the dangers of conflating feminist goals with imperialist agendas. Central to this scholarship was the emphasis on the "politics of location" in claiming a feminist politics and feminist subject rooted in specific contexts and experiences. In essence, Zia's argument constitutes the other side of this politics of location. She suggests that when feminist individuals in Pakistan involve themselves with "post-secularist" scholarship amidst a backdrop of growing religious and military influence within imperialist geopolitics, the rights of women and minorities are further restricted. Zia argues that this interaction is a reciprocal one, as "Islamists too use the same tool (women's sexual freedom) to launch cultural assaults on the West and to reaffirm the sovereignty of (an imagined) Muslim *ummah* (global community, represented by male clerics) through a commitment to protect society and women from their own collective sexualities."[2]

This chapter unpacks and problematizes this popularized notion of Muslim women's pietist agency, a topic that has faced significant scrutiny as Islam gained more prominence globally. In her book *Politics of Piety*, Saba Mahmood challenges liberal accounts of the relationship between religion, women, and agency. She argues for the need to move beyond the binary conceptions of resistance versus subservience to understand the ways in which Muslim women express their "agency." While recognizing the significance of her book, this chapter highlights the problematic ways in her application of post-secular theory and its ramifications in Muslim settings. The chapter also discusses the difficulties such conceptualizations pose for secular Muslim feminist advocacy within and beyond Muslim contexts. The majority of the secular Muslim feminists mentioned in this study express how such theorizations and celebrations of Muslim women's pietist agency have not only marginalized them but also sought to erase their contributions to feminist movements in Muslim societies. These are individuals whose activism is not rooted in theological beliefs, motivations, or slogans.

Theorizing "Agency"

I think it would be fair to argue that the exploration of women's agency has been central to the research of Muslim feminist scholars since the late 1960s, coinciding with the introduction of feminist studies into academic discourse. In Muslim, primarily Middle Eastern societies, the issue of access was particularly significant due to the prevailing gender segregation norms of the time. The integration of women into academia initially seemed to address this challenge. However, it soon became apparent that the issue was far more complex than mere access. Like much of the early feminist scholarship, Muslim women's scholarship identified and critically explored "male bias" in research. As mentioned earlier, this scholarship has also aimed to challenge oversimplified portrayals of women in non-western Muslim societies, emphasizing women's capacities of resistance and activism. However, this approach has varied over time. Sertaç Sehlikoglu categorizes the conceptualizations of "agency" in the study of Muslim women into four distinct waves.

From the late 1960s to the early 1970s, the initial wave resembled western mainstream feminist theory by addressing methodological constraints that marginalized women and critiquing the male bias in early anthropological theories. During this first wave, Sehlikoglu argues that the foundation of agency emerged, primarily tied to acts of resistance. Activities like women's social gatherings such as reception days, formal teas, and religious ceremonies were identified as significant in fostering this sense of agency.[3] These events, arranged and attended by women of higher social status and viewed as spaces for interaction and empowerment, became central areas of interest for the early feminists.

The second wave, from the late 1980s to the early 2000s, coincided with two major theoretical turns: the postcolonial critique introduced by Edward

Said and the increased attention to gender and sexuality studies influenced by works like Michel Foucault's *History of Sexuality* (1978) and later Judith Butler's work, like *Gender Trouble: Feminism and the Subversion of Identity* (1990) and *Bodies That Matter: On the Discursive Limits of "Sex"* (1993). During this period, the early theorizations of agency among Muslim feminists began manifesting within discussions on subjectivity.[4] Saba Mahmood refers to this work as the "analysis of subaltern gendered agency." Furthermore, the second wave marked a departure from a purely geographical focus toward delving into the fundamental principles of comprehending women's subjectivity in the region, laying the groundwork for the third wave.[5] The third wave placed emphasis on the Muslim identity of women both within and beyond the region, including Muslim female immigrants residing in Europe. This transition resulted in a more systematic approach to constructing gender and Islam, representing the first non-western feminist theoretical progression and offering a more substantial critique of male-centric viewpoints in orientalist research (termed colonialist male bias by Sehlikoglu). This wave witnessed a proliferation of literature challenging and countering ethnocentrism, contributing to the evolution of postcolonial feminist theory. A significant issue that plagued the second wave, later tackled by the forthcoming generation of feminist scholars focusing on the Middle East, was the complex dynamic between secular feminists and female supporters of Islamic resurgence in the 1990s. This wave, according to Sehlikoglu, coincided with the revival of colonialist male bias manifested in the "Islam and terror" discourse. Simultaneously, some influential work examining the engagement of secular Muslim feminists in activism emerged.[6] These developments offered the necessary theoretical framework (and urgency) to reexamine topics on Islam and women. This wave ultimately heightened the capacity to acknowledge agency. While the first and third waves focused on Muslim women's agency, the third wave conceptualized the notion. Mahmood's contributions marked the inception of this new stream of thought, as she acknowledged the process of religious self-formation and highlighted the long-overlooked feminist agency of devout Muslim women.

The theoretical framework crafted by Mahmood stemmed from a fusion of three paradigmatic turns. Sehlikoglu outlines them as (1) a critical assessment of anthropology as a secular system of knowledge production, exemplified in Talal Asad's reevaluation of Islam as a "discursive tradition" rather than a set of beliefs or practices;[7] (2) the performative turn in feminist theory, following Judith Butler's exploration of gender and performance in the late 1990s arguing that gender is not an inherent characteristic;[8] and (3) the shift toward agency within social theory, seeking to understand how individuals actively participate in and influence the social world.[9] According to Sehlikoglu, Mahmood's scholarship bridged these three turns, notably emphasizing the agency of devout Muslim women. Post-2000s, influenced by Mahmood's work, Muslim women's subjectivity started to be perceived as agentive, albeit diverging from traditional liberal expectations. Mahmood's impactful contributions have sparked a new trend in scholarly works, paving the way for a unique concept known as the "Piety Turn."[10]

The focus on Muslim women's agency by postcolonial feminist scholars and the acknowledgment of their capabilities and resilience in navigating societal transformations marks a significant shift in the realm of Islamic and gender studies. However, the implications of these theories warrant scrutiny, particularly concerning their practicality and the obstacles they present for secular feminist advocacy in Muslim settings, especially in the aftermath of the post-9/11 period. The fourth wave, thus, emerged with a call to go beyond the piety turn, aiming to uncover subjectivities not exclusively tied to piety. Lara Deeb refers to this departure as a scholarly endeavor to scrutinize Mahmood's influence, as her writings were widely interpreted in a way that reduced the visibility of Muslims solely to pious individuals.[11] Within this wave, researchers started exploring agency within a broader array of contexts in the lives of Muslim women. Some of these works delve into topics like fashion, youth culture, art, leisure, desire, sports, and the routines of everyday life. This will be explored further toward the end of this chapter. Still, before I delve into the critique, I would like to further explore how the Pakistani émigré and the cultural anthropologist professor Saba Mahmood theorize Muslim women's agency.

"Piety" and the "Agency" Turn

The ethnography, published in 2004 by Saba Mahmood, examines the women's pietist movements in Egypt from 1995 to 1997 in what has been described by many as the "Islamic revival" and by Mahmood as "the mosque movement." In this study, Mahmood delves into the motivations behind Muslim women's choice to embrace religious norms that seemingly place them in a subordinate position. To address this inquiry, she had to rethink the assumptions of secular-liberal feminism, which posit that the desire for freedom is universal and crucial to an understanding of agency. Throughout her ethnography, she states that she has come to realize an entirely new understanding of piety and its meaning to the women she studied. She reveals how these women navigate the intricate relationship between religion and feminist ideals within the context of the mosque movement. Their participation, while occurring within a system that privileges male authority, presents a novel case of how religious devotion and feminist aspirations can coexist and challenge one another simultaneously. By exploring complex ideas and relationships, Saba Mahmood brings new understandings to topics such as ethics, agency, and identity. Her work has been recognized with the prestigious 2005 Victoria Shuck Award, a testament to its transformative impact on the liberal post-secular discourse.

In this seminal work, Saba Mahmood challenges the limitations of western feminist theory and secular liberal politics in explaining the participation of women in religious revival movements in non-western contexts. Drawing on a reappropriation of poststructuralist feminist theory and her ethnographic research on the urban women's mosque movement in Cairo (1995–7), she argues for a broader conception of women's political agency, recognizing the transformative potential of religious spaces in offering new leadership opportunities and participatory roles for women. She highlights how women's didactic efforts within the mosque movement fostered new forms of sociability and solidarity, enabling them to express their interests effectively within the framework of Islamic tradition. She challenges scholars to recognize and value women's agency beyond the "usual forms and institutions of politics" such as state, legal systems, and public protests.[12] Her work emphasizes the diverse ways women navigate power dynamics and carve out spaces for self-expression and collective action within their sociocultural contexts. This groundbreaking work has significantly impacted the study of *da'wa* and religious movements, prompting scholars to reconsider their assumptions and explore women's agency within diverse cultural and religious contexts.

Mahmood begins her inquest by examining the question of "freedom," challenging its conception within western secular-liberal practices and traditions. She argues that the secular-liberal tradition, of which western feminism is a part, often assumes freedom as an inherent and universal human attribute. She critiques the notion of freedom being intrinsically linked to individual autonomy, which places the individual as the ultimate authority over their destiny. Within the secular-liberal tradition, two distinct interpretations of freedom emerge: negative and positive. Negative freedom focuses on freedom from interference, coercion, or oppression, for example, freedom of speech, freedom of religion, freedom from arbitrary arrest, and so on. Positive freedom emphasizes the individual's capacity to act and achieve their goals effectively, such as self-mastery, self-determination, and the ability to shape one's destiny. Central to both types of freedom is the concept of individual autonomy, or the ability to choose one's desires regardless of the content of the desire. This emphasis on individual choice is often considered universal and transferable across different contexts. Mahmood argues that this universalized notion of individual autonomy clashes with poststructuralist feminist perspectives, especially when applied to the study of religious movements in non-western contexts like Egypt. She critiques the assumption that individual autonomy is the sole determinant of agency and freedom, particularly in contexts where social structures, cultural norms, and religious beliefs shape individual desires and possibilities.

Mahmood contends that the women involved in the Egyptian mosque movement exercise agency through their conscious choice to participate and embrace certain practices and virtues (a term used almost seventy times in her book) associated with piety. This engagement with piety, emphasizing internal struggles, sacrifices, and personal growth, provides a public expression of their beliefs and desires. For Mahmood, agency in this context arises from the practice of piety itself, which involves a form of "submission toward acquiring a higher end."[13] While western feminist tradition, Saba Mahmood remarks, interprets female agency too narrowly to suggest the resistance of patriarchal structures and norms, it fails to fully grasp the agency exercised by the pious women in her study. These women, who consciously choose to live a submissive and modest life, believe this is essential for embodying authentic Islamic norms. Their agency, therefore, is not solely driven by individual desires but is deeply intertwined with their religious beliefs and commitment to a particular way of life. Mahmood's arguments are grounded in her ethnographic research conducted in six Cairo mosques frequented by *da'wa* practitioners and teachers. She provides vivid examples of the deliberations of women who seek recognition within secular and nationalistic contexts that often challenge their religious identity. These women grapple not with abstract theological concepts but with tangible everyday concerns that shape their lives: "how to deal with anger; how to cultivate habits of shyness or modesty when these don't feel natural; how to handle a husband who drinks alcohol and views pornography; how to work in close physical contact with men; and so forth."[14] Mahmood emphasizes that those female *da'wa* practitioners are not driven by a desire to alter gender relations or reform Islamic theology. Rather, they aim to strengthen and uplift society by bridging the gap between religious beliefs and daily practices. Their engagement with religious norms and virtues presents a significant challenge to the secular liberal framework that underpins western feminist notions of agency.

Mahmood proposes a framework that examines "how different modalities of moral actions and embodied practices are performed and permeated in the process of self-development and subject construction."[15] She approaches "ethics" as a practice of self-cultivation and transformation shaped by the specific cultural and religious contexts in which individuals live. She emphasizes the role of embodied practices, such as rituals, devotional acts, and everyday routines, in shaping individuals' ethical sensibilities and moral development. These practices are not merely external actions but are deeply intertwined with the formation of one's internal self and character. Rather than viewing ethics as a fixed set of rules, Mahmood conceptualizes it as a dynamic process of becoming: an ongoing process that requires constant effort and self-reflection. She argues that ethical practices and understandings are not universal or absolute but are situated within specific cultural, religious, and historical contexts. This conception of ethics, in her argument, is closely linked to her understanding of agency. This approach, according to its proponents, allows for a more nuanced understanding of the diverse ways individuals exercise agency within their sociocultural contexts, taking into account the complex interplay of internal and external influences.

Mahmood also argues that the actions of women in the mosque movement cannot be solely understood through the lens of resistance to male authority or pursuit of gender equality. Her concept of "docile agency" captures the paradoxical engagement of these women with religious tradition, where they simultaneously embrace, reinterpret, and occasionally innovate within its confines. This paradoxical engagement acknowledges their prescribed marginalization within certain interpretations of Islam.[16] Thus, "docile agency" allows us to understand how women can exercise agency even within structures that appear to limit or constrain them. This framework expands our understanding of agency beyond simple resistance, acknowledging its potential to both reinforce and subvert dominant structures, depending on the specific context and motivations of the actors involved. Mahmood further challenges the narrow definitions of both religious and feminist traditions, arguing that they often fail to account for the rich diversity and cultural variations among women globally. She emphasizes that the embracing of "docile agency" reveals the limitations of both traditions and their inability to capture the nuanced ways in which women navigate religious and cultural norms within their specific lived experiences. In response to the question of why women would choose to adhere to traditional virtues associated with their subordination, Mahmood cautions against imposing western feminist understandings of resistance onto the motivations of these women. She uses her case study to argue that the conflation of agency with resistance is a fundamental flaw of feminism, blinding it to other forms of agency that can meaningfully shape women's lives. Drawing inspiration from Judith Butler's notions of performativity and subjectivation,[17] Mahmood redefines agency "not as a synonym for resistance to relations of domination, but as a capacity for action that historically specific relations of subordination enable and create."[18] Her focus shifts from acts of subversion to examining "what resources and capacities does a pious lifestyle make available"[19] for these women to navigate their lives, express their beliefs, and contribute to society within the framework of their chosen path. In effect, by drawing on "performativity," the idea that identity is constructed through repeated actions and behaviors (e.g., gender performativity), and "subjectivation," how individuals become subjects through power relations, shaping their identities and capacities, Mahmood reinterprets agency as the ability to act, shaped and facilitated by specific historical contexts, including relationships of subordination. In other words, agency is not just about opposing power but also about navigating and utilizing the conditions created by power structures.

Saba Mahmood's anthropological insights have profoundly impacted feminist scholarship, inspiring a growing body of scholarly and ethnographic work exploring the concept of "docile agency." Theresa Saliba views it as a potentially new revolutionary paradigm facilitating the entry of feminism into the post-secular landscape. Rosi Braidotti emphasizes that the post-secular perspective recognizes the role of religious piety in shaping agency and political subjectivity, even embracing spirituality as a source of empowerment. She argues that the post-secular turn "makes manifest the notion that agency, or political subjectivity, can be conveyed through and supported by religious piety, and may even involve significant amounts of spirituality."[20] Similarly, Sarah Bracke expands the parameters of active-based subjectivities to include (1) non-liberal and non-secular understandings of agency, acknowledging the diverse ways in which individuals and groups can exert agency beyond the confines of liberal and secular frameworks, and (2) understandings of agency that are rooted in cultural traditions and spiritual beliefs, recognizing that individuals can exercise agency within the context of their own traditions, shaping and transforming those traditions from within. She highlights the disjunction between the secular and the modern, arguing that the theoretical link between modernization and secularization needs to be reexamined. She proposes that the post-secular represents a new detachment between these concepts, challenging the assumption that secularism is an inevitable outcome of modernization. Not only these, but Mahmood's work has inspired numerous scholars working in various disciplines, including anthropology, sociology, religious studies, gender studies, and political science. Her ideas have contributed to ongoing debates on agency, subjectivity, and the role of religion in the lives of women and other marginalized groups globally. However, while these scholars share some common ground with Mahmood's arguments and offer their unique perspectives and contributions to the field, their work collectively demonstrates the rich and diverse ways scholars engage with the complexities of agency, ethics, and religion in contemporary societies. Saba Mahmood's work has also sparked various critiques from scholars in diverse fields, which I discuss in the following section.

The Limits of Pietist "Agency"

Since 2005, *Politics of Piety* has had a remarkably successful distribution and circulation within Euro-American academia. Saba Mahmood—a feminist social anthropologist with left-wing, secular political values—looked to understand why women would become active participants in a movement that ostensibly encouraged their subjugation. Inspired by Mahmood's work, in her ethnographic account of Islamic activist women in rural Egypt, Sherine Hafez portrays women's Islamic activism as "a form of worship."[21] She argues that the "desires and subjectivities" driving Islamic women's activism are a response to and rejection of the secularism and state modernization schemes that sought to forcibly transform them into "modern" citizens. In her book *An Islam of Her Own*, on extensive fieldwork with a Cairo-based grassroots Islamic organization, she aims to dismantle the dichotomous distinction between Islamic and secular values. She argues that contemporary Muslim desires and subjectivities are best understood as stemming from the convergence of multiple historical trajectories. By using the concept of "desire," she proposes we can move beyond the idea of the "unitary individual" typically "assumed in modern liberal discourse."[22] However, a problem that she recognizes is that the insistence on "merging" discourses can inadvertently reproduce the very dichotomy she aims to dismantle. She writes, "One of the challenges I face is that to clarify the mutual embeddedness of Islam and secularism in the activist women's desires, I risk reifying these discourses and presenting them as contradictory."[23]

Mahmood's evidence from her fieldwork suggests that her participants cultivate docility, piety, and submission to the Islamic authority as practices of ethical self-realization. She posits that the critical distinction between her subjects' genuine desires and socially prescribed norms is problematic when considering

Islam. For the mosque movement, these socially prescribed norms are essential for developing the pious self. In other words, the separation between individual desire and social norms is obscured or nonexistent in non-western, non-liberal cultures. The question, then, is how we can comprehend individual freedom in a context where the distinction between personal desires and socially prescribed norms cannot be assumed and where submission is a prerequisite for achieving self-realization. Mahmood proposes separating agency from politics, arguing that the desire for freedom from norms is not an inherent drive that universally affects all cultures. She contends that both liberal and poststructuralist feminism fail to consider the historical applicability of their norms to the "Other," thus overlooking forms of agency not driven by a desire for autonomy. This approach is problematic because, when the link between oppositional consciousness and agency is severed, subjectivity is reduced to an "unreflective, embodied experience of the norms of one's religious culture."[24] Rosa Vasiliky argues that

> what stems from Mahmood's argument is not only that subjectivities are cultural or discursive products, or that agency is more diverse than acknowledged in theories of resistance, but that there are (pre)determined, fixed subjectivities specific to particular cultures, which is a typically essentialist understanding of culture.[25]

Vasiliky's critique raises important concerns about the implications of Saba Mahmood's arguments on agency and subjectivity. She contends that Mahmood's perspective can be interpreted as suggesting that subjectivities are not just culturally or discursively constructed but also as inherently predetermined and fixed within particular cultural contexts. Vasiliky points out that this view risks falling into cultural essentialism, which runs contrary to the more dynamic and interactionist views of culture, which see cultural identities as fluid and continuously evolving. She also acknowledges Mahmood's valuable contribution to expanding the understanding of agency beyond western-centric theories of resistance but expresses concern about the broader implications. However, emphasizing culturally specific and seemingly fixed forms of subjectivity, Vasiliky argues, runs the risk of overgeneralization, which could inadvertently reinforce stereotypes. The idea that there are predetermined, fixed subjectivities within particular cultures can undermine the agency and variability of individuals within those cultures, suggesting that individuals have little room for maneuver or change. As a sociologist dedicated to collaborating with and supporting Muslim communities, I maintain that highlighting the role of religion in daily life requires a shift away from the prevailing binary perspectives often found in studies on Muslim societies and women. It is not awfully hard to understand why scholars working on Muslim societies find themselves compelled to connect their findings to Islam or to elucidate the distinctions between Muslim and western lifestyles. However, it is crucial to recognize that privileging religion as the primary perspective can also constrain alternative understandings of the self, potentially overshadowing "the fact that selves are contradictory, multiple, and fragmented."[26] I am particularly familiar with the research concerning how religious women perceive and navigate their daily experiences, having witnessed this directly during my fieldwork for my master's in Cairo in 2005. Nevertheless, as I elaborate further in the following pages, I argue for a critical need to move past the concept of pietist agency to fully grasp the diverse nature of subjectivity and acknowledge the fluidity of Muslim women's identities. Needless to say, Mahmood's analysis presents notable efforts of women's pursuit of ethical cultivation as a means of challenging conventional liberal viewpoints. However, it is widely recognized that patriarchy comprises not a singular but multiple systems that impact women. Hence, it is logical to acknowledge that women's maneuvering within diverse patriarchal frameworks (like neoliberalism, nationalism, religion, etc.) is a complex, nonlinear, and multidimensional process. Therefore, by overly focusing on the religious aspect of Muslim women's lives, the piety turn neglects the variety of agencies that Muslim women utilize to navigate through various social structures, opportunities, and pressures in their day-to-day experiences. This oversight is surprising, given that scholars have long studied women's negotiations with these patriarchal structures.

In her journal article "Bargaining with Patriarchy," Deniz Kandiyoti introduces the concept of the "patriarchal bargain," which describes a woman's choice to comply with patriarchal expectations in exchange for certain advantages, such as financial security, emotional well-being, or social status. Kandiyoti asserts that these patriarchal bargains manifest in diverse ways, shaped by the unique experiences of women stemming from factors like race, socioeconomic status, religion, and more. An issue associated with patriarchal bargains is that they pressure women to adopt and internalize patriarchal beliefs, consequently perpetuating patriarchy in their daily routines, whether consciously or unconsciously. While observing how women engage in negotiations with patriarchy, there may be a tendency to assign blame to women for their "choices." However, it is imperative to situate these choices within the broader context of patriarchy, capitalism, and neoliberalism. In an article for *The Conversation* entitled "No, Feminism Is Not about Choice," Meagan Tyler writes, "Yes, we make choices, but these are shaped and constrained by the unequal conditions in which we live." Therefore, while examining how women adapt and function within patriarchal systems or religious frameworks is crucial, it is equally vital to bear in mind that this apparent "agency" is intrinsically linked to the specific context in which it is situated. In various of her writings, Joan Wallach Scott critiques Mahmood's conceptualization of agency, suggesting that it might be too accommodating of traditional and patriarchal structures. In her critique of poststructuralism, Nancy Fraser argues that the poststructuralist frameworks Mahmood employs might risk legitimizing certain forms of oppression by framing them as agency or choice.

Despite Mahmood's explicit argument that she does not advocate for "abandon[ing] our critical stance towards what we consider to be unjust practices in the situated context of our own lives, or … uncritically embrac[ing] and promot[ing] the pious lifestyles of the women"[27] she worked with, there remains an unexamined aspect in her portrayal of the gender disparities inherent in these devout practices. The challenge with Mahmood's work goes beyond identifying "agency" within one's oppression. A closer examination of her article "Secularism, Hermeneutics, and Empire" reveals that her broader agenda extends beyond establishing a comparison between the religious aspects of the mosque movement and various secular outlooks, delving into discrediting secular and reformist Muslims entirely. To support this claim, she contends that both "secularism" and "reform" are components of a narrative facilitated by US political interests. Consequently, she argues that Muslims advocating for reform, whether from a religious or secular standpoint, are complicit with US imperialism. Nawal El Saadawi argues that Mahmood's objective extends beyond merely illuminating the "agency" within the *da'wa* movement members. Instead, it aims to "undo the project of any kind of secular feminism as an agent of social reform in Muslim contexts, and at the same time to mount a defense of the most conservative varieties of Islamism by mounting a critique of reformist Muslims."[28] This is problematic considering the long and vibrant history of feminist activism within countries where Islam is predominant.

Perhaps the most challenging task, an unaddressed dilemma in Mahmood's work, is not solely comprehending how religious devotion can shape diverse forms of agency but also defining and contextualizing this religiosity within a broader sociopolitical landscape. Ostensibly, it may seem that scholarly theorizing generally has little to do with women's lives worldwide. However, it is crucial to approach with caution those who brand modernity as a threat to tradition, constructing narratives that entail essentialist views of religious customs. It is, in fact, vital that we do not overlook the pluralities and malleability of religious traditions. However, it is equally questionable to presume that modernity and secularism are inherently intertwined. In her book, *An Enchanted Modern*, Lara Deeb introduces the idea of an "enchanted modern" to illustrate how modernity can be envisioned without losing its enchantment. She stresses the significance of the material and the spiritual aspects as integral elements.[29] By exploring the various ways in which modernity and piety may overlap in people's daily social practices, she shows that an "enchanted modern" acts as a critique of the binary logic that categorizes Islam as "anti-modern" and the west as "modern." Deeb suggests that breaking free from this division allows us to perceive spiritual growth as a feasible component of modernity.[30] Similarly, in her book, *The Politics of the Veil*, Joan Wallach Scott highlights and challenges the notion that the liberation of women stems exclusively from secularization within modern societies. This perspective often reinforces the perceived opposition between religion and secularism. Against this backdrop, she refuses such a binary by referring to the relation between the state and its religions and how this relation can be more helpful to the notion of agency, particularly if it neither represses religion nor relinquishes democracy—"which remains a place where political resolution is never achieved on the grounds of religious truth."[31] In the same vein, Zahra Ali's article, which delves into contemporary feminisms and women's activisms in present-day Iraq, suggests analyzing the secular and the religious perspectives in relation to each other rather than treating them as separate. The focus is on moving beyond the simplistic Islamist or secular divide and exploring the nuances that exist between these rigid categories. In her critique of Mahmood's emphasis on religious piety, she writes that it "fails to capture the complex and often contradictory nature of everyday experiences, thereby oversimplifying the nuanced negotiations involved in daily moral practices."

In recent decades, inspired by Saba Mahmood's work, a prevailing theme within the discussions around Muslim women highlighting binaries like traditional versus modern, Islamic versus secular, and east versus west has emerged. Nadia Fadil and Mayanthi Fernando draw attention to the opposition between piety and the everyday, arguing that it is an opposition "between textual norm and individual practice" and, therefore, "untenable."[32] In other words, the rigid adherence to textual norms may not always align with the nuanced and varied individual practices observed in everyday life. Recognizing that not all Muslims prioritize religious aspects in their day-to-day lives is crucial. The issue lies in Mahmood's primary goal of confronting western secular liberal narratives influencing the Muslim world, potentially at the expense of women's autonomy in the pursuit of revitalizing an authentic version of Islam. In a review of Saba Mahmood's book, Lama Abu-Odeh questions, "If the liberal secular is open to Islamist intervention, why not the Islamist one?"[33] This question sheds light on a significant drawback in Mahmood's work, as it fails to consider individuals who do not adhere to religious beliefs. While acknowledging the valuable contributions that Mahmood's work offers in challenging orientalist interpretations of Muslim societies, the issue with her thesis and the subsequent post-secularist research is the viewpoint that analyzing the lives of Muslim women should primarily involve considerations of faith-based politics. In a subtle critique of Saba Mahmood's work, Asef Bayat argues that the turn to religion within the pietist movement, which Mahmood describes, may well have enhanced individuals' autonomy, but in reproducing patriarchal constraints, this turn effectively demarcates the agential possibilities available for Muslim women from other social strata and ideologies. In the accounts of most post-secular scholarship that followed Mahmood's thesis, the portrayal of Muslim women activists as possessing "agency" continues to overlook the constraints imposed by patriarchal norms. However, if agency is defined as the ability of individuals to act independently and make free choices, then the latter framing becomes problematic. The notion of "agency" described may not truly represent freedom of choice; rather, it might be a strategic effort to attain a certain level of autonomy sanctioned by individuals who hold authority, typically seen as their male superiors. Haideh Moghissi challenges this celebration of Muslim women's agency by insisting on the inclusion of a conscious resistance against oppressive forces in order to counter the perception of women as mere instruments of patriarchal control and domination.[34] That is to say, agency should be acting on behalf of women and for their benefit. In her words, she stresses:

> For women, having agency should include moving in the direction of identifying the forces that limit their capacity to have control over their lives and make informed choices within specific cultural and political contexts, to transform the conditions that reduce and weaken that capacity. Obviously, resistance against domination is central to this definition of agency regardless of the form and intensity of the resistance.[35]

This quote underscores a crucial aspect of women's agency, emphasizing the importance of recognizing and challenging the factors hindering women's ability to control their lives and make informed decisions within diverse cultural and political frameworks. Thus, the notion of resistance against domination is pivotal in this understanding of agency. I echo Moghissi's emphasis on the importance of critically analyzing religious-based reform movements, which often portray

Muslim women as a homogeneous group defined solely by their faith, regardless of variations in their religious practices. It is vital not to overlook the diverse struggles of women globally who are also struggling against patriarchal norms. It is essential to recognize that the quest for emancipation and equality by Muslim women extends beyond their religious identity, reflecting broader challenges faced by women worldwide. As the question of the compatibility of religion and feminism is frequently posed among scholars, I suggest that as well as situating women within their unique historical, social, and ideological contexts, we must acknowledge the commonalities in women's struggles regardless of their religious affiliations. One way to move beyond such limitations, classifications, and binaries, Sertaç Sehlikoglu suggests, is to "embrace fluidities, temporalities, shifts, and instabilities as they exist in the lives of individuals."[36] And while Mahmood critiques the limited "situated analysis" of Islamist movements, which often portrays them narrowly as militant, patriarchal, and undemocratic organizations,[37] Afia Zia argues that suspending political critique while focusing solely on the cultural and religious contexts of these movements falls short of genuine critical engagement.[38] She questions whether, at this point, it is worthwhile even to call it "agency" anymore. She also questions why this form of agency is exclusively associated with gender, as it could be just as relevant to male pietist movements.

Beyond Faith and Agency

The literature that emerged during the "piety turn" often depicted Islam as a "perfectionist ethical project of self-discipline,"[39] overshadowing the diversity within the Muslim community, including those who are not particularly pious and who adhere to various moral perspectives. To rectify this imbalance, some scholars have shifted their focus to the everyday lives of ordinary Muslims. One such effort to move away from the emphasis on piety-related agency is the body of work that explores the realm of fashion to highlight the pleasures and diverse experiences in Muslim women's lives.[40] While some of this work sought to find ways to link pleasure to piety, others used the fashion industry that caters to visibly Muslim women to challenge the binary of Islam versus the west.[41] Another body of work that goes beyond pietist agency is the work that focus on youth culture,[42] leisure,[43] desire,[44] sports,[45] and the ordinary everyday life.[46] The edited volume *Islam, Politics and Anthropology* by Benjamin Soares and Filippo Osella is a significant contribution to this critique. This work contends that prioritizing religious agency in the literature has often overlooked other facets of Muslim women's everyday lives. The chapters in this book challenge the tendency to overemphasize religion when examining Muslim cultures, arguing that this focus leads to the "othering" and homogenizing of Muslims. Their theorization expands on the definition of human agency while questioning the legitimacy of attributing every action performed by Muslims to Islam, as though it should be the central element defining their identity. For instance, Lara Deeb and Mona Harb examine the interplay between leisure, morality, and geography through the concept of "multiple moral rubrics" to extend their critique of Mahmood's perspectives. Drawing on Samuli Schielke's study of Muslim youth in Egypt, they contend that Mahmood's emphasis on piety as a "primary motivator" is problematic. They argue that ethical subjectivities are essentially based on the coexistence of various motivations, goals, and identities, which may sometimes appear contradictory but are not entirely oppositional. Another example that focuses on everyday life in relation to the politics of war is Aitemad Muhanna's ethnography on women in Gaza. Muhanna explores the intricate dynamics of gendered agency amidst siege, insecurity, and conflict. Her work draws on rich interviews and a life history approach, arguing that women's sense of agency has shifted from domestic providers to being publicly reliant on humanitarian aid.

Another body of literature suggests that understanding the dynamics of agency involves exploring realms of fantasy, desire, and fear. A few decades ago, in her book *A Passion for Difference*, Henrietta Moore noted that "any approach to the analysis of agency must include a consideration of the role of fantasy and desire, both with regard to questions of compliance and resistance and in connection with the construction of a sense of self."[47] According to Moore, these elements represent the innovative dimensions in the theorization of "agency." In her subsequent works, she highlights the correlation between fantasy, desire, and pleasure by characterizing the unconscious as a dynamic space that links the societal realm to the individual. This view, as she argues, "provides the basis for the assertion that the social and the psychic are not isomorphic, that the self can never be wholly determined by culture."[48] This implies that to understand agency, it is crucial to recognize that desire, as an inherent human capability, serves as a platform through which individuals seek possibilities. In her article "Learning Desire," Souad Joseph argues that traditional interpretations of desire in western contexts have tended to overlook non-western manifestations of desire. She advocates for an exploration of how local conceptions of desire, rooted in ideas of interconnected selfhood, are cultivated, imparted, and enacted within their specific environments.[49] She delves into how desires are shaped by historical, religious, familial, and societal influences, emphasizing that these desires are "configured within notions of relational selfhood, [and are] … learned, taught, and practiced in the context of intimate patriarchal familial and communal relationships."[50]

In this chapter, I have argued that post-secular conceptualizations of Islam and Muslims in the anthropology of Saba Mahmood are premised on the proposition that Islam and Islamic traditions represent a counterpoint to western secularity. Mahmood's perspective defines Muslims mainly within Islamic traditions and their connections to foundational texts. However, this approach seems inadequate for a comprehensive anthropological understanding of contemporary Muslims in a globalized, hybrid world where religious and secular elements and Islamic and non-Islamic influences intersect. Furthermore, it raises questions on the viability of sustainable feminist politics within this framework. While Mahmood challenges assumptions of secular feminism and calls for a deeper comprehension of pious Muslim women and a transformation of ethical and cultural perceptions underlying western legal contexts, there seems to be a lack of tangible solutions to current challenges. Critiques ponder on the effectiveness of Mahmood's approach in addressing issues like FGM and question the potential of her work inadvertently promoting relativism that could undermine condemning oppressive practices. Robin May Schott wonders how far Mahmood's conceptualization can help address worries about the effects of practices such as FGM.[51] This naturally leads to the argument that without normative critique, Mahmood's work just falls into a relativism that would make it hard to justify calling any practice oppressive.

This leads to the consideration of alternatives for feminist anthropology regarding Muslim women. A practical starting point would involve steering away from reducing ethnographies of real Muslim women to mere tools for ideological criticisms. The recent anthropological efforts mentioned earlier, exploring the lives of everyday Muslims across various contexts, strive to move beyond the binaries that Mahmood's work heavily depends on. Therefore, ethnographic studies on Muslim societies need to adapt in a way that can capture the dynamic nature of agency, which may not always resist patriarchal ideologies outright but can find alternative ways to escape from them. Consequently, in feminist scholarship concerning Muslim societies, while viewing Muslim women's agency as an epistemological issue, it is crucial not to overlook the diversity in women's subjectivity that encompasses elements like ambition, desire, and pleasure. This complexity also underscores the importance of offering a nuanced understanding of the spectrum between the religious and the secular, avoiding rigid dichotomies that can inadvertently reinforce Islamist perceptions of secularist opposition to religion. Nevertheless, it is important to recognize that a significant portion of these recent works continue to associate religious aspects with the daily experiences of Muslim women in some way. To truly grasp the agency, desires, and subjectivities of Muslim women, it is crucial to transcend the prevailing binaries that often shape research on Muslim women within both Muslim-majority societies and Muslim communities in the west, like Europe and the United States. Current scholars exploring the daily lives, desires, aspirations, and pleasures of Muslim women face the risk of being constrained by the same dichotomous secular versus religious mindset, that even when they attempt to challenge it, they tend to propose a new version of the same binary inadvertently. Nonetheless, ongoing discussions are shifting toward more nuanced insights, aiming to move beyond these initial controversies and deepen our understanding of the diverse ways in which Muslim women navigate challenges across various aspects of their lives beyond religion, finding joy not solely tied to religious realms. This book aspires to contribute to these efforts.

6

Islam, Secularism, and the Woman's Question

Within the contentious discourse surrounding theories of "secularism," "secularization" and the "secular age," and their intricate interplay with religion and gender, little attention has been paid to exploring the foundational connections between secularism and gender equality and the implications of this relationship. The correlation between secularism and feminism emerges amidst a confluence of notable occurrences: the surge of the "clash of civilizations" theory, the emergence of postmodern critiques of Enlightenment rationality, and the ongoing scrutiny of the "secularization thesis." This is further complicated by the prominence of the "woman question" amidst the upsurge of Islamist movements, which is often framed in cultural terms and linked to social transformations. In recent years, cultural theorists and sociologists have shown a growing interest in exploring the connection between secularism and gender equality. The primary objective of these studies is to critically reassess established theories that portray secularism as a consistent framework for gender equality. Previous critiques of secularism, predominantly limited to the secular-religious binary, failed to challenge secularism as an autonomous normative framework for women's rights issues. This was partly influenced by the close interplay between patriarchy and religion, leading to the assumption that secularizing gender perceptions rooted in religion would diminish patriarchy, paving the way for gender equality. By reexamining how secularism and gender equality intersect, this chapter aims to contribute to the discourse exploring the "inherent" link between gender equality and secularism, a pivotal inquiry of this book. It traces the evolution of the meaning of secularism over the past centuries, transitioning from a historical narrative of enlightenment prevailing over religion to being viewed as a favorable alternative not to all faiths but to Islam, in particular. This paradigm shift has led to the categorization of Muslims both as abstract citizens and as a distinct minority, contributing to the complexity of their societal positioning.

Examining the intricate dynamics at play where secularism intersects with gender equality, this chapter incorporates recent feminist critiques that challenge traditional narratives, revealing instances where secular states have perpetuated gender inequalities akin to religious systems. The chapter also examines how Muslim women pose a challenge to the secular narrative on gender equality, shedding light on how they struggle to find a place within its framework. Exposing how the secular discourse on gender equality remains entangled within secular or religious dichotomies, this examination highlights the constraints limiting alternative female expressions or empowerment pathways. Furthermore, the chapter delves into the challenges posed by current developments to secular-oriented feminist ideologies and practices. By analyzing the evolving contexts of secularism, the intention is to uncover the complexities inherent in the position of Muslim women within secular discourse, highlighting the constraints and ideological contradictions tied to the presumed association between secularism and gender equality. Exploring the controversies surrounding secularism in Islamic political thought, partly due to historical colonial legacies and western interventions, underscores the nuanced complexities at play. In the Muslim world, secularism has been associated with failed authoritarian political systems and has often been conflated with ideas of "modernity," recalling the colonial history by the "Christian" world. This has resulted in alienating the voices of secular Muslims in general and secular Muslim feminists in particular, which made it harder for many to associate with the term. Looking at secularism beyond the west, the chapter discusses the limits and possibilities of secularism in enabling and protecting choice and ethics of coexistence. I argue that a new critical engagement with secularism as a normative principle in democratic, multicultural societies may help bridge common ground amidst politically diverse orientations. Emphasizing "democracy" and its underlying values as the framework for redefining secularism underpins this argument. In adopting a perspective that views secularism not as a rigid analytical category but as a dynamic "discursive operation of power," I argue for the necessity of historical scrutiny.[1] I draw on Michel Foucault's "genealogical" method, which involves scrutinizing how the term has been deployed and the consequences of its utilization. Instead of assuming a preset definition of secularism, I explore how its interpretation has varied across diverse contexts and time periods, acknowledging the diverse articulations and applications it has undergone. Understanding why gender inequality persists within secular societies sheds light on the inconsistencies and constraints inherent in the prevailing secular narrative, offering an opportunity to reframe this relationship more cohesively. The crux lies in recognizing gender equality as a multilayered phenomenon shaped by cultural, political, economic, and psychological dynamics, where the assumption that secularization alone can eradicate inequality warrants scrutiny, especially amid the enduring influence of religion.

Secularism in a Post-secular Age

It has been thirty years since Samuel Huntington first published his famous article "The Clash of Civilizations?" followed by a comprehensive book addressing the same topic three years later. As part of this rhetoric, a renewed attention to secularism has taken place in Europe and the west. Undoubtedly, there is an extensive academic history on secularization, exploring the ways through which the western world is believed to have transcended obstacles to disbelief and developed, or discovered, substitute moral foundations apart from God. Within this process, it is said that western states controlled organized religion, integrated bureaucratic structures into their administration, and validated their legitimacy through republican or democratic ideologies.[2] Secularism has often been equated with these developments, symbolizing the victory of enlightenment principles over religious influences. Several scholarly works presume that secularism, commonly understood as the division of religion and state, is a fundamental element for the advancement and prosperity of contemporary "Western" nation-states.[3] They frame *secularism* as a "linear evolution of ideas and institutions that brought us modernity," describing *secular* as simply synonymous with "nonreligious," *secularization* as the historical process by which religious authority is replaced with knowledge produced by human reasoning, and *secularity* as a nonreligious state of being.[4]

While the term "secular," derived from the Latin word *saeculum*, meaning worldly or temporal, has existed since the thirteenth century,[5] referring to "secular priests" who left the clergy for a worldly life, the concept of "secularism" is considered relatively modern. In its early uses, "secularism" carried negative connotations, reflecting its position within "religiously centered discourses," as Joan Wallach Scott argues, where the religious was "defined (positively)" in opposition to the worldly. The differentiation between the sacred and the worldly existed even in non-western cultures, predating the term "secular." This reflected a new consciousness in human history that distinguished myth from science, God from the monarch, religion from politics, and so on. The French term for secularism, *laïcité*, derived from the Greek word *Laos*, meaning "the common people," was initially used by the church to refer to the people of a parish or the church's subjects in general. In this context, secularism was not the opposite of religion but simply a religious term used for practical, nonideological purposes. However, it was not until 1851 that George Holyoake coined the term as a philosophical concept.[6] Holyoake's secularism was not a rejection of religion but rather a broad philosophy that accommodated some forms of religion while excluding others.[7] As a matter of fact, the understanding of secularization as a transition from religious belief to autonomous human reason emerged later in the nineteenth century. In her book *Sex and Secularism*, Scott identifies three key waves in the development of the concept of secularism and its uses. During the first wave, secularism was seen as "the progressive alternative to religion— the sign of the advance of civilization."[8] Scott notes, "It was initially used as a polemic during nineteenth-century anticlerical campaigns in England and France when it stood for free speech and the moral autonomy of individuals against the pressures of organized religion."[9] The second wave, emerging in the early twentieth century, witnessed a decline in explicit references to the term in the west. This shift can be attributed to the diminishing political relevance of the concept amidst the Cold War context.[10] The relationship between the state and religion was redefined, with the Soviet Union becoming the antithesis of religious freedom in the "Christian" democratic west.[11] The focus shifted to the ideological struggle between communism and capitalism, with the Soviet Union, a predominantly atheist state, becoming the symbol of religious oppression. The Soviet Union's rejection of religion became a rallying point for the "Christian" democratic west, emphasizing its commitment to religious freedom. Secularism reemerged as a key concept in the late twentieth century with the resurgence of religion as a social and political force, particularly with Islam replacing Soviet communism as a perceived threat to the west.[12]

In recent years, scholars have questioned the historical account of this seemingly inevitable triumph of the secular. This intellectual wave has its roots in the revival of religion as a social and political force, challenging the assumptions of secularism, particularly the notion that religion should be excluded from the public sphere due to its potential negative impact on social and political order. Moreover, the conventional association of religion with the supernatural, the irrational, and the regressive, and its presumed decline under the pressure of science, rationality, and modernity, has been questioned. Talal Asad takes a different approach to the study of secularism, emphasizing its discursive formation rather than focusing on its historical emergence. He argues that "the secular is neither singular in origin nor stable in its historical identity, although it works through a series of particular oppositions," among which are the political and the religious, the public and the private.[13] Critiquing the conventional opposition between the secular and the religious, Asad examines another well-known dichotomy: the sacred and the profane. He notes that "the sacred" evolved from being associated with specific "places, objects, and times, each requiring specific conduct" to a "unitary domain" constructed through culturally and historically particular settings. This construction of "the sacred" as a realm rather than a quality signaled the formation of "the secular." Asad suggests that this understanding of the sacred became intertwined with Europe's imperial endeavors. This led to labeling elements of the European post-Enlightenment political structure as justifications for colonial "tutelage." At the same time, "superstition" came to classify practices deemed in need of regulation in the pursuit of (European) "civilization."[14] Asad establishes a connection between secularism and colonial expansions, where the western perspective interpreted it vis-à-vis "religion." The understanding of these beliefs and practices was grounded in Protestant Christianity as the context for developing western secularism.[15] Intrinsically, Asad argues that the concept of "the secular" is not a neutral space but rather a space shaped by particular values and assumptions that reflect the interests of those in power.

Meanwhile, the classic secularization thesis, as Rectenwald and Almeida argue, has recently faced mounting challenges, with some scholars questioning the very notion of secularizing the modern world. They point to the resurgence of churchgoing in the United States, the rise of New Age spirituality in Western Europe, the growth of fundamentalist movements and religious and political parties in the Muslim world, the widespread evangelical revival in Latin America, and the rise of ethnoreligious conflicts in international affairs. These developments, they argue, following Peter Berger, that the world may be undergoing a process of "de-secularization":

> The assumption that we live in a secularized world is false. The world today with some exceptions is as furiously religious as it ever was, and in some places more so than ever. This means that a whole body of literature by historians and social scientists loosely labeled "secularization theory" is essentially mistaken.[16]

This statement directly confronts the secularization thesis, claiming that its central premise of a declining role of religion in modern societies is fundamentally flawed. Echoing this argument, Jürgen Habermas emphasizes the enduring presence of religion in the public sphere and calls for a renewed role for it in politics and public life. Popularizing the term "post-secularism," he poses the question: "If modernity no longer implies a secular outlook, and secularism, by definition, cannot generate any values beyond an indifferent tolerance of all belief, what role will religion play in the 21st century?"[17] A post-secular society, in Habermas's argument, is a society that accommodates itself to the existence of religious communities in an increasingly secularized environment. He attributes the "post-secular" to three key factors contributing to a change in consciousness. First, the prevalence of global conflicts, often framed in terms of religious discord, has challenged the secular belief in the inevitable disappearance of religion. Second, religion continues to play a significant role in national-level debates, as evidenced by controversies surrounding abortion, euthanasia, genetic engineering, animal protection, and climate change. These issues often involve ethical and moral considerations deeply intertwined with religious beliefs and values. Third, migration and globalization have led to unprecedented religious diversity in many societies, bringing together Christians, Muslims, Hindus, and individuals of other faiths. This increased interaction between religious and secular communities provides evidence that religious communities can adapt and thrive in a secular environment.[18] Habermas agrees with Casanova that religious communities need to engage in continuous self-reflection and seek connections between their faith and secular views. He advises secular citizens to refrain from judging the truth of religious claims, recognizing the separation between the domains of faith and knowledge or scientific reasoning. However, he emphasizes that changes in mentality cannot be forced or manipulated but must emerge organically as a learning process. However, Habermas's focus on western nations having undergone secularization excludes the non-western world from full participation in post-secularity. Aakash Singh Rathore critiques Habermas's "revivalist endeavor," seeing it as "a rather conservative one"[19] in retaining the western liberal separation between religion and politics.

While post-secular critiques challenge the universal applicability of secularism, especially in non-western contexts, the debate continues regarding its potential to foster social cohesion, establish democratic governance, and promote individual rights and freedoms. Some argue that secularism, despite its limitations, remains a viable framework for managing religious diversity, resolving sectarian conflicts, and ensuring the separation of religion from state affairs. They emphasize the importance of a neutral public sphere, free from the influence of any particular religious doctrine, to guarantee equal rights and opportunities for all citizens, regardless of their faith or beliefs. However, others contend that secularism, particularly as promoted by western nations, often carries the baggage of colonialism and imposes a eurocentric understanding of modernity onto diverse cultural and religious contexts. They argue that this approach can be exclusionary and fails to acknowledge the complex relationship between religion and society in many parts of the world, leading to tensions and misunderstandings. A key point of contention lies in the interpretation and implementation of secularism. While proponents of a strict separatist model advocate for a clear distinction between religion and the public sphere, others favor a more inclusive approach that recognizes the potential contributions of religious communities and individuals to civic engagement and public discourse. Rectenwald and Almeida assert that secularism is not a simple advancing of an "Enlightenment universal," but the secular and the religious are integral to the construction of one another; thus, secularism is always dependent upon "its relationship with the particularity of its religious other." This debate highlights the need for context-specific understandings of secularism, acknowledging different societies' unique historical, cultural, and religious realities. The new generation of social theorists, including Casanova, argue that secularization does not necessarily entail the decline of religion or the regression of its social and political influence, instead, the reduction of its ability to infringe other spheres, allowing each one to a separate internal autonomy. The definition of secularization as the "functional differentiation between different spheres" thus "liberates the theory from the ideological load of the Enlightenment critique of religion." In other words, people can still maintain their religious beliefs, which serve social and spiritual purposes, whilst also being able to identify as secular, as long as they recognize the boundaries between those spheres. Yahya Akalay argues that divorcing secularism from its "ideological anti religiousness inclinations" clarifies the distinction between secularism and atheism and "transforms secularism into an inclusive theory that is neutral in matters of religiousness and non-religiousness or belief and disbelief." This does not imply a singular interpretation of "differentiation" or a uniform relationship between religious and secular realms. While advocates of the separatist model of secularism are entitled to their views, we need not succumb to a universalizing conceptualization. The importance of context-specific understandings in this debate cannot be overstated, as it allows us to appreciate the diverse ways in which secularism is interpreted and practiced worldwide.

Secularism Confronts Islam

The encounter between Islam and the west spans a millennium, with the first Muslim minorities appearing under western Christian rule in Sicily during the eleventh century. However, the second half of the twentieth century witnessed a significant shift with the large-scale migration of millions of Muslims from various regions, including the Middle East, Southeast Asia, Turkey, Africa, and India, to western societies. Today and especially since the attacks of September 11, secularism has become a central theme in debates surrounding immigration in Western Europe, advanced by politicians from both the right and left, using it as a tool to address concerns about integration, often ignoring the global resurgence of religion beyond Islam. Within these debates, a persistent association prevails between Islam and incompatibility with western secularism and Christian identity. This assumption rests on the historical narrative of Christianity's receptiveness to secularizing forces, while Islam or "Islamism" is portrayed as inherently resistant to secular modernity. This association of Christianity and western democracy is a persistent feature of the contemporary discourse of secularism, stemming from the legacy of the Treaty of Westphalia in 1648, which ended the European wars of religion and established the principle of state sovereignty for all Christian nations.[20] Consequently, state sovereignty and Christian practices became inextricably linked.

This constitution of modern Europe as a "secular" civilization leads to treating Muslims as abstract citizens on the one hand and as a distinctive minority on the other. They are either tolerated (the liberal orientation) or restricted (the national orientation), depending on the prevailing political stance. In France, for example, the growing Islamic revival is largely seen by the "secular" majority as a threat to the cultural integrity of France and to the secular values of "freedom," gender equality, and tolerance that supposedly define the nation.[21] This is evident in the 2004 headscarf ban and the court's note that it was influenced by "questions linked to Islam and to the place and status of Muslim women in society."[22] This is despite the fact that from 1905 until 1987, the French court had assumed that religion had little bearing on the "woman question."[23] Following France's lead, in Switzerland in 2009, a referendum led to the amendment of the Swiss Constitution to ban the construction of new minarets, justified by proponents as preserving Swiss secular values and culture. This move was widely seen as a discriminatory act against the Muslim community. In Britain, despite a generally more permeable attitude toward public affirmations of religion, multicultural policies have been under attack since the late 1980s, a period marked by the

Rushdie affair,[24] which heightened tensions between "the 'freedom to' assert religious beliefs and make demands for religious recognition, and the need to safeguard people's 'freedom from' religion – the right to critique and live free from the influence of religion, religious leaders and religious organisations."[25] This manifests with many spokespersons of the liberal establishment beginning to use the term "secularism" to characterize the backwardness of migrant communities. In the United States, even before the emergence of al-Qaeda and ISIS, policymakers in Washington began to warn of a new threat to the "secular liberal" order after the Soviet Union's collapse. That threat was Islam. Vice President Dan Quayle, serving from 1989 to 1993, considered Islam a major ideological threat to western culture, akin to Nazism or Communism. Relations between Islam and the west worsened after the September 11 attacks, prompting a war against so-called homegrown Muslim extremists. Under the Obama administration, the United States "engaged in the extrajudicial killing of its citizens, including the sixteen-year-old son of Anwar al-Awlaki, Abdurrahman."[26] The law, reserved for the civilized, was not extended to those held in indefinite military detentions without trial, such as in Guantanamo Bay. Quintan Wiktorowicz, who shaped the Obama administration's counter-radicalization policies, collaborated closely with the British government to implement a series of draconian measures, including planting informants, conducting surveillance, and spreading propaganda aimed at the Muslim community in America.[27] In the name of national security, secularism took an aggressive trajectory, equating violence and terrorism with Muslims' adherence to an "alien ideology" that does not conform to the principles of the secular order.[28]

In critiquing the essentialist perspective of secularism, Olivier Roy highlights the legal and methodological challenges it poses. He argues that this view, particularly concerning western conceptions of secularism, faces several key hurdles. Firstly, it questions the conventional separation of church and state, challenging western and European states' presumed "secular" nature. Secondly, it presupposes that western political culture is underpinned by "Christian" values universally shared among western populations. Thirdly, it characterizes Islam as a rigid set of norms and values inherently embedded in the consciousness of every Muslim, including nonbelievers, asserting their inevitable influence by Islamic "culture." As Roy argues, this overlooks the diverse daily practices of individual Muslims striving to adapt their traditions and customs in ways that allow them to engage with western societies. It is itself complex and often divided on many issues. The War on Terror is not merely a military campaign but is also steeped in the propagation of an essentialist secular ideology. By expanding this influence, western powers aspire to reshape Islam to align with their secular or Christian principles, a process largely driven by what Roy labels as a "theological predicament."[29] This sets the foundation for the perceived necessity to educate "suitable" *imams* in France, introduce a "revised" curriculum for Islamic studies in public schools in the German region of North Rhine-Westphalia, or support a foundation dedicated to "developing a Muslim identity at home in, and with the West" and "reprogramming Muslims"[30] in Britain. Recently, the search for a moderate or secular Muslim has become a discernible pursuit, with several government and nongovernment bodies deliberating on the ideal traits of such individuals. The "Hearts, Minds, and Dollars" report highlights these endeavors, providing examples, such as the Muslim World Outreach program, which was allocated $1.3 billion to work toward "transforming Islam from within."[31] Despite these efforts, religious fundamentalism continues to flourish amidst the erosion of cultural identity: "The young radicals are indeed perfectly 'Westernised.'"[32] This loss of cultural identity, according to Roy, serves as the premise for both assimilation and the emergence of novel fundamentalist ideologies. Whether manifested in Muslim, Christian, or Jewish contexts, the resurgence of religious fervor prompts contemplation on the role of religion in the public domain, as highlighted by Roy:

> The debates about prayers in school, the display of the Ten Commandments in courthouses, or the creation of an eruv following the request of Haredi Jews to privatize public space on Shabbat show that the recasting of the relation between the religious and the public sphere is not specific to Islam.[33]

This quote implies that reevaluating the interaction between religious practices and the public sphere is not unique to Islamic contexts. Instead, it points out that multiple faith traditions grapple with how their beliefs and customs fit within or intersect with the secular public domain, highlighting a universal challenge diverse religious communities face in navigating the balance between personal faith practices and public life. The reframing of the relations between religion and politics is a challenge for the west, as well as countries that grapple with issues related to the application of "secular" values to mull over, and this is not only because of Islam. The conditions of post-secularism are, as Roy argues, the very foundation of the contemporary religious revival: the Jesus Army from the Baptist tradition of Protestant Christianity;[34] the New Jerusalem claim to represent the true Orthodox tradition;[35] the International Society for Krishna Consciousness and the Brahma Kumaris[36] which have their roots in Hinduism, and many more. One crucial point about these new religious movements lies in their diverse nature, making any sweeping generalization about them potentially inaccurate. Current debates around whether we are observing a trend toward secularization or a resurgence of religious fervor hold increasing significance. In my view, the reality suggests both phenomena are concurrently unfolding. Therefore, rather than viewing them as conflicting concepts, analyzing them as interconnected processes that influence each other may be more fruitful. At present, a growing area of research seeks to transcend binary labels like "western" and "non-western," "Muslim" and "non-Muslim," and "secular" and "religious." The term "Islam mondain," introduced by Benjamin Soares and René Otayek, describes the coexistence of Islam and secularism. These discussions reflect a shift in acknowledging Muslims' diverse engagements with secularity and religion, moving beyond traditional categorizations. In understanding transformations among Muslims in western secular contexts, we must reconsider our frameworks and categories to recognize the nuanced ways in which Muslims navigate between secular and religious realms.

The "Muslim" Woman's Question

Despite its variations, the essence of secularism has often been characterized by a fundamental dichotomy between the traditional and the modern, the oppressive and the emancipatory. Given that many self-proclaimed secular nation-states emerged from historical conflicts within religious factions, secularism—whether in countries like the United States, Turkey, Germany, or Norway—is intricately entwined with specific religious discourses. In Egypt, Hussein Agrama characterizes secularism as a "problem space" that necessitates a continual evaluation of the boundary separating the religious realm from the political sphere. According to this binary view, secularism is commonly assumed to be inherently liberating for women, often seen as the pathway to women's emancipation in the face of religious conservatism, the best path to "closing the gender gap."[37] However, this simplistic distinction overlooks the pervasiveness of gender inequality within secular societies themselves, ignoring the complex interplay of cultural, economic, and political factors that shape gendered power dynamics, even in the absence of overt religious influence. This binary also ignores the diverse forms of patriarchy and their complex relationship with both secularism and religion, failing to recognize that neither religion nor secularism is inherently patriarchal or liberating. By framing the debate as "whether religion (or secularism) can offer a better path to gender equality than the other"—a common theme in policy debates—we prioritize religious and secular frameworks over examining power dynamics among different genders and sexual identities.

Traditional works on secularism often disregarded gender as a topic of study or confined it to a fixed category primarily associated with women. Linda Woodhead, one of the earliest scholars to critically examine the intersection of secularism and gender theory, highlights the absence of gender perspectives in discussions around secularization theories. She emphasizes examining restrictive forms of secularism that limit freedom of choice, justifying the marginalization of women and minority groups due to their religious beliefs conflicting with prevailing secular values. Although she takes a more open approach to dealing with religion in the public sphere, Woodhead's analysis does not sufficiently address the impact of this reevaluation of secularism on gender equality. She stops short of presenting an alternative conception of secularism, simply arguing that it has fallen short of eliminating religion and fulfilling its promises regarding women's rights. Joan Wallach Scott, renowned for her work in gender history, critically questions the assumptions linking secularism to sexual liberation and gender equality. In *Sex and Secularism*, she extends this argument by suggesting that secularism is a dynamic discourse that has embraced concepts such as freedom, equality, colonialism, white supremacy, and, fundamentally, the political marginalization of women from the political sphere. She maintains that during the eighteenth and nineteenth centuries, gender inequality served as a foundational element in shaping the structures of nation-states, "the allocation of citizenship, and the justification for imperial rule."[38] She argues that in the nineteenth century, proponents of secularism, predominantly men, placed high regard on public reason, which they viewed as masculine, contrasting it with what they perceived as women's private emotions linked to their sexuality, uncontrollable fertility, and religious fervor. For instance, Scott's examination of the French historian Jules Michelet's advocacy for secularism reflects his concern that in the nineteenth century, priests were spiritually, if not literally, undermining husbands across France by confiding in their female parishioners during confession. Michelet contends that husbands must regain authority over their wives, supported by a pseudoscientific notion that women's menstrual cycle inherently rendered them wounded and naturally subservient to men. In her examination of anti-suffrage arguments in nineteenth-century Britain, Scott references a Scottish biologist who opposed granting women the right to vote, basing his stance on the belief that ova were less active and "hungry" compared to sperm. Adding a Cold War element to the discourse, she highlights

American anxieties that a Soviet triumph could result in the sterilization of all men. By emphasizing the diverse and unique ways in which bodies are depicted to serve political objectives, Scott reveals that gender, race—often emphasizing whiteness—and sexual distinctions are fundamental elements in the narrative of secularism.

Currently, Scott argues that "secularism has become synonymous with (an ill-defined) gender equality that distinguishes west from east, the Christian secular from the Islamic."[39] Her work, alongside that of other postcolonial feminists, illustrates how women in the contemporary western world have historically faced and still confront exclusion from active participation in politics and are frequently relegated to subordinate roles within both the family structure and the workforce. Reflecting on the situation in France, she recalls the significant resistance, primarily from male politicians, against the passing of the parity law in the 1990s, which aimed to ensure equal opportunities for women seeking political office. Recent studies have highlighted pervasive discrimination against women in western nations: unequal pay for women—with working-class and immigrant women often marginalized into lower-paying "care" roles—compared to men; underrepresentation of women in leadership roles, particularly in politics; persistent rates of domestic violence affecting women of all backgrounds; an increase in misogynistic behaviors; prevalent instances of sexual harassment in various settings like workplaces, schools, and public spaces; and ongoing challenges to women's access to contraception and abortion rights by religious fundamentalists and their political supporters.[40] In an earlier publication featuring an essay titled "Sexularism," Scott highlights the continual postponement of secularism's pledges as they relate to gender equality. She points out, "The promise of equality espoused by secularism has always been hindered by sexual distinctions, grappling with the challenging—and sometimes insurmountable—task of attributing ultimate significance to bodily variances between women and men."[41] Challenging the notion of secularism's egalitarian principles is a complex endeavor—advocates have campaigned for various rights such as access to contraception, fairer divorce regulations, and the legalization of same-sex marriage by leveraging a secular argument centered on the separation of church and state. However, the pursuit of these goals within a secular framework, exemplified by figures like contraception advocate Margaret Sanger, does not preclude the possibility that aspects of secularism can also cultivate racist xenophobia or uphold white privilege grounded in historical colonial property laws, which even permitted slavery. Even within a secular context that embraces sexual liberation, as Scott posits, there remains a gendered aspect to this "freedom" that may not inherently translate to genuine equality. In a sexually liberated society, issues like sexual harassment and exploitation persist, particularly affecting individuals who hold less societal power.

This is not to say that gender inequalities are the same everywhere, but that the idea that gender inequality exists only in Islam is simply not accurate. Issues such as gender inequality, gender-based violence, stigmatization, marginalization of sexual minorities, and rigid constructions of masculinity are prevalent globally, cutting across contexts that might be categorized as "religious," "secular," or neither, given the inherent complexities associated with these labels. In today's society, public scrutiny and potential repercussions based on attire extend far beyond Muslim women. Female athletes often encounter criticism regarding their appearance even before their performance begins. The realm of politics is no exception, with women facing relentless scrutiny over their fashion choices. Female politicians are constantly under the microscope, from Theresa May's shoe selection to Hillary Clinton's pantsuits, Angela Merkel's understated style, and Julia Gillard's hair. Furthermore, judgments frequently transcend appearance, with women in various fields evaluated based on how they speak rather than the substance of their words. This phenomenon extends even to female academics, who navigate a delicate balance between looking engaging enough to captivate students while remaining professional enough to garner respect from their colleagues.

Despite making clear that gender inequality transcends the experiences of Muslim women alone, the heightened attention on the status of Muslim women within western and Muslim-majority societies has thrust secularism into the heart of discussions on the challenges faced by this increasingly visible demographic. The contentious headscarf controversy in France has led to a common association between Muslim women and secularism, making it difficult to overlook the intersection between the two. However, the debate surrounding Muslim women in the context of secularism predates the headscarf controversy in France, reflecting a discourse that often shapes Muslim women's identities within a western-centric framework. This discourse tends to portray Muslim women as passive victims without agency, contrasting them with western religious women, seen as more autonomous individuals with intricate intersecting identities. The concept of secularism, when wielded in this manner, contributes to a dichotomy that renders Muslim women as symbols in a clash between the east and west, measuring their "progress" based on their secularization. Scott argues that the connection between the secularism discourse's insistence on gender equality today and its anti-Islamic stance is rooted in its colonial history. She writes:

The discourse of secularism, gender, and race operate differently in the articulation of the national identities of Western European nation-states. The difference of race works to establish the outsider status of those others who aren't part of the presumed homogeneity of the national body—they are not only others but outsiders. The difference of sex poses another set of problems. It is a difference that can't be extruded; indeed, it is necessary for the very future of the nation. Women may be men's others, but they are intimate and necessary others. Their standing as insiders, as members (and reproducers) of the national body, elevates them above racial outsiders; their subordination is not of a piece with the subordination either of race or, for that matter, of class. If secularism is a discourse about the articulation of the sovereign identity of Western European nation-states, then a racialized gender (the attribution of meaning to the difference of sex) is at the heart of that discourse.[42]

Moreover, Scott argues that the alignment of secularism with gender equality stemmed from the increased visibility of Muslim women, prompting western societies to reassess the influence of religion in public spheres. She highlights that in this context, religion refers specifically to Islam and is depicted as a new threat to the west post-Soviet communism's decline. This evolving narrative leads to a reinterpretation of the concept of secularism, with Muslim women viewed as a means to regulate religion in the pursuit of gender equality. Consequently, the focus on issues like sexual freedom, critical in Muslim societies, prevails over addressing broader concerns such as economic equality, political representation, misogyny, sexual harassment, and domestic violence prevalent in both secular and religious settings, diminishing the unique position of Muslim women. The promotion of gender equality within the context of secularism is utilized to emphasize the dominant and superior identity of the west in the post-Cold War era. This contrasts with the previous era when the correlation between secularism and gender equality was deemed insignificant due to the Soviets, who, as a secular entity, already granted women equal rights and empowerment. Post-Cold War, the focus of discussions on secularism and gender equality shifted toward emphasizing a contrast with Islam. Muslim women were portrayed as carriers of dangerous religious values that challenged western norms and were depicted as victims of their restrictive religion. Emancipation, in this context, shifted from removing barriers to women's freedom to conforming to western ideals of sexual and gender relations. The debate surrounding the headscarf marked a pivotal moment within this discourse, reflecting the struggle to define boundaries between religious and secular values, particularly concerning the visibility of women's bodies in public spaces. In 2001, for instance, a Swiss federal court made a ruling against a teacher's desire to wear a *hijab* in class, arguing that "it is difficult to reconcile the wearing of the headscarf with the principle of gender equality—which is a fundamental value of our society enshrined in a specific provision of the Federal constitution."[43] It is worth mentioning that women in Switzerland only gained the right to vote in 1971. In 2003, the leader of the French commission recommending a ban on Islamic headscarves in public schools justified their stance by invoking the principle of *laïcité* (French secularism), emphasizing that "France cannot allow Muslims to undermine its core values, which include a strict separation of religion and state, equality between the sexes, and freedom for all."[44] The same year, American political scientists Ronald Inglehart and Pippa Norris argued that the clash of civilizations revolved around gender equality and sexual liberation.[45] These instances illustrate how conflicts between the west and Islam are used to mask persistent inequalities within western societies. The narrative that equates contemporary secularism with gender equality is shown to be misleading. By framing Islam in opposition to secular values with gender equality as the focal point, attention is diverted from the entrenched gender inequality issues within the "secular" Christian west and elsewhere. The ongoing focus on "liberating" Muslim women not only perpetuates the objectification of western women but also deflects attention from racialized gender disparities in various societal domains. Furthermore, it falsely assumes homogeneous experiences for all western and Muslim women. Despite that postcolonial feminists have and continue to contest such stereotypes, the discourse of secularism persists in using these misrepresentations as evidence of the superiority of the west.

By perpetuating such stereotypes, we endorse a mindset that shields secularism from critical scrutiny, thereby allowing existing inequalities to persist unchallenged. These inequalities are often portrayed as contradictory to the promised ideals of emancipation and equality within secularism. The debate around the headscarf exemplifies how Muslim women's attire is targeted as a symbol of defiance against "western" secular values. Scott contends that the secular perspective on the veil asserts that "uncovering" is synonymous with ensuring equality between genders, disregarding the inherent obstacle of sexual difference, regardless of whether women choose to reveal or conceal their bodies. She further argues that neither religious nor secular women have complete autonomy as societal norms and pressures influence their choices, whether under the guise of values or fashion. The issue of Muslim women challenges the idea that secularism is the sole framework for women's liberation and questions its alleged universality. Thus, there is a need to reconsider secularism beyond its western-centric context. Here, I would suggest a framework within which secularism is not viewed as counter to religious tradition but as a system that acknowledges diversity and capacity for adaptation. Furthermore, reevaluating the relationship between feminism and secularism should move beyond critiques of patriarchal religious influences in the Global South to also address Islamophobia and racism in western societies. Instead of asking whether "religion" or "secularism" is the more effective path to women's equality, the question should then be: How can individuals and groups, regardless of their religious or secular beliefs, development status, or political systems, collaborate to achieve greater equality and emancipation for all women?

Secularism in the Muslim World

In many Muslim communities, the concept of secularism is often viewed with strong negative undertones, a sentiment rooted in historical complexities. One key source of this perception stems from the colonial era, where the term became synonymous with the erasure of Islamic influence from legal and political domains by imperial forces. western powers, through their conquest of Muslim territories, conflated race and religion, depicting Muslims as inferior while positioning Christians as symbols of white superiority.

The association of "modernity" with "secularism" and "the west" invokes memories of colonial impositions on the Muslim world by predominantly Christian western nations.[46] Among the array of western ideas enforced on Muslims, secularism stands out as the most formidable challenge to traditional Islamic norms. Consequently, many Muslims harbor deep skepticism toward western cultural imports, including secularism, viewing them as threats to their beliefs. Even moderate or "enlightened" Islamists advanced serious arguments against adopting secularism, which they perceive as a foreign concept imposed by the west. Critics question proponents of secularism in Muslim societies, accusing them of blind admiration for European values and superiority complex toward western ideologies. The other key point of contention arises from the religious interpretation of secularism among Islamists, who often equate it with *kufr* (disbelief) and *irtidad* (apostasy). In Egypt, Muhammad al-Ghazali, a leading Egyptian theologian, perceives secularism as "unadulterated *kufr*."[47] In Iran, Ayatolla Khomeini claims that secularism "means the abandonment of Islam; it means burying Islam in our cells in the *madrasa*."[48] Even a moderate scholar like Fazlur Rahman, who devoted himself to educational reform and the revival of independent reasoning, asserts, "Secularism destroys the sanctity and universality (transcendence) of all moral values ... Secularism is necessarily atheistic."[49] However, according to Tamara Sonn, this assessment is not confined solely to Islamic perspectives, as some fundamental Christians express comparable views. She describes this interpretation as "an unfortunate misunderstanding of the essence of secularism and its significance in shaping stable national political structures."[50] In her view, this signifies a retreat from the strides taken by pre-First World War Islamic reformers, and early modernists like Rifa'a al-Tahtawi,[51] and their contemporaries. The third key contention arises from the belief held by many Muslims that, unlike Christianity, Islam does not advocate for a separation of religion from the state. A significant portion of Muslims worldwide support the idea of Islam playing a pivotal role in the political affairs of their nations. In their perspective, Islam is "a faith and a law, a sharia that envisages a religio-political community (*umma*) governed by God's rules."[52] This view underscores the inseparability of Islam from state affairs, with the notion of religion and state (*din wa dawla*) being a common assertion among many Muslim scholars. Consequently, there is widespread apprehension that secularism would fundamentally challenge the core tenets of Islam. Many within the Muslim intellectual sphere vehemently oppose the notion that the secular principle of separating religion and state could be harmoniously integrated into Islam without compromising its intrinsic identity as a religion, a community, a moral code, and a legal system.[53] Interestingly, the notion of religion holding political power is not exclusive to Islam, as seen in historical Christianity. In the Christian domains of antiquity, God served as the cornerstone of moral values, with the expansion of territories viewed not only as permissible but as a moral duty. For instance, in Christian Rome, full citizenship rights were often granted solely to adherents of the Christian faith, while individuals maintaining different religious convictions faced suspicion and marginalization.[54] This historical parallel sheds light on the intricate relationship between religion and political authority, a subject of debate and contention across various religious traditions. A fourth argument, advocated by some contemporary Muslim scholars, asserts that Islam inherently encompasses its version of secularism, thereby averting the necessity to mirror western interpretations of the concept. Muhammed Imara (1931–2020), a renowned Islamic scholar influenced by the teachings of early Muslim reformists like Jamal al-Din al-Afghani (1838–1897)[55] and Muhammad Abduh (1849–1905), contends, "We do not reject secularism because it has been imported from the west. We need only examine our circumstances in light of our Islamic religion and its nature to find out whether secularism would mean progress for us in the same way it did for Europe or whether it would prove to be inappropriate and harmful."[56] Imara's argument emphasizes the significance of evaluating secular principles through an Islamic lens, focusing on their relevance within the context of Islamic traditions and societal norms rather than blindly replicating western models. By asserting that Islam inherently supports public interest, progress, rationality, and a balanced approach to tradition, he questions the necessity and relevance of adopting secular principles. Fauzi M. Najjar further elaborates on his arguments:

> In his effort to demonstrate that secularism is either inimical, extrinsic or inappropriate to Islam, Imara... [argues] (1) Whereas Islam gives priority to public interest, even over a religious text, and sanctions what the Muslim community considers good and beneficial in its worldly affairs, Western secularism is utilitarian, with self-interest as its primary value. (2) It is true that secular society stands for change and innovation ... so does Islam; its endorsement of progress knows no limit. Why then, he wanders, should Muslims look to secularism for inspiration? (3) Lack of interest in the supernatural and emphasis on human reason is another distinguishing feature of secularism. Well, Islam's partiality to reason and rationality is quite clear, certain, and decisive ... (4) Secular society is indifferent to traditional values and conservative tendencies. Islam, on the other hand, distinguishes between reactionary values that are inimical to progress and development, and those which play a positive role in the life of society, rejecting the former and accepting the latter, even if they were ancestral and traditional.[57]

Imara's stance challenges the assumption that secularism is a universal solution, suggesting instead that Islamic principles are sufficient and perhaps more aligned with the moral and societal needs of Muslim communities. His critique invites a deeper reflection on the unique elements of Islamic governance and philosophy, advocating for an indigenous approach to modernization and development.

Due to these factors, Muslim liberal thinkers, secularists, and writers have often been viewed as renegades within their communities. One of these progressive voices, a pioneering figure in the modern Muslim world, was Rifa'a al-Tahtawi (1801–1873), renowned for his efforts to reform education under Muhammad Ali and his successors.[58] While his methods remained traditional, al-Tahtawi introduced a novel emphasis, arguing that Islamic law had the potential to foster a "modern" society capable of achieving scientific and technological progress. However, the first Muslim religious scholar to openly advocate for secularism was Shaykh Ali Abd al-Raziq (1888–1966). In his seminal and controversial work, *al-Islam wa 'usul al-hukm* (*Islam and the Fundamentals of Political Rule*), published in 1925, he argues that Islam "was a religion and not a state, a message not a government, a spiritual edifice not a political institution," a proposition that led to his dismissal by the Azhar Committee of the *Ulamā'*.[59] Taha Husayn (1889–1976), Egypt's renowned blind literary figure, faced a similar fate following the publication of his *Fi al-shi'r al-jahili* (*On Pre-Islamic Poetry*) in 1926. In this book, Husayn contends that "religious motives had contributed to the forging of so-called pre-Islamic poems" and that the Qur'ānic stories of Ibrahim and Ismail[60] were myths.[61] These controversial views led al-Azhar University to label him an "apostate," while a magazine called *al-Manar* demanded his dismissal.[62] Currently, Muslims continue to grapple with the challenge of balancing their Islamic identity with the demands of modernity. There remains a lack of consensus on which aspects of Islamic tradition to preserve and how to integrate elements of modernity. Moreover, the rise of militant Islamists, who staunchly oppose western influences and resort to indiscriminate violence and terrorism, has complicated the ongoing discourse on this issue. With the pressures from Islamists and fundamentalists, proponents of a "moderate" Islam find themselves hesitant to assert their visions for a renewed Islam in contemporary times. This reluctance is partly fueled by an apprehension to engage in further discord. The prevalent situation reflects a confluence of factors contributing to unrest in the Muslim world. For obvious reasons, there is a tendency to view the propositions put forth by Islamic secularists as a continuation of these ongoing debates. Present circumstances demonstrate that the political, social, and economic landscape in the Muslim world is inadvertently benefiting militant Islamists, perpetuating political and social turmoil, and obstructing crucial economic and political advancement. In my perspective, recent works by Islamic secularists, such as Abdullahi Ahmed An-Na'im, a Sudanese-born scholar based in the United States teaching at Emory University, offer a glimmer of hope for the progression of these discussions. He advocates secularism as a political order that does not violate Islam, coupled with constitutionalism and human rights, could potentially offer a more harmonious fit with Islamic history than the prevailing notions of an Islamic state. In his words,

> Since the legitimacy of the secular state among believers depends on its ability to mediate the public role of religion rather than relegate religion to the so-called private domain, it is misleading and counterproductive to define the secular state by the negative quality of being the opposite of religious. It is equally important to emphasize that the dynamic and multiple roles of religion for believers should

never be at the expense of unbelievers. It is as wrong to deny unbelievers their commitment to whatever beliefs they choose to adopt as it is to impose those beliefs on believers.[63]

An-Na'im's quote raises significant points about the role of religion within a secular state and underscores the importance of effectively navigating the relationship between the two. By highlighting that a secular state's legitimacy hinges on its ability to manage the public presence of religion rather than completely relegating it to a private realm, the quote challenges the simplistic notion of secularism solely as the absence of religion in governance. Furthermore, it stresses the need to recognize and respect the diverse beliefs of both believers and unbelievers within society. Ultimately, this underscores the need for a nuanced understanding of secularism that fosters a space where diverse religious and nonreligious perspectives can coexist harmoniously, promoting tolerance, inclusivity, and mutual understanding within society, taking into account historical, cultural, and religious factors.

Beyond Western Conceptualizations

While Islamists and secularists may have a few shared ideas, the consensus on obtaining cultural significance, crafting religious identities, defining practices, and integrating beliefs remains elusive. The interpretation and implementation of religious-secular interactions vary among religious and secular groups and governmental and judicial bodies.[64] Postcolonial scholars, influenced by the focus on the Christian roots of secularism and the stereotyping of non-western cultures, have come to view secularism as a form of homogenization and oppression.[65] Therefore, many non-western scholars have delved into the diverse interpretations, adaptations, and implications of secularism outside the confines of western perspectives. Postcolonial scholars argue that secularism is "plural, that various secularisms have developed in various contexts and from various traditions around the world, and that secularism takes on different social and cultural meanings and political valences wherever it is expressed."[66] As I have previously emphasized, secular societies do not align exclusively with atheist or irreligious perspectives. Instead, they intricately intertwine religious and secular elements, reshaping the dynamics of their interaction.

In instances such as communist regimes, where enforced secularism formed a core part of the political doctrine, the juxtaposition of social progress and national cohesion often solidified the divide between the secular and the religious. Interestingly, these regimes have recently witnessed a resurgence of religious sentiments. Consequently, the culture of secularism had to undergo adaptations to accommodate these evolving circumstances. Simultaneously, new institutionalized secular structures and novel modes of social engagement have emerged to challenge and address these shifting trends. In another instance, Turkey and Albania, both European countries with Muslim-majority populations dating back to the post-Ottoman period, have sought to regulate and control Islam. Turkey, in particular, has often intertwined Islam with a dominant and, at times, overbearing state structure that monitors and governs religious expressions in the supposedly "liberated and rationalized" public domain.[67] During this transformation, the state has also attempted to restructure and modernize Islam itself. In Albania, since the fall of communism in the early 1990s, the country has transitioned toward a more pluralistic society. The country's constitution guarantees freedom of religion and separation of church and state, establishing a secular legal framework. In present-day Albania, Arolda Elbasani and Murat Somer argue that secularism has been presented in terms of interreligious equality. At the same time, in contemporary Turkey, a dominant Islam has been endorsed for a cohesive national identity and social uniformity. Therefore, in Turkey, secularism carries an element of "Islamic" influence, whereas in Albania, secularism exhibits a multireligious quality. Islamic figures in both countries have demonstrated flexibility in engaging with and navigating various forms of secularism, challenging, negotiating, adapting, and competing for acknowledgment within distinct contexts. It is, thus, evident that the dynamic interplay between secularism and religion evolves differently based on the sociopolitical and historical circumstances at play. These developments make clear the need to rethink and maybe "radically redefine" secularism, as Charles Taylor suggests in his later works.

In a similar vein, political theorist Rajeev Bhargava recounts the narrative of a unique Indian secularism that emerged independently of western colonial influence. Bhargava suggests that this model could offer valuable insights for western democracies. He posits that, contrary to the common view, secularism should not merely serve as a hollow separation between the state and the public realm on one side and religious beliefs and rituals on the other.[68] Rather, he views secularism as a crucial and adaptable concept capable of fostering and strengthening modernity. The uniqueness of India's secularism stems from its acknowledgment that profound religious diversity is inherent to the social and cultural fabric. This recognition has facilitated the acceptance of rights specific to various communities and blurred the lines between the public and private spheres. Due to India's divergence from the western trajectory of secularization, religion has consistently held a pivotal role in political discussions. In contrast to the notion of the post-secular, religion in India has never resurfaced; it has continuously been a prominent feature of the public domain. Moreover, governmental authority has never been aligned with any specific faith. Following independence from British colonial rule, multiple dialogues reshaped the concept of secularism in India, independent of tenets of western secularism. In his journal article "Reimagining Secularism," Bhargava advocates for a departure from the conventional church-versus-state paradigms of secularism, emphasizing the importance of viewing secularism as a reaction to religious pluralism. He argues that diversity is intricately linked with power dynamics, underscoring the importance of recognizing the potential for religious-based dominance. This perspective, according to him, rebukes the charge that secularism is intrinsically anti-religious. Secularism is not intended to be and should not be anti-religion; instead, its aim should be to resist the domination of institutionalized religion. Reading secularism through this lens allows for the envisioning of a secular state that upholds a discerning respect for all religious and philosophical perspectives. Bhargava suggests that such a stance is achievable only through maintaining what he describes as a "principled distance" from each of them. The concept of "principled distance," as introduced by Bhargava, offers a dynamic perspective on how the state interacts with religion, encompassing both inclusion and exclusion, as well as engagement and disengagement. It emphasizes the need to maintain a respectful distance while engaging with religious matters thoughtfully. Principled distance thus underscores the importance of inclusivity without allowing any single religion to dominate state affairs. Bhargava's approach involves a strategic balance between engaging with religious communities to address their needs and concerns while refraining from endorsing specific religious doctrines. By upholding this principle, the state can safeguard individual rights and freedoms, promote tolerance and respect for diverse beliefs, and navigate the complexities of governance in multicultural societies effectively.

Bhargava's scholarship on Indian secularism has sparked debates and discussions, with critics questioning the adaptation of secularism to the Indian context and its potential dilution of original principles. The concept of "principled distance" has also been challenged for its potential inconsistencies in application. Additionally, concerns have been raised about the extent of state intervention in religious matters and its potential impact on religious freedoms and autonomy. Other critics of Indian secularism contend that, given the profound influence of religion in Indian society, the notion of secularism defined as the separation of state and religion is impractical and foreign to the Indian context. This misinterpretation disregards the nuanced approach outlined in the distinctive Indian constitution, which mandates the state to be impartial toward all religions, necessitating a careful avoidance of both extremist religious interpretations and the typical "separation" concept of secularism. It is true that the practical application of secularism in India has recently faced distortion as right-wing Hindu groups advocate for a form of political Hinduism that threatens to dominate, endangering minority freedoms and interreligious equality. Critics argue that the BJP's Hindu nationalist leanings demonstrate a bias toward the majority Hindu community, eroding the diverse fabric of Indian society. However, the core issue here lies not in the interpretation of secularism but in the dangerous endeavors of radical groups aiming to manipulate its implementation.

In his book *Secularism on the Edge*, Jacques Berlinerblau suggests that the academic field of secularism is in need of a period of discovery, emphasizing the necessity of gathering more data before drawing definitive conclusions.[69] Rectenwald and Almeida counter this suggestion arguing that the potential for secularism cannot be predetermined, rather intricately linked to its cultural, political, regional, and religious contexts, with its effectiveness largely contingent on effectively advocating for its value as both an ideology and a political tool. The challenge, however, lies in articulating the meaning of secularism on the theoretical level and the way it is implemented on the political level. Researchers need to reexamine religious-secular distinctions across the entire range of institutional domains, not only the political domain but also in law, arts, education, and so on. We must also remember that secularism is not confined to institutional structures alone but is also evident in public discourse, media practices, and everyday life.[70] For a successful articulation of secularism, some form of what Habermas calls "post-secularism" may be necessary. While I am not advocating for scrapping secularism and adopting post-secularism outright, the complexities of both concepts need to be acknowledged. Embracing post-secularism presents challenges, as does sustaining secularism. This intricate balance reflects varied manifestations of secularism globally and underscores that broader post-secular frameworks might be fostering softer institutional secularisms. Taking the case of France, a radical exemplar of secularism, where tensions have risen due to Islam challenging its strict secular model, addressing the ongoing struggle may involve eventually accommodating religious expression and observance. Broadly speaking, the evolving landscape of global secularisms appears to be gravitating toward more adaptable, inclusive, and diverse frameworks as they grapple with expanding and diversified religious realms. Perhaps the so-called crisis of secularism could potentially catalyze its transformation and diversification over time.

Secularism, as a worldview, does not necessitate the complete rejection of religion. But it does necessitate safeguarding against the religious right's attempts to dictate how individuals should live and express themselves, whether in public or private spheres. This echoes An-Na'im's work, which underscores the importance of acknowledging religion as a fundamental element of contemporary secular political modernity, serving "as a source of cultural identity, framework for organizing social life, and fount of collective or individual meaning and psychological motivation."[71] The insistence that refugees from France's former colonies should assimilate begs the question of what exactly is it to which they should assimilate. In response, An-Na'im's theorization envisions a secular political modernity that strives to strike a delicate balance between these domains, recognizing the two "exist in tension or even in possible antagonism."[72] Similarly, Scott proposes a perspective where democratic states and religions are seen as parallel systems of interpretation. This approach, she argues, "opens the relationship between the state and its religions to negotiation without either forcibly repressing religion or giving up democracy—which remains a place where political resolution is never achieved on the grounds of religious truth."[73] Rohit Chopra advocates an equilibrium that "can simultaneously rejuvenate religion as a source of public life, while [secularizing] it to ensure that it can be freely debated and criticized without any fear of the part of interlocutors that they might be accused of blasphemy."[74] With that said, it remains imperative to explore the potential challenges that may arise within "post-secular" societies. Drawing from the context of India, Rajeev Bhargava argues, it may have "always been post-secular." With the pursuit of religious neutrality, India's objective of embracing and maintaining equidistance from all faiths has garnered controversy. This stems from inconsistencies in the judiciary's approach toward reforming diverse religious traditions. For instance, the judiciary's hesitance to address gender equality issues within Islam was perceived as favoritism toward Muslims by the Hindu majority, while some Muslims saw the state's actions as aligning more with Hindu interests despite advocating for secularism overtly.[75] Under the leadership of Narendra Modi, India has witnessed a systematic erosion of minority rights, particularly targeting Muslims through discriminatory policy measures like the Citizenship Amendment Act of 2019, mentioned earlier. The media as well as the corporate sector have only strengthened Modi's authoritarian grip on political power in India.⁷⁶ In both practice and theory, Chopra argues, India has now started to look like a Hindu religious state. It is exactly for these reasons that the value of secularism must be reaffirmed, and a workable and sustainable secularism reimagined. It is for these reasons that secularism as a social value and as a principle that regulates the actions of the state should be invested in. In order to protect the rights of religious minorities, secularism, indeed, becomes a "necessary condition for the meaningful exercise of religious belief, practice."⁷⁷ At the same time, An-Na'im invites us to rethink religion, too.

Reimagining Secularism

The aim of this chapter is to underscore the significance of secularism as a framework that enables and safeguards choices and promotes ethical coexistence. From my perspective, the key to achieving religious harmony and political stability lies in the principles of secularism and democracy. However, because the concept of secularism has been challenged as a western imposition that marginalizes local beliefs and values, its viability has been questioned. My aim here is not to delve into the ongoing secular debates of modern western nations but to reexamine the specific connotations and implementation of secularism as a contemporary discourse in a global context. This exploration takes place in a milieu where religion is closely intertwined with individual experiences, especially in light of the growing influence of religious movements. Addressing the challenge of accommodating religion while comprehending the symbolic significance of secular practices raises critical questions, as the essence of secularization traditionally signifies a division between state and religion. As previously highlighted, it is important to treat the idea that there is a definitive original definition of secularism with caution. While the concept originates from the west historically, its adaptation into global contexts is generating fresh interpretations. The intricate presence of religious symbols in contemporary multicultural, multi-faith societies makes the division between religion and secularism a challenging task. The debate on reconciling Islam with secularism gained momentum in the late 1980s due to conflicts arising from the publication of Salman Rushdie's novel. This was ignited by Women Against Fundamentalism (WAF), a feminist organization in London established in 1989, which underscored the significance of secular spaces in upholding equality for all individuals. Their argument was influenced by Homi Bhaba's work, in which he supports the crucial role that secularism plays in facilitating and safeguarding the evolutionary nature of religions over time. Bhaba's work also underscores the various forms of religious practices that evolve as populations move within and across different countries. By drawing from a version of secularism rooted in the historical and cultural contexts of migration, diaspora, and resettlement that characterize today's multicultural societies, Bhaba introduces the concept of "subaltern secularism." This alternative perspective moves beyond the constraints of traditional "liberal" secularism, aiming to support communities and individuals who have historically been marginalized or excluded from the principles of liberal individualism.[78] Drawing on Gita Sahgal's work on the experiences of Asian women organizing in Britain, he uses the notion of "the subaltern" to describe marginalized minority groups that challenge the dominant authority structures. He highlights that women from religious minority backgrounds often find themselves navigating the complexities of a multi-faith, multicultural society where decisions are predominantly dictated by male community leaders who are seen as the public faces of the community. This situation limits their autonomy and contradicts the foundational principles of liberal secularism, but as Sahgal argues, they require secular spaces to guarantee freedom of choice and ethical coexistence.

In Chapter 2, I analyzed the narratives secular Muslim feminists draw on to articulate their ideologies and political viewpoints. I have argued that secular Muslim feminists find themselves constrained within limited roles and perspectives, often misunderstood by various factions. In a separate segment, I have demonstrated how "secular" and "religious" feminisms among Muslim women portray the "other" as monolithic and fixed, lacking in nuance, diversity, and evolution. In Chapters 3 and 4, I have highlighted the ways both "secular" and "religious" feminisms within Muslim communities depict the "other" as singular and unchanging, neglecting nuances, intricacies, and the dynamic nature of individuals. This oversimplified categorization obstructs meaningful dialogue between secular and religious feminists and diminishes the opportunity for forming united strategic alliances in advancing gender equality. The feminists whose narratives and ideologies are recounted here advocate for women's rights to challenge religious, cultural, traditional, and normative practices. They do not oppose religion but prioritize the necessity of secular spaces in guaranteeing equal treatment for all, regardless of religious affiliations. They articulate a need for "secular" spaces that acknowledge their unique historical and cultural backgrounds, providing them with unfettered freedom of choice that is not predetermined or dictated. These spaces should be inclusive of diverse perspectives, fostering solidarity not just through shared similarities but through the acknowledgment and appreciation of differences. In this sense, "secularism" is still defined by the clear division between religion and state while simultaneously upholding equal respect for the human rights of all individuals. This interpretation of secularism advocates for a framework where nobody faces undue advantages or disadvantages based on their beliefs. It encapsulates a vision of secularism as a universal principle that champions the fundamental freedoms of every human being, aligning with the ongoing quest for basic human rights. As Amina Jamal puts it, "To engage the diversity of the vast majority of [Muslim] women who are unlikely to identify exclusively with oppressive forms of religiosity or anti-Muslim secularism, we need painful and painstaking ethnographies of secularism in religious spaces and of the presence of religion in secular spaces."[79]

7

Can the Secular Muslim Feminist Speak?

In 2023, Iranian women's rights advocate Narges Mohammadi was honored with the Nobel Peace Prize for her unwavering dedication to combating the systemic oppression women face in Iran. Mohammadi, currently serving multiple prison sentences in Tehran's Evin prison, has been charged with offenses such as spreading propaganda against the state. This prestigious award was announced amid ongoing women-led protests both in Iran and around the world, sparked in part by the tragic death of Mahsa Amini, a young woman who died while in police custody for allegedly violating Iran's compulsory *hijab* law. The #WomanLifeFreedom movement draws inspiration from the enduring advocacy and resilience of Iranian figures such as Azar Nafisi, Shirin Ebadi, a Nobel Peace Prize laureate, Nasrin Sotoudeh, a renowned human rights lawyer, Leyla Qasim, a prominent Kurdish women's rights activist and politician, who founded the Free Women's Organization of Kurdistan and played a key role in establishing women's shelters, and many more. These courageous women have long challenged oppressive norms and championed gender equality and human rights in Iran, imprinting their legacy on the ongoing struggle for justice and empowerment. This enduring protest movement, representing decades-long battles by Iranian women against religious authoritarianism, seems poised to instigate an unprecedented shift in confronting one of modern history's most repressive regimes. Despite its achievements, the movement faces challenges, from silencing to imprisonment. This raises significant concerns about the unique and multifaceted challenges that Muslim women face when advocating for their rights. In countries like Taliban-controlled Afghanistan or socially conservative Saudi Arabia, Muslim women who reveal their experiences or advocate for gender equality often find their efforts and experiences misrepresented or stereotyped, both within their own countries and in the international arena. In previous chapters of this book, I have critiqued the limits of religious empowerment for Muslim women. I have also delved into the problematic aspect of the "rescue" narrative used by western policies, right-wing factions, and fundamentalist Islamic groups. While the wider western societies continue to identify them as the "Muslim" other, turning them into targets of intensified prejudice. They are situated as "enemy outsiders" as the public repeatedly reconstructs their status as "non-white," immigrant women, rendering them "incapable of transcending their Muslim difference."[1] Notably, it is not only Islamists who view secular Muslim feminists as a threat to the societies they aspire to create or right-wing groups who harbor their suspicions about them merely by virtue of being Muslim; other factions, including feminists and those on the political left, fail to grasp the significance of their narrative. They do not believe these women are the "right" kind of Muslim, both religiously and politically. At the same time, while postcolonial feminists aim to carve out platforms for solidarity and amplify marginalized viewpoints, they have overlooked the opportunity for women, similar to the ones highlighted in this book, to share their narratives.

This chapter begins with a summary of the overlooked secular feminist movements in Muslim nations to explore how these voices are often misconstrued as either simply mimicking western ideals or betraying their own cultural and religious identities. In their countries, their voices frequently go unheard in mainstream dialogue, with their efforts toward social transformation downplayed or disregarded. Surveillance, harassment, and arrests are also common, with prosecutions under broadly interpreted laws criminalizing opposition. Alongside legal consequences, outspoken Muslim women often encounter direct threats that range from death threats and online abuse to physical attacks. In severe instances, they and their families become targets of violence, instilling a climate of fear that suppresses activism. Meanwhile, the chapter also delves into the ways postcolonial feminists perceive these feminists. They label them "native informants" for airing their country's dirty laundry for personal or political gain. They question the very applicability of a "secular" framing and accuse them of being compromised, biased, culturally inappropriate, imperialist, and so on. The chapter then delves into a critical examination of the somewhat restricted approaches and tactics of purportedly progressive factions in Europe—namely western feminists and the left. These groups exhibit hesitancy in backing individuals who challenge Islamist ideologies, succumbing to influences from both Islamic fundamentalist pressures and the lingering shadow of colonial legacies. The chapter further delves into the complex debate surrounding cultural relativism versus universalism in the context of women's rights advocacy. It explores the tensions between respecting cultural differences and upholding universal human rights standards, shedding light on the nuances of navigating these ideological challenges within the sphere of Muslim women's activism. In closing, the chapter asks how diverse forms of feminist organizing can accommodate differences and absorb conflict while allowing for the solidarity necessary for collective action.

Silenced Voices in Their Homelands

In a previous chapter, I have outlined vital discussions and strategies that have influenced feminist movements within Muslim communities since the early 2000s, aiming to trace the historical thread of feminist consciousness among Muslim women. Although women's movements in Muslim-majority regions have maintained a continuous presence, they have frequently operated discreetly, with their voices at times marginalized, misconstrued, or dismissed. In Iran, for instance, state-controlled media, academic spheres, and official political narratives have consistently undermined, silenced, and patronized feminists advocating for women's rights. Following the 1979 Revolution, Islamic clerics, led by Ayatollah Ruhollah Khomeini, tightened their grip on the government, ushering in a series of oppressive laws that specifically targeted women. Despite enduring brutality from the regime, women emerged as significant figures in the resistance against oppression. These feminist voices are not only repressed within Iran but also deliberately ignored by the global community. Mouri and Batmanghelichi aptly observe, "In the absence of substantive dialogues concerning theory and practical application, particularly concerning 'the woman question' in contemporary Iran, a noticeable void and mutual detachment persist between Iranian activists and feminist scholars based in America and Europe."[2]

The systematic oppression of women has remained a consistent element within modern Iranian society. Since the late nineteenth century, Iranian women have tirelessly campaigned for advancements in their familial, political, and societal status, encountering both successes and challenges throughout their journey. The late nineteenth and early twentieth centuries saw the establishment of Iran's earliest women's rights organizations, championing education, legal reforms, and social progress. Despite the Constitutional Revolution of 1906 not culminating in a constitutional monarchy, women actively engaged in the public arena, advocating for political rights and challenging conventional norms. During the reign of Reza Shah Pahlavi (1925–1941), substantial reforms were introduced, including the unveiling of women, establishing girls' schools, and granting voting rights. Nevertheless, these reforms often faced opposition from conservative factions. In the aftermath of the 1979 Islamic Revolution, women experienced a severe setback in their rights, marked by compulsory *hijab* enforcement, restrictions on employment and education, and the establishment of a patriarchal legal framework. Despite these obstacles, women persisted in organizing and pushing for their rights within the constraints of the altered political landscape. The reformist era under President Mohammad Khatami (1997–2005) briefly witnessed a relative liberalization, with women achieving advancements in education, employment, and political participation. By 2009, feminists, including previously marginalized secular feminists, began gaining visibility and influence. Recent years have seen women at the forefront of the fight, engaging in activities such as public commemorations of International Women's Day, protesting injustices and activist repression in events like the twin June 12 demonstrations of 2005 and 2006, initiating the One Million Signatures Campaign in 2006, and displaying solidarity between secularist and Islamic feminists in 2007. Before this coalition, Islamic feminists struggled to elevate women's issues, yet western media predominantly focused on them when discussing the status of women in Iran. Hassan Rouhani's 2013 presidential election led to a transient period of moderate liberalization, with women making strides in education, employment, and political participation. However, conservatives resisted many of these reforms, which hindered progress and resulted in slow and inconsistent developments. The 2017 election of hardliner Ebrahim Raisi as president marked a critical moment for women's rights in Iran, as the new government enforced stringent policies further restricting women's liberties, including mandatory *hijab* regulations, limited job opportunities, and travel constraints. These measures were met with widespread opposition from women and civil society organizations.

Currently, the #WomenLifeFreedom movement, sparked by the tragic death of Mahsa Amini in September 2022, stands as a powerful symbol of resistance against Iran's oppressive regime. Originating from the Kurdish women's movement *Jin, Jiyan, Azadî* (Women, Life, Freedom), the slogan champions women's rights, freedom, and equality. Initially adopted by the Kurdistan Workers' Party (PKK) in the 1990s during their quest for Kurdish autonomy and gender liberation, the slogan gained broader recognition during the 2019 Rojava protests in northern Syria. It echoed through the voices of Kurdish women defiantly confronting the Turkish invasion and the Islamic State group. This rallying cry transcended borders and resonated in Iran, becoming pivotal during the 2022 nationwide protests. Journalists Niloofar Hamedi and Elaheh Mohammadi were among the earliest reporters of Amini's death, instigating nationwide demonstrations. Hamedi, affiliated with the reformist publication *Shargh* (East), poignantly shared an image online depicting Amini's grieving father and grandmother, captioned: "The black dress of mourning has become our national flag."[3] Elaheh Mohammadi, associated with *Ham-Mihan* (Compatriot), covered Amini's funeral in Saqqez, emphasizing the mourners' chant of "Woman, Life, Freedom."[4] Both journalists faced arrest for their reporting but were later released on bail. Their commitment to truth has inspired many to join the movement. Narges Mohammadi, a stalwart in the fight for women's rights since the early 1990s as a student, encountered thirteen arrests and five convictions, leading to a cumulative thirty-one-year prison sentence and 154 lashes. During the 2022 surge of #WomenLifeFreedom protests, she orchestrated gestures of solidarity within Tehran's infamous prison. Despite authority-imposed restrictions on her interactions, Mohammadi managed to smuggle an article to the *New York Times*, published in September 2023, bearing the headline: "The More They Lock Us Up, the Stronger We Become."[5] Renowned human rights lawyer and women's rights advocate Sepideh Rashno, who has adamantly opposed Iranian governmental human rights abuses, faced multiple arrests and imprisonments in defense of her convictions. Student activist Shima Babaei, who actively engaged in the #WomenLifeFreedom demonstrations, encountered detainment for her advocacy but persisted in her fight for women's rights and free expression. Acclaimed actress and filmmaker Roya Piraei, who utilized her platform to endorse the protests and denounce the governmental clampdown on dissent, endured a work ban in Iran due to her activism. These accounts are just a fraction of the countless women courageously challenging the oppressive Iranian regime. They are a testament to the power of collective action and the steadfast perseverance of those unwilling to remain silenced.

In Pakistan, the independence movement culminated in the partition of British India on August 14, 1947, leading to the establishment of the new state of Pakistan. The partition was largely a response to deep-seated religious and political divisions between the Muslim-majority regions and the Hindu-majority areas in British India. Since gaining independence, Pakistan has navigated through various political, social, and economic challenges while striving to preserve its national identity, promote "democracy," and address issues related to governance, development, and regional stability. Despite aspirations for democracy, soon after independence, the nation witnessed a crackdown on women's activism. The initial enthusiasm for democracy was accompanied by challenges in upholding women's rights and ensuring gender equality. Activists advocating for women's empowerment, education, and social participation faced suppression and censure from societal norms and conservative forces. The nascent democratic institutions grappled with entrenched patriarchal structures that hindered the progress of women's activism and limited the scope for gender-inclusive policies and reforms. Moreover, society has largely turned a blind eye to women seeking empowerment through education, employment, or autonomy in selecting a life partner. NGOs dedicated to supporting women have faced allegations of manipulation and "brainwashing" them.[6] Following General Zia ul-Haq's implementation of the *Hudood* Ordinances in the 1980s, the situation for women's activism in Pakistan deteriorated further. The ordinance's implementation led to increased restrictions on women's rights, particularly regarding issues such as sexual assault and adultery, with severe punishments that disproportionately affected women. The establishment of the Women's Action Forum (WAF) in September 1981 marked a pivotal moment, with members lobbying and advocating on behalf of women. WAF openly opposed the bill, voiced dissent against the government through media channels, organized street protests, conducted educational initiatives in schools, and popularized the potent slogan "Men, Money, Mullahs, and Military."[7] This phrase gained prominence during the 2011 demonstrations against the then-military ruler Pervez Musharraf, resonating as a concise and pointed critique of Pakistan's predominant power structures. The elements of "men," "money," "mullahs," and "military" encapsulate the societal dynamics critiqued by the slogan: "men" symbolizes the entrenched patriarchy resulting in women's marginalization and limited prospects; "money" signifies the influence of the economic elite and their control over resources; "mullahs" points to the authoritative religious establishment impacting social and political realms; and "military" denotes the pervasive role of the armed forces in Pakistan's political landscape and historical interventions in civilian governance.

Similar to many Muslim-majority nations, Islamic and secular feminism are the prominent feminist discourses in Pakistan. Islamic feminism resonates strongly with various social strata in the country, ranging from the lower to the upper-middle class, where individuals often turn to religion for guidance and solutions. Secular feminism, as in other contexts, face criticism and are usually labeled as adherents of western ideologies. An advocate of secular feminism in Pakistan, Bina Shah, contends, "Pakistan needs a feminism that elegantly marries both strands of feminism, secular and Islamic."[8] But in Pakistan, secular feminists continue to face demonization and scrutiny as a unifying coalition akin to that in Iran has not materialized to offer collective support and protection. Despite the lack of solidarity between secular and Muslim feminists, in 2021, Pakistani women staged demonstrations across the country on International Women's Day, demanding an end to violence against women and gender minorities. Subsequently, members of Pakistan's Taliban movement accused the participating women of blasphemy—a charge frequently used to target minorities and incite violence. Currently, Pakistani women confront an array of challenges, from entrenched patriarchal norms and societal biases to limited access to education and healthcare, gender-based violence encompassing domestic abuse, honor killings, and sexual harassment, as well as discrimination in professional and political spheres. In the face of these obstacles, Pakistani feminists remain steadfast in advancing women's rights through diverse advocacy strategies. Noteworthy figures like Asma Jahangir, an unrelenting human rights lawyer and activist, have fearlessly championed women's rights and social equity in Pakistan, enduring threats, harassment, and imprisonment for their advocacy. A politician and human rights advocate, Shireen Mazari has assumed various ministerial roles and confronted opposition for her progressive stance against human rights violations in Pakistan. Equally commendable is the work of Hina Jilani, a lawyer and human rights defender. Despite facing threats and intimidation for her activism, she is renowned for her involvement in pivotal cases regarding women's rights, religious liberties, and freedom of expression. Yet, amidst these struggles and sacrifices by Pakistani feminists, the international community's response remains conspicuously muted, as many scholars observe.

In North Africa and the Middle East, the feminist movement, which dates back to the late nineteenth and early twentieth centuries, gained prominence specifically after independence. It began by tying women's issues to the secular nationalist and anti-colonial movements of the time, but the relationship between early feminists and male nationalists was far from harmonious. This has taught feminists that efforts to achieve gender equality can no longer be gained through the power of male elites. Since then, feminists have navigated a complex landscape of social reform, political oppression, and a resurgent religious conservatism. In Egypt, the Nasser government's repression of religious and political movements and parties resulted in a reactionary religious resurgence, which further divided the women's movement into secular and Islamic camps. Similarly, Morocco, Tunisia—despite its progressive stance—and Algeria among others, for instance, Jordan and Lebanon, have also witnessed a divide within the women's movement, with some groups advocating for a secular approach to women's rights while others seeking to interpret Islamic teachings in a more feminist way. This division, however, did not diminish the ability of

North African and Middle Eastern women to organize and advocate for their goals. Both camps continued to engage in critical debates on women's issues and their impact on broader political questions. While the 2011 revolution initially brought hope for greater gender equality, the rise of Islamist parties in the subsequent elections in many MENA regions led to concerns about potential rollbacks on women's rights. Yet, particularly in the aftermath of the 2011 Arab Spring, women, especially young women, have become increasingly vocal in their demands for political reforms and gender equality. Harnessing the power of social media, they have used platforms like Twitter, Instagram, and Facebook to amplify their voices. Yet, despite the feminist movement's apparent strides forward, some MENA governments have implemented measures to curb women's autonomy. In Egypt, in 2016, human rights organizations, particularly those advocating for women's rights, faced severe restrictions. Prominent activists, including founders of leading women's organizations, had their assets frozen and travel bans imposed, preventing them from participating in crucial international conferences. Among those are Mozn Hassan, the founder of Nazra for Feminist Studies, and Azza Soliman, Director of the Center for Egyptian Women's Legal Assistance (CEWLA). In 2020, the arrest of at least fifteen people, including a seventeen-year-old girl, for posting a video about being beaten and raped further illustrates the deteriorating state of women's rights in Egypt. Instead of proactively addressing pervasive issues like domestic violence, sexual harassment, and overall violence, Egyptian authorities seem to be prioritizing the persecution of women and girls based on their online presence or speech. In January 2021, the Egyptian cabinet approved a personal status bill requiring the consent of a male guardian for a woman to get married, register a child's birth, or travel abroad. Nehad Abu El Komsan, head of the Egyptian Center for Women's Rights, called the bill "repressive" and "patriarchal," and "takes us back 200 years." Nonetheless, the steadfast resilience and bravery demonstrated by Egyptian feminists in confronting adversity stand as a beacon of inspiration for women and activists globally.

Dismissed by the International Community

The previous brief evaluation of some of the current women's movements in Muslim-majority countries highlights the presence of both secular and Islamic feminists and activists across various Muslim countries. Despite this diversity, scholarly works examining women's activism in Muslim societies predominantly focus on Islamic feminism. According to Mouri and Batcmanghelichi, "the figure of the 'Islamic feminist' ... has uncritically become the central protagonist and spokesperson to describe what is, in actuality, a hybrid movement of secularists, feminists, and the religiously devout, among many other characters and strains."[9] This tendency to prioritize Islamic feminism over other forms of activism has resulted in the marginalization and suppression of secular Muslim feminists not only in Iran but also in various regions. This bias is evident in the limited academic attention given to non-faith-based activism in Muslim contexts. As a consequence, many voices within secular Muslim women activists' circles struggle to establish impactful movements due to continuous marginalization. Some critics even suggest that feminists who choose not to intertwine every aspect of their lives with religion are a "non-representative minority, ignorant of the dangers and effects of neoliberal imperialism, and therefore, complicit in imperialist wars/violence."[10] Other similar assumptions broadly categorize all liberal and secular Muslim feminists in Muslim-majority regions and the western world as "elite" and far removed from the realities of everyday life for Muslim women. Afia Zia critiques this perspective as a form of racialization, insinuating that women of color lack their independent agendas, implying they either unquestionably follow white feminist principles or adhere strictly to their religious doctrines.

On top of that, the global media frequently neglects to adequately report on women's movements in Muslim-majority nations. They often concentrate on specific narratives that align with their audience's preconceived notions or geopolitical interests, overshadowing the intricate and varied struggles of these movements. Even when coverage does exist, it tends to be framed through a lens of cultural essentialism, emphasizing oppression while downplaying agency and resistance. Despite the portrayal of Muslim women as oppressed victims, international aid and funding often do not prioritize grassroots women's movements in Muslim-majority countries.[11] Donors commonly favor allocating funds for immediate humanitarian crises, neglecting long-term support for women's movements. Furthermore, funding often comes with strings attached to specific agendas that may not harmonize well with the local context or the priorities of these movements. As I have discussed in an earlier chapter, women's rights become politicized in global discourse, serving to rationalize broader geopolitical objectives linked to the "War on Terror," resulting in selective advocacy where some movements are amplified while others are disregarded based on strategic interests. In addition to these challenges, women's movements within Muslim-majority countries face internal fragmentation: varying ideologies and priorities create obstacles in presenting a united front, and limited resources foster competition rather than solidarity. Ultimately, these movements face not only silencing within their own countries but also struggle to gain recognition on a global stage.

The "Native Informant" Conundrum

During the 2010 Women of Courage Award ceremonies in Washington, homage was given to the Iranian activist Shadi Sadr, alongside ten other women hailed as "courageous" from across the globe. Residing in Germany at the time, Sadr addressed the audience through a prerecorded video. When asked about the reason for her physical absence, she shared her explanation with Leila Mouri:

> the award enables me to publicize the systematic human rights abuses in Iran ... [but] to be honest, since the Iranian regime declares that all human rights activists ... are spies and puppets for the West ... I initially worried that to dedicate this award to Shiva [Nazar Ahari][12] alone might increase the pressure and hostility of her interrogators and the judicial forces and make matters worse for her.[13]

This statement from Shadi Sadr highlights the cautious approach taken by women activists in Muslim societies, particularly those with a secular orientation, in avoiding direct ties with the west, notably the United States, to preempt any potential repercussions such connections may entail. Just two months following the Awards Ceremony, Mouri and Batmanghelichi reported that Sadr was found guilty by Tehran's Revolutionary Court for involvement in activities deemed detrimental to Iran's national security. Subsequently, in that same year, she was handed a sentence of six years imprisonment and seventy-four lashes for various charges, including "acting against national security through gathering and collusion to disrupt public security, disturbing public order and insurgence against officials."[14] Sadr's ordeal sheds light on a broader pattern observed among women activists in similar circumstances. In 2023, an independent women's rights group called "Bidarzani" reported that Iranian security forces conducted several home raids and arrested twelve individuals, consisting of eleven women's rights advocates and one political activist, under the accusation of scheming to disrupt public security.[15] In Egypt, Nawal El Saadawi, a renowned Egyptian feminist writer, activist, and physician often dubbed as "the Simone de Beauvoir of the Arab World," faced allegations of "defaming religions" in her statements to the BBC.[16] El Saadawi, a lifelong campaigner against Female Genital Mutilation (FGM), has argued that this practice serves as a tool for oppressing women. On *Without Limits* TV program, the alleged interview, she advocated for the need to update religious doctrines, such as those found in the Qur'ān, Bible, and Torah, to better align with people's changing interests across different eras.[17] The resurgence of political Islam globally since the late 1970s has led to accusations against many women activists of collaboration with "western imperialism" by allegedly introducing foreign ideas and practices into society. Additionally, the emergence of the Islamic feminist approach created "a lack of balance in most of the affirmative accounts of Muslim women's activism."[18] By stipulating Islam as the "only" viable alternative to western feminism, the possibility of hearing different voices in different cultural and political contexts becomes deterred. Consequently, forms of women's activism that challenge the authority of sharia law often do not receive adequate attention, documentation, or discussion. In some instances, as illustrated by the examples above, secular women activists have even faced imprisonment as a consequence of their advocacy.

While it is true that Muslim women activists in western countries espousing secular ideologies are unlikely to face the same level of threat of imprisonment as their counterparts in authoritarian theocratic regimes, they encounter a complex web of challenges. In their Muslim communities in the west, these activists confront dual layers of restrictions: first, entrenched patriarchal traditions that subjugate them as women, and second, a newly embraced religious "Muslim" identity that often vilifies them for embracing "secularism." They are frequently dismissed and accused of holding anti-Islamic sentiments and being apologists for imperialist agendas by Islamists. They are also labeled inauthentic, theoretically uninformed, and members of privileged classes by postcolonial feminists. While postcolonial feminist depictions of Muslim women as both subjects and agents have effectively created a space for challenging the oppressive colonial portrayals of Muslim women as perpetual victims of patriarchal religious practices and male dominance, new complexities and dilemmas have emerged, dividing Muslim women into categories such as feminist versus fundamentalist, secular versus religious, and diasporic versus native. Shāhnaz Khan argues that the western-based Muslim "native informant" is compelled to "present true accounts of experience in relation to her own racial/cultural group from a position of fixed identity."[19] Her argument highlights the pressure experienced by secular Muslim feminists to conform to predetermined narratives and perceptions that the broader society or academic circles hold about their cultural or religious background. In other words, these individuals are seen as representatives who must provide authentic, insider perspectives that fit into established frameworks of understanding. This preconceived positioning, as highlighted by Jasmin Zine, "implicates the space of Muslim women's theorizing and praxis by containing it within static notions of Islam and Islamic identity."[20] Simply put, this obligation often limits their ability to convey the full complexity and diversity of their experiences and identities, as they are boxed into delivering accounts that meet external expectations of their "authentic" self. In her journal article, "'Good' and 'Bad' Muslim Citizens," Sunaina Maria describes Muslims who question their culture as "native informants" who, as "good Muslims," need "bad Muslims" to stay in business.[21] Those seen as "moderate," "progressive," and aligned with western norms are depicted by their respective western states as "good Muslims," in her argument, gain validation or legitimacy through their opposition to "bad Muslims," those portrayed as extremists, fundamentalists, or those who do not conform to western ideals and values. She characterizes Irshad Manji's portrayal of herself as a "moderate" Muslim in her book as "both profitable and strategic," labeling her writing as "hysterical ranting."[22] Additionally, she describes other secular Muslim feminists as self-centered "native informants" advocating for neoliberalism.[23] In response to such accusations, Sadia Abbas raises important questions:

> Are secular or reformist Muslim feminists allowed to talk about patriarchal structures that draw upon Islam, or are they always to be subjected to disciplining by the metropolitan gaze ... In other words, are Muslims always to remain caught between the distortions, misrepresentations and bigotries of the media-empire-neocon and the high-minded apologias of this configuration's left-liberal critics?[24]

This quote underscores the tension between the right of Muslim feminists to engage in self-critique within their communities and the external pressures that may suppress such discourse. It highlights the problematic extremes that ensnare Muslim voices between conflicting narratives, each with its agenda, which ultimately stifles genuine, nuanced, and independent discourse. In addition, the systematic discrediting of Muslim feminists who critique practices within their communities often uses a specific lexicon aimed at delegitimizing these efforts. This is largely rooted in a post-colonial feminist framework within academia that grapples with multiculturalism and community-imposed standards of female behavior. While an awareness of issues impacting various demographics should always be encouraged, labeling groups critical of their communities as "native informants" is concerning.

If we begin to dismiss and marginalize the voices of Muslim feminists who bring uncomfortable truths to light, "dirty laundry" that we would rather keep concealed, branding them as "native informants"—regardless of the term's intended meaning—we risk excluding a significant portion of Muslim women's perspectives. This is especially detrimental to those who may not be "esteemed scholars" but instead express their views through blogs or self-publishing. By doing so, we effectively silence half of the voices within Muslim feminism, limiting the movement's diversity and depth.

The Impasse of Apologism

Despite the expectation that secular Muslim feminists, due to their alignment with the west, would receive support and amplification from western feminist, academic, and political circles, the reality paints a different picture. Evidence of this discrepancy is seen in the limited coverage or discussion of secular Muslim feminists in academic writings, journalism, or other media forms. According to Angel Rabasa and colleagues, secular Muslims in the Middle East or the diaspora are assumed to be "peripheral figures having no real influence or appeal."[25] While it is accurate that certain "radical" secular Muslim feminists, such as those exemplified by figures like Ayaan Hirsi Ali, who attribute all issues of Muslim women to Islam and align themselves with western politics against the religion, receive recognition and backing from western governments and even far-right groups, the situation is more complex. The broader group of secular Muslim feminists who strive against the homogenization of Muslim women, and as previously detailed, do not fundamentally oppose Islam, face significant marginalization both from western policies and scholarly circles. These overlooked secular feminists do not fit the narrative of being the "good" Muslim opposing the "bad Muslim." As they do not fuel anti-Muslim sentiments and their advocacy does not align with western agendas surrounding the War on Terror, they are often sidelined and viewed with suspicion. Meanwhile, under the guise of respecting and embracing "other" cultures, various entities pressure secular Muslim feminists not to oppose practices that violate basic human rights, including "honor" crimes, forced marriages, and domestic violence. Marieme Hélie-Lucas points out that "progressive" groups in Europe often shy away from endorsing secular Muslim feminism, fearing accusations of Islamophobia and racism, but above all, they are hesitant to challenge Muslim fundamentalists. She notes, "It follows suit that numerous organisations of civil society, including women's rights organisations, who struggle against anti-women and anti-secular ... actions of Christians or Jewish fundamentalism in Europe keep cowardly quiet in front of similar actions of Muslim fundamentalism."[26] By shining a light on these disparities, she prompts reflection on the potential biases and challenges within civil society organizations when navigating complex and sensitive issues related to religious fundamentalism and women's rights advocacy. In the French context, particularly, she argues that the left has compromised secularism by adopting the fundamentalists' viewpoint that social issues should be approached and tackled through the lens of religious discrimination.[27] Traditionally, the left has treated Muslim fundamentalism "as a social movement of the oppressed and the legitimate representative of "Muslims."[28] By essentializing "Muslim culture" without critical evaluation of who defines such cultural norms, the left unwittingly falls into the trap of multiculturalism.

In the realm of social policy and discourse, multiculturalism stands as a beacon of inclusivity, aiming to celebrate diverse cultures and foster social cohesion within pluralistic societies. However, beneath the surface lie debates and critiques that question the efficacy and implications of multicultural approaches. One of the central criticisms is its tendency to essentialize cultures, oversimplifying complex identities into rigid stereotypes. This reductionist approach runs the risk of homogenizing diverse communities, failing to capture the individuality and diversity within cultural groups. Furthermore, the principle of cultural relativism, which I discuss in more detail in the next section, often associated with multiculturalism, raises concerns about the prioritization of cultural sensitivity over universal human rights standards. The reluctance to challenge harmful cultural practices in the name of tolerance can perpetuate inequalities, particularly regarding gender rights and marginalized voices within communities. Gender equality remains a focal point of contention within multicultural frameworks, as the prioritization of cultural norms can sometimes conflict with fundamental rights. Driven by multicultural principles, sections of the left as well as some western feminists often find themselves engaging with Islamist groups or ideologies under the guise of combatting Islamophobia and promoting cultural understanding. Secular voices, particularly secular Muslim feminists, have voiced concerns about the pro-Islamist left's adherence to multicultural principles overshadowing the need to challenge regressive practices within some religious communities. They argue that the pro-Islamist left's association with Islamist groups invites scrutiny regarding alliances that may inadvertently compromise liberal democratic values, such as gender equality and LGBTQ+ rights. Sara Khan, for instance, expresses concerns about the "pro-Islamist left" in the UK, which assumes that Islamist leaders are the arbiters of normative Islam and that their ideology represents all Muslims. This faction is quick to label secular Muslim feminists as Islamophobic. Human rights organizations around the world are largely following the same path as leftists in the name of human rights, religious rights, cultural rights, community rights, and so on. Human rights organizations are thus denying Muslim women their fundamental human rights: freedom of belief, freedom of thought, and freedom of speech. They are denying those who do not choose religion as the main marker of their identity or those who want their faith to remain a private affair, their basic human rights.

In this climate, the term "Islamophobia" has become a contentious point with accusations that it is wielded by Islamists to deflect legitimate criticism of extremism. Nova Daban, in a piece for the National Secular Society, cautions against the manipulative use of the term, expressing concerns that labeling critiques of religious norms as "Islamophobic" could lead to the imposition of a quasi-blasphemy code that undermines free speech and a secular, liberal democracy. This manipulation of the term has had a cascading effect on the discourse around secular Muslim feminists, who have found themselves unjustly labeled as "Islamophobic" for their outspoken criticism of fundamentalist interpretations of Islam that oppress women and girls. CAGE, an advocacy organization based in London that purports to empower communities affected by the War on Terror, denounced the involvement of Southall Black Sisters and Inspire in the gender segregation case discussed in an earlier chapter as "Islamophobic," alleging alignment with the "Prevent" agenda. Meanwhile, the Council of Ex-Muslims of Britain, for which Mariam Namazie serves as a spokesperson, endured an eight-month investigation by Pride in London due to accusations of Islamophobia leveled by East London Mosque and Mend, an organization aiming to facilitate greater participation of British Muslims in local media and politics. Subsequently, Mariam Namazie faced exclusion from Warwick University, harassment from Islamic Society students at Goldsmiths, and the cancellation of her speaking engagement at Trinity College amidst similar allegations.[29] This raises an important question: does challenging fundamentalist interpretations of Islam that violate the rights of Muslim women and girls classify secular Muslim feminists as Islamophobes? The current apprehension among secular Muslim feminists is that instances of abuse, harassment, and intimidation, as asserted by Pragna Patel, are "conveniently ignored by the police and prosecutorial services precisely because the dominant understanding of 'Islamophobia' as defined by fundamentalists and conservatives precludes this."[30]

Patel's assertion that such actions are overlooked due to the prevailing narrative of "Islamophobia" underscores the chilling effect this labeling has on meaningful discourse and activism. Criticizing political Islam, challenging patriarchal and heterosexual structures within Islam, questioning sharia laws and gender segregation, scrutinizing prominent Muslim leaders, and advocating for atheism and secularism are all forms of legitimate free speech that warrant protection. However, amidst an environment of religious intolerance across various faiths, there exists a risk of succumbing to pressure to persecute those who are seen as offending religious sensitivities for fear of being branded as "Islamophobic."

Moreover, the term "Islamophobia" itself is contentious, carrying implications of a rigid and exclusive understanding of Muslim identity that stifles dissent and diversity within Muslim communities. Mariam Namazie's critique of "Muslimness" as a concept of exclusion sheds light on the harmful impact of such narrow definitions, which marginalize voices that do not conform to traditional expectations of Muslim identity. She argues that it tends to exclude anyone not authentically "veiled enough … segregated enough … submissive enough … pro-sharia enough … modest enough."[31] Limiting the definition of Muslimness based on outward appearances or behaviors overlooks the reality faced by women who encounter significant instances of anti-Muslim hatred from various segments of society—spanning the political spectrum from the left and the right to Islamists. These women, despite not conforming to stereotypical perceptions of authentic "Muslim-ness," should not be subjected to unwarranted hostility or discrimination. Along these same lines, western feminists remain divided. Only a few put women's rights first in the hierarchy of human rights, while others seem "not only petrified by the fear of being seen as anti-Islam but also cornered by the longstanding support of the feminist movement for diversity."[32] Some critics argue that feminists—both western and Islamic—who adopt apologetic tones toward Muslim women disapprove of secular Muslim feminists for framing Muslim women as victims. The complexities surrounding "Islamophobia," particularly as it pertains to secular Muslim feminists, underscore the multilayered challenges faced by individuals who navigate the intersections of secularism, feminism, and Muslim identity. The confluence of various forces—left-wing reluctance, right-wing extremism, and Islamist agendas—creates a complex landscape where critical voices advocating for secularism and gender equality are criticized and marginalized. The juxtaposition of political pressures, fear of offense, and the imperative to uphold free expression underscores the intricate path these activists tread in forwarding their vital causes. As if "one could not struggle at the same time against both the traditional extreme right and the new fundamentalist extreme right," as Marieme Hélie-Lucas argues.[33] Ending on a poignant excerpt from Sara Khan's *The Battle for British Islam*, I invite readers to ponder the formidable hurdles facing secular Muslim feminists as they navigate the intricate terrain of "secular," "Muslim," and "feminist" identities. It illuminates the challenges and dilemmas inherent in their advocacy efforts and the need to navigate these complex waters delicately and firmly in the pursuit of equality and justice:

> My work ... has resulted in me experiencing abuse, harassment, threats, online stalking and character assassination ... As a Muslim countering Islamist extremist who justify hatred and violence in the name of my faith, I am accused of being an "Islamophobe." I am a "sell-out" or a "native informant" because I have delivered projects supported by the UK authorities to dissuade young Muslims from joining ISIS. Speaking out ... has led to my being declared an apostate ... When I turned to liberals and some on the Left for solidarity, instead I found painful rejection; some had clearly allied themselves with Islamists. Those on the Right wondered why I even bothered to be a Muslim in the first place when my faith was so "backward." The leading light of New Atheism, Richard Dawkins tweeted in 2014 ...: "You pick your peaceful verses, but ISIS can find verses to justify their vile acts. Why not just give up your faith and join the 21st century?"[34]

The Limits of Relativism (and) Universalism

Amid the surge of migration from the Global South to the Global North, the discourse on the peaceful coexistence among individuals from diverse backgrounds has gained prominence, particularly in western nations. The contemporary debate between universalism and cultural relativism traces back to the inception of the Universal Declaration of Human Rights in 1947, with the acknowledgment that "values and standards are relative to the culture from which they derive."[35] Proponents of cultural rights at the time argued that this statement was not enough to ensure that the declaration's focus on individual-oriented "universal" norms would not clash with local cultural values. Advocates of universal rights, however, assert that the declaration's formulation involved diverse cultural representations, and with numerous countries signing the document, its principles should be viewed as universally applicable. This debate peaked in the 1990s, particularly evident after the Bangkok Declaration produced by a group of Asian nations ahead of the Vienna World Conference on Human Rights. While the declaration claimed to support the universality of human rights, it emphasized self-determination, national sovereignty, and economic development, suggesting that human rights should be considered in the context of national and regional particularities and historical, cultural, and religious backgrounds. Although the argument was explicitly rejected in Vienna, it spurred widespread debate about whether a universal set of human rights could indeed be asserted, leading to varied responses. Some advocated for greater attention to regional human rights instruments, and others criticized the western focus on certain non-western practices labeled as "human rights violations," arguing that this approach lacked an understanding of cultural and social contexts while proponents of universal human rights defended their stance by citing the shared human experience and suffering, critiquing essentialist assertions of cultural differences.[36]

The debate over universalism versus cultural relativism in human rights is particularly contentious concerning women's rights. The depiction of non-western women as needing liberation often perpetuates western superiority, reminiscent of colonial civilizing missions. Uma Narayan points out the tension that while combating western cultural arrogance, silence on women's issues in non-western cultures is not a solution.[37] Dianne Otto highlights that human rights frameworks often reflect colonial paradigms that exclude non-European women's experiences. This imperialistic nature of human rights makes postcolonial critics cautious in addressing discrimination perpetuated under the guise of tradition.[38] This framing of the debate as a binary between the west, perceived as prioritizing autonomy and individual rights, and the non-west, seen as more devoted to culture and tradition, is largely perpetuated by the ongoing legacies of colonialism discussed earlier in this book. In this light, Kiran Grewal argues, efforts to "respect cultural differences" often mirror the demands for adherence to universal (western liberal) human rights. Both sides uncritically accept what are often colonial constructions of non-western culture and tradition, creating an overly homogenized, collectivist non-west that stands in contrast to the diverse and heterogeneous west.[39] A promising development in recent human rights scholarship, Grewal notes, has been the shift from debates over the ontological foundations of human rights toward examining their practical impacts in specific contexts. This shift has been driven by and contributed to a growing body of anthropological and sociological human rights studies. However, these ethnographic interventions have been met with backlash from within the "mainstream" of human rights.

Wary of being accused of siding with imperialism and labeled "Islamophobic" factions of the left, some western feminists choose to adopt a cultural relativist position when it comes to Islam. They view western criticisms of certain Islamic practices as a continuation of colonial power dynamics, perpetuating negative stereotypes and undermining self-determination. They prioritize solidarity with marginalized groups, including Muslims, even if it means overlooking certain cultural practices that might be viewed as problematic. Social justice activists, too, have used cultural relativism to "record discriminatory grievances and demand tolerability and fairness."[40] This position can be problematic, as it can lead to overlooking human rights violations that occur within certain cultures, including those against women, LGBTQ+ individuals, and religious minorities. It also leads to the assumption that Islam and political Islam are the sole representatives of all those who are deemed or labeled Muslims, regardless of their individual experiences and diverse perspectives. When it comes to women's rights, more is at stake because certain societies continue to defend their unequal treatment in the name of preserving culture. The consequence of this approach is the division of women worldwide based on religion, ethnicity, nationality, and other particularisms. This creates a fragmented landscape where women's struggles are pitted against each other, obscuring the commonalities of their experiences and hindering collective action for global justice. Moreover, proponents of cultural relativism, while often opposing violence and discrimination in principle, "often remain silent about it, especially when it is perpetrated by 'others' whom they cannot judge because of cultural differences."[41] This reluctance to criticize harmful practices, even when they violate fundamental human rights, effectively silences the voices of women who suffer under such practices and perpetuates a culture of impunity for those who commit such violations. In her article on the Norwegian Government's policy toward forced marriage, Sherene Razack makes this point very clear:

> I argue that social and political responses to violence against women in Muslim communities have been primarily culturalist. That is, the violence is understood as originating entirely in culture, an approach that obscures the multiple factors that give rise to and sustain the violence. The culturalist approach enables the stigmatization and surveillance of Muslim communities.[42]

As a feminist and a woman with Muslim origins, Razack states, this situation leaves her in "an impossible bind."[43] She questions how one can address and confront patriarchal violence in Muslim migrant communities without resorting to oversimplified cultural interpretations and without unintentionally encouraging stigmatization, surveillance, and control measures.[44] To truly move in a different direction, it is necessary to step beyond the confines of cultural relativism. Simply labeling Muslim women solely by their religious identity neglects the long-standing battle that Muslim women have fought against patriarchy for over a century. Cultural relativists, in their resistance to universal principles, often end up aligning themselves with nationalist, Islamist, and nativist viewpoints, interpreting the resistance of Muslim women as a reflection of "western ideologies" incompatible with Islam and not inherent to local customs. Mojab and ElKassam argue:

> It is understandable, then, why academics and activists in the cultural relativist position prefer silence or fail to condemn violence against women of the "other" culture. They are more concerned about being labeled "racist," "Orientalist," "ethnocentric," "essentialist" or "neocolonialist" than in being able to deeply challenge their own thoughts on the inter dynamics of diverse and even contradictory factors in understanding and explaining the diversity of the role of Islam as a religion and a culture in women's lives.[45]

Cultural relativism, while well-intentioned, presents several problematic aspects. One glaring issue is the internal inconsistency inherent in many of its formulations, leading to tautological statements incapable of providing a cohesive framework for understanding cultural differences. This results in a confused landscape where the boundaries between respect for diverse cultures and condoning harmful practices become blurred. Let's take, for example, the erection of a sixteen feet steel statue of a woman in an Islamic veil in Birmingham, UK, with a statement at its base saying "The Strength of the *hijab*," amidst global mourning for Mahsa Amini, a young woman who died in the custody of Iran's "morality police" for not wearing *hijab* "correctly," raises critical questions about cultural relativism, women's rights, and the complex relationship between Islam and the west. On the one hand, the statue can be interpreted as a symbol of tolerance and respect for diversity, recognizing the right of Muslim women to choose to wear *hijab* as an expression of their faith. On the other hand, in the context of the ongoing struggle of countless women around the world who face oppression for defying compulsory *hijab* laws, the statue appears tone-deaf and insensitive. It risks silencing the voices of those who oppose *hijab* as a symbol of patriarchal control and erasing the experiences of women who have suffered under its imposition. The simplistic assumption that *all* Muslim women support *hijab* plays directly into Islamist narratives that seek to control women's bodies and choices. It ignores the diversity of perspectives within Muslim communities, where countless women are actively challenging patriarchal interpretations of their faith and advocating for their right to choose what they wear. This monolithic representation further marginalizes those who defy *hijab* and undermines their courageous struggle for autonomy and self-determination. The statue's erection also reflects a concerning trend of ignorance and an unwillingness to think critically about religious practices that are at odds with democratic values. By shying away from a nuanced and critical examination of *hijab* and its implications for women's rights, the statue risks perpetuating harmful stereotypes and overlooking the complex realities of Muslim women's experiences.

However, the universalist approach also poses limitations for Muslim women striving for equal rights. By overlooking cultural diversity, it tends to oversimplify the experiences of Muslim women, portraying them solely as victims of patriarchal and misogynistic cultures who require saving through the lens of "universal human rights." Though some scholars are making efforts to adopt more balanced stances that recognize both the value of human rights and the importance of culture, intergovernmental discussions and many UN bodies are primarily dominated by extreme perspectives from culturalists, universalists, or a mix of both.[46] How much longer must feminists, like those mentioned earlier, endure abuse, harassment, and bullying just for speaking out against outdated and unfair religious and cultural practices? In countries with a Muslim majority, such as Syria, Algeria, and Kazakhstan, there have been instances where full-face veils (*niqābs* and *burqas*) have been prohibited in specific situations under the argument that they pose security risks and symbolize discrimination against women. Interestingly, in western societies, suggesting similar actions can swiftly result in accusations of Islamophobia. A significant dilemma arises when many human rights activists and western feminists view religion as inherently patriarchal. Being forced to make a choice between Islam and human rights, or between identifying as Muslim and feminist, only serves to divide us for political reasons. In reality, we, as Muslim women, a diverse group with varying beliefs, styles of dress, and lifestyles, embody the modern interpretation of what it means to be Muslim in the twenty-first century.

Of course, far-right terrorism targeting Muslims in many countries, such as the oppression of Muslims in Xinjiang, China since 2014, the vilification (mock public beheading and pig roasting aimed at offending Muslims) in Australia in 2015, the Rohingya Genocide since 2016, Quebec City Mosque Shooting in 2017, the Bayonne Mosque Shooting in France in 2019, and the Christchurch

Mosque shooting in New Zealand in 2020, should not be tolerated in any way. Equally, human rights violations that take place in Muslim-majority countries in the name of Islam, such as the so-called honor killings which continue to take place in Jordan, Iraq, Kuwait, and Palestine, with the authorities failing to take action to prosecute the perpetrators, the failure to define domestic violence, criminalize marital rape and child marriage in Iran, the failure to provide protection for women and girls from rape and other sexual and gender-based violence as well as killings, torture and unlawful deprivation of liberty by militias, armed groups, and other non-state actors in Libya should be strongly condemned. Furthermore, the backlash faced by many secular Muslim feminists for critiquing such actions in a manner divergent from mainstream expectations, under the guise of apologism, cultural relativism, or religious fundamentalism, should not be endorsed. Grewal calls for a more nuanced and critical understanding of human rights that takes into account both universal and particular perspectives. But finding a balance between respecting cultural diversity and upholding universal human rights is a complex challenge. This requires engaging in respectful dialogue with diverse perspectives, including those within Muslim communities, to understand the complexities of cultural practices and their impact on individuals, situating critiques of specific practices within a broader framework of human rights and social justice, avoiding generalizations and recognizing the diversity of interpretations within Islam, and empowering voices within Muslim communities who advocate for reform and challenge harmful practices, fostering dialogue and change from within.

Solidarity across Difference Is Possible!

Movements led by women have a long history of effectively fueling democratic change. This is evident in various periods of history and still holds true today. In Argentina, the #NiUnaMenos (Not One Less) movement led by women and girls seeking justice for femicide exerted considerable influence. In 2019, this movement directly prompted the government of President Alberto Fernández to set up a new Ministry of Women, Gender, and Diversity, marking a pivotal step toward progress. Thanks to the tenacity of Argentinian women in raising their voices, the country has set on a path toward change. In Chile, women have played prominent roles in the rights movement, both pre and post the Pinochet dictatorship. The current feminist movement, particularly advocating for abortion rights, draws strong inspiration from the #NiUnaMenos movement.

Their activism bore fruit as legal protections for abortion were included in a new constitution drafted in 2022 to replace the long-standing Pinochet-era constitution. Although a plebiscite rejected the constitutional redraft in September 2022, women persist as vanguards of rights protests, keeping the discourse alive. In Iran, women continue to march for their rights amidst challenging circumstances. Hashtags like #SayHerName, #Mahsa_Amini, and #Jina_Amini served as poignant images of Amini's motionless figure. During her funeral, the powerful chant of "Jin, Jiyan, Azadî" (Woman, Life, Freedom) reverberated among the gathered women, who spontaneously shed their headscarves, an act that struck a chord with many across Iran. This act of solidarity prompted more women to join, removing their *hijabs*, cutting their hair, and setting fire to their headscarves as acts of mourning and indignation. The collective expression of grief and anger not only triggered a surge in gender consciousness and emotions within the populace but also galvanized a movement that mobilized masses to the streets in a bold attempt to challenge and dismantle the ruling Islamic Republic regime in Iran. Women of diverse backgrounds, both veiled and unveiled, united shoulder to shoulder, reveling in solidarity, love, and happiness as they assert ownership of their bodies and cast off the shackles of shame. Proud graffiti decorating the walls boldly declares, "No matter how much you try to harm me, I will not be wounded; I will keep sprouting."[47] A notable moment in this uprising is the vocal endorsement of the feminist movement by men, particularly those from working-class, ethnic, and diverse religious backgrounds.[48] Shirin Assa describes this solidarity as

> refusing to be mere victims, women in Iran assert their agency and position a "relational essence" (Zack 2005, 8) between themselves, which not only brings educated, poor, devout and veiling women together, but also transcends hegemonic values, showcasing how commonalit-ies bridge differences (Hancock 2016; Yuval-Davis 1997).

A year after the emergence of the movement, the outcome remains uncertain in the face of brutal repression from the clerical establishment and its conservative allies. Nonetheless, the regime's aura of invincibility—and women's marginalization from politics—has been categorically disrupted.[49] Even as the security services try to crack down on protesters, the ongoing struggle against the patriarchal regime persists. The voices of women demanding freedom of expression, bodily autonomy, and political participation have already begun reshaping Iran's societal and political landscape. This burgeoning challenge posed by women's voices is becoming a substantial threat to the legitimacy of the Iranian theocracy. While skeptics may point to the regime's past tactics of violence and censorship to quash dissent, this new wave of protests has captured global attention, amplifying the fight for women's rights on Iranian streets and inspiring women worldwide to advocate for their own freedoms and equality. These strides have been managed, despite the divide between Islamic and secular feminists. By focusing on shared goals such as freedom of speech, bodily autonomy, and political engagement, Iranian women could unite their voices and amplify their demands, showcasing the power of solidarity in driving social and political change. This is not to undermine other barriers to protest; for example, the financial strain of detaining a provider presents a substantial sacrifice, particularly amid uncertainties surrounding the movement's potential for effecting tangible change. But highlighting the power of solidarity across difference has the potential to unite women within diverse backgrounds challenging the gendered apparatus of the Islamic regime. We must foster a spirit of solidarity, transcending competition for leadership roles and resisting opportunistic external influences. The core principles of the Woman, Life, Freedom movement—humanism, existentialism, egalitarianism, liberation, inclusivity, and pluralism—should serve as our guiding light as we strive to overcome the global patriarchy that continues to dictate our lives.

The debate over Islamists and secularists' roles in Muslim women's rights is often marred by extreme viewpoints. Faith-based and secular Muslim feminists clash on issues like veiling, with many secular feminists viewing it as an undeniable example of religious fundamentalism. Yet, not all faith-based activists see it as purely religious. Scholars also note the veil's multifaceted social and political meanings across diverse contexts. Joan Wallach Scott frames the European *hijab* ban within an anti-racist lens, connecting it to broader Islamophobia, Xenophobia, and the War on Terror's focus on Muslim women's bodies. However, her French context, where *hijab* opposes secular values, leads her to view those opposing the ban as exercising agency through their choice to wear it. This overlooks potential coercion, especially for young girls wearing headscarves. While acknowledging the existence of patriarchy in Muslim contexts, Scott hastily dismisses its severity by comparing it to the French case of coercing women to remove *hijab*. Amidst prevalent multicultural policies and discussions of immigration, gender, and sexuality in the west, the feminists studied here offer a voice that refuses to speak from a subaltern position aspiring to move to the center, where it could reconstruct an ideal that transcends the strict separation between the modern, secular, western world and the cultural, Islamic voice. Their position avoids cultural relativism and apologia. They neither celebrate *hijab* as a form of "empowerment" nor strongly condemn its forced removal. They wish to be integrated into "an open, liberal space." However, despite their adamant rejection of imposed narratives, they continue to be viewed as victims or villains by various groups. This discrepancy between their self-perception and external perceptions hinders their ability to find solidarity amongst themselves and with others. They are forced to choose between religiously defined communities or nations and universalistic narratives of feminism and gender. This ignores the interconnectedness of gender, power, agency, and desire, crucial for any meaningful debate. By selectively acknowledging and celebrating specific subjectivities over others, we deny the possibility of shared desires for freedom and autonomy among diverse women.

While it is unsurprising that many postcolonial and third world feminists emphasize solidarity based on shared assumptions, arising from their unique historical connections and disconnections, this idea can make it difficult to build solidarity on other grounds. Sara Salem argues that true solidarity requires difficult conversations and an understanding of unequal power relations. We must move beyond simplistic notions of universal sisterhood and acknowledge the diverse challenges that separate women, but without viewing these differences as insurmountable barriers to solidarity. As Chandra Mohanty argues, solidarity should be based on a recognition that women's oppression worldwide could be both comparable and specific as it is constantly shaped by local histories and politics. However, Ella Shohat reminds us in *Talking Visions* of the reality of "multicultural feminisms," where "connections, borders, and passports" under surveillance is a constant reminder that some connections are easier to make than others in a world "simultaneously undergoing globalization and fragmentation."[50] So, how can feminist scholarship redefine the boundaries of transnational feminist solidarity when its terms are so contested? Amanda Lock Swarr and Richa Nagar emphasize that transnational feminist studies is a "necessary unstable field" that must continuously question its definition to remain relevant.[51] They argue that the focus on individual activists should not overshadow the collective nature of activism. Along these lines, they suggest that transnational feminist collaboration must be critically interrogated as we work and that this should be done with the primary purpose of generating new debates that may bring together feminists from various locations. By recognizing connections without homogenizing diversity, we can challenge dominant narratives that portray *all* Muslim women as victims yet do not position them as a single simplistic identity—it's not a flipside of Muslim women are not oppressed but liberated. Kiran Grewal writes:

> It is we who assert a commitment to both anti-racism and feminism that must find appropriate ways to respond to [contested voices] in order not to fall into the very trap of doing what we have so long worked to critique: silencing a different and challenging voice.[52]

Grewal's quote emphasizes the interconnectedness of anti-racism and feminism, rejecting the separation of these struggles, acknowledging the existence of contested voices and the importance of engaging with them constructively. In addition to those appeals, I advocate for a nuanced understanding of the ways in which Muslim feminists engage with diverse discourses in their daily lives. I believe transnational feminist approaches can capitalize on the political potential of "affective dissonance"—the discrepancy between self-perception and external perception—to forge a new understanding of solidarity. This can foster a feminist movement striving for political transformation and opening avenues for solidarity across boundaries. I draw on Clare Hemmings' concept of "affective dissonance" as a distinction between embodied self and expected social self. As she suggests, affective dissonance can be processed in different ways. It may be suppressed, or it could be "utilised to justify political action."[53] Judith Lakämper further argues that the dissonance arising from a mismatch between individual experience and available identity models can trigger a desire to influence these dominant narratives. In the context of this work, the "onto-epistemological gap" that these feminists experience may "fulfil the premise for political mobilisation,"[54] a potential they themselves seem to be unaware of. By shifting our focus from identity politics to modes of engagement that originate from "affective dissonance," we can begin to bridge this gap and build solidarity. Hemmings emphasizes the importance of moving from "affective dissonance" to "affective solidarity," acknowledging that dissonance itself is crucial for feminist politics to emerge. This realization can become the basis for seeking solidarity with others who share similar experiences of being misperceived. Through recognizing not only differences but also commonalities—a shared sense of "having had enough" with how we are perceived—feminists can develop mutual understanding and strengthen the basis for a collective struggle. By collectively acknowledging their shared experience of dissonance, they can spark a solidarity "premised not on a false idea of homogeneity ... but on th[is] shared knowledge of each other."[55] In other words, rather than being the enemy of solidarity, difference may become the foundation for building a collective. Therefore, instead of viewing difference as an obstacle to solidarity, we can embrace it as the foundation for building a collective feminist movement—one that recognizes its collective strength in the face of misrepresentation and strives for political transformation.

While most feminists experience affective dissonance, evidenced by their narratives of being misunderstood, misrepresented, or both, many often neglect that this experience is not unique to them. This neglect of shared experiences can lead to narratives of alienation and isolation, undermining the potential for solidarity. Clare Hemmings acknowledges this possibility but argues against it being the inevitable outcome. Ignoring that all feminists, regardless of their ideological stance, experience a gap between discursive constructions and lived realities perpetuates the very binary of "us" versus "them" that they reject. If Muslim feminists, across their diverse perspectives and locations, recognize this shared experience of dissonance, they can harness it to build affective solidarity. This requires acknowledging the commonality of feeling misunderstood and misrepresented, transcending the limitations of group identity and its impact on solidarity. As Chandra Mohanty urges, we must seek a concept that allows women to express solidarity despite their varied experiences of oppression.[56] Given the ongoing debates around solidarity in transnational spaces, group identity continues to heavily influence the potential for solidarity among women. However, by recognizing and embracing the shared experience of affective dissonance, we can move beyond these limitations and build a collective feminist movement that is truly inclusive and transformative. Judith Lakämper argues, "A feminist solidarity that draws on experiences of affective dissonance could derive its sense of belonging not from the commitment to an ideal ... but from an investment in the conversation with others who struggle in similar, yet also different, ways"[57] with the encounters of discrepancy between how they perceive themselves and how others perceive them. Postcolonial and transnational feminists, thus, should take into account the turn to affect, recognizing its crucial role in analyzing experiences of discontent and their systemic origins. Black feminists have long championed the broad tradition of affect in their work, addressing its historical neglect of questions of race and their crucial contributions.[58] While currently being called for by western feminism, affective dissonance can pave the way for greater understanding and solidarity among diverse groups, including third world, postcolonial, Islamic feminists, and those who do not identify with any specific label. By highlighting the significance of affect in creative and political lives, we emphasize the emotional labor that is often undervalued and unsupported. Muslim feminists, by acknowledging their shared experiences of affective dissonance despite their ideological differences and modes of activism, can open up new possibilities. This may eventually boost their capacity for creating a social movement strengthened, rather than diminished, by diversity and disagreement. Solidarity and sameness are not the same thing. As Audre Lorde writes in *Sister Outsider*: "You do not have to be me … for us to fight alongside each other."[59] Starting with the realization that affective dissonance is just the first step on a long journey toward true solidarity, we can chart a path toward a solidarity that confronts and heals from the injustices that weigh heavily upon us. As M. Jaqui Alexander powerfully reminds us in *Pedagogies of Crossing*,

> We are not born women of color. We become women of color. In order to become women of color, we would need to become fluent in each other's histories, to resist and unlearn an impulse to claim first oppression, most-devastating oppression, one-of-a-kind oppression, defying comparison oppression. We would have to unlearn an impulse that allows mythologies about each other to replace knowing about one another. We would need to cultivate a way of knowing in which we direct our social, cultural, psychic, and spiritually marked attention on each other. We cannot afford to cease yearning for each other's company.[60]

Concluding Remarks

This book draws on my two decades of experience as a feminist activist, researcher in renowned NGOs, and facilitator of dialogues with trailblazing founders and leaders of diverse organizations across Europe and the Middle East. It draws on a plethora of autobiographies and sociological works penned by and about secular Muslim feminists worldwide. My intention is not to perpetuate binary divisions or simplistic oppositions. Instead, I have deliberately disregarded the myriad of local variations and struggles to illuminate the intricate complexities, embracing contradictions as inherent parts of the narrative. This work is an unapologetic response to those who claim westerners instrumentalize Muslim women's emancipation to attack Islam. It is true, but I remind them, Islamists have wielded the same tool in their own battles against the west. In this book, I challenge the uncritical celebration of Muslim women's religious agency by scholars like Saba Mahmood, who present it as an indigenous alternative to western secularism. I argue that such celebrations inadvertently accommodate patriarchal and conservative aims, ultimately hindering women's true emancipation. Within the global context, the secular Muslim feminist agenda has been co-opted by the far-right, whose anti-Muslim sentiments masquerade a "concern" for the subjugated Muslim woman. This hypocrisy fuels the reluctance of the liberal left to support secular Muslim feminists who condemn Islamism, while readily extending such support against other forms of religious fundamentalism. This phenomenon mirrors the hesitation to condemn Israel or Zionist politics, driven by the fear of being labeled anti-Semitic.

I have been writing this book while women in Gaza, a land enduring under relentless siege and suffering immense hardship, navigate a perilous landscape, confronting not just the systemic challenges faced by women in other Muslim societies but also the brutal realities of a conflict-ridden zone. Their stories offer a stark reminder of the intersections of gender, faith, and geopolitical conflict, amplifying the urgency for solidarity and support. The women of Gaza, like their sisters across the Muslim world, grapple with patriarchal traditions, societal expectations, and the complexities of religious interpretations. They bear the brunt of war, displacement, and economic devastation, facing a daily struggle for survival amid ongoing violence and instability. Despite the despair, their resilience shines through—they are educators, entrepreneurs, artists, and activists—their voices refusing to be silenced. Their narratives intertwine with the broader themes explored throughout this book—the tension between secularism and religious interpretations, the struggle against fundamentalist forces, and the yearning for self-determination and equality. But the quest for solidarity with women in Gaza confronts a complex reality. While the international community recognizes the gravity of their plight, a pervasive fear of being labeled anti-Semitic often clouds the narrative, hindering crucial support and amplifying the challenges they face. This fear stems from the complex geopolitical landscape surrounding the Israeli-Palestinian conflict, where accusations of anti-Semitism are frequently weaponized to silence criticism of Israel's policies. Consequently, western entities, organizations, and individuals often tread cautiously, fearing repercussions that could jeopardize their legitimacy or expose them to public backlash. This apprehension stifles critical dialogue and undermines efforts to provide comprehensive support for women in Gaza, whose voices are often muted amidst the cacophony of political agendas and external interests. Amid this complex landscape, it is imperative to remember that supporting women in Gaza is not synonymous with taking sides in a political conflict. It is a fundamental human rights issue that transcends geopolitical tensions. These women are not pawns in a political game; they are human beings enduring immense suffering and yearning for a life free from violence, oppression, and discrimination. To truly support women in Gaza, we must disentangle the narratives of anti-Semitism (and Islamophobia) from the legitimate pursuit of justice and equality. We must reject the weaponization of such accusations and prioritize the human rights of those caught in the crossfire.

The narratives recounted in the second chapter of this book demonstrate that a close examination of individual experiences reveals crucial points of connection and convergence. These stories, deeply personal and meaningful, merge into a powerful collective when considered together. The patterns that emerge from these situated and particular narratives—the repetition of general themes, the challenges of validating emotions, and the continuous negotiation of belonging and meaning-making—transcend individual experiences and forge a shared narrative. This stands as a resounding response to those who dismiss secular Muslim feminists as insignificant. As Charles Tilly argues, political identities are "always, everywhere relational and collective,"[1] even when they are articulated by individuals, for they are inescapably embedded in the social fabric. Identities are constantly in flux, continuously shaping themselves "through the combined processes of being, belonging and longing to belong."[2] In the words of Petra

Munro, "how individuals construct their stories, the tensions, the contradictions and the fictions, signifies the very power relations against which we write our lives."[3] In other words, our individual narratives, shaped by the "toolkit" of cultural constructs available to us, express our positions in relation to dominant narratives. Francesca Polletta argues:

> Hegemony operates not by way of a single canonical story repeated over and over again in identical form, but rather by way of many stories that are quite different from each other but navigate similarly between the poles of familiar symbolic oppositions. Against that backdrop, stories that challenge those oppositions are either disbelieved or assimilated to more familiar stories.[4]

Inspired by Francesca Polletta, I argue that the credibility of narratives stems from their inherent "ubiquity and diversity." Narrative power, therefore, emerges from its complexity and the multifaceted experiences it captures. Women who openly denounce harmful practices within their communities while critiquing western policies that fuel their oppression often find themselves ostracized, distrusted by both sides. Shedding light on their narratives unveils the intricate and nuanced realities of their lives, challenging simplistic generalizations and offering a more authentic and holistic portrayal. The bulk of academic research on Muslim women's lives has often homogenized their experiences, erasing the rich pool of diversity and individual stories. This book challenges that approach, arguing that while experiences may share some similarities, they are ultimately multifaceted and richly textured. Uncovering these complex narratives requires attuning our ears to the unique stories each woman carries. Through the act of listening, we can better support these discursive spaces and open avenues for new knowledge and political possibilities. By delving into the nuances and complexities of women's discursive resistance, we position ourselves to advocate for liberatory changes in policies and practices. Polletta's work brilliantly bridges my research interests in narrative and activism, revitalizing and reconceptualizing their interconnectedness. It emphasizes that stories can equally mobilize and fail to mobilize, their success or failure often hinging on the storytelling context: "who tells them, when, for what purpose and in what setting."[5] However, Polletta's keen focus rests on the inherent ambiguity and openness to interpretation of narratives. We often perceive stories as unique, told by exceptional individuals in extraordinary circumstances. Yet, we also recognize their universality, told by everyone, everywhere. Ultimately, Polletta argues for embracing this inherent ambiguity of narrative and activism rather than seeking to resolve it.

My intention here is not to make a case for enlightenment, secularism, or modernity as the definitive solution. I acknowledge that not all Muslim women embrace or desire universal human rights and women's rights guidelines grounded in secular principles. Instead, I argue that secular resistance can provide a strategic interlude, disrupting the ways tools of control are wielded. It marks a return to the feminist discourse of the early Muslim activists (c. 1930s), predating the rise of secular and religious ideologies that polarized the cultural and political spheres. This return necessitates questioning the foundational ideologies of both secular and Islamic feminism, beginning with a critical rereading of secularism. It also entails exploring the relationship between religion and the legal system within the specific social, political, and cultural contexts of each country. These contexts possess their own distinct dynamics and should not be ignored. In my vision, secular Muslim feminism prioritizes the protection of individual freedom of religion, including the right to develop personal religious interpretations. It de-emphasizes identity politics, focusing instead on issues of mutual concern to both secular and religious factions, such as political representation, education, employment, and practical matters. This approach embraces the complexity of culture, recognizing religion as a vital component without confining culture solely to the realm of religion. Chapter Six of this book underscores the significance of secularism as a framework for enabling choices, safeguarding ethical coexistence, and promoting religious harmony and political stability. While acknowledging the challenges to secularism, particularly its perceived imposition of western values and the difficulty of separating religion from individual experiences, I draw on Homi Bhaba's concept of "subaltern secularism," rooted in the diverse historical and cultural contexts of multicultural societies. This approach recognizes the evolving nature of religions and seeks to support marginalized communities, including women from minority backgrounds, in navigating a multi-faith world where male community leaders often hold dominant authority. The "secular spaces" I aspire to see one day are spaces guaranteeing equal rights, freedom of choice, and unfettered self-determination for all, regardless of religious affiliation, while acknowledging diverse experiences and promoting solidarity through the acknowledgment and respect for differences.

As I pen these concluding words, a remarkable question pierces the air: "Who are you writing about?," asks a bright young Iranian student, my resilient compatriot. I offer names of Iranian feminists who have carved their paths in the struggle for justice and equality. Yet, her recognition remains elusive. As the name Masih Alinejad falls from my lips, her response is swift: "I hate her, she's a mouthpiece." "This," I counter, "is precisely what they want you to believe, my dear." In this final reflection, I lay bare the essence of this book's journey. We (I say "we" not to homogenize but to acknowledge the commonalities of our struggles), Muslim women activists, particularly those with secular aspirations, tread a treacherous path. Each step is fraught with challenges, demanding careful navigation. Engaging with the west often invites suspicion, accusations of betrayal, and the specter of national security threats. Those forced to flee their homelands, like myself, have no choice but to engage with the west. By doing so, they are often branded as traitors for seeking refuge and advocating for change. Am I a traitor for choosing a western publisher to amplify the voices of feminists who are often ignored or dismissed by feminists, academic, and activist circles? This narrative, meticulously crafted by those who seek to silence dissent, aims to discredit those who challenge the status quo. They, the fundamentalists yearning for a caliphate and the west exploiting women's liberation for neocolonial ambitions, benefit from stifling our voices. They seek to paint those like Alinejad as mouthpieces, traitors, to dissuade young women like my beautiful student, from demanding their rightful place in the world. While international support, encompassing moral, political, and technological aid, plays a vital role, the current struggle for solidarity and gender equality among diverse Muslim women can only be truly transformed by the women themselves. Women, particularly young women, are the primary agents of change. They are the embodiment of hope, the driving force for a brighter future.

I urge postcolonial feminists to reject the reduction of real Muslim women's narratives to mere tools for ideological critiques. To truly understand Muslim women's agency, desires, and subjectivities, we must shatter the persistent binary frameworks that constrain our understanding of Muslim women, both within Muslim-majority societies and Muslim communities in the west. The way forward demands introspection, candid dialogue, and a concerted effort to identify more effective ways to support Muslim women globally. Let us embrace this challenge with open minds, unwavering solidarity, and a shared commitment to forging a world where all women, regardless of faith, background, or identity, can exercise their agency and claim their rightful place in the world.

Notes

Preface

1 Neil Gross, "Charles Tilly and American Pragmatism," *American Sociologist* 41, no. 4 (2010): 351.
2 Nira Yuval-Davis, "Intersectionality and Feminist Politics," *European Journal of Women's Studies* 13, no.1 (2006): 201.
3 Petra Munro, *Subject to Fiction: Women Teachers' Life History Narratives and the Cultural Politics of Resistance* (Buckingham, PA: Open University Press, 1998), 5.
4 Francesca Polletta, *It Was Like a Fever: Storytelling in Protest and Politics* (Chicago: University of Chicago Press, 2006), 52.
5 Ibid., 3.

1

1 Hamid Dabashi is a renowned Iranian American scholar, public intellectual, and literary critic. Born in 1951, he currently holds the Hagop Kevorkian Professor of Iranian Studies and Comparative Literature at Columbia University. Dabashi is a prominent figure in postcolonial studies, critiquing western hegemony and its impact on non-western cultures. Dabashi draws on Islamic philosophical and theological traditions to engage with contemporary issues. He argues for a reinterpretation of Islam that is compatible with democratic values and human rights. Dabashi's outspoken views and provocative critiques have generated controversy. He has been accused of anti-Semitism and of romanticizing the Iranian regime.
2 Hamid Dabashi, "Native Informers and the Making of the American Empire," *Al-Ahram Weekly Online* (2006), available at https://www.meforum.org/campus-watch/10542/native-informers-and-the-making-of-the-american.
3 Jasmin Zine, Lisa K. Taylor, and Hilary E. Davis, Reading Muslim Women and Muslim Women Reading Back: Transnational Feminist Reading Practices, Pedagogy and Ethical Concerns," *Intercultural Education* 18, no. 4 (2007): 271.
4 See Hind Elhinnawy, "The Role of Difference in Feminist Transnational Solidarity: Secular Muslim Feminists in the United Kingdom and France," *International Feminist Journal of Politics* 25, no. 4 (2023): 593–612.

5 Rebecca Durand and Myk Zeitlin, "Women against Fundamentalism: Stories of Dissent and Solidarity," *Feminist Dissent* 1 (2013): 132.
6 For examples of scholars presenting the Muslim woman as an agent of her liberation, see Dunya Maumoon, "Islamism and Gender Activism: Muslim Women's Quest for Autonomy," *Journal of Muslim Minority Affairs* 19, no. 2 (1999); Saba Mahmood, *Politics of Piety: The Islamic Revival and the Feminist Subject* (Princeton: Princeton University Press, 2005); Sherine Hafez, *An Islam of Her Own: Reconsidering Religion and Secularism in Women's Islamic Movements* (New York: New York University Press, 2011); Anabel Inge, *The Making of a Salafi Muslim Woman: Paths to Conversion* (New York: Oxford University Press, 2017). For examples of scholars presenting Muslim women as victims of their patriarchal societies, see Maria Rosa Cutrufelli, *Women of Africa: Roots of Oppression* (London: Zed Books, 1984); Emily Eden, *Up the Country: Letters from India* (London: Virago Press, 1983).
7 See Anouar El Younssi, "Maajid Nawaz, Irshad Manji, and the Call for a Muslim Reformation," *Politics, Religion & Ideology* 19, no. 3 (2018): 305–22.
8 Amna Akbar and Rupal Oza, "'Muslim Fundamentalism' and Human Rights in the Age of Terror and Empire," in *Gender, National Security, and Counter-Terrorism: Human Rights Perspectives*, ed. Margaret L. Satterthwaite and Jayne Huckerby (London: Routledge, 2013), 152.
9 Mahmood Mamdani, "Good Muslim, Bad Muslim: A Political Perspective on Culture and Terrorism," *American Anthropologist* 104, no. 3 (September 2002): 766.
10 Sukhwant Dhaliwal and Nira Yuval-Davis, *Women against Fundamentalism: Stories of Dissent and Solidarity* (London: Lawrence and Wishart, 2014).
11 Azza Karam, *Women, Islamists and the State: Contemporary Feminisms in Egypt* (London: Palgrave Macmillan, 1998), 13.
12 Ibid., 5–6.
13 Margot Badran, *Feminists, Islam and the Nation* (Princeton: Princeton University Press, 1995), 246.
14 Ernest Renan (1823–1892) was a French philosopher, historian, and orientalist known for his influential work on the history of religions, including Islam. Renan's views on Islamic reformation were rooted in his belief in rationalism and progress. He saw Islam as a religion that needed to adapt to modernity and undergo a reformation similar to what Christianity had experienced.
15 Ignaz Goldziher (1850–1921) was a Hungarian orientalist and scholar of Islam who made significant contributions to the study of Islamic history and culture. Goldziher's work on Islamic reformation focused on the historical development of Islamic law and theology. He emphasized the need for a reinterpretation of Islamic texts and traditions to reconcile the teachings of Islam with modern values and principles.

16 Muhammad Abduh (1849–1905) was an influential Egyptian Islamic scholar and reformer who sought to modernize Islamic thought by blending traditional Islamic principles with contemporary values and scientific progress. A disciple of Jamal al-Din al-Afghani, Abduh championed educational reforms, rationality, and the practice of ijtihad (independent interpretation of Islamic law). As the Grand Mufti of Egypt, his work significantly impacted the modernization of Islamic societies and inspired future generations of scholars.

17 Rashid Rida (1865–1935), a disciple of Muhammad Abduh, was a prominent Islamic scholar and reformer who significantly influenced modern Islamic thought and activism. Through his influential journal *al-Manar*, he advocated for a return to the *Qur'an* and *Sunnah*, challenging traditional interpretations and promoting a more progressive approach. Rida emphasized Pan-Islamism and social reform, believing that Islam could address contemporary challenges. His legacy is celebrated for his contributions to Islamic scholarship, activism, and the advancement of Muslim unity.

18 See Osman Bakar, "Islam and the Challenge of Diversity and Pluralism: Must Islam Reform Itself?," *ICR Journal* 1, no. 1 (2009): 55–73.

19 Jarmila Drozdíková, "Review Article: Progressive Muslims," *Asian and African Studies* 14, no. 1 (2005): 83.

20 Omid Safi (ed.), *Progressive Muslims: On Justice, Gender, and Pluralism* (Oxford: Oneworld, 2003), 18.

21 Drozdíková, "Review Article: Progressive Muslims," 84.

22 See Faisal Gazi, "The First Muslim Secularist," *The Guardian* (2009), available at https://www.theguardian.com/commentisfree/belief/2009/apr/09/religion-islam-secularism-egypt.

23 Diane Reay, "Future Directions in Difference Research: Recognizing and Responding to Difference in the Research Process," in *Handbook of Feminist Research: Theory and Praxis*, ed. Sharlene Nagy Hesse-Biber (London: Sage, 2012), 628.

24 Marianne H Marchand, "The Future of Gender and Development after 9/11: Insights from Postcolonial Feminism and Transnationalism," *Third World Quarterly* 30, no. 5 (2009): 921.

25 Tina Miller, Maxine Birch, Melanie Mauthner and Julie Jessop (eds.), *Ethics in Qualitative Research* (London: Sage, 2012), 6.

2

1 See Yasmine Mohamed's bio on her webpage https://www.yasminemohammed.com/bio.

2 Ibid.

3 See https://twitter.com/i/events/1079102742755303424.
4 An interview with Masih Alinejad, "Iranian Influential Women: Masih Alinejad (1976–Present)," *Iranwire* (2023), available at https://iranwire.com/en/women/120868-iranian-influential-women-masih-alinejad-1976-present/.
5 Irshad Manji, *Don't Label Me: How to Do Diversity without Inflaming the Culture Wars* (New York: St. Martin's Press, 2019), xiii.
6 Ibid., 30.
7 Ibid., 31.
8 Ibid., 33.
9 See Nandini Archer, "Muslim Women Are Stuck between Islamophobes and Islamic Fundamentalists," *Open Democracy* (2019), available at https://www.opendemocracy.net/en/5050/muslim-women-stuck-between-islamophobes-and-islamic-fundamentalists/.
10 Ibid.
11 Maryam Namazie, "Mariam Namazie," in *Islamophobia: An Anthology of Concerns*, ed. Emma Webb (London: Civitas, 2019), 77.
12 See for example, Leila Mouri and Kristin Soraya Batmanghelichi, "Can the Secular Iranian Women's Activist Speak?: Caught between Political Power and the Islamic Feminist," in *Gender and Sexuality in Muslim Cultures*, ed. Gul Ozyegin (Aldershot: Ashgate, 2015) and Afia S. Zia, *Faith and Feminism in Pakistan: Religious Agency or Secular Autonomy* (Brighton: Sussex Academic Press, 2018).
13 Amy Gutmann, *Identity in Democracy* (Princeton: Princeton University Press, 2003).
14 See Julia Serran, "Prejudice, 'Political Correctness,' and the Normalization of Donald Trump," *Medium* (2016) available at https://juliaserano.medium.com/prejudice-political-correctness-and-the-normalization-of-donald-trump-28c563154e48#.sypha7app.
15 Lani Guinier and Gerald Torres, *The Miner's Canary: Enlisting Race, Resisting Power, Transforming Democracy* (Cambridge, MA: Harvard University Press, 2002). It is important to point out that not all politically salient identities are emancipatory, progressive, or sympathetic to democrats. Not all people are seeking simply inclusion for a group that has been marginalized.
16 See Ibtissame Bouachrine, *Women and Islam: Myths, Apologies, and the Limits of Feminist Critique* (Lanham, MD: Lexington Books, 2014) and Shāhnaz Khan, "Reconfiguring the Native Informant: Positionality in the Global Age," *Signs* 30 no.4, Special Issue (New Feminist Approaches to Social Science Methodologies) (2005): 2017–37. Hamid Dabashi dedicates his entire book to critique scholars whom he sees as accomplices of western imperialist politics. See Hamid Dabashi, *Brown Skin, White Masks* (London: Pluto Press, 2011).

17 Saʿdiyya Shaikh, "Transforming Feminisms: Islam, Women and Gender Justice," in *Progressive Muslims: On Justice, Gender and Pluralism* (Oxford: Oneworld Press, 2006), 148.
18 Ibtissam Bouachrine, *Women and Islam: Myths, Apologies, and the Limits of Feminist Critique* (Lanham, MD: Lexington Books, 2014), xii.
19 Kiran Grewal, "Reclaiming the Voice of the 'Third World Woman': But What Do We Do When We Don't Like What She Has to Say? The Tricky Case of Ayaan Hirsi Ali," *Interventions* 14, no. 4 (2012): 572.
20 See Hind Elhinnawy, "Contested Voices: Secular Muslim Women Activists in the Age of ISIS," PhD dissertation, University of Kent (2019).
21 Mona Eltahawy, *Headscarves and Hymens: Why the Middle East Needs a Sexual Revolution* (London: Weidenfeld & Nicolson, 2016), 29.
22 See Mariz Tadros, "Stop Homogenising Us: Mixing and Matching Faith and Beliefs in India and Beyond," *IDS* (2021), available at https://www.ids.ac.uk/opinions/stop-homogenising-us-mixing-and-matching-faith-and-beliefs-in-india-and-beyond/.
23 Shaikh, "Transforming Feminisms," 148.
24 Haideh Moghissi, *Feminism and Islamic Fundamentalism: The Limits of Postmodern Analysis* (London: Zed Books, 1999), 127.
25 Ibid., 7.
26 See Kylie Cheung, Shoniqua Roach, Benita Roth, Jamia Wilson, and Rafia Zakaria, "Rafia Zakaria's Against White Feminism," *Signs: Short Takes: Provocations on Public Feminism* (n. d), available at http://signsjournal.org/zakaria/#:~:text=Agai nst%20White%20Feminism%20requires%20Western,thoughtfully%20offering%20 answers%20for%20each.
27 See Khadija Khan, "Islamic Feminism is a Myth," *Areo* (2018), available at https://areomagazine.com/2018/05/02/islamic-feminism-is-a-myth/.
28 Margot Badran, "From Islamic Feminism to Muslim Holistic Feminism," *IDS Bulletin* 42, no. 1 (2011): 82.
29 Zia, *Faith and Feminism in Pakistan*, 21
30 See Khan, "Islamic Feminism is a Myth."
31 In the early 1980s in Turkey, the number of university students wearing headscarves increased substantially, and in 1984, the first widespread application of headscarf ban came into effect at the universities. In 1997, the law extended the ban to the wearing of headscarves in all universities in Turkey. Since then, the debate over headscarves in universities has become an important element in the politics of Turkey.
32 In Austria a ban on full-face veils took place in 2017. The ban comes from a deal to save coalition government. The ban prohibits full-face veils such as the niqāb and burqa in courts and schools. Austria is also investigating the possibility of banning headscarves for women employed in public service. In Belgium, several

municipalities have used municipal bylaws on face-covering clothing to ban public wearing of the niqāb and burqa. The town of Maaseik was the first to implement a ban in October 2004. On 31 March 2010 the Belgian Chamber Committee on the Interior unanimously approved legislation instating a nationwide ban on wearing the burqa in public. The proposal was accepted by the Chamber of Representatives on 27 April 2010 with only two abstentions from Flemish Socialist MPs. A law was finally voted by both federal parliamentary chambers on 28 April 2011, as the parliamentary process had been interrupted by elections in June 2010. One Flemish Green MP voted against; two French-speaking Green MPs abstained. Amnesty International Brussels has criticized the proposed legislation, stating that it is "being presented as an act to combat discrimination against women, whereas it is an act of discrimination in itself." In 2016, a legal ban on face-covering Islamic clothing was adopted by the Bulgarian parliament. A Danish law banning the public wearing of a niqāb or burqa has taken effect on 1 August 2018. The Dutch government parliament, in January 2012, enacted a ban on face-covering clothing, popularly described as the "burqa ban." These are only a handful of examples.

33 Ziv Orenstein and Itzchak Weismann, "Neither Muslim nor other: British Secular Muslims," *Islam and Christian–Muslim Relations* 27, no. 4 (2016): 387.

34 See Chris Marsden and Julie Hyland, "Britain: Jack Straw's Anti-Muslim Provocation," *WSWS* (2006), available at https://www.wsws.org/en/articles/2006/10/ukin-o07.html.

35 Sahar Amer, *What Is Veiling?* (North Carolina: University of North Carolina Press, 2014), 113.

36 Ibid., 115.

37 See, for example Sukhada Tatke, "Not French Enough: What It Means to Be an Immigrant in France," *Aljazeera* (2021), available at https://www.aljazeera.com/features/2021/3/2/not-french-enough-what-it-means-to-be-an-immigrant-in-france; Cady Lang, "Who Gets to Wear a Headscarf? The Complicated History behind France's Latest Hijab Controversy," *Time* (May 19, 2021), available at https://time.com/6049226/france-the hijab-ban; Aala Abdelgadir and Vicky Fouka, "France's headscarf ban: the effects on Muslim integration in the West," *The Forum: ERF Policy Portal* (May 14, 2019), available athttps://theforum.erf.org.eg/2019/05/07/frances-headscarf-ban-effects-muslim-integration-west/.

38 Mayanthi L. Fernando, "Exceptional Citizens: Secular Muslim Women and the Politics of Difference in France," *Social Anthropology* 17 (4) (2009).

39 Orenstein and Weismann, "Neither Muslim nor Other," 387.

40 See Haroon Siddique, "Muslim Women: Beyond the Stereotype," *The Guardian* (2011), available at https://www.theguardian.com/lifeandstyle/2011/apr/29/muslim-women-fighting-islamic-extremism.

41 Ibid.

42 Chahdortt Djavann, *Que ponse Allah de l'Europe?* (Paris: Gallimard, 2004), 25.
43 See Pioneer Press, "Mona Eltahawy: Rending the Veil—with a Little Help," *Twin Cities* (2010), available at https://www.twincities.com/2010/07/19/mona-eltahawy-rending-the-veil-with-a-little-help/.
44 See Kia Abdulla, "It Is Possible to Be a Secular Muslim," *Inews* (2020), available at https://inews.co.uk/opinion/secular-muslim-islam-faith-484560.
45 See Milad Milani, "Cultural Muslims, Like Cultural Christians, Are a Silent Majority," *The Conversation* (2014), available at https://theconversation.com/cultural-muslims-like-cultural-christians-are-a-silent-majority-32097.
46 Ibid.
47 Ruth Mas, "Compelling the Muslim Subject: Memory as Post-colonial Violence and the Public Performativity of 'secular and cultural Islam'," *Muslim World* 96, no. 4 (2006): 586.
48 See Pragna Patel and Uditi Sen, "Cohesion, Faith and Gender: A Report on the Impact of the Cohesion and Faith-Based Approach on Black and Minority Women in Ealing," *Southall Black Sisters* (2011). Available at http://comodino.peacelink.org/tdt/docs/1933.pdf.
49 Irshad Manji, *Don't Label Me: How to Do Diversity without Inflaming the Cultural Wars* (New York: St. Martin's Griffin, 2020), 25.
50 Maryam Namazie, "Religion Is a Private Affair: One Law for All," *Dossiers* 30–1 (2011): 150.
51 See Milad Milani, "Cultural Muslims, Like Cultural Christians, Are a Silent Majority," *The Conversation* (September 2014).
52 See Abdulla, "It Is Possible to Be a Secular Muslim."
53 Ibid.
54 See http://faithinfeminism.com/secular-muslims-womens-rights/?doing_wp_cron=1536840804.1862609386444091796875.
55 Angel Rabasa, Cheryl Benard, Lowell H. Schwartz, and Peter Sickle, *Secular Muslims: A Forgotten Dimension in the War of Ideas* (Santa Monica, CA: RAND: Center for Middle East Public Policy), 135.
56 Paul Cliteur, "Female Critics of Islamism: Liberal or Secular Islam?," *Feminist Theology* 19, no. 2 (2011): 157.
57 See Nano GoleSorkh, "Political Activist Homa Arjomand on One Secular Education for All," YouTube (2014) https://www.youtube.com/watch?v=gc0uK1vD5zw.https://www.youtube.com/watch?v=gc0uK1vD5zw.
58 Ibid.
59 Kiran Grewal, *Racialised Gang Rape and the Reinforcement of Dominant Order: Discourses of Gender, Race and Nation* (London: Routledge, 2017), 194.
60 Nadje al-Ali, *Secularism, Gender and the State in the Middle East: The Egyptian Women's Movement* (Cambridge: Cambridge University Press, 2000), 130.

61 Nikki R. Keddie, "Secularism and the State: Towards Clarity and Global Comparison," *New Left Review* (1997): 24.
62 Mas, "Compelling the Muslim subject," 586.
63 Sukhwant Dhaliwal and Nira Yuval-Davis, *Women against Fundamentalism: Stories of Dissent and Solidarity*, London: Lawrence and Wishart,15.
64 Homi K. Bhabha, "On Subaltern Secularism," in *Women against Fundamentalism* 6 (1995): 5–7.
65 Ibid., 6.
66 Gita Sahgal, "Secular Spaces: The Experience of Asian Women Organizing," in *Refusing Holy Orders: Women and Fundamentalism in Britain*, ed. Gita Sahgal and Nira Yuval-Davis (London: WLUML, 2000), 169–203.
67 Bhabha, "On Subaltern Secularism," 7.
68 Azza Karam, *Women, Islamisms and the State: Contemporary Feminisms in Egypt* (London: Palgrave Macmillan, 1998), 13.
69 Mohammed A. Salih and Marwan M. Kraidy, "Islamic State and Women: A Biopolitical Analysis," *International Journal of Communication* 14 (2020): 1933.
70 See Suzie Mackenzie, "Meet the Woman Taking on Isis," *Vogue World Paris* (2017), available at https://www.vogue.co.uk/article/sara-khan-we-will-inspire-muslim-group.
71 Orenstein and Weismann, "Neither Muslim nor Other," 384.
72 See Emma Pearce, "'Gender Apartheid' Is Real in UK Universities. So Why Aren't More People Fighting It?," *The Telegraph*, available at https://www.telegraph.co.uk/women/womens-life/10510284/Gender-apartheid-segregation-is-real-in-UK-universities.-So-why-arent-more-people-fighting-it.html.
73 See Sara Khan "Segregating Men and Women at University Events Won't Lead to Equality," *Independent* (2019), available at https://www.independent.co.uk/voices/comment/segregating-men-and,-women-at-university- events-wont-lead-to-equality-8962984.html.
74 Ibid.
75 Orenstein and Weismann, "Neither Muslim nor Other," 383.
76 See Feminist Resources, "Chahla Chafiq: 'Choosing the Veil Is Not Equivalent to Choosing a Lipstick," Feminist Resources (2020), available at https://ressourcesfeministes.fr/2020/08/13/chahla-chafiq-choosing-the-veil-is-not-equivalent-to-choosing-a-lipstick/.
77 Ibid.
78 Peter Tatchell, "Peter Tatchell," in *Islamophobia: An Anthology of Concerns*, ed. Emma Webb (London: Civitas, 2019), 21.
79 See Nova Daban, "'Islamophobia' Distracts from Tackling Anti-Muslim Bigotry," *National Secular Society* (2021), available at https://www.secularism.org.uk/opinion/2021/11/islamophobia-debate-distracts-from-tackling-anti-muslim-bigotry.

80 The Prevent agenda in the UK refers to a government strategy aimed at preventing radicalization and extremism. It involves various initiatives, such as working with schools, healthcare providers, local authorities, and other institutions to identify individuals at risk of being drawn into extremist ideologies. The goal of Prevent is to intervene early to safeguard vulnerable individuals and redirect them away from radical influences.

81 See Rachel Blundy, "London Schoolgirl Who Recruited Three Classmates to Join IS in Syria 'Was Radicalised at East London Mosque,'" *The Standard* (2020), available at https://www.standard.co.uk/news/london/london-schoolgirl-who-recruited-three-classmates-to-join-is-in-syria-was-radicalised-at-east-london-mosque-10433150.html.

82 https://www.thetimes.co.uk/article/muslim-lobby-group-promotes-extremism-muslim-engagement-and-development-mend-hkm87fx35.

83 See Richard Adams, "Student Union Blocks Speech by 'Inflammatory' Anti-sharia Activist," The Guardian (2015), available at https://www.theguardian.com/education/2015/sep/26/student-union-blocks-speech-activist-maryam-namazie-warwick.

84 See Aine McMahon, "Activist Claims Trinity Speech on Apostasy and Islam Cancelled," *Irish Times* (2015), available at https://www.irishtimes.com/news/politics/activist-claims-trinity-speech-on-apostasy-and-islam-cancelled-1.2149050.

85 Pragna Patel, "Pragna Patel," in *Islamophobia: An Anthology of Concerns*, ed. Emma Webb (London: Civitas, 2019), 54.

86 Ibid.

87 Jo Woodiwiss, Kate Smith, and Kelly Lockwood, eds., *Feminist Narrative Research: Opportunities and Challenges* (London: Palgrave Macmillan, 2017), 21.

88 Francesca Poletta, *It Was Like a Fever: Storytelling in Protest and Politics* (London: University of Chicago Press, 2006), 41.

3

1 Sevinc Karaca, "Feminism in the Muslim world," *Red and Black Revolution* 15 (2009), 522.

2 Harriet Tubman was an American abolitionist and social activist. After escaping slavery, Tubman made some thirteen missions to rescue approximately seventy enslaved people, including her family and friends, using the network of antislavery activists and safe houses known collectively as the Underground Railroad.

3 Marilyn Booth, "Activism through Literature: Arguing Women's Rights in the Middle East," *Yale Review* 93 (2005): 3.

4 Ibid., 2.

5 See Amna Nasir, "Begum Rokeya: The Writer Who Introduced Us to Feminist Sci-Fi #IndianWomenInHistory," *Feminism in India* (2017), available at https://feminisminindia.com/2017/07/06/begum-rokeya-essay/.
6 Ibid., xvi.
7 Leila Ahmed, *Women and Gender in Islam: Roots of a Modern Debate* (New Haven: Yale University Press, 1992), 171.
8 Ibid., 183.
9 Marilyn Booth, "Activism through Literature," 12.
10 A mark of the growth in scholarly attention to women in Muslim societies is a two-volume bibliography compiled by Yvonne Haddad and others. The first volume, *The Contemporary Islamic Revival*, which covers works published between 1970 and 1988. In this volume, only eight pages were needed to list writing dealing with "women." While the second volume, *The Islamic Revival since 1988*, covering works published between 1988 and 1997, expanded the category of "women" to almost forty pages.
11 See, for example, Kumari Jayawardena, *Feminism and Nationalism in the Third World* (New Delhi: Kali for Women, 1986); Suha Sabbagh, *Arab Women: Between Defiance and Restraint* (New York: Olive Branch Press, 1997); Lila Abu-Lughod, ed. *Remaking Women: Feminism and Modernity in the Middle East* (Princeton, NJ: Princeton University Press, 1998).
12 Partha Chaterjee, "Colonialism, Nationalism, and Colonialized Women: The Contest in India," *American Ethnologist* 16, no. 4 (1989): 631.
13 Ibid.
14 Afia S. Zia, *Faith and feminism in Pakistan: Religious Agency or Secular Autonomy* (Brighton: Sussex Academic Press, 2018), 4.
15 See, for example, Gayatri Chakravorti Spivak, "Can the Subaltern Speak?" in *Colonial Discourse and Post-colonial Theory: A Reader*, ed. Patrick Williams and Laura Chrisman (New York: Columbia University Press, 1983); Ranajit Guha, ed., *A Subaltern Studies Reader, 1986-1995* (Minneapolis, MN: University of Minnesota Press, 1997).
16 Valentine M. Moghadam, *Globalizing Women: Transnational Feminist Networks* (Baltimore, MD: Johns Hopkins University Press, 2005), 82.
17 Islamic modernism is one of the of several Islamic movements—including Islamic secularism, Islamism, and Salafism—that emerged in the mid-nineteenth century in reaction to western colonialism in the Muslim world (see Richard C. Martin, *Encyclopedia of Islam and the Muslim World* (New York: Macmillan Reference USA, 2016). The movement attempts to reconcile the Islamic faith with modern values of democracy, civil rights, equality, and progress through a critical reexamination of the classical conceptions and methods of jurisprudence (see Mansoor Moaddel, *Islamic Modernism, Nationalism, and Fundamentalism: Episode and Discourse* (Chicago: University of Chicago Press, 2005).

18 Huma Ahmed-Gosh, "Dilemmas of Islamic and Secular Feminists and Feminisms," *Journal of International Women's Studies* 9, no. 3 (2008): 4.
19 Zia, *Faith and Feminism in Pakistan*, 5.
20 Haideh Moghissi, *Feminism and Islamic Fundamentalism: The Role of Postmodern Analysis* (London: Zed Books, 1999), 127.
21 Chandra Talpade Mohanty, "'Under Western Eyes' Revisited: Feminist Solidarity through Anticapitalist Struggles," *Signs: Journal of Women in Culture and Society* 28, no. 1 (2002): 509.
22 Sa'diyyah Shaikh, "Transforming Feminism: Islam, Women and Gender Justice," in *Progressive Muslims: On Justice, Gender and Pluralism*, ed. Omid Safi (Oxford: One World, 2003), 155.
23 Valentine M. Moghadam, *Globalizing Women: Transnational Feminist Networks* (Baltimore, MD: Johns Hopkins University Press, 2005), 196.
24 Jasmin Zine, "Between Orientalism and Fundamentalism: The Politics of Muslim Women's Feminist Engagement," *Muslim World Journal of Human Rights* 3, no. 1 (2006): 17.
25 Ibid., 18.
26 Peter Mandaville, *Global Political Islam* (New York: Routledge, 2001), 51.
27 Moghissi, *Feminism and Islamic Fundamentalism*, 127.
28 Haleh Afshar, "Women and Politics in Iran," *European Journal of Development Research* 12 (2000): 188–205.
29 Moghissi, *Feminism and Islamic Fundamentalism*, 127.
30 Margot Badran, "Independent Women: More than a Century of Feminism in Egypt," in *Arab Women: Old Boundaries, New Frontiers*, ed. Judith Tucker (Bloomington: Indiana University Press, 1993), 135.
31 Zaid Edayat, "Islamic Feminism: Roots, Development and Policies," *Global Policy* 4, no. 4 (2013): 361.
32 Yahya Akalay, "Re-reading the Relationship between Secular and Islamic Feminism(s) in Morocco: The Third Way as an Alternative Feminist Paradigm," *Feministische Studien* 39, no. 1 (2021).
33 Ibid., 131.
34 Margot Badran, "Competing Agenda: Feminists, Islam and the State in Nineteenth- and Twentieth Century Egypt," in *Women, Islam and the State*, ed. Deniz Kandiyoti (Philadelphia: Temple University Press, 1991), 214.
35 Moghissi, *Feminism and Islamic Fundamentalism*, 132–3.
36 Ibid., 132.
37 Nayera Tohidi, "Women's Rights and Feminist Movements in Iran," in *Women's Movements in the Global Era: The Power of Local Feminisms*, ed. Amrita Basu (New York: Routledge, 2017), 77.

38 Asef Bayat, *Street Politics: Poor People's Movements in Iran* (New York: Columbia University Press, 1997): 162.
39 Zia, *Faith and Feminism in Pakistan*, 20.
40 Margot Badran, "From Islamic feminism to a Muslim holistic feminism," *IDS Bulletin* 42, no. 1 (Gender, Rights and Religion at the Crossroads, 2011), 81.
41 Ibtissam Bouachrine, *Women and Islam: Myths, Apologies, and the Limits of Feminist Critique* (Lanham, MD: Lexington Books, 2014), 51.
42 Fatima Mernissi, *The Veil and the Male Elite: A Feminist Interpretation of Women's Rights in Islam* (Cambridge: Perseus Books, 1991), ix.
43 Amina Wadud, *Inside the Gender Jihad: Women's Reform in Islam* (Oxford: One World, 2006), 190.
44 Ibid.
45 Valentine M. Moghadam, "Islamic Feminism and Its Discontents: Toward a Resolution of the Debate," *Signs: Journal of Women in Culture and Society* 27, no. 4 (2002): 22.
46 Haideh Moghissi, "Islamic Feminism Revisited," *Comparative Studies of South Asia, Africa and the Middle East* 31, no. 1 (2011): 77.
47 Zia, *Faith and Feminism in Pakistan*, 22.
48 Ibid.
49 Lila Abu-Lughod. "Do Muslim Women Need Saving?," *Ethnicities* 15 (2013): 759–77.
50 Nawal El Saadawi, *The Nawal El Saadawi reader* (London: Zed Books, 1997), 246.
51 Nadje al-Ali, *Secularism, Gender and the State in the Middle East: The Egyptian Women's Movement* (Cambridge: Cambridge University Press, 2000), 59.
52 Margot Badran. "From Islamic Feminism to a Muslim Holistic Feminism," *IDS Bulletin* 42 (2011): 78–87.
53 Zia, *Faith and Feminism in Pakistan*, 22.
54 Shahrzad Mojab. "Theorizing the Politics of 'Islamic Feminism,'" *Feminist Review* 69 (2001): 124–46.
55 Moghissi, "Islamic Feminism Revisited," 77.
56 Priscilla Offenhauer, "Women in Islamic Societies: A Selected Review of Social Scientific Literature," a report prepared by the federal Research Division, Library of Congress (2005): 15.
57 Zia, *Faith and Feminism in Pakistan*, 24.
58 Nadje al-Ali, *Secularism, Gender and the State in the Middle East*, 83–4.
59 Zia, *Faith and Feminism in Pakistan*, 24.
60 Merieme Hélie-Lucas, "Introduction," *Women Living Under Muslim Laws*, Dossier 30–1(July 2011): 2.
61 Nawar Al-Hassan Golley, "Is Feminism Relevant to Arab women?," *Third World Quarterly* 25, no. 3 (2004): 522.

62 Rohan Gunaratna, "Global Threat Forecast The Rise of ISIS," *Counter Terrorist Trends and Analyses* 8, no. 1 (January 2016): 6.
63 Ibid.
64 Ibid.
65 Zia, *Faith and Feminism in Pakistan*, 179, 180.
66 Zia, *Faith and Feminism in Pakistan*, 181.

4

1 See Steve McCurry, "Afghan Girl Revealed," National Geographic (1985), available at https://www.nationalgeographic.com/magazine/article/afghan-girl-revealed.
2 al-Qaeda, Arabic al-Qā'idah ("the Base"), is a militant Islamist organization founded by Osama bin Laden in the late 1980s. The organization began as a logistical network to support Muslims fighting against the Soviet Union during the Afghan War. When the Soviets withdrew from Afghanistan in 1989, the organization dispersed but continued to oppose what its leaders considered corrupt Islamic regimes and foreign (i.e., US) presence in Islamic lands. The group eventually reestablished its headquarters in Afghanistan (c. 1996) under the support of the Taliban militia.
3 https://www.nationalgeographic.com/magazine/article/afghan-girl-revealed.
4 Maryam Khalid, "Gender, Orientalism and Representations of the 'Other' in the War on Terror," *Global Change, Peace and Security* 23, no. 1 (2011): 19.
5 Ziauddin Sardar, *Orientalism* (Buckingham: Open University Press, 1999), 2.
6 Khalid, "Gender, Orientalism and Representations of the 'Other' in the War on Terror," 19.
7 Edward W. Said, *Orientalism* (New York: Vintage Books, 1979), 3.
8 Ibid., 10.
9 Ibid., 8.
10 Ibid., 27.
11 Shehla Burney, "Chapter One: Orientalism: The Making of the Other," *Counterpoints* 417 (2012): 24.
12 See https://gabesibenglishgost.weebly.com/macauley--the-english-canon.html.
13 Roger Owen. "The Brismes Annual Lecture 2004: Biography and Empire: Lord Cromer (1841–1917) Then and Now," *British Journal of Middle Eastern Studies* 32 (2005): 3–12.
14 Burney, "Orientalism: The Making of the Other," 23.
15 Thisaranie Herath, "Women and Orientalism: 19th Century Representations of the Harem by European Female Travelers and Ottoman Women," *Constellations* 7, no. 1 (2016): 32.

16 Ibid.
17 Said, *Orientalism*, 9–10.
18 Ibid., 30.
19 Ibid., 11.
20 Nikita Dhawan, Elisabeth Fink, Johanna Leinius, and Rirhandu Mageza-Barthel, "Normative Legitimacy and Normative Dilemmas: Postcolonial Interventions," in *Negotiating Normativity: Postcolonial Appropriations, Contestations, and Transformations*, ed. Nikita Dhawan, Elisabeth Fink, Johanna Leinius, and Rirhandu Mageza-Barthel (New York: Springer, 2016), 8–9.
21 Said, *Orientalism*, 13.
22 Ibid., 11.
23 Nadje al-Ali, *Secularism, Gender and the State in the Middle East: The Egyptian Women's Movement* (Cambridge: Cambridge University Press, 2000), 22.
24 See, for example, Lisa Lowe, *Critical Terrains: French and British Orientalisms* (Ithaca, NY: Cornwell University Press, 1994); Reina Lewis, *Gendering Orientalism: Race, Femininity and Representation* (London: Routledge, 1996); Meyda Yegenoglu, *Colonial Fantasies: Toward a Feminist Reading of Orientalism* (Cambridge: Cambridge University Press, 1998): Ziauddin Sardar, *Orientalism* (Buckingham: Open University Press, 1999).
25 Khalid, "Gender, Orientalism and Representations of the 'Other' in the War on Terror," 23.
26 Nadje al-Ali, *Secularism, Gender and the State in the Middle East*, 23.
27 Ibid., 24.
28 See, for example, James Donald and Ali Rattansi, *Race, Culture, Difference* (London: Sage, 1992); Homi K. Bhaba, *The Location of Culture* (London: Routledge, 1994); Reina Lewis, *Gendering Orientalism*; Meyda Yegenoglu, *Colonial Fantasies*.
29 Lisa Lowe, *Critical Terrains*, 20.
30 Avtar Brah, "Women of South Asian Origin in Britain: Issues and Concerns," *South Asian Research* 7, no. 1 (1987): 136.
31 Mohja Kahf, *Western Representations of the Muslim Woman: From Termagant to Odalisque* (Austin: University of Texas Press, 1999), 9.
32 Zine, "Between Orientalism and Fundamentalism," 5.
33 Herath, "Women and Orientalism," 4
34 Khalid, "Gender, Orientalism and Representations of the 'Other' in the War on Terror," 18.
35 Ibid., 33.
36 Chandra Talpade Mohanty, "Under Western Eyes: Feminist Scholarship and Colonial Discourse," *Boundary 2* 12, no. 3 (1984): 335.
37 Miriam Cooke, "Saving Brown Women," *Signs* 28, no. 1 (2002): 468.

38 Frantz Omar Fanon was a Francophone Afro-Caribbean psychiatrist, political philosopher, and Marxist from the French colony of Martinique. His works have become influential in the fields of postcolonial studies, critical theory, and Marxism.
39 Mohandas Karamchand Gandhi was an Indian lawyer, anti-colonial nationalist, and political ethicist who employed nonviolent resistance to lead the successful campaign for India's independence from British rule. He inspired movements for civil rights and freedom across the world.
40 Francis Kwame Nkrumah was a Ghanaian politician, political theorist, and revolutionary. He was the first prime minister and president of Ghana, having led the Gold Coast to independence from Britain in 1957.
41 Shaminder Takhar, *Gender, Ethnicity, and Political Agency: South Asian Women Organizing* (London: Routledge, 2013), 45.
42 Partha Chatterjee, "Colonialism, Nationalism, and Colonialized Women: The Contest in India," *American Ethnologist* 16, no. 4 (1989): 623.
43 Miriam Cooke, *Deconstructing War Discourse: Women's Participation in the Algerian Revolution* (Michigan: Michigan State University Press, 1989), 2.
44 See Danièle Djamila Amrane-Minne and Farida Abu-Haidar, "Women and Politics in Algeria from the War of Independence to Our Day," *Research in African Literatures* 3, no. 3 (1999).
45 Shaminder Takhar, *Gender, Ethnicity, and Political Agency: South Asian Women Organizing* (London: Routledge, 2013), 55.
46 Chatterjee, "Colonialism, Nationalism, and Colonialized Women," 627.
47 Kedar Vishwanathan, "Aesthetics, Nationalism, and the Image of Woman in Modern Indian Art," *CLCWeb: Comparative Literature and Culture* 12, no. 2 (2010): 4.
48 Renata Pepicilli, "Rethinking Gender in Arab Nationalism: Women and the Politics of Modernity in the Making of Nation-States. Cases from Egypt, Tunisia and Algeria," *Oriente Moderno* 97, no. 1 (2017): 204.
49 Neil Macmaster, "The Colonial 'Emancipation' of Algerian Women: The Marriage Law of 1959 and the Failure of Legislation on Women's Rights in the Post-independence Era," *Vienna Journal of African Studies* 12 (2007): 92.
50 Leila Ahmed, *Women and Gender in Islam: Roots of a Modern Debate* (New Haven: Yale Unversity Press, 1992), 164.
51 Helie-Lucas, Marie-Aimee, "Women, Nationalism, and Religion in the Algerian Liberation Struggle," in *Opening the Gates: An Anthology of Arab Feminist Writing*, ed. Margot Badran and Miriam Cooke (Bloomington: Indiana University Press, 1990), 108.
52 See Kumari Jayawardena's article "Feminism and Nationalism in the Third World," in Progressive International, available at https://progressive.international/wire/2023-08-31-kumari-jayawardena-feminism-and-nationalism-in-the-Third world/e.

53 Khalid, "Gender, Orientalism and Representations of the 'Other' in the War on Terror," 18.
54 Ibid.
55 Avtar Brah, "Women of South Asian Origin in Britain: Issues and Concerns," *South Asian Research* 7, no. 1 (1987): 139.
56 Kiran K. Grewal, *The Socio-Political Practice of Human Rights: Between the Universal and the Particular* (London: Routledge, 2016), 23.
57 Brah, "Women of South Asian Origin in Britain: Issues and Concerns," 144.
58 Gita Sahgal and Nira Yuval-Davis, "Introduction: Fundamentalism, Multiculturalism and Women in Britain," in*Refusing Holly Orders: Women and Fundamentalism in Britain*, ed. Gita Sahgal and Nira Yuval Davis (London: Women Living Under Muslim Laws, 2000), 8.
59 Ibid.
60 George W. Bush, Statement by the President in his Address to the Nation, September 11, 2001; and Address to a Joint Session of Congress and the American People, September 20, 2001.
61 Nacira Guénif-Souilamas, "The Other French Exception: Virtuous Racism and the War of the Sexes in Postcolonial France," *French Politics, Culture and Society* 24, no. 3 (2006): 27.
62 Khalid, "Gender, Orientalism and Representations of the 'Other' in the War on Terror," 21.
63 See http://www.whitehouse.gov/news/releases/2002/01/20020129-11.html.
64 Khalid, "Gender, Orientalism and Representations of the 'Other' in the War on Terror," 21.
65 Tashfeen Malik was one of the perpetrators of the 2015 San Bernardino shooting in California. Along with her husband Syed Rizwan Farook, Malik carried out an attack at a holiday party held by Farook's employer, killing fourteen people and injuring twenty-two others. The couple, who were reportedly radicalized for some time before the attack, died in a shootout with law enforcement later on the same day. The incident raised concerns about homegrown radicalization and terrorism, sparking debates about gun control, security measures, and the motives behind the attack. The event also intensified discussions about the portrayal of Muslim individuals in the media and broader societal perceptions of Islam and extremism.
66 Constantine Gidaris. "Victims, Terrorists, Scapegoats: Veiled Muslim Women and the Embodied Threat of Terror," *Postcolonial Text* 13 (2018).
67 Zine, "Between Orientalism and Fundamentalism," 8.
68 Ibid., 9.
69 Ibid.
70 See, for example, Margaret L. Satterthwaite and Jayne C. Huckerby, eds., *Gender, National Security, and Counter-Terrorism: Human Rights Perspectives* (London:

Routledge, 2013); Kiran K. Grewal, *Racialized Gang Rape and the Reinforcement of Dominant Order: Discourses of Gender, Race and Nation* (London: Routledge, 2017); Sara R. Farris, *In the Name of Women's Rights: The Rise of Femonationalism* (Durham, NC: Duke University Press, 2017).

71 See, for example, Joan Wallach Scott, *The Politics of the Veil* (Princeton: Princeton University Press, 2007); Katherine Bullock, *Rethinking Muslim Women and the Veil: Challenging Historical and Modern Stereotypes* (London: International Insititute of Islamic Thought, 2010); Marnia Lazreg, *The Eloquence of Silence: Algerian Women in Question* (London: Routledge, 2018).

72 See, for example, Fazila Bhimji, *British Asian Muslim Women: Multiple Spacialities and Cosmopolitanism* (London: Palgrave Macmillan, 2012); Sariya Contractor, *Muslim Women in Britain: Demystifying the Muslimah* (London: Routledge, 2012); Danièle Joly and Khursheed Wadia, *Muslim Women and Power: Political and Civic Engagement in Western European Societies* (London: Palgrave Macmillan, 2017).

73 See, for example, Danielle Zimmerman, "Young Arab Muslim Women's Agency Challenging Western Feminism," *Affilia* 30 (2015); Anderson Beckmann Al Wazni, "Muslim Women in America and the Hijab: A Study of Empowerment, Feminist Identity, and Body Image," *Social Work* 60 (2015) and Simra Bilge, "Beyond Subordination vs. Resistance: An Intersectional Approach to the Agency of Veiled Muslim Women," *Journal of Intercultural Studies* 31 (2010).

74 See Abir M. Ismail. "Muḥajababes, Meet the New Fashionable, Attractive and Extrovert Muslim Woman: A Study of the Hijāb Practice among Individualized Young Muslim Women in Denmark," *Scandanivian Journal of islamic Studies* 9, no. 2 (2017).

75 Dhawan, Fink, Leinius, and Mageza-Barthel, "Normative Legitimacy and Normative Dilemmas," 11.

76 See, for example, Afshar Haleh, "Can I See Your Hair? Choice, Agency and Attitudes," *Ethnic and Racial Studies* 31, no. 2 (2008); Irene Zempi, "'It's a Part of Me, I Feel Naked Without It': Choice, Agency and Identity for Muslim Women Who Wear the Niqab," *Ethnic and Racial Studies* 30, no. 10 (2016).

77 See, for example, Pnina Werbner, "Divided Loyalties, Empowered Citizenship? Muslims in Britain," *Citizenship Studies* 4, no. 3 (2000); Narzanin Massoumi, "'The Muslim Woman Activist': Solidarity across Difference in the Movement against the 'War on Terror,'" *Ethnicities* 15, no. 5 (2015), and Aleksandra Lewicki and Theresa O'Toole, "Acts and Practices of Citizenship: Muslim Women's Activism in the UK," *Ethnic and Racial Studies* 40, no. 1 (2016).

78 See, for example, Katherine Brown, "Realizing Muslim Women's Rights: The Role of Islamic Identity among British Muslim Women," *Women Studies International Forum* 29, no. 4 (2006); Naaz Rashid, "Giving the Silent Majority a Stronger Voice? Initiatives to Empower Muslim Women as Part of the UK's War on Terror," *Ethnic*

and *Racial Studies* 37, no. 4 (2014); Narzanin Massoumi, "The Muslim Woman Activist."
79 Sara R. Faris, *In the Name of Women's Rights: The Rise of Femonationalism* (Durham: Duke University Press, 2017), 117.
80 Ibid., 11.
81 Cited in Zine, "Between Orientalism and Fundamentalism," 13.
82 Shāhnaz Khan, "Performing the Native Informant: Doing Ethnography from the Margins," *Canadian Journal of Women and the Law* 13, no. 2 (2001), 269.
83 France has decided to proclaim 2003 as "The Year of Algeria," and under the official label of "*Djazair 2003—Algerie au Coeur* (Algeria at Heart)," has set in motion a series of year-long events to mark Franco-Algerian friendship.
84 Mireille Rosello, *France and the Maghreb: Performative Encounters* (Florida: University of Florida Press, 2005), 87.
85 Dhawan, Fink, Leinius, and Mageza-Barthel, "Normative Legitimacy and Normative Dilemmas," 10.
86 See, for example, Patricia Jeffrey, *Frogs in a Well: Indian Women in Purdah* (London: Zed Books, 1979), Juliette Minces, *The House of Obedience: Women in Arab Society* (London: Zed Books, 1982), Maria Rosa Cutrufelli, *Women of Africa: Roots of Oppression* (London: Zed Books, 1983).
87 Ania Loomba, *Colonialism/Postcolonialism* (London: Routledge, 2005), 187.

5

1 Afia Zia, *Faith and Feminism in Pakistan: Religious Agency or Secular Autonomy* (Brighton : Sussex Academic Press, 2018), 2.
2 Ibid., 37.
3 Ibid., 74.
4 Ibid., 77.
5 Sertaç Sehlikoglu, "Revisited: Muslim Women's Agency and Feminist Anthropology of the Middle East, *Contemporary Islam* 12 (2018): 73–92. https://doi.org/10.1007/s11562-017-0404-8.
6 The most influential work on the activism of secularist feminists in the Muslim world was that of Nadje al-Ali's *Secularism, Gender and the State*.
7 Talal Asad's critique of anthropology questions the assumptions and biases inherent in the field's study of religion, particularly Islam. He argues that anthropology has historically approached Islam from a western-centric, secular perspective, often overlooking the diverse and dynamic nature of Islamic traditions. By reframing Islam as a discursive tradition rather than a static set of beliefs or practices, Asad encourages scholars to consider the multiplicity of voices and interpretations within

Islamic contexts. This approach challenges the dualistic frameworks often imposed on non-western religions and underscores the need for a more culturally sensitive and historically grounded analysis of Islam. See Talal Asad, *Formations of the Secular: Christianity, Islam, Modernity* (Stanford, CA: Stanford University Press, 2003).

8 Judith Butler's exploration of performativity in gender theory revolutionized the way gender is understood and studied. Butler contends that gender is not something innate or predetermined but rather a continual performance shaped by social norms, institutions, and cultural practices. By highlighting the performative nature of gender, Butler disrupts traditional notions of fixed gender identities and opens up space for considering gender as a dynamic and socially constructed phenomenon. This shift has profound implications for feminist theory, challenging essentialist views of gender and advocating for a more fluid and intersectional understanding of identity. See Judith Butler, *Bodies That Matter: On the Discursive Limits of "Sex"* (New York: Routledge, 1993).

9 The focus on agency within social theory shifts attention to the ways in which individuals and groups actively engage with and shape their social environments. This perspective emphasizes the capacity of individuals to exercise choice, make decisions, and influence social structures. Understanding agency involves exploring how people navigate power dynamics, resist oppression, and enact change within their communities. By centering agency in social theory, scholars seek to unpack the complexities of human action, agency, and empowerment, offering insights into how individuals mobilize resources, challenge norms, and participate in social transformation. See Margaret Scotford Archer, *Culture and Agency: The Place of Culture in Social Theory* (Cambridge: Cambridge University press, 1996) and Barry Barnes, *Understanding Agency: Social Theory and Responsible Action* (New York: Sage, 2000), to name a few.

10 See, for example, Asef Bayat, "Piety, Privilege and Egyptian Youth," *Isim Newsletter* 10, no. 23 (2002); Lara Deeb, *An Enchanted Modern: Gender and Public Piety in Shi'i Lebanon* (Princeton: Princeton University Press, 2006); Sherine Hafez, *An Islam of Her Own: Reconsidering Religion and Secularism in Women's Islamic Movements* (New York: New York University Press, 2011); Noorhaidi Hasan, "The Making of Public Islam: Piety, Agency, and Commodification on the Landscape of the Indonesian Public Sphere," *Cont Islam* 3 (2009).

11 See Lara Deeb, "Thinking Piety and the Everyday Together: A Response to Fadil and Fernando," *HAU: Journal of Ethnographic Theory* 5, no. 2 (2015): 95.

12 Saba Mahmood, *Politics of Piety: The Islamic Revival and the Feminist Subject* (Princeton, Oxfordshire: Princeton University Press, 2005), 152.

13 Ibid.

14 Ibid.

15 Saleh Chaoui, "Embodied Faith and the Limits of Female Agency in Randa Abdel-Fattah's Does My Head Look Big in This?," *Fudan Journal of the Humanities and Social Sciences* 16 (2023): 25.
16 Atalia Omer, "Is 'Docile Agency' Good for Women?," *Berkley Center* (2014), available at https://berkleycenter.georgetown.edu/posts/is-docile-agency-good-for-women.
17 In her seminal book *Gender Trouble* (1990), Butler applies the concept of performativity to gender, arguing that gender identity is not something one is born with but something one performs through repetitive behaviors, actions, and speech. Subjectivation refers to the process by which individuals are shaped as subjects within specific power contexts. It's about how one internalizes and responds to the norms and expectations imposed by society. While subjectivation involves subjection to power, it also entails the possibility of agency. Individuals are not merely passive recipients of social norms but can actively engage with and potentially transform them. Through the process of subjectivation, individuals can find ways to resist and negotiate the norms that constitute their identities. Mahmood uses these concepts to explore how Muslim women in pietist movements exercise agency within religious and patriarchal frameworks.
18 Mahmood, *Politics of Piety*, 103.
19 Ibid., 168.
20 Theresa Saliba, "Introduction: Gender, Politics and Islam," in *Gender, politics and Islam*, ed. Theresa Saliba, Carolyn Allen, and Judith A. Howard (Chicago: University of Chicago Press, 2002), 2.
21 Hafez, *An Islam of Her Own*, 97.
22 Ibid., 4.
23 Ibid., 79.
24 Rosa Vasilaki, "The Politics of Post-secular Feminism," *Theory, Culture & Society* 33, no. 2 (2016): 114.
25 Ibid.
26 Sehlikoglu, "Revisited," 84.
27 Mahmood, *Politics of Piety*, 39.
28 Cited in Sadia Abbas, "The Echo Chamber of Freedom: The Muslim Woman and the Pretext of Agency," *Boundary 2* 40, no. 1 (2013): 184.
29 Lara Deeb, *An Enchanted Modern*, 5.
30 Ibid., 18.
31 Ibid., 95–6.
32 Nadia Fadil and Mayanthi Fernando, "Rediscovering the 'Everyday' Muslim: Notes on an Anthropological Divide," *HAU: Journal of Ethnographic Theory* 5, no. 2 (2015): 63.

33 Lama Abu-Odeh, "Post-secularism and the Woman Question," *Georgetown Law Faculty Publications and Other Works* (2019), 5.
34 Haideh Moghissi, "Islamic Feminism Revisited," *Comparative Studies of South Asia, Africa and the Middle East* 31, no. 1 (2011): 80.
35 Ibid.
36 Sehlikoglu, "Revisited," 84.
37 Mahmood, *Politics of Piety*, 224.
38 Zia, *Faith and Feminism in Pakistan*, 42.
39 Ibid., 92.
40 See, for example, Noor Al-Qasimi, "Immodest Modesty: Accommodating Dissent and the 'Abaya-as-Fashion in the Arab Gulf States," *Journal of Middle East Women's Studies* 6, no. 1 (2010); Banu Gökarıksel and Anna Secor, "Islamic-ness in the Life of a Commodity: Veiling-Fashion in Turkey," *Transactions of the Institute of British Geographers* 35, no. 3 (2010); Emma Tarlo and Annelies Moors, eds., *Islamic Fashion and Anti-Fashion: New Perspectives from Europe and North America* (London: Bloomsbury Academic, 2013).
41 See, for example, Reina Lewis, *Modest Fashion: Styling Bodies, Mediating Faith* (New York: IB Tauris, 2013).
42 See, for example, Asef Bayat, "Piety, privilege and Egyptian youth," *ISIM Newsletter* 10 (1) (2002); Pascal Menoret, *Joyriding in Riyadh: Oil, Urbanism, and Road Revolt* (Cambridge: Cambridge University Press, 2014).
43 See, for example, Lara Deeb and Mona Harb, *Leisurely Islam: Negotiating Geography and Morality in Shi'ite South Beirut* (Princeton: Princeton University Press, 2013).
44 See, for example, Gul Ozyegin, *New Desires, New Selves: Sex, Love, and Piety among Turkish Youth* (New York: New York University Press, 2015).
45 See, for example, Homa Hoodfar, *Women's Sport as Politics in Muslim Contexts* (London: Women Living Under Muslim Laws, 2015); Sertaç Sehlikoglu, "Exercising in Comfort: Islamicate Culture of Mahremiyet in Everyday Istanbul, *Journal of Middle East Women's Studies* 12, no. 2 (2016).
46 See, for example, Asef Bayat, *Life as Politics: How Ordinary People Change the Middle East* (Palo Alto: Stanford University Press, 2103).
47 Henrietta L. Moore, *A Passion for Difference* (Cambridge: Polity Press, 1994), 5.
48 Henrietta L. Moore, *The Subject of Anthropology: Gender Symbolism and Psychoanalysis* (Cambridge: Polity Press, 2007), 57.
49 Souad Joseph, "Learning Desire: Relational Pedagogies and the Desiring Female Subject in Lebanon," *Journal of Middle East Women's Studies* 1, no. 1 (2005): 80.
50 Ibid.
51 Robin May Schott, "The Politics of Piety and the Norms of Analysis," in *Pieties and Gender*, ed. Hilda Rømer Christensen and Lene Sjørup (Leiden: Brill, 2009), 53.

6

1. Joan Wallach Scott, *Sex and Secularism* (Princeton, Oxford: Princeton University Press, 2017), 4.
2. Ibid., 1.
3. To name a few, see, for example, Charles Taylor, *A Secular Age* (Cambridge, MA: Belknap Press of Harvard University Press, 2007); Ronald Inglehart and Pippa Norris, *Sacred and Secular: Religion and Politics Worldwide* (Cambridge: Cambridge University Press, 2004); John Lardas, *Modern, Secularism in Antebellum America* (Chicago: University of Chicago Press, 2011); Linell E. Cady and Elizabeth Shakman Hurd, eds., *Comparative Secularisms in a Global Age* (New York: Palgrave Macmillan, 2010).
4. Scott, *Sex and secularism*, 5.
5. According to the Oxford English Dictionary, the earliest known use of the word "secular" is in the Middle English period (1150–1500). OED's earliest evidence for secular is from around 1290, in St. Edmund.
6. See Linell E. Cady and Elizabeth Shakman Hurd, "Comparative Secularisms and the Politics of Modernity: An Introduction," in *Comparative Secularisms in a Global Age*, ed. Linell E. Cady and Elizabeth Shakman Hurd (New York: Palgrave Macmillan, 2010) and Andrew Copson, *Secularism: A Very Short Introduction* (Oxford: Oxford Academic, 2019).
7. See Cady and Shakman Hurd, "Comparative Secularisms and the Politics of Modernity: An Introduction."
8. Scott, *Sex and secularism*, 9.
9. Ibid., 10.
10. Ibid., 28.
11. Ibid., 123.
12. Ibid., 14.
13. Talal Asad, *Formations of the Secular: Christianity, Islam, Modernity* (Stanford CA: Stanford University Press, 2003), 25.
14. Ibid., 91.
15. Michael Rectenwald and Rochelle Almeida, "Introduction: Global Secularisms in a Post-secular Age," in *Global Secularisms in a Post-secular Age*, vol. 2, ed. Michael Rectenwald, Rochelle Almeida, and George Levine (Boston, MA: De Grutyer, 2015), 6.
16. Rectenwald and Almeida, "Introduction," 1.
17. Jürgen Habermas, "Notes on Post-secular Society," *New Perspectives Quarterly* 25 (2008): 17.
18. Ibid., 20.

19 Aakash Singh Rathore, "Habermas's Post-secularism: The Penetration /Preservation of the (European) Political Public Sphere," in *Discoursing the Post-secular: Essays on the Habermasian Post-secular Turn*, ed. Aakash Singh Rathore and Peter Losonczi (Wien: Lit Verlag, 2010), 78.
20 Scott, *Sex and secularism*, 18.
21 See Mayanthi L. Fernando, "Exceptional Citizens: Secular Muslim Women and the Politics of Difference in France," *Social Anthropology* 17 (4 Special Issue: Muslim Women in Europe) (2009)."
22 Scott, *Sex and Secularism*, 16.
23 Ibid.
24 The Salman Rushdie affair began with the 1988 publication of his novel *The Satanic Verses*, which many in the Muslim community deemed blasphemous for its critical references to Islam and the Prophet Muhammad. The backlash included global protests, some violent, and reached a peak when Iranian Supreme Leader Ayatollah Ruhollah Khomeini issued a fatwa on February 14, 1989, calling for Rushdie's assassination and targeting those involved in the book's publication. This led Rushdie to live under British government protection for years, and despite Iran's later attempts to distance itself from the fatwa, hardline factions have maintained it. The controversy resulted in attacks on translators and publishers, bookstore bombings, and the book's ban in several countries. The affair underscored the clash between free speech and religious sensitivity, highlighting deep cultural and ideological divides, and it remains a significant case in discussions on these themes.
25 Sukhwant Dhaliwal, "Women against Fundamentalism: 25 Years of Anti-racist, Anti-fundamentalist Feminism," *Feminist Review* 108, no. 1 (2014): 10.
26 See Traversing Traditon, "The US State and the Making of a Secular Islam," *Traversing Tradition* (2019), https://traversingtradition.com/2019/04/15/the-us-state-and-the-making-of-a-secular-islam/.
27 See Pew Research Center, "U.S. Muslims Concerned about Their Place in Society, but Continue to Believe in the American Dream," *Pew Research Center* (2017), available at http://www.pewforum.org/2017/07/26/findings-from-pew-research-centers-2017-survey-of-us-muslims/.
28 Ibid.
29 Ibid.
30 The Quilliam Foundation was put into liquidation on April 9, 2021. The same day, Nawaz posted on Twitter: "Due to the hardship of maintaining a non-profit during COVID lockdowns, we took the tough decision to close Quilliam down for good ... looking forward to a new post-covid future." The report "Re-programming British Muslims" itself does not exist online anymore, however a summary of it could be found here: https://www.media-diversity.org/re-programming-british-muslims-a-study-of-the-islam-channel-by-the-quilliam-foundation/.

31 See https://www.globalissues.org/article/584/hearts-minds-and-dollars.
32 See Olivier Roy, "Secularism confronts Islam," *Open Democracy* (2007) available at https://www.opendemocracy.net/en/34938/.
33 Ibid.
34 The Jesus Army, originating from the Baptist tradition of Protestant Christianity in the UK during the 1960s, combined evangelical fervor with communal living inspired by early Christian communities. Emphasizing shared living spaces, evangelism, charismatic practices, and social justice advocacy, the movement aimed to embody the teachings of Jesus through communal living, outreach efforts, and social service. Despite facing controversies and internal challenges, the Jesus Army dissolved in 2019, leaving a legacy of blending Baptist evangelicalism with communal living, spiritual gifts, and a commitment to social justice.
35 The New Jerusalem movement traces its roots to the Russian Orthodox Church in the early twentieth century, particularly during a period of upheaval following the Russian Revolution of 1917. The movement was influenced by a desire to preserve traditional Orthodox practices amidst significant social and political changes in Russia. The central figure associated with the movement is Archbishop Ioann (John) Maximovich, known for his staunch traditionalism and advocacy for upholding Orthodox traditions. The New Jerusalem movement sought to maintain Orthodoxy in its original form, emphasizing adherence to historical liturgical practices, conservative theological teachings, and a strict interpretation of Orthodox doctrine. Over time, the movement expanded beyond Russia, gaining followers who shared their commitment to preserving what they saw as the authentic Orthodox tradition. The New Jerusalem movement continues to be a prominent force in contemporary Orthodox Christianity, dedicated to upholding and promoting the traditional values and practices of the Orthodox faith.
36 The International Society for Krishna Consciousness (ISKCON), also known as the Hare Krishna movement, was founded in 1966 in New York City by A. C. Bhaktivedanta Swami Prabhupada. ISKCON is a worldwide spiritual organization that follows the teachings of the Bhagavad Gita and promotes the worship of Lord Krishna as the Supreme Personality of Godhead. The Brahma Kumaris, on the other hand, is a spiritual movement that originated in India in the 1930s. Founded by Lekhraj Kripalani, who later became known as Brahma Baba, the Brahma Kumaris teach a form of Raja Yoga meditation as a means of connecting with the divine and achieving self-realization.
37 Daniel Steinmetz-Jenkins, "Do Secularism and Gender Equality Really Go Hand in Hand?," *The Guardian* (2017), available at https://www.theguardian.com/commentisfree/2017/dec/30/secularism-gender-equality-joan-wallach-scott.
38 Scott, *Sex and Secularism*, 15.
39 Ibid., 14.

40 Ibid., 17.
41 Joan Wallach Scott, *The Fantasy of Feminist History* (Duke: Duke University Press, 2011), 95.
42 Scott, *Sex and Secularism*, 21.
43 Ibid.
44 Cited in Scott, *Sex and Secularism*, 2.
45 See Ronald Inglehart and Pippa Norris, "The True Clash of Civilizations," *Foreign Policy*, no. 135 (March–April 2003): 62–70, available at https://www.jstor.org/stable/3183594.
46 Abdullah F. Alrebh, "Islamic Authority: A Matter of Guardianship," *Athens Journal of Social Sciences* 5, no. 2 (2018): 172.
47 Fauzi M. Najjar, "The Debate on Islam and Secularism in Egypt," *Arab Studies Quarterly* 18, no. 2 (1996): 3.
48 Tamara Sonn, "Secularism and National Stability in Islam," *Arab Studies Quarterly* 9, no. 3 (1987): 284.
49 Ibid.
50 Ibid.
51 Rifa'a al-Tahtawi was an influential Egyptian scholar and early modernist reformer who played a key role in the intellectual and cultural developments in the Islamic world during the nineteenth century. He is renowned for his contributions to modernizing Islamic educational systems and promoting societal reforms.
52 Fauzi Najjar, "The Debate on Islam and Secularism in Egypt," *Arab Studies Quarterly* 18, no. 2 (1996): 6.
53 Ibid.
54 Ibid.
55 Jamal al-Din al-Afghani (1838–1897) was a key nineteenth-century Muslim intellectual and reformer, known for advocating Pan-Islamism to counter European colonialism. He promoted modern scientific and educational reforms within an Islamic framework and traveled widely to engage in intellectual and political activism. His ideas significantly influenced subsequent Islamic reformers, including Muhammad Abduh, and remain pivotal in discussions on Islam's relationship with modernity and anti-colonial resistance.
56 Cited in Najjar, "The Debate on Islam and Secularism in Egypt," 7.
57 Najjar, "The Debate on Islam and Secularism in Egypt," 7.
58 Sonn, "Secularism and National Stability in Islam," 287.
59 Najjar, "The Debate on Islam and Secularism in Egypt," 1.
60 The story of Prophet Ibrahim as told in the Quran is a story of sacrifice. The Prophet Ibrahim had a series of dreams where he was being instructed to sacrifice his beloved son, Ismail. He was deeply disturbed by them and confided in his son, who comforted his father and encouraged him to follow

the commands of Allah. Once on Mount Arafat, Prophet Ibrahim decided to blindfold himself while he carried out the slaughter so to ease his own pain. When Ibrahim removed his blindfold, he saw that by the divine grace of Allah, Ismail was safe beside him, and a ram lay in the place of his son! Since then, Muslims have been sacrificing an animal, as Ibrahim did—preferably a goat, sheep, cow, or camel, during the celebration of the Bairam to echo Ibrahim's deed of devotion, obedience, and submission to Allah.

61 Najjar, "The Debate on Islam and Secularism in Egypt," 3.
62 *al-Manar* was an influential Islamic journal founded in 1898 by Muhammad Rashid Rida, a disciple of Muhammad Abduh. The magazine aimed to modernize Islamic thought by reconciling traditional teachings with contemporary ideas, promoting ijtihad (independent reasoning) over taqlid (blind adherence). It covered religious reform, education, politics, and social issues, playing a crucial role in the intellectual and reformist movements of the Muslim world during the late nineteenth and early twentieth centuries. Despite its progressive stance, *al-Manar* sometimes sparked controversies, such as calling for the dismissal of Taha Husayn from the university due to his contentious views on pre-Islamic poetry. The magazine remains a key historical source for studying the evolution of modern Islamic thought.
63 Abdullahi Ahmed An-Na`im, "Islam and Secularism," in *Comparative Secularisms in a Global Age*, ed. Linell E. Cad and Elizabeth Hurd Shakman (New York: Palgrave Macmillan, 2010), 218.
64 Marian Burchardt, Monika Wohlrab-Sahr, and Matthias Middell, *Multiple Secularities beyond the West: Religion and Modernity in the Global Age* (Boston, MA: De Grutyer, 2015).
65 Ibid., 4.
66 Rectenwald and Almeida, "Introduction," 6.
67 Arolda Elbasani and Murat Somer, "Muslim Secularisms in the European Context," in *Global Secularism in a Post-secular Age*, ed. Michael Rectenwald, Rochelle Almeida, and George Levine (Boston, MA: De Grutyer, 2015), 173.
68 Rectenwald and Almeida, "Introduction," 6.
69 Jacques Berlinerblau, "Introduction: Secularism and Its Confusions," in *Secularism on the Edge: Church-State Relations in the United States, France, and Israel*, ed. Jacques Berlinerblau, Sarah Fainberg, and Aurora Nou (New York: Palgrave Macmillan, 2014), 9.
70 Rectenwald and Almeida, "Introduction," 21.
71 Cited in Rohit Chopra, "Secularism, Religion, and the State in a Time of Global Crisis: Theoretical Reflections on the Work of Abdullahi An-Na'im," *Emory International Law Review* 36, no. 4 (2022): 651.
72 Ibid., 655.

73 Joan Wallach Scott, *The Politics of the Veil* (Princeton, NJ: Princeton University Press, 2007), 96.
74 Chopra, "Secularism, Religion, and the State in a Time of Global Crisis," 655.
75 Ibid., 657.
76 See Arun Kumar, "Five Years Later, It's Even More Clear that Demonetization Was a Disaster for India," Scroll.in (November 6, 2021), available at https://scroll.in/article/1009871/five-years-later-its-even-more-clear-that-demonetisation-was-a-disaster-for-india#:~:text=There%20has%20been%20growing%20unemployment,after%20the%20goalposts%20were%20shifted.
77 Rohit Chopra, "Secularism, Religion, and the State in a Time of Global Crisis," 659.
78 Homi K. Bhabha, "On Subaltern Secularism," *Women against Fundamentalism* 6 (1995): 6.
79 Amina Jamal, "The Entanglement of Secularism and Feminism in Pakistan," *Meridians* 20, no. 2 (2021): 390.

7

1 Mayanthi L. Fernando, "Exceptional Citizens: Secular Muslim Women and the Politics of Difference in France," *Social Anthropology* 17, no. 4 (Special Issue: Muslim Women in Europe) (2009): 381.
2 Leila Mouri and Kristin Soraya Batmanghelichi, "Can the Secular Iranian Women's Activist Speak? Caught between Political Power and the 'Islamic feminist'," in *Gender and sexuality in Muslim cultures*, ed. Gul Ozyegin (London: Routledge, 2015), 334.
3 See Lipika Pelham "Iran Frees Niloufar Hamedi & Elaheh Mohammadi, Jailed for Covering Mahsa Amini Death," *BBC* (2023), available at https://www.bbc.co.uk/news/world-middle-east-67975811.
4 Ibid.
5 See Narges Mohammadi, "The More They Lock Us Up, the Stronger We Become," *New York Times* (2023), available at https://www.nytimes.com/2023/09/16/opinion/narges-mohammadi-iran-women.html.
6 See Mehreen Ovais, "Feminism in Pakistan: A Brief History," *Tribune* (2010), available at https://tribune.com.pk/story/764036/feminism-in-pakistan-a-brief-history.
7 Ibid.
8 See Bina Shah, "The Fate of Feminism in Paksitan," *New York Times* (2014), available at https://www.nytimes.com/2014/08/21/opinion/bina-shah-the-fate-of-feminism-in-pakistan.html#:~:text=A%20feminist%20movement%20can%20succeed,both%20Islamic%20and%20secular%20principles.

9 Mouri and Soraya Batmanghelichi, "Can the Secular Iranian Women's Activist Speak," 333–4.
10 Afia S. Zia, *Faith and Feminism in Pakistan: Religious Agency or Secular Autonomy* (Brighton: Sussex Academic Press, 2018), 135. See also Jasmin Zine, "Between Orientalism and Fundamentalism: The Politics of Muslim Women's Feminist Engagement," *Muslim World Journal of Human Rights* 3, no. 1 (2006) and Amna Akbar and Rupal Oza, "Muslim Fundamentalism and Human Rights in an Age of Terror and Empire," in *Gender, National Security and Counter-Terrorism: Human Rights Perspectives*, ed. Margaret L. Satterthwaite and Jayne Huckerby (London: Routledge, 2012).
11 See Deniz Kandiyoti, "Between the Hammer and the Anvil: Post-conflict Reconstruction, Islam and Women's Rights," *Third World Quarterly* 28, no. 3 (2007). See also Nehaluddin Ahmad, "Modern Debate on the Socio-Political Rights of Muslim Women," *Asia-Pacific Journal on Human Rights and the Law* 13, no. 1 (2012): 42–64 and Maryam Ahmad and James Deshaw Rae, "Women, Islam, and Peacemaking in the Arab Spring," *Peace Review* 27, no. 3 (2015).
12 Shiva Nazar Ahari is an Iranian human rights activist and a founding member of the Committee of Human Rights Reporters. She has been jailed several times by the Iranian government. At the time of Shadi Sadr's interview with Leila Mouri, Ahari, who was twenty-seven then, was being held in Tehran's Evin prison.
13 Mouri and Soraya Batmanghelichi, "Can the Secular Iranian Women's Activist Speak," 334–5.
14 See Lawyers for Lawyers, "Iran Shadi Sadr Convicted to 6 Years and 74 Lashes," *Lawyers for Lawyers* (2010), available at https://lawyersforlawyers.org/en/iran-shadi-sadr-convicted-to-6-years-and-74-lashes/.
15 See Human Rights Watch, "Iran: Mass Arrests of Women's Rights Defenders," *Human Rights Watch*, available at https://www.hrw.org/news/2023/08/19/iran-mass-arrests-womens-rights-defenders.
16 See Cairo Scene, "Egyptian Activist Nawal El-Saadawi Accused of Blasphemy Again," *Cairo Scene* (2018), available at https://cairoscene.com/buzz/nawal-saadawi-blasphemy-bbc.
17 See Egypt Today, "Complaint Filed against Nawal el-Saadawi for Defaming Religions," *Egypt Today* (2018), available at https://www.egypttoday.com/Article/1/53701/Complaint-filed-against-Nawal-el-Saadawi-for-defaming-religions.
18 Haideh Moghissi, "Islamic Feminism Revisited," *Comparative Studies of South Asia, Africa and the Middle East* 31, no. 1 (2011): 77.
19 Shahnaz Khan, "Performing the Native Informant: Doing Ethnography from the Margins," *Canadian Journal of Women and the Law* 13, no. 2 (2001): 269.
20 Zine, "Between Orientalism and Fundamentalism," 11–12.

21 See Sunaina Maria, "'Good' and 'Bad' Muslim Citizens: Feminists, Terrorists, and U.S. Orientalism," *Feminist Studies* 35, no. 3 (2009).
22 Ibid., 635–44.
23 Ibid.
24 Sadia Abbas, "The Echo Chamber of Freedom: The Muslim Woman and the Pretext of Agency," *Boundary 2* 40, no. 1 (2013): 169.
25 Ibid.
26 Ibid.
27 Marieme Hélie-Lucas, "A South-North Transfer of Political Competence," *Women Living Under Muslim Laws*, July, Dossier 30–1 (2011): 61.
28 Ibid.
29 Mariam Namazie, "Mariam Namazie," in *Islamophobia: An Anthology of Concerns*, ed. Emma Webb (London: Civitas, 2019), 76.
30 Pragna Patel, "Pragna Patel," in *Islamophobia: An Anthology of Concerns*, ed. Emma Webb (London: Civitas, 2019), 54.
31 Namazie, "Mariam Namazie," 77.
32 Hélie-Lucas, "A South-North Transfer of Political Competence," 62.
33 Marieme Hélie-Lucas, "Introduction," *Women Living Under Muslim Laws*, July, Dossier 30–1(The Struggle for Secularism in Europe and North America, 2011): 1.
34 Sara Khan and Tony McMahon, *The Battle for British Islam: Reclaiming Muslim Identity from Extremism* (London: Saqi, 2016), 113.
35 Michael Freeman, *Human Rights: An Interdisciplinary Approach* (Cambridge: Polity Press, 2010), 120.
36 Ibid.
37 Uma Narayan, *Dislocating Cultures: Identities, Traditions, and Third World Feminism* (London: Routledge, 1997), 135.
38 Dianne Otto, "Lost in Translation: Re-scripting the Sexed Subjects International Human Rights Law," in *International Law and Its Others*, ed. Anne Orford (Cambridge: Cambridge University Press, 2006), 335.
39 Kiran Kaur Grewal, *The Socio-Political Practice of Human Rights: Between the Universal and the Particular* (London: Routledge, 2016), 25.
40 Shahrzad Mojab and Nadeen El-Kassem, "Cultural Relativism: Theoretical, Political and Ideological Debates," *Women Living Under Muslim Laws*, Dossier 30–1 (2011): 191.
41 Mojab and El-Kassem, "Cultural Relativism," 192.
42 Sherene H. Razack, "Imperilled Muslim Women, Dangerous Muslim Men and Civilised Europeans: Legal and Social Responses to Forced Marriages," *Feminist Legal Studies* 12, no. 2 (2004): 130.
43 Ibid., 131.
44 Ibid.

45 Ibid., 194.
46 István Lakatos, "Thoughts on Universalism versus Cultural Relativism, with Special Attention to Women's Rights," *Pécs Journal of International and European Law* 1 (2018): 25.
47 Shirin Assa, "Unveiling a Feminist Strike: The Case of 'Woman, Life, Freedom' in Iran," *Atlantis* 44, no. 2 (2023): 59.
48 See Nayera Tohidi, "Iran in a Transformative Process by Woman, Life, Freedom," *Freedom of Thought Journal*, no. 13 (2023): 29–57. See also Shakib Zarbighalehhammami and Fatemeh Abbasi, "The Demand for Freedom and Equality in the Street Below the Movement of Woman, Life, Freedom," *Journal of Advanced Research in Social Sciences* 6, no. 3 (2023).
49 Despite slim evidence of substantial fractures within the ruling echelons or significant discord among the repressive armed forces loyal to the Iranian regime, a growing sense of disenchantment, alienation, and disillusionment is evident among various influential factions and personalities. There have been notable denunciations of "immoral policies," escalating corruption, economic mismanagement, mistreatment of political detainees, and the execution of protestors from entities closely linked to the establishment, some even calling for the supreme leader's resignation. Moreover, the diminishing number of seminary students and aspiring clergy underscores an increased distrust and aversion toward the clergy. Statesmen have openly expressed concerns regarding the diminishing number of mosque attendees, religious service participants, and Friday prayer attendees. These concerns highlight a potential decline in religious observance and engagement within certain communities. See Nayera Tohidi, "Iran in a Transformative Process by Woman, Life, Freedom."
50 Ella Shohat, ed., *Talking Visions: Multicultural Feminism in a Transnational Age* (New York: MIT Press, 1998), 15.
51 Amanda Lock Swarr and Richa Nagar, "Theorizing Transnational Feminist Praxis," in *Critical Transnational Feminist Praxis*, ed. Amanda Lock Swarr and Richa Nagar (New York: State University of New York Press, 2010), 12.
52 Kiran K. Grewal, "Reclaiming the Voice of the 'Third World Woman': But What Do We Do When We Don't Like What She Has to Say? The Tricky Case of Ayaan Hirsi Ali," *Interventions* 14, no. 4 (2012): 589.
53 Judith Lakämper, "Affective Dissonance, Neoliberal Postfeminism and the Foreclosure of Solidarity," *Feminist Theory* 18, no. 2 (2017): 125.
54 Ibid.
55 Leah Bassel and Akwugo Emejulu, *Minority Women and Austerity: Survival and Resistance in France and Britain* (Bristol: Policy Press, 2017), 28.
56 Chandra Talpade Mohanty, "Transnational Feminist Crossings: On Neoliberalism and Radical Critique," *Signs* 38, no. 4 (2013): 967–91.

57 Ibid.
58 For a prime example, see Jennifer C. Nash, *Black Feminism Reimagined: After Intersectionality* (Durham, NC: Duke University Press, 2019); see also Cynthia Burack, *Healing Identities: Black Feminist Thought and the Politics of Groups* (Ithaca, NY: Cornell University Press, 2004); Nydia A. Swaby, "'Disparate in Voice, Sympathetic in Direction': Gendered Political Blackness and the Politics of Solidarity," *Feminist Review*, no. 108 (2014).
59 Audre Lorde, *Sister Outsider: Essays and Speeches* (Trumansburg, NY: Crossing Press, 1984), 142.
60 M. Jacqui Alexander, *Pedagogies of Crossing: Meditations on Feminism, Sexual Politics, Memory, and the Sacred* (Durham, NC: Duke University Press, 2006), 269.

Concluding Remarks

1 Debbie Horsefall, "Black Holes in the Writing Process: Narratives of Speech and Silence," in *Critical Moments in Qualitative Research*, ed. Debbie Horsfall and Joy Higgs (Woburn: Butterworth-Heinemann, 2001), 84.
2 The label "Cultural Muslim" has lately been used in the literature to describe those Muslims who are religiously unobservant, secular or nonreligious individuals who still identify with the Muslim culture due to family background, personal experiences, or the social and cultural environment in which they grew up. This concept acknowledges the diverse ways in which individuals engage with their cultural and religious backgrounds, recognizing that one's cultural identity can be intertwined with religious heritage in complex ways. Cultural Islam allows individuals to express their sense of belonging to a particular cultural and historical tradition without strictly adhering to the religious doctrines and practices associated with Islam. However, it is important to note that the term "cultural Islam" is subject to interpretation and may vary among individuals based on their personal experiences, upbringing, and understanding of their cultural and religious identities.
3 Deniz Kandiyoti coined the term "patriarchal bargain" in her 1988 article "Bargaining with Patriarchy." The term refers to a decision a woman takes to conform to the demands of patriarchy in order to gain some benefit, be that financial, psychological and emotional, or social.
4 A political prisoner is someone imprisoned for their political activity. There is no internationally recognized legal definition of the concept, although numerous similar definitions have been proposed by various organizations and scholars. In Egypt, political prisons still exist until this day, and thousands of political activists are held in these prisons, sometimes for years.

5 Since the early 2000s, there has been a rise in various political movements, which inspired many youths to participate in protests. The Kifaya movement was established in 2004 through an unlikely alliance of fifteen different organizations and activists. Following Kifaya, a new wave of social movements emerged, in particular the "March 9" movement calling for the Independence of the University; the "Youth for Change" movement, an adjunct of Kifaya, which focused on the socioeconomic problems facing youth, such as unemployment and housing; and the "Workers for Change movement," which demanded an independent labor union. See, for example Tarek Osman, *Egypt on the Brink: From Nasser to Mubarak* (New Haven, London: Yale University Press, 2010). "April 6" movement started in the spring of 2008, when over 100,000 Facebook users joined an online group to express solidarity with workers protesting in the Delta industrial city of al-Mahalla al-Kubra. As the protests escalated into a nationwide strike, the Facebook group gained momentum and eventually coalesced into a political movement known as the "April 6 Youth Movement."

6 Since its early onset, feminism in Muslim societies was directly influenced by Western feminism and thus was seen by some as a vessel of continued colonial influence. As a result, the use of the term was, generally, not welcomed.

7 Until the present day, the Egyptian Laws consider homosexuality and sexual relations out of wedlock as illegal.

8 In Egypt, at the time I gave birth to my daughter, whilst a man can register a child with or without a marriage certificate, a woman needs to present a marriage certificate in order to register her child. This suggests that the main issue isn't having a child out of wedlock, but rather it revolves around the father's approval or disapproval in the registration process.

9 In Egypt, the law, based on Islamic Sharia, stipulates that children must be named after their fathers and only through a proven marriage relationship. In my case, as the father has denied the entire relationship and the paternity rights of my daughter, I had to take the matter to the courts to prove the rights of my daughter to carrying his name. It was not that his name was so precious to me, but in Egypt a child cannot take their mother's name. I am named after my father just like every Egyptian.

10 See, for example, Neil MacFarquhar, "Paternity Suit against TV Star Scandalizes Egyptians," *New York Times* (2005), available at http://www.nytimes.com/2005/01/26/world/middleeast/paternity-suit-against-tv-star-scandalizes-egyptians.html; *New York Times*, "Virgin Territory for Egypt as Paternity Suit Filed," *Sunday Morning Herald* (2005), available at https://www.smh.com.au/news/World/Virgin-territory-for-Egypt-as-paternity-suit-filed/2005/01/28/1106850110497.html.

11 See, for example, May Allam, "Meet Hind Elhinnawy, the Egyptian Woman Who Defied the Social Norms," Women of Egypt Network (2018), available at https://womenofegyptmag.com/2018/07/21/meet-hind-elhinnawy-the-%D9%90%D9%90egyptian-woman-who-defied-the-social-norms/.
12 See Ghadeer Ahmed, "Outlawed Pregnancy: The Consequences of Pregnancy Outside Marriage for Egyptian Women," *Sister-hood* (2017), available at http://sister-hood.com/ghadeer-ahmed/outlawed-pregnancy/.
13 Nawal El Saadawi, *The Nawal El Saadawi Reader* (London: Zed Books, 1997), 2.
14 In 2005, I worked as a researcher at the "New Woman's Organization" in Cairo. My main role was developing awareness campaigns and promoting programs. From 2006 to 2008, I worked at the "Ibn Khaldun Center for Developmental Studies," owned by the notorious Saad Eddin Ibrahim. At the Ibn Khaldun, I managed a project called "The Egyptian Democracy Support Network."
15 See https://www.hindelhinnawy.org/ for a list of blog posts I've written.
16 Examples are *Elbeit Beitak* (Feel at Home) program, a show that has tremendous popularity and very high viewership in Egyptian television. See https://en.wikipedia.org/wiki/El_beit_beitak; *Sireh wo Infatahit* (Open for Discussion) hosted by Zaven Kouyoumdjian and considered to be the highest rating talk show in the Arab World.
17 Souad Salih (1942–2007) was a prominent Egyptian TV presenter, journalist, and religious commentator known for her outspoken and controversial views within the Islamic sphere. She rose to fame as a television presenter on Egyptian TV Channel 1, hosting a popular religious program named *Mo'mineen'* (Believers).
18 Born in Egypt in 1946, Safwat Hegazy gained prominence as a prominent Islamic preacher and scholar. Hegazy was known for his conservative interpretations of Islam and his strong advocacy for Islamic law. He was a regular fixture on Egyptian television, appearing on numerous religious programs.
19 The term "Islam is the solution" gained prominence in the late 1970s and early 1980s, particularly in the context of political movements and ideologies in the Middle East. In regions where nationalist movements did not adequately address societal challenges or where nationalist governments failed to deliver on promises of progress and development, some segments of the population turned to Islamic movements as an alternative solution. Islamic movements often presented themselves as offering a more authentic, moral, and just alternative to the perceived shortcomings of nationalist ideologies, garnering support from those who felt disillusioned with nationalist governments or movements. See, for example, Saeed Rahnema, "Radical Islamism and Failed Developmentalism," *Third World Quarterly* 29, no. 3 (2008): 483–96, available at http://www.jstor.org/stable/20455053.

20 Dina Wahba, "Gendering the Egyptian Revolution," in *Women's Movements in Post-"Arab Spring,"* ed. Fatima Sadiqi (New York: Palgrave Macmillan, 2016), 61–76.
21 See Lauren Bohn, "9 faces of the New Egypt," *The Atlantic* (2012), available at https://www.theatlantic.com/international/archive/2012/02/9-faces-of-the-new-egypt/253003/.
22 Rahel R. Wasserfall, "Reflexivity, Feminism and Difference," in *Reflexivity and Voice*, ed. Rosanna Hertz (Thousand Oaks, CA: Sage, 1997), 154.
23 Shāhnaz Khan, "Performing the Native Informant: Doing Ethnography from the Margins," *Canadian Journal of Women and the Law* 13, no. 2 (2001): 268.
24 Cited in Shāhnaz Khan, "Reconfiguring the Native Informant: Positionality in the Global Age," *Signs* 30, no. 4 (2005): 2017–37.
25 Khan, "Performing the native Informant," 275.
26 Ibid., 265.
27 See Hind Elhinnawy, "Afghanistan: The West Needs to Stop Seeing Women as in Need of 'Saving,'" *The Conversation* (2021) https://theconversation.com/afghanistan-the-west-needs-to-stop-seeing-women-as-in-need-of-saving-170731.
28 See Hind Elhinnawy, "Nobel peace prize: Narges Mohammadi wins on behalf of thousands of Iranian women struggling for human rights," *The Conversation* (2023), available at https://theconversation.com/nobel-peace-prize-narges-mohammadi-wins-on-behalf-of-thousands-of-iranian-women-struggling-for-human-rights-215190.
29 Khan, "Performing the Native Informant," 270.
30 Kiran Grewal, "Reclaiming the Voice of the 'Third World Woman': But What Do We Do When We Don't Like What She Has to Say? The Tricky Case of Ayaan Hirsi Ali," *Interventions* 14, no. 4 (2012): 571.
31 Ibid., 581

Glossary

al-Azhar: Literally meaning "most luminous," al-Azhar is the world's oldest mosque-university and Sunnī Islam's foremost seat of learning. It was founded by Jawhar, the Sicilian commander of the army sent by the Fāṭimid caliph-imam (r. 953–975 CE), in 970 CE after having laid the foundations of a new capital, al-Qāhira (the victorious), now the city of Cairo. al-Azhar remains a focal point of Islamic religious and cultural life for Egypt and the entire Muslim world.

Ashkenazi Jews: Also known as Ashkenazic Jews or Ashkenazim, the Jewish diaspora that lived in Central and Eastern Europe. The term was initially used to define a distinct cultural group of Jews who settled in the tenth century in Western Germany. Eventually, most Ashkenazi Jews relocated to the Polish Commonwealth (today's Poland, Lithuania, Latvia, Ukraine, and Belarus).

Banlieue: A French word that means a disadvantaged inner-city area, with roughly the same meaning as cité. While the term translates literally as "suburb," it is often more accurately equated with the term "ghetto": underprivileged, state-subsidized housing estates on the outskirts of major cities in France.

Burqa: An outer garment worn by some Muslim women to cover the body and face. It is also known as chadaree or chador in Pakistan and Afghanistan and Parnja in Central Asia. The term is sometimes conflated with the niqāb, a face veil. The term is usually used in Asia, not in the Arab world.

Caliphate: Known in the English language as "Islamic State," political-religious state comprising the Muslim community, the lands, and the people under its domination in the centuries following the death of the Prophet Muhammed. Ruled by a caliph (Arabic khalīfah, "successor"), who held temporal and sometimes a degree of spiritual authority, the empire of the Caliphate grew rapidly through conquest during its first two centuries to include most of Southwest Asia, North Africa, and Spain. Later, the Mongol destruction of Baghdad in 1258 brought about its decline, and it ceased to exist as a functioning political institution.

Da'wa: Also written as Da'wah, an Arabic word that literally means "issuing a summon" or "making an invitation." The term is often used to describe how Muslims teach others about the beliefs and practices of their Islamic faith. For certain groups within Islam, da'wa is also considered a political activity, a duty to actively encourage fellow Muslims to pursue greater piety in all aspects of their lives, a definition that has become central to contemporary Islamic thought.

Eid: The word means "feast" or "festival." Each year, Muslims celebrate two festivals: Eid al-Fitr and Eid al-Adha. Eid al-Fitr means "festival of the breaking of the fast" and is celebrated at the end of the holy month of Ramadan when many adult Muslims fast. Eid al-Adha means "feast of the sacrifice" and is celebrated just over two months after Eid al-Fitr, coinciding with the end of Hajj, the annual Islamic pilgrimage to Mecca in Saudi Arabia.

Fatwa: A nonbinding legal opinion on the point of sharia given by a qualified jurist in response to a question posed by a private individual, judge, or government. The jurist issuing fatwas is called a mufti. Fatwas are usually issued in response to questions from individuals or Islamic courts. A requester who finds a fatwa unconvincing is permitted to seek another.

Fiqh: Often described as the human understanding of sharia. Fiqh expands and develops sharia through the interpretation of the Qur'ān and Hadīth and is implemented by the rulings of jurists on questions presented to them. Whereas sharia is "divine," thus fixed, fiqh is created by humans and thus amendable.

Foreign Fighters: According to the International Association of Chiefs of Police, foreign fighters are individuals recruited to travel to a conflict zone or choose to do so to train and fight with a particular group. This trend has become an increasing concern in the last decade as individuals from Europe and North America have sought to train and fight al-Qaeda, ISIS, and their affiliates in places such as Afghanistan, Pakistan, Somalia, and Yemen.

Hadīth: Refers to what most Muslims and the mainstream schools of Islamic thought believe to be a record of the words, actions, and silent approvals of the Islamic prophet Muhammad as transmitted through chains of narrators.

Hajj: An annual Islamic pilgrimage to Mecca, Saudi Arabia, the holiest Muslim city. Hajj is a mandatory religious duty for Muslims that must be carried out at least once in a lifetime by all adult Muslims who are physically and financially capable of undertaking the journey and supporting their families during their absence from home.

Haram: An Arabic word meaning "sinful" often refers to an act forbidden in Islam, such as pork-related products, alcohol, gambling, extramarital sex, and pornography.

Harem: Although usually associated in western thought with Muslim practices, harems are known to have existed in the pre-Islamic civilizations of the Middle East; there, the harem served as the secure, private quarters of women who nonetheless played various roles in public life.

Hijab: An Arabic word meaning barrier or partition. In Islam, the term is widely used to refer to the head covering that many Muslim women wear. Popular schools of Islamic thought assert that Muslim women are required to wear it in front of any man they could theoretically marry.

Hudood: The Arabic term hadd (plural: hudood or hudud) is defined as a punishment stated in Islamic law for impinging the limits set by Allah. Specific punishments are stated in the Qur'ān and the Sunnah as applicable to certain crimes, such as adultery, theft, drinking alcohol, highway robbery, and more. Hudood punishments range from public lashing and stoning to death, amputation of hands, and more. These punishments were applied in premodern Islam, and their use in some modern states has been controversial.

Ijtihād: Arabic for "effort" in Islamic law, the independent or original interpretation of problems not precisely covered by the Qur'ān, Hadīth, and ijmā' (scholarly consensus). In the early Muslim community, every adequately qualified jurist had the right to exercise such original thinking, mainly in ra'y (personal judgment) and qiyās (analogical reasoning). But with the crystallization of madhhabs (legal schools) under the Abbāsids (750–1258), jurists of the majority Sunnī branch of Islam came to be associated with one or another of the schools of law.

Imam: An Islamic leadership position, commonly used as the title of a worship leader of a mosque and community, who leads prayers and provides religious guidance among Sunnī Muslims. For Shi'a, imams are leaders of the Umma (Islamic community) after the Prophet.

Irtidad: An Arabic word that means to cause to revert, reject, repel, avert, or return. It originates from the root word radd, which, among other connotations, means to retreat, retire, withdraw, or fall back from. In the context of Muslim fiqh, it is equated with renunciation or abonnement of Islam by a Muslim. The apostate is called murtad. For Muslim jurists, the terms irtidad or ridda are generally used to describe the act of a convert, a blasphemer, or a heretic.

Jihad: The word's literal meaning in the Arabic language is struggle or effort. Muslims at large use it to describe three different meanings: a believer's internal struggle to live out the Muslim faith "as well as possible," a struggle to build a good Muslim society, and broadly used by fundamentalists, signifying a holy war, a struggle to defend Islam. With the rise of Islamic fundamentalism, the term and its relevance for modern-day Muslims became highly contested.

Kufr: The literal meaning is to hide. Ingratitude is also called kufr because the recipient hides the bounties of the giver (by denying it or not acknowledging it). In sharia, kufr refers to the denial of anything Allah obliges belief in. A person who does not consider any of the definite teachings of the Prophet, Qur'ān, or both to be true or disapproves of them is called a kafir (disbeliever).

Laïcité: Olivier Roy defines it as a philosophy, a political principle, and a legislative tool. But the concept is far more complex than it might appear. Laïcité was fully developed under the Third Republic, with the 1905 law that separated the state and the church, and it continues to govern the relations between the two to the present day. In English, it is referred to as "French secularism."

Madrasa: Sometimes transliterated as madrasah or madrassa, the Arabic word for any type of educational institution, secular or religious (of any religion), whether for elementary or higher education. In a historical context, the term generally refers to a particular kind of institution in the Muslim world, which primarily taught Islamic law and jurisprudence and other subjects on occasion.

Maghreb: The Maghreb (Arabic: "West"), also spelled Maghrib, is a region of North Africa bordering the Mediterranean Sea. The ancients' Africa Minor once included Moorish Spain and now comprises the Atlas Mountains and the coastal plains of Morocco, Algeria, Tunisia, and Libya.

Niqāb: A black veil worn by some Muslim women in public, covering the entire face apart from the eyes. According to the majority of Muslim scholars, face veiling is not a requirement of Islam. However, a minority assert that women are required to cover their faces in public.

Purdah: A custom practiced in some Muslim and Hindu societies in which women either remain in a particular part of the house or cover their faces and bodies to avoid being seen by men who are not related to them.

Sati: Also spelled Su-thi or Suttee, a traditional Hindu practice of a widow immolating herself on her husband's funeral pyre. The Sati tradition was prevalent among certain sects of society in ancient India, who either took the vow or deemed it a great honor to die on the funeral pyres of their husbands.

Shāh: In old Persian, shāh refers to the title of the kings of Iran or Persia. When compounded as shāhanshāh, it denotes "king of kings," or emperor, a title adopted by the twentie-century Pahlavi dynasty in evocation of the ancient Persian "king of kings," Cyrus II the Great (r. 559–c. 529 BC).

Sharia: An Arabic term that refers to wide-ranging moral and broad ethical principles drawn from the Qur'ān and the Hadīth (practices and sayings of Prophet Muhammad). These broad principles are interpreted by jurists who produce specific legal rulings and moral prescriptions, commonly referred to as fiqh (see above).

Sheikh: Also spelled sheik, shaikh, or shaykh, an honorary title of respect dating to pre-Islamic antiquity. It usually refers to a venerable man of more than fifty years of age, literally meaning "elder." In a monarchical context, it is also translated as "Lord or Master." It commonly designates a chief of a tribe or a royal family member in the Gulf Arab states, or a Muslim religious scholar.

Shi'i /Shiite: A branch of Islam that, similar to the Sunnī branch, strives to live according to the Sunna (the example of Prophet Muhammad, as interpreted by the teachings of their hereditary imams). In addition, they recognize the ongoing leadership and strive to follow the guidance of the imams, who are responsible for interpreting the faith. Shi'i Muslims believe that the Prophet declared his nephew Ali as his successor to lead the Muslim community on several occasions. This is, perhaps, one of the major differences between Shi'i and Sunnī Muslims, who believe that the successor is the prophet's companion, Abu Bakr.

Sufi/Sufism: A mystical Islamic belief and practice in which Muslims seek to find the truth of divine love and knowledge through direct personal experience of God. It consists of a variety of mystical paths designed to discover the nature of humanity and God and facilitate the experience of the presence of divine love and wisdom in the world.

Sunnī: The largest branch of the Muslim community. The name is derived from the Sunnah, the exemplary behavior of the Prophet Muhammed. Sunnī life is guided by four schools of legal thought—Hanafi, Maliki, Shafi'I, and Hanbali—each of which strives to develop practical applications of revelation and the Prophet's example.

Ulamā': Singular 'ālim, also spelled Ulemā', the learned of Islam, those who possess the quality of 'ilm (knowledge) in its widest sense. From the 'ulamā' who are versed theoretically and practically in the Muslim sciences, come the religious teachers of the Islamic community—theologians, muftis (canon lawyers), qadis (judges), professors—and high state religious officials. In a narrower sense, 'ulamā' may refer to a council of learned men holding government appointments in a Muslim state.

Umma: Sometimes spelled Ummah is an Arabic word usually translated in English as "nation." However, Umma does not only define a group of people with common ancestry or in the same geographical region; it also means "the Islamic community," seen by many Muslims as a community without borders united under the guidance of the one God.

Zina: An Islamic legal term referring to unlawful sexual intercourse. According to traditional jurisprudence, zina can include adultery, fornication, prostitution, rape, sodomy, and incest. Zina must be proved by testimony of four Muslim eyewitnesses to the actual act of penetration or a confession repeated four times and not retracted later. Making an accusation of zina without presenting the required eyewitnesses is itself a hudood offense.

Bibliography

Abbas, Sadia. 2013. "The Echo Chamber of Freedom: The Muslim Woman and the Pretext of Agency." *Boundary 2* 40 (1): 155–89. doi:10.1215/01903659-2072909.

Abbas, Tahir, and Imran Awan. 2016. "Limits of UK Counterterrorism Policy and Its Implications for Islamophobia and Far Right Extremism." *International Journal for Crime, Justice and Social Democracy* 4 (3): 16–29. doi:10.5204/ijcjsd.v4i3.241.

Abdelgadir, Aala, and Vicky Fouka. 2019. "France's Headscarf Ban: The Effects on Muslim Integration in the West." *The Forum: ERF Policy Portal*. May 14. Accessed June 6, 2024. https://theforum.erf.org.eg/2019/05/07/frances-headscarf-ban-effects-muslim-integration-west/.

Abdel-Malek, Anouar. 1963. "Orientalism in Crisis." *Diogenes* 11 (44): 103–40. doi:10.1177/039219216301104407.

Abdulla, Kia. 2020. "It Is Possible to Be a Secular Muslim." *Inews*. 6 July. Accessed Jun 6, 2024. https://inews.co.uk/opinion/secular-muslim-islam-faith-484560.

Abu-Lughod, Leila, ed. 1998. *Remaking Women: Feminism and Modernity in the Middle East*. Princeton, NJ: Princeton University Press.

Abu-Lughud, Leila. 2013. *Do Muslim Women Need Saving?* Cambridge, MA: Harvard University Press.

Abu-Odeh, Lama. 2019. "Post Secularism and the Woman Question." *Georgetown Law Faculty Publications and Other Works* (2142): 1–6. https://scholarship.law.georgetown.edu/facpub/2142.

Adams, Richard. 2015. "Student Union Blocks Speech by 'Inflammatory' Anti-sharia Activist." *The Guardian*. 26 September. Accessed June 6, 2024. https://www.theguardian.com/education/2015/sep/26/student-union-blocks-speech-activist-maryam-namazie-warwick.

Afshar, Haleh. 2008. "Can I See Your Hair? Choice, Agency and Attitudes." *Ethnic and Racial Studies* 31 (2): 411–27.

Afshar, Haleh, and Mary Maynard. 1994. *The Dynamics of Race and Gender: Some Feminist Interventions*. London: Taylor & Francis Group.

Agadjania, Alexander. 2014. "Vulnerable Post-Soviet Secularities: Patterns and Dynamics in Russia and Beyond." In *Multiple Secularities beyond the West: Religion and Modernity in the Global Age*, ed. Marian Burchardt, Monika Wohlrab-Sahr, and Matthias Middell, 241–60. Boston: De Gruyter.

Ahmad, Maryam, and James Deshaw Rae. 2015. "Women, Islam, and Peacemaking in the Arab Spring." *Peace Review* 27 (3): 312–19. doi:10.1080/10402659.2015.1063373.

Ahmad, Nehaluddin. 2012. "Modern Debate on the Socio-Political Rights of Muslim Women." *Asia-Pacific Journal on Human Rights and the Law* 13 (1): 42–64. doi:10.11 63/138819012X13323234709785 .

Ahmed, Ghadeer. 2017. "Outlawed Pregnancy: The Consequences of Pregnancy outside Marriage for Egyptian Women." *Sister-hood*. 18 July. Accessed June 5, 2024. https://sister-hood.com/ghadeer-ahmed/outlawed-pregnancy/.

Ahmed, Leila. 1992. *Women and Gender in Islam: Roots of a Modern Debate*. New Haven: Yale Unversity Press.

Ahmed, Leila. 2011. *A Quiet Revolution: The Veil's Resurgence, from the Middle East to America*. New Haven: Yale Univcrsity Press.

Ahmed, Sara. 2000. *Strange Encounters: Embodied Others in Post-coloniality*. London: Routledge.

Ahmed, Sara. 2010. *The Promise of Happiness*. Durham, NC: Duke University Press.

Ahmed, Sara. 2012. *On Being Included: Racism and Diversity in Institutional Life*. Durham, NC: Duke University Press.

Ahmed-Gosh, Huma. 2008. "Dilemmas of Islamic and Secular Feminists and Feminisms." *Journal of International Women's Studies* 9 (3): 99–116. https://vc.brid gew.edu/jiws/vol9/iss3/7.

Akalay, Yahya. 2021. "Re-reading the Relationship between Secular and Islamic Feminism(s) in Morocco: The Third Way as an Alternative Feminist Paradigm." *Feministische Studien* 39 (1): 17–35. doi:https://doi.org/10.1515/fs-2021-0002.

Akalay, Yahya. 2022. "Secularism and the Muslim Women Question: A Critique of Secularism as a Frame of Reference for Gender Equality." *Journal of Gender, Culture and Society* 2 (1): 57–67. https://al-kindipublisher.com/index.php/jgcs/article/view/3320.

Akbar, Amna, and Rupal Oza. 2012. "'Muslim Fundamentalism' and Human Rights in an Age of Terror and Empire." In *Gender, National Security and Counter-Terrorism: Human Rights Perspectives*, ed. Margaret L. Satterthwaite and Jayne Huckerby, 52–182. London: Routledge.

Akhtar, Aasim Sajjid. 2016. "Dreams of a Secular Republic: Elite Alienation in Post-Zia Pakistan." *Journal of Contemporary Asia* 46 (4): 641–58. doi:10.1080/00472336.2016 .1193214.

Al Wazni,Anderson Beckmann. 2015. "Muslim Women in America and the Hijab: A Study of Empowerment, Feminist Identity, and Body image." *Social Work* 60 (4): 325–33. http://www.jstor.org/stable/24881182.

Alaa, Fathimath, Sariburaja Kennimrod, Arvin Tajari, and Muhammad Ammar Hisyam Mohd Anuar. 2022. "India's Citizenship Amendment Act (CAA) Of 2019: A Case Study of Anti-Muslim Sentiment in India: Akta Pindaan Kewarganegaraan 2019 India: Kajian Kes Sentimen Anti-Muslim Di India." *Journal of Interdisciplinary and Strategic Studies* 3 (5) (2022): 268–82. doi:10.47548/ijistra.2022.51.

al-Ali, Nadja. 2000. *Secularism, Gender and the State in the Middle East: The Egyptian Women's Movement*. Cambridge: Cambridge University Press.

al-Ali, Nadje. 2002. *Women's Movements in the Middle East: Case Studies of Egypt and Turkey*. Centre for Gender Studies, SOAS, University of London, Geneva: United Nations Research Institute for Social Development.

Alexander, M. Jacqui. 2005. *Pedagogies of Crossing: Meditations on Feminism, Sexual Politics, Memory, and the Sacred*. Durham, NC: Duke University Press.

Alghamdi, Sameha. 2020. *Orientalism and Its Challenges: Feminst Critique of Orientalist Knowledge Production*. Toronto: York University.

Ali, Ayaan Hirsi. 2007. *Infidel*. New York: Simon & Schuster.

Ali, Faiza, and Jawad Syed. 2018. "'Good Muslim Women' at Work: An Islamic and Postcolonial Perspective on Ethnic Priviledge." *Journal of Management & Organization* 24 (5): 679–97.

Ali, Inbisat, and Taimur Ali. 2019. "Beyond Pakistani Harem: Women's Spaces, Neo-Colonial Patriarchy and Agency in My Feudal Lord by Tehmina Durrani." *American International Journal of Contemporary Research* 9 (2): 82–7. doi:10.30845/aijcr.v9n2p10.

Ali, Zahra. 2019. "Feminisms in Iraq: Beyond the Religious and Secular Divide." *Gender a výzkum / Gender and Research* 20 (2): 47–67. doi:http://dx.doi.org/10.13060/257 065 78.2019.20.2.483.

Alinejed, Masih. 2018. *The Wind in My Hair: My Fight for Freedom in Modern Iran*. London: Virago.

Allam, May. 2018. "Meet Hind Elhinnawy, the Egyptian Woman Who Defied the Social Norms." *Women of Egypt Network*. 21 July. Accessed June 5, 2024. https://womenofegyptmag.com/2018/07/21/meet-hind-elhinnawy-the-%D9%90%D9%90egyptian-woman-who-defied-the-social-norms/.

Alosh, Islam. 2018. "Rationality and Resentment in the Egyptian Critique of Orientalism; The Example of Anouar Andel-Malek and Hasan Hanafi." The University of Arizona. chrome-extension://efaidnbmnnnibpcajpcglclefindmkaj/https://repository.arizona.edu/bitstream/handle/10150/630557/azu_etd_16659_sip1_m.pdf?sequence=1&isAllowed=y.

Al-Qasimi, Noor. 2010. "Immodest Modesty: Accommodating Dissent and the 'Abaya-as-Fashion in the Arab Gulf States." *Journal of Middle East Women's Studies* 6 (1): 46–74. https://www.researchgate.net/publication/285046311_Immodest_Modesty_Accommodating_Dissent_and_the_%27Abaya-as-Fashion_in_the_Arab_Gulf_States?enrichId=rgreq-daf0e7834f294800d0d87aa8b0e666c3-XXX&enrichSource=Y292ZXJQYWdlOzI4NTA0NjMxMTtBUzo1MjgwOTEwNDg5MzEz.

Alrebh, Abdullah F. 2018. "Islamic Authority: A Matter of Guardianship." *Athens Journal of Social Sciences* 5 (2): 167–88. doi:https://doi.org/10.30958/ajss.5-2-3.

Alrebh, Abdullah F. 2019. "Muslims, Secularism, and the State." In *Handbook of Contemporary Islam and Muslim Lives*, ed. R. Lukens-Bull and M. Woodward, 1–17. Cham: Springer.

Amara, Fadela, and Sylvia Zappi. 2006. *Breaking the Silence: French Women's Voices from the Getto*. Berkley, CA: University of California Press.

Amer, Sahar. 2014. *What Is Veiling?* North Carolina: University of North Carolina Press.

Amrane-Minne, Danièle Djamila, and Farida Abu-Haidar. 1999. "Women and Politics in Algeria from the War of Independence to Our Day." *Research in African Literatures* 3 (3, Dissent Algeria): 62–77. https://www.jstor.org/stable/3821017.

An-Na`im, Abdullahi Ahmed. 2010. "Islam and Secularism." In *Comparative Secularisms in a Global Age*, ed. Linell E. Cady and Elizabeth Shakman Hurd, 217–18. New York: Palgrave Macmillan.

Ansari, Sarah. 2009. "Polygamy, Purdah and Political Representation: Engendering Citizenship in 1950s Pakistan." *Modern Asian Studies* 43 (6): 1421–61. http://www.jstor.org/stable/40285018.

Anthias, Floya, and Nira Yuval-Davis. 1992. *Racialized Boundaries: Race, Nation, Gender, Colour and Class and the Anti-Racist Struggle*. London: Routledge.

Archer, Margaret Scotford. 1996. *Culture and Agency: The Place of Culture in Social Theory*. Cambridge: Cambridge University Press.

Archer, Nandini Naira. 2019. "Muslim Women Are Stuck between Islamophobes and Islamic Fundamentalists." *Open Democracy*. February 7. Accessed June 6, 2024. https://www.opendemocracy.net/en/5050/muslim-women-stuck-between-islamophobes-and-islamic-fundamentalists/.

Asad, Talal. 2003. *Formations of the Secular: Christianity, Islam, Modernity*. Stanford, CA: Stanford University Press.

Assa, Shirin. 2023. "Unveiling a Feminist Strike: The Case of 'Woman, Life, Freedom' in Iran," *Atlantis* 44, no. 2 (2023): 53–71. https://atlantisjournal.ca/index.php/atlantis/article/view/5787.

Badran, Margot. 2005. "Between Secular and Islamic Feminism/s: Reflections on the Middle East and Beyond." *Journal of Middle East Women's Studies* 1 (1): 6–28. https://www.jstor.org/stable/40326847.

Badran, Margot. 1991. "Competing Agenda: Feminists, Islam and the State in Nineteenth- and Twentieth Century Egypt." In *Women, Islam and the State*, ed. Deniz Kandiyoti. Philadelphia: Temple University Press.

Badran, Margot. 2009. *Feminism in Islam: Secular and Religious Convergences*. Oxford: One World.

Badran, Margot. 1995. *Feminists, Islam and Nation: Gender and the Making of Modern Egypt*. Princeton, NJ: Princeton University Press.

Badran, Margot. 2011. "From Islamic Feminism to a Muslim Holistic Feminism." *IDS Bulletin* 42 (1: Gender, Rights and Religion at the Crossroads): 78–87. doi:10.1111/j.1759-5436.2011.00203.x.

Badran, Margot. 1993. "Independent Women: More than a Century of Feminism in Egypt." In *Arab Women: Old Boundaries, New Frontiers*, ed. Judith E. Tucker. Bloomington: Indiana University Press.

Badran, Margot. 2010. "Re/plcing Islamic Feminism." *Critique Internationale* (Presses de Sciences Po) (46): 25–44. http://www.sciencespo.fr/ceri.

Badran, Margot, and Miriam Cooke. 1990. *Opening the Gates: A Century of Arab Feminist Writing*. Bloomington: Indiana University Press.

Bahi, Riham. 2011. "Islamic and Secular Feminisms: Two Discourses Mobilized for Gender Justice." *EUI Working Papers* (European University Institute) 25. https://hdl.handle.net/1814/17294.

Bakar, Osman. 2009. "Islam and the Challenge of Diversity and Pluralism: Must Islam Reform Itself?" *ICR Journal* 1 (1): 54–73.

Balchin, Cassandra. 2007. *Religious Fundamentalisms on the Rise: A Case for Action*. AWID, 1–31.

Bano, Samia. 2012. *Muslim Women and Shari'ah Councils: Transcending the Boundaries of Community and Law*. London: Palgrave Macmillan.

Baran, Zeyno, ed. 2010. *The Other Muslims: Moderate and Secular*. London: Palgrave Macmillan.

Barlas, Asma. 2013. "Uncrossed Bridges: Islam, Feminism and Secular Democracy." *Philosophy and Social Criticism* 39 (4–5): 417–25. doi:10.177/0191453713477346.

Barnes, Barry. 2000. *Understanding Agency: Social Theory and Responsible Action*. New York: Sage.

Bassel, Leah, and Akwugo Emejulu. 2017. *Minority Women and Austerity: Survival and Resistance in France and Britain*. Britol: Policy Press.

Basu, Amrita, ed. 1995. *The Challenge of Local Feminisms: Women's Movements in Global Perspective*. Colorado: Westview press.

Bayat, Asef. 2007. "A Women's Non-movement: What It Means to Be a Woman Activist in an Islamic State." *Comparative Studies of South Asia, Africa and the Middle East* 27 (1): 160–72. doi:10.1215/1089201x-2006-050.

Bayat, Asef. 2013. *Life as Politics: How Ordinary People Change the Middle East*. Palo Alto: Stanford University Press.

Bayat, Asef. 2007. *Making Islam Democratic: Social Movements and the Post-Islamist Turn*. Stanford: Stanford University Press.

Bayat, Asef. 2002. "Piety, Privilege and Egyptian Youth." *ISIM Newsletter* 10 (1): 23. https://hdl.handle.net/1887/16791.

Bayat, Asef. 1997. *Street Politics: Poor People's Movements in Iran*. New York: Columbia University Press.

Berger, Peter L. 1999. "The De-secularization of the World: A Global Overview." In *The De-secularization of the World: Resurgent Religion and World Politics*, ed. Peter L. Berger, 1–18. Grand Rapids, MI: William B. Eerdmans.

Berlinerblau, Jacques. 2014. "Introduction: Secularism and Its Confusions." In *Secularism on the Edge: Church-State Relations in the United States, France, and Israel*, ed. Jacques Berlinerblau, Sarah Fainberg, and Aurora Nou, 1–16. New York: Palgrave Macmillan.

Berman, Sheri. 2003. "Islamism, Revolution, and Civil Society." *Perspectives on Politics* 1 (2): 257–72. doi:10.1017/S1537592703000197.

Bhabha, Homi K. 1995. "*On Subaltern Secularism.* " in *WAF Journal* (6): 5–7.
Bhabha, Homi K. [1994] 2004. *The Location of Culture*. London: Routledge.
Bhargava, Rajeev. 2013. "Reimagining Secularism: Respect, Domination and Principled Distance." *Economic and Political Weekly* 48 (50): 79–92. https://www.jstor.org/stable/24479049.
Bhargava, Rajeev. 2011. "Religion, State, and Secularism: How Should States Deal with Deep Religious Diversity." In *The Handbook of Communications Ethics*, ed. George Cheney, Steve May, and Debashish Munshi, 401–13. London: Taylor & Francis..
Bhargava, Rajeev. 2010. *The Promise of India's Secular Democracy*. Oxford: Oxford University Press.
Bhargava, Rajeev. 2015. "We (in India) Have Always Been Post-secular." In *Global Secularisms in a Post-secular Age*, ed. Michael Rectenwald, Rochelle Almeida and George Levine, 109–36. Boston, MA: De Gruyter.
Bhimji, Fazila. 2012. *British Asian Muslim Women: Multiple Spacialities and Cosmopolitanism*. London: Palgrave Macmillan.
Bilge, Simra. 2010. "Beyond Subordination vs. Resistance: An Intersectional Approach to the Agency of Veiled Muslim Women." *Journal of Intercultural Studies* 31 (1: Women, Intersectionality and Diasporas): 28–9. doi:10.1080/07256860903477662.
Blair, Tony. 2001. "Leader's Speech, Brighton 2001." *Briths Political Speech*. Accessed June 6, 2024. http://www.britishpoliticalspeech.org/speech-archive.htm?speech=186.
Blundy, Rachel. 2015. "London Schoolgirl Who Recruited Three Classmates to Join IS in Syria 'Was Radicalised at East London Mosque." *The Standard*. August 2. Accessed June 6, 2024. https://www.standard.co.uk/news/london/london-schoolgirl-who-recruited-three-classmates-to-join-is-in-syria-was-radicalised-at-east-london-mosque-10433150.html.
Bohn, Lauren. 2012. "9 Faces of the New Egypt." *The Atlantic*. February 13. Accessed June 5, 2024. https://www.theatlantic.com/international/archive/2012/02/9-faces-of-the-new-egypt/253003/.
Booth, Marilyn. 2005. "Activism through Literature: Arguing Women's Rights in the Middle East." *The Yale Review* 93 (1): 1–26. doi:10.1111/j.0044-0124.2005.00873.x.
Booth, Marylin. 1995. "Exemplary Lives, Feminist Aspirations: Zaynab Fawwāz and the Arabic Biographical Tradition." *Journal of Arabic Literature* 26 (1/2: The Quest for Freedom in Modern Arab Literature): 120–46. https://www.jstor.org/stable/4183369.
Bouachrine, Ibtissam. 2014. *Women and Islam: Myths, Apologies, and the Limits of Feminist Critique*. Lanham, NC: Lexington Books.
Bracke, Sarah. 2008. "Conjugating the Modern/Religious, Conceptualizing Female Religious Agency: Contours of a 'Post-secular' Conjuncture." *Theory, Culture and Society* 25 (6): 51–67. doi:10.1177/0263276408095544.
Bracke, Sarah. 2011. "Subjects of Debate: Secular and Sexual Exceptionalism, and Muslim Women in the Netherlands." *Feminist Review* 98 (Islam in Europe): 28–46. doi:10.1057/fr.2011.5.

Brah, Avtah. 1987. "Women of South Asian Origin in Britain: Issues and Concerns." *South Asia Research* 7 (1): 39–54. doi:10.1177/026272808700700103.

Braidotti, Rosi. 2008. "In Spite of the Times: The Postsecular Turn in Feminism." *Theory, Culture and Society* 25 (6): 1–24. doi:10.1177/0263276408095542.

Brown, Katherine. 2006. "Realizing Muslim Women's Rights: The Role of Islamic Identity among British Muslim Women." *Women's Studies International Forum* 29 (4): 417–30. doi:10.1016/j.wsif.2006.05.002.

Bullock, Katherine. 2010. *Rethinking Muslim Women and the Veil: Challenging Historical and Modern Stereotypes*. London: International Insititute of Islamic Thought.

Burack, Cynthia. 2004. *Healing Identities: Black Feminist Thought and the Politics of Groups*. Ithaca, NY: Cornell University Press.

Burchardt, Marian, Monika Wohlrab-Sahr, and Matthias Middell. 2015. *Multiple Secularities beyond the West: Religion and Modernity in the Global Age*. Boston, MA: De Gruyter.

Burney, Shehla. 2012. "CHAPTER ONE: Orientalism: The Making of the Other." *Counterpoints* 417 (PEDAGOGY of the Other: Edward Said, Postcolonial Theory, and Strategies for Critique): 23–39. https://www.jstor.org/stable/42981698.

Butler, Judith. 1993. *Bodies That Matter: On the Discursive Limits of "Sex."* New York: Routledge.

Butler, Judith. 2006. *Gender Trouble: Feminism and the Subversion of Identity*. New York: Routledge.

Cady, Linell E., and Elizabeth Shaknman Hurd. 2010. *Comparative Secularisms in a Global Age*. New York: Palgrave Macmillan.

Çaha, Ömer. 2020. *The "Islamic women's" Movement: Transition from the Private Domain to the Public Sphere*. Vol. 1, in *Economic Empowerment of Women in the Islamic world: Theory and Practice*, ed. Toseef Azid and Jennifer L. Ward-Batts, 289–308. Singapore: World Scientific.

Cairo Scene. 2018. "Egyptian Activist Nawal El-Saadawi Accused of Blasphemy Again." *Cairo Scene*. July 12. https://cairoscene.com/buzz/nawal-saadawi-blasphemy-bbc.

Casanova, José. 1994. *Public Religions in the Modern World*. London: University of Chicago Press.

Chafiq, Chahla. 2011. *Islam politique, sexe et genre: À la lumière de l'expérience iranienne*. Paris: Presses Universitaires de France.

Chaoui, Saleh. 2023. "Embodied Faith and the Limits of Female Agency in Randa Abdel-Fattah's Does My Head Look Big in This?" *Fudan Journal of the Humanities and Social Sciences* 23–9. doi:10.1007/s40647-022-00359-5.

Chatterjee, Partha. 1989. "Colonialism, Nationalism, and Colonialized Women: The Contest in India." *American Ethnologist* 16 (4): 622–33. https://www.jstor.org/stable/645113.

Cheung, Kylie, Shoniqua Roach, Benita Roth, Jamia Wilson, and Rafia Zakaria. n.d. "Rafia Zakaria's against White Feminism." *Signs: Short Takes: Provocations on Public*

Feminism. Accessed June 6, 2024. https://signsjournal.org/zakaria/#:~:text=Agai nst%20White%20Feminism%20requires%20Western,thoughtfully%20offering%20 answers%20for%20each.

Chishti, Maliha. 2002. "The International Woman's Movement and the Politics of Participation for Muslim Women." *American Journal of Islamic Social Sciences* 19 (4): 80–99. doi:10.35632/ajis.v19i4.1917.

Chopra, Rohit. 2022. "Secularism, Religion, and the State in a Time of Global Crisis: Theoretical Reflections on the Work of Abdullahi An-Na'im." *Emory International Law Review* 36 (4): 647–59. https://scholarlycommons.law.emory.edu/ eilr/vol36/iss4/3?utm_source=scholarlycommons.law.emory.edu%2Feilr%2Fvo l36%2Fiss4%2F3&utm_medium=PDF&utm_campaign=PDFCoverPages.

Cimino, Richard, and Christopher Smith. 2007. "Secular Humanism and Atheism beyond Progressive Secularism." *Sociology of Religion* 66 (8): 407–24. doi:https://doi. org/10.1093/socrel/68.4.407.

Clarke, Janine, and Samah Krichah. 2021. "Secular Feminism in Tunisia: A Political Generations Approach." *Globalizations*. doi:https://doi-org.ntu.idm.oclc. org/10.1080/14747731.2021.2009309.

Cliteur, Paul. 2011. "Female Critics of Islamism: Liberal or Secular Islam?" *Feminist Theology* 19 (2): 154–67. doi:10.1177/0966735010384328.

Contractor, Sariya. 2012. *Muslim Women in Britain: Demystifying the Muslimah*. London: Routledge.

Cooke, Miraim. 1989. *Deconstructing War Discourse: Women's Participation in the Algerian Revolution*. Michigan: Michigan State University Press.

Cooke, Miriam. 2002. "Saving Brown Women." *Signs* 28 (1): 468–73.

Cooke, Miriam. 2001. *Women Claim Islam: Creating Islamic Feminism through Literature*. New York: Routledge.

Copson, Andrew. 2019. *Secularism: A Very Short Introduction*. Oxford: Oxford Academic.

Cutrufelli, Maria Rosa. 1983. *Women of Africa: Roots of Oppression*. London: Zed Press.

Daban, Nova. 2021. "'Islamophobia' Distracts from Tackling Anti-Muslim Bigotry." *National Secular Soceity*. November 30. Accessed May 31, 2022. https://www.secular ism.org.uk/opinion/2021/11/islamophobia-debate-distracts-from-tackling-anti-mus lim-bigotry.

Dabashi, Hamid. 2011. *Brown Skin, White Masks*. London: Pluto Press.

Dalaman, Zeynep Banu. 2021. "From Secular Muslim Feminism to Islamic Feminism(s) and New Generation Islamic Feminists in Egypt, Iran and Turkey." *Border Crossing* 77–91. doi:10.33182/bc.v11i1.1042.

Davis, Joseph E. 2002. "Narrative and Social Movements: The Power of Stories." In *Stories of Change: Narrative and Social Movements*, ed. Joseph E. Davis, 3–29. Albany: State Unversty of New York Press.

Davis, Nira Yuval. 2006. "Intersectionality and Feminist Politics." *European Journal of Women's Studies* 13 (3): 193–209. doi:10.1177/1350506806065752.

de Wenden, Catherine Wihtol. 2014. "Second-Generation Immigrants: Citizenship and Transnationalism/Inmigrantes de Segunda Generación: Ciudadanía y Transnacionalismo." *Araucaria* 16 (31): 147–70. https://revistascientificas.us.es/index.php/araucaria/article/view/813.

Deeb, Lara. 2006. *An Enchanted Modern: Gender and Public Piety in Shi'i Lebanon*. Princeton: Princeton University Press.

Deeb, Lara. 2015. "Thinking Piety and the Everyday Together: A Response to Fadil and Fernando." *HAU: Journal of Ethnographic Theory* 5 (2): 93–6.

Deeb, Lara, and Mona Harb. 2013. *Leisurely Islam: Negotiating Geography and Morality in Shi'ite South Beirut*. Princeton: Princeton University Press.

Deramo, Michele C. 2014. "Reflecting on the Politics of Piety." *SPECTRA: The Social, Political, Ethical, and Cultural Theory Archives* 3 (1).

Dhaliwal, Sukhwant. 2014. "Women against Fundamentalism: 25 Years of Anti-Racist, Anti-Fundamentalist Feminism." *Feminist Review* 108 (1): 88–9. https://www.jstor.org/stable/24571922.

Dhaliwal, Sukhwant, and Nira Yuval-Davis. 2014. *Women against Fundamentalism: Stories of Dissent and Solidarity*. London: Lawrence and Wishart.

Dhawan, Nikita, Elisabeth Fink, Johanna Leinius, and Rirhandu Mageza-Barthel. 2016. "Normative Legitimacy and Normative Dilemmas: Postcolonial Interventions." In *Negotiating Normativity: Postcolonial Appropriations, Contestations, and Transformations*, ed. Nikita Dhawan, Elisabeth Fink, Johanna Leinius and Rirhandu Mageza-Barthel, 1–23. New York: Springer.

Djavan, Chahdortt. 2004. *Que Pense Allah de l'Europe?* Paris: Gallimard.

Djavann, Chahdortt. 2016. *Les putes voilées n'iront jamais au paradis*. Paris: Grasset and Fasquelle.

Dokumacı, Pınar. 2022. "The Question of Collaboration between Secular Feminists and Pious Feminists in Turkey." *Digest of Middle East Studies: DOMES* 31 (4). doi:https://doi-org.ntu.idm.oclc.org/10.1111/dome.12275.

Donald, James, and Ali Rattansi. 1992. *Race, Culture and Difference*. London: Sage.

Drozdíková, Jarmila. 2005. "Review Article: Progressive Muslims." *Asian and African Studies* 14 (1): 83–95. https://www.jstor.org/stable/24571922.

Durand, Rebecca, and Myk Zeitlin. 2016. "Review: Women against Fundamentalism: Stories of Dissent and Solidarity." *Feminist Dissent* 1: 132–5.

Easat-Daas, A., and S. Ounissi. 2013. *European Muslim Youth and the Rise of the Far-right Anti-Muslim Narrative*. Brussels: Forum of Eurpoean Muslim Youth and Student Organisations.

Ebadi, Shirin. 2007. *Iran Awakening: A Memoir of Revolution and Hope*. London: Rider.

Edayat, Zaid. 2013. "Islamic Feminism: Roots, Development and Policies." *Global Policy* 4 (4): 359–68. doi:10.1111/1758-5899.12057.

Edwin, Shirin. 2016. *Privately Empowered: Expressing Feminism in Islam in Northern Nigerian Fiction*. Evanston, IL: Northwestern University Press.

Egypt Today. 2018. "Complaint Filed against Nawal el-Saadawi for Defaming Religions." *Egypt Today*. July 10. Accessed June 6, 2024. https://www.egypttoday.com/Article/1/53701/Complaint-filed-against-Nawal-el-Saadawi-for-defaming-religions.

Eickelman, Dale F., and Jon W. Anderson. 2003. "Redefining Muslim Publics." In *New Media in the Muslim World: The Emerging Public Sphere*, ed. Dale F. Eickelman and Jon W. Anderson, 1–18. Bloomington: Indiana University Press.

El Guindi, Fadwa. 2005. "Gendered Resistance, Feminist Veiling, Islamic Feminism." *Ahfad Journal* 22 (1): 53–78.

EL Guindi, Fadwa. 1999. *Veil: Modesty, Privacy, Resistance*. New York: Berg.

El Younssi, Anouar. 2018. "Maajid Nawaz, Irshad Manji, and the Call for a Muslim Reformation." *Politics, Religion and Ideology* 19 (3): 305–25. doi:10.1080/21567689.2018.1524327.

Elbasani, Arolda, and Murat Somer. 2015. "Muslim Secularisms in the European Context." In *Global Secularisms in a Post-Secular Age*, ed. Michael Rectenwald, Rochelle Almeida, and George Levine, 171–88. Boston, MA: De Grutyer.

Elhinnawy, Hind. 2021. "Afghanistan: The West Needs to Stop Seeing Women as in Need of 'Saving.'" *The Conversation*. 28 August. https://theconversation.com/afghanistan-the-west-needs-to-stop-seeing-women-as-in-need-of-saving-170731#comment_2643302.

Elhinnawy, Hind. 2020. *Contested Voices: Secular Muslim Women Activists in the Age of ISIS*. Canterbury: University of Kent. https://kar.kent.ac.uk/id/eprint/82264.

Elhinnawy, Hind. 2021. "Mothers of Intervention: The Politics of Motherhood in the Battle against ISIS." In *The Fourth International Conference on Gender Research*, ed. Elisabeth T. Pereira, Carlos Costa and Zelia Breda. Reading: Academic Conferences International Limited. 97–103. https://tinyurl.com/ICGR2021.

Elhinnawy, Hind. 2023. "Nobel Peace Prize: Narges Mohammadi Wins on Behalf of Thousands of Iranian Women Struggling for Human Rights." *The Conversation*. 6 October. Accessed June 5, 2024. https://theconversation.com/nobel-peace-prize-narges-mohammadi-wins-on-behalf-of-thousands-of-iranian-women-struggling-for-human-rights-215190.

Elhinnawy, Hind. 2012. *Rethinking Gender in the New Muslim Public Sphere: New Egyptian Religious Satellite Television in Relation to Young Female Viewers*. Saarbrücken: LAP Lambert Academic.

Elhinnawy, Hind. 2022. "Surviving Academia at the Times of COVID-19: A Critical Autoethnography of a Woman of Colour." *New Horizons in Adult Education and Human Resources Development*, 34 (3): 54–68. doi:10.1002/nha3.20364.

Elhinnawy, Hind. 2023. "The Role of Difference in Feminist Transnational Solidarity: Secular Muslim Feminists in the United Kingdom and France."

International Feminis Journal of Politics 25 (4): 593–614. doi:10.1080/14616742.2023.2206828.

Ellsworth, Elizabeth. 1992. "Why Doesn't This Feel Empowering? Working through the Repressive." In *Feminisms and Critical Pedagogy*, ed. Carmen Luke and Jennifer Gore, 90–119. New York: Routledge.

El Saadawi, Nawal. 1997. *The Nawal El Saadawi Reader*. London: Zed Books.

Eltahawy, Mona. 2016. *Headscarves and Hymens: Why the Middle East Needs a Sexual Revolution*. London: Widenfeld & Nicolson.

Eltahawy, Mona. 2010. "Rending the Veil—with a Little Help." *Twin Cities: Pioneer Press*. July 19, Accessed June 6, 2024. https://www.twincities.com/2010/07/19/mona-eltahawy-rending-the-veil-with-a-little-help/.

Emerson, Michael O., and David Hartman. 2006. "The Rise of Religious Fundamentalism." *Annual Review of Sociology* 32: 127–44. https://www.jstor.org/stable/29737734.

Esposito, John L., and Francois Burgat. 2003. *Modernizing Islam: Religion in the Public Sphere in the Middle East and Europe*. London: Hurst.

Esposito, John L., Yvonne Y. Haddad, and John O. Voll. 1991. *The Contemporary Islamic Revival: A Critical Survey and Bibliography*. Westport, CT: Greenwood.

Fadil, Nadia, and Mayanthi Fernando. 2015. "Rediscovering the 'Everyday' Muslim: Notes on an Anthropological Divide." *HAU: Journal of Ethnographic Theory* 5 (2): 59–88. doi:10.14318/hau5.2.005.

Fanon, Frantz. [1963] 2001. *The Wretched of the Earth*. New edition. Trans. Constance Farrington. London: Penguin.

Farris, Sara R. 2017. *In the Name of Women's Rights: The Rise of Femonationalism*. Durham, NC: Duke University Press.

Fayard, Nicole, and Yvette Rocheron. 2009. "Ni Putes ni Soumises: A Republican Feminism from the Quartiers Sensibles." *Modern and Contemporary France* 17 (1): 1–18. doi:10.1080/09639480802639736.

Felski, Rita. 1989. *Beyond Feminist Aesthetics: Feminist Literature and Social Change*. Cambridge, MA: Harvard University Press.

Feminist Translations. 2020. "Chahla Chafiq: 'Choosing the Veil Is Not Equivalent to Choosing a Lipstick.'" *Feminist Resources*. August 13. Accessed June 6, 2024. https://ressourcesfeministes.fr/2020/08/13/chahla-chafiq-choosing-the-veil-is-not-equivalent-to-choosing-a-lipstick/.

Fernando, Mayanthi L. 2009. "Exceptional Citizens: Secular Muslim Women and the Politics of Difference in France." *Social Anthropology* 17 (4 Special Issue: Muslim Women in Europe): 379–92. doi:10.1111/j.1469-8676.2009.00081.x.

Fernando, Mayanthi L. 2014. *The Republic Unsettled: Muslim French and the Contradictions of Secularism*. Durham, NC: Duke University Press.

Fernando, Mayathni L. 2010. "Reconfiguring Freedom: Muslim Piety and the Limits of Secular Law and Public Discourse in France." *American Ethnologist* 37 (1): 19–35. doi:10.1111/j.1548-1425.2010.01239.x.

Field, Nathan, and Ahmed Hamam. 2009. "Salafi Satellite TV in Egypt." *Arab, Media & Society*: 1–11.
Foucault, Michel. 1980. *Power/Knowledge: Selected Interviews and Other Writings, 1972–1977*. Brighton: Harvester Press.
Foucault, Michel. 1998. *The History of Sexuality*. New York: Pantheon.
Foucault, Michel. 1982. "The Subject and Power." *Critical Inquiry* 8 (4): 777–95.
Fraser, Nancy. 1990. "Rethinking the Public Sphere: A Contribution to the Critique of Actually Existing Democracy." *Social Text* 25–6: 56–80. http://www.jstor.org/stable/466240?origin=JSTOR-pdf.
Freeman, Michael. 2010. *Human Rights: An Interdisciplinary Approach*. Cambridge: Polity Press.
Gabesid English Gost. n.d. "Macaulay & the English Canon." *Gabesid English Gost*. Accessed June 6, 2024. https://gabesibenglishgost.weebly.com/macauley--the-english-canon.html.
Gatenby, Bev, and Maria Humphries. 2000. "Feminist Participatory Action Research: Methodological and Ethical Issues." *Women's Studies International Forum* 23 (1): 89–105.
Gazi, Faisal. 2009. "The First Muslim Secularist." *The Guardian*. April 9. Accessed June 5, 2024. https://www.theguardian.com/commentisfree/belief/2009/apr/09/religion-islam-secularism-egypt.
Gökarıksel, Banu, and Anna Secor. 2010. "Islamic-ness in the Life of a Commodity: Veiling-Fashion in Turkey." *Transactions of the Institute of British Geographers* 35 (3): 313–33. doi:10.1111/j.1475-5661.2010.00384.x.
GoleSorkh, Nano. 2014. "Political Activist Homa Arjomand on One Secular Education for All." *YouTube*. October 30. Accessed June 6, 2024. https://www.youtube.com/watch?v=gc0uK1vD5zw.
Golley, Nawar Al-Hassan. 2004. "Is Feminism Relevant to Arab Women?" *Third World Quarterly* 25 (3): 521–36. https://www.jstor.org/stable/3993823.
Grewal, Inderpal, and Caren Kaplan. 2001. "Global Identities: Theorizing Transnational Studies of Sexuality." *GLQ: A Journal of Lesbian and Gay Studies* 7 (4): 663–79.
Grewal, Inderpal, and Caren Kaplan. 1998. *Scattered Hegemonies: Postmodernity and Transnational Feminist Practices*. Minneapolis: University of Minnesota Press.
Grewal, Kiran Kaur. 2017. *Racialised Gang Rape and the Reinforcement of Dominant Order: Discourses of Gender, Race and Nation*. London: Routledge.
Grewal, Kiran Kaur. 2016. *The Socio-Political Practice of Human Rights: Between the Universal and the Particular*. London: Routledge.
Grewal, Kiran. 2012. "Reclaiming the Voice of the 'Third World Woman': But What Do We Do When We Don't Like What She Has to Say? The Tricky Case of Ayaan Hirsi Ali." *Interventions* 14 (4): 569–90. doi:10.1080/1369801X.2012.730861.
Grewal, Kiran. 2007. "The Threat from Within: Representations of the Banlieue in French Popular Discourse." In *Europe: New Voices, New Perspectives: Proceedings*

From the Contemporary Europe Research Centre Postgraduate Conference, 2005/2006, ed. Matt Killingsworth, 41–67. Melbourne: Contemporary Europe Research Centre, University of Melbourne.

Gross, Neil. 2010. "Charles Tilly and American Pragmatism." *American Sociologist* 41 (4, Remembering Charles Tilly): 337–57. https://www.jstor.org/stable/40983484.

Guénif-Souilamas, Nacira. 2006. "The Other French Exception: Virtuous Racism and the War of the Sexes in Postcolonial France." *French Politics, Culture and Society* 24 (3): 23–41. https://www.jstor.org/stable/42843464.

Guest, Carly. 2016. *Becoming Feminist: Narratives and Memories*. London: Palgrave Macmillan.

Guha, Ranajit, ed. 1997. *A Subaltern Studies Reader, 1986–1995*. Minneapolis: University of Minnesota Press.

Guinier, Lani, and Gerald Torres. 2002. *The Miner's Canary: Enlisting Race, Resisting Power, Transforming Democracy*. Cambridge, MA: Harvard University Press.

Gutmann, Amy. 2003. *Identity in Democracy*. Princeton: Princeton University Press.

Habermas, Jurgen. 2011. "'The political': The Rational Meaning of a Questionable Inheritance of Political Theology." In *The Power of Religion in the Public Sphere*, ed. Eduardo Mendieta and Jonathan Vanantwerpen, 15–33. New York: Columbia University Press.

Habermas, Jürgen. 2008. "Notes on Post-secular Society." *New Perspectives Quarterly* 25: 17–29. doi:https://doi.org/10.1111/j.1540-5842.2008.01017.x.

Haddad, Yvonne Yazbeck, John L. Esposito, and Elizabeth Hiel. 1997. *The Islamic Revival since 1988: A Critical Survey and Bibliography*. Westport, CT: Greenwood Press.

Hafez, Sherine. 2011. *An Islam of Her Own: Reconsidering Religion and Secularism in Women's Islamic Movements*. New York: New York University Press.

Harfouch, Ali, and Abdur-Rafay. 2019. "The US State and the Making a Secular Islam." *Traversing Tradition*. April 15. Accessed June 6, 2024. https://traversingtradition.com/2019/04/15/the-us-state-and-the-making-of-a-secular-islam/.

Hartley, Gemma. 2018. *Fed Up: Emotional Labor, Women, and the Way Forward*. New York: HarperCollins.

Hasan, Noorhaidi. 2009. "The Making of Public Islam: Piety, Agency, and Commodification on the Landscape of the Indonesian Public Sphere." *Contemporary Islam* 3: 29–250.

Helie-Lucas, Marie-Aimee. 1990. "Women, Nationalism, and Religion in the Algerian Liberation Struggle." In *Opening the Gates: An Anthology of Arab Feminist Writing*, ed. Margot Badran and Miriam Cooke,105–14. Bloomington: Indiana University Press.

Hélie-Lucas, Marieme. 2011. "A South-North Transfer of Political Competence." *Women Living under Muslim Laws* Dossier 30–1 (The Struggle for Secularism in Europe and North America): 43–85.

Hélie-Lucas, Marieme. 2011. "Introduction." *Journal of Women Living under Muslim Laws* Dossier 30-1 (The Struggle for Secularism in Europe and North America): 1-7.

Hélie-Lucas, Marieme, ed. 2011. "Introduction." In The Struggle for Secularism in Europe and North America." *Women Living under Muslim Laws*. Dossier 30-1.

Hemmings, Clare. 2012. "Affective Solidarity: Feminist Reflexivity and Political Transformation." *Feminist Theory* 13 (2): 147-61. doi.org/10.1177/1464700112442643.

Herath, Thisaranie. 2016. "Women and Orientalism: 19th Century Representations of the Harem by European Female Travellers and Ottoman Women." *Constellations* 7 (1): 31-40. doi:10.29173/cons27054.

Herr, Ranjoo Seodu. 2014. "Reclaiming Third World Feminism: Or Why Transnational Feminism Needs Third World Feminism." *Meridians* 12 (1): 1-30. https://www.jstor.org/stable/10.2979/meridians.12.1.1.

Hesová, Zora. 2019. "Secular, Islamic or Muslim Feminism? The Place of Religion in Women's Perspectives on Equality in Islam." *Gender a výzkum / Gender and Research* 20 (2): 26-46. doi:http://dx.doi.org/10.13060/25706578.2019.20.2.482.

Hogben, Alia. 2011. "Introduction of Religious Family Laws in Canada: A Case Study." *Women Living under Muslim Laws* Dossier 30-1 (The Struggle for Secularism in Europe and North America): 183-90.

Holstein, James A. 2000. *The Self We Live By: Narrative Identity in a Post-modern World*. Oxford: Oxford University Press.

Hoodfar, Homa. 2015. *Women's Sport as Politics in Muslim Contexts*. London: Women Living under Muslim Laws.

Hoodfar, Homa, and Fatemah Sadeghi. 2009. "Against all Odds: The Women's Movement in the Islamic Republic of Iran." *Development* 52 (2): 215-23. doi:10.1057/dev.2009.19.

Hoodfar, Homa, and Shadi Sadr. 2010. "Islamic Politics and Women's Quest for Gender Equality in Iran." *Third World Quarterly* 31 (6): 885-903.

Horsfall, Debbie. 2001. "Black Holes in the Writing Process: Narratives of Speech and Silence." In *Critical Moments in Qualitative Research*, ed. Debbie Horsfall, Hilary Bryne-Armstrong, and Joy Higgs, 82-91. Woburn: Butterworth-Heinemann.

Human Rights Watch. 2023. "Iran: Mass Arrests of Women's Rights Defenders." *Human Rights Watch*. August 19. Accessed June 6, 2024. https://www.hrw.org/news/2023/08/19/iran-mass-arrests-womens-rights-defenders.

Huntington, Samuel P. 1993. "The Clash of Civilizations?" *Foreign Affairs* 72 (3): 22-49.

Hussein, Shakira. 2019. *From Victims to Suspects: Muslim Women since 9/11*. Yale: Yale University Press.

Inge, Anabel. 2017. *The Making of a Salafi Muslim Woman: Paths to Conversion*. New York: Oxford University Press.

Inglehart, Ronald, and Pippa Norris. 2003."The True Clash of Civilizations." *Foreign Policy* (135): 62-70. https://www.jstor.org/stable/3183594.

Inglehart, Ronald, and Pippa Norris. 2004. *Sacred and Secular: Religion and Politics Worldwide*. Cambridge: Cambridge University Press.
Iranwire. 2023. "Iranian Influential Women: Masih Alinejad (1976–Present)." *Iranwire*. September 25. https://iranwire.com/en/women/120868-iranian-influent ial-women-masih-alinejad-1976-present/.
Ismail, Abir M. 2017. "Muḥajababes, Meet the New Fashionable, Attractive and Extrovert Muslim Woman: A Study of the Hijāb Practice among Individualized Young Muslim Women in Denmark." *Scandanivian Journal of Islamic Studies* 9 (2): 106–29. doi:10.7146/tifo.v9i2.25355.
Ismail, Salwa. 1998. "Confronting the Other: Identity, Culture, Politics, and Conservative Islamism in Egypt." *International Journal of Middle East Studies* 30: 199–225. https://www.jstor.org/stable/164700.
Jaiswal, Anuradha. 2018–19. "The Evolution of Women's Movements in Colonial India." *Proceedings of the Indian History Congress. Proceedings of the Indian History Congress*: 577–82. https://www.jstor.org/stable/26906294.
Jamal, Amina. 2021. "The Entanglement of Secularism and Feminism in Pakistan." *Meridians: Feminism, Race, Transnationalism* 20 (2): 370–95. https://muse-jhu-edu.ntu.idm.oclc.org/article/856879.
Jansen, Yolande. 2013. *Secularism, Assimilation and the Crisis of Multiculturalism: French Modernist Legacies*. Amsterdam: Amsterdam University Press.
Jayawardena, Kumari. 1986. *Feminism and Nationalism in the Third World*. New Delhi: Kali for Women.
Jayawardena, Kumari. 2023. "Feminism and Nationalism in the Third world." *Progressive International*. August 31. Accessed June 6, 2024. https://progressive.international/wire/2023-08-31-kumari-jayawardena-feminism-and-national ism-in-the-Third world/en.
Jeffrey, Patricia. 1979. *Frogs in a Well: Indian Women in Purdah*. London: Zed Press.
Jelodar, Esmaeil Zeiny, Noraini Md Yusof, and Ruzy Suliza Hashim. 2014. "Muslim Women's Memoirs: Disclosing Violence or Reproducing Islamophobia?" *Asian Social Science* 10 (14): 215–23. doi:http://dx.doi.org/10.5539/ass.v10n14p215.
Jenkins, Richard. 1997. *Rethinking Ethnicity*. London: Sage.
Joly, Danièle. 2017. "Muslim Women's Politcal Participation in British and French Society." *Revue Européenne de Migrations Internationales* 33 (2–3): 157–81.
Joly, Danièle, and Khursheed Wadia. 2017. *Muslim Women and Power: Political and Civic Engagement in West European Societies*. London: Palgrave Macmillan.
Joseph, Souad. 2005. "Learning Desire: Relational Pedagogies and the Desiring Female Subject in Lebanon." *Journal of Middle East Women's Studies* 1 (1): 79–109. https://www.jstor.org/stable/40326850.
Jouili, Jeanette S., and Schirin Amir-Moazami. 2006. "Knowledge, Empowerment and Religious Authority among Pious Muslim Women in France and Germany." *Muslim World* 96: 617–42. doi:10.1111/j.1478-1913.2006.00150.x.

Kahf, Mohja. 1999. *Western Representations of the Muslim Woman: From Termagant to Odalisque*. Austin: University of Texas Press.

Kandiyoti, Deniz. 1988. "Bargaining with Patriarchy." *Gender and Society* 2 (3): 274–90. https://www.jstor.org/stable/190357.

Kandiyoti, Deniz. 2007. "Between the Hammer and the Anvil: Post-conflict Reconstruction, Islam and Women's Rights." *Third World Quarterly* 28 (3): 503–17. https://www.jstor.org/stable/20454943.

Kandiyoti, Deniz, ed. 1996. *Gendering the Middle East: Emerging Perspectives*. London: I.B. Tauris.

Kandiyoti, Deniz. 1991. "Identity and Its Discontents: Women and the Nation." *Millenium* 20 (3): 429–43. doi:10.1177/03058298910200031501.

Kaplan, David E. 2005. "Hearts, Minds and Dollars." *Global Issues*. April 5. Accessed June 6, 2024. https://www.globalissues.org/article/584/hearts-minds-and-dollars.

Kapoor, Ilan. 2003. "Acting in a Tight Spot: Homi Bhabha's Postcolonial Politics." *New Political Science* 25 (4): 561–77. doi:10.1080/0739314032000145233.

Karaca, Sevinc. 2009. "Feminism in the Muslim World." *Red and Black Revolution* 15: 1–7.

Karam, Azza. 1998. *Women, Islamisms and the State: Contemporary Feminisms in Egypt*. London: Palgrave Macmillan.

Keddie, Nikki R. 1997. "Secularism and the State: Towards Clarity and Global Comparison." *New Left Review* 21–40. https://newleftreview.org/issues/i226/articles/nikki-r-keddie-secularism-and-the-state-towards-clarity-and-global-comparison.pdf.

Keddie, Nikki R. 2007. *Women in the Middle East: Past and Present*. Princeton: Princeton University Press.

Kennedy, Dominic. 2017. "Muslim Lobby Group Promotes Extremism: Muslim Engagement and Development MEND." *The Times*. October 31. Accessed June 6, 2024. https://www.thetimes.com/uk/politics/article/muslim-lobby-group-promotes-extremism-muslim-engagement-and-development-mend-hkm87fx35.

Kernaghan, Jennifer. 1993. "Lord Cromer as Orientalist and Social Engineer in Egypt: 1882–1907." University of British Columbia, April. http://hdl.handle.net/2429/2378.

Khalid, Maryam. 2011. "Gender, Orientalism and Representations of the 'Other' in the War on Terror." *Global Change, Peace and Security* 23 (1): 15–29. doi:10.1080/14781158.2011.540092.

Khan, Khadija. 2018. "Islamic Feminism is a Myth." *Areo*. May 2. Accessed June 6, 2024. https://areomagazine.com/2018/05/02/islamic-feminism-is-a-myth/.

Khan, Sara. 2013. "Segregating Men and Women at University Events Won't Lead to Equality." *Independent*. November 25. Accessed June 6, 2024. https://www.independent.co.uk/voices/comment/segregating-men-and-women-at-university-events-won-t-lead-to-equality-8962984.html.

Khan, Sara. 2018. "We Are Still Ignoring Victims of Anti-Muslim Prejudice." *The Huffingtom Post*. December 3. Accessed June 2, 2022. https://www.huffingtonpost.co.uk/entry/islamophobia-extremism-hate-crime-racism_uk_5c0566e8e4b066b5cfa475a3.

Khan, Sara, and Tony McMahon. 2016. *The Battle for British Islam: Reclaiming Muslim Identity from Extremism*. Kindle Edition. London: Saqi.

Khan, Shahnaz. 2001. "Performing the Native Informant: Doing Ethnography from the Margins." *Canadian Journal of Women and the Law* 13 (2): 266–84.

Khan, Shahnaz. 2005. "Reconfiguring the Native Informant: Positionality in the Global Age." *Signs* 30 (4 (Special Issue) New Feminist Approaches to Social Science Methodologies): 2017–37.

Kienle, Eberhard. 1998. "More than a Response to Islamism: The Political Deliberalization of Egypt in the 1990s." *Middle East Journal* (Middle East Institute) 52 (2): 219–35. https://www.jstor.org/stable/4329187.

Killian, Caitlin. 2006. *North African Women in France: Gender, Culture and Identity*. Stanford: Stanford University Press.

Kolluri, Satish, and Ali Mir. 2002. "Redefining Secularism in Postcolonial Contexts: An Introdcution." *Cultural Dynamics* 14 (1): 7–20. doi:10.1177/09213740020140010601.

Kumar, Arun. 2021. "Five Years Later, It's Even More Clear that Demonetisation Was a Disaster." *Scroll In*. November 6. Accessed June 6, 2024. https://scroll.in/article/1009871/five-years-later-its-even-more-clear-that-demonetisation-was-a-disaster-for-india#:~:text=There%20has%20been%20growing%20unemployment,after%20the%20goalposts%20were%20shifted.

Kumar, Randha. 1993. *The History of Doing, an Illustrated Account of Movements for Women's Rights and Feminism in India, 1800–1990*. London: Verso.

Kwall, Roberta Rosenthal. 2015. *The Myth of the Cultural Jew: Culture and Law in Jewish Tradition*. Oxford: Oxford University Press.

Lakämper, Judith. 2017. "Affective Dissonance, Neoliberal Postfeminism and the Foreclosure of Solidarity." *Feminist Theory* 18 (2): 119–35. doi:10.1177/1464700117700041.

Lakatos, István. 2018. "Thoughts on Universalism versus Cultural Relativism, with Special Attention to Women's Rights." *Pécs Journal of International and European Law* 1: 6–25.

Lang, Cady. 2021. "Who Gets to Wear a Headscarf? The Complicated History behind France's Latest Hijab Controversy." *Time*. May 19. Accessed June 6, 2024. https://time.com/6049226/france-hijab-ban/.

Lardas, John. 2011. *Modern Secularism in Antebellum America*. Chicago: University of Chicago Press.

Lassalle, Didier. 2011. "French laïcité and British Multiculturalism: A Convergence in Progress?" *Journal of Intercultural Studies* 32 (3): 229–43. doi:10.1080/07256868.2011.565734.

Lawyers for Lawyers. 2010. "Iran Shadi Sadr Convicted to 6 Years and 74 Lashes." *Lawyers for Lawyers*. May 31. Accessed June 6, 2024. https://lawyersforlawyers.org/en/iran-shadi-sadr-convicted-to-6-years-and-74-lashes/.

Lazreg, Marnia. 1988. "'Feminism and Difference: The Perils of Writing as a Muslim Woman on Women in Algeria." *Feminist Studies* 14 (1): 81–107. doi:10.2307/3178000.

Lazreg, Marnia. 2021. *Islamic Feminism and the Discourse of Post-liberation: The Cultural Turn in Algeria*. London: Routledge.

Lazreg, Marnia. 2018. *The Eloquence of Silence: Algerian Women in Question*. London: Routledge.

Leonard, Keith D. 2012. "'Which Me Will Survive': Rethinking Identity, Reclaiming Audre Lorde." *Callaloo* 35 (3): 758–77. https://www.jstor.org/stable/23274338.

Lewicki, Aleksandra, and Theresa O'Toole. 2016. "Acts and Practices of Citizenship: Muslim Women's Activism in the UK." *Ethnic and Racial Studies* 40 (1): 152–71. doi:10.1080/01419870.2016.1216142.

Lewis, Reina. 1996. *Gendering Orientalism: Race, Femininity and Representation*. London: Routledge.

Lewis, Reina. 2013. *Modest Fashion: Styling Bodies, Mediating Faith*. New York: I.B. Tauris.

Liddle, Joanna. 1985. "Gender and Colonialism: Women's Organisation under the Raj." *Women's Studies International Forum* 8 (5): 521–9. doi:10.1016/0277-5395(85)90083-4.

Loomba, Ania. 2005. *Colonialism/Postcolonialism*. London: Routledge.

Lorde, Audre. 1984. *Sister Outsider: Essays and Speeches*. Trumansburg, NY: Crossing Press.

Lowe, Lisa. 1991. *Critical Terrains: French and British Orientalisms*. Ithaca, NY: Cornell University Press.

Luke, Carmen. 1992. "What We Can Do for You! What Can 'We' Do for 'You'? Struggling Over." In *Feminisms and Critical Pedagogy*, ed. Carmen Luke and Jennifer Gore, 54–73. New York: Routledge.

MacFarquhar, Neil. 2005. "Paternity Suit against TV Star Scandalizes Egyptians." *New York Times*. January 26. Accessed June 6, 2024. https://www.nytimes.com/2005/01/26/world/middleeast/paternity-suit-against-tv-star-scandalizes-egyptians.html.

Mackenzie, Suzie. 2017. "Sara Khan: Meet the Woman Taking on Isis." *Vogie World: Paris*. May 23. Accessed June 6, 2024. https://www.vogue.co.uk/article/sara-khan-we-will-inspire-muslim-group.

Macmaster, Neil. 2007. "The Colonial 'Emancipation' of Algerian women: The Marriage Law of 1959 and the Failure of Legislation on Women's Rights in the Post-independence Era." *Vienna Journal of African Studies* 12: 91–116.

MacNell, Lillian, Adam Driscoll, and Andrea N. Hunt. 2015. "What's in a Name: Exposing Gender Bias in Student Ratings of Teaching." *Innovative Higher Education* 40: 291–303. doi:10.1007/s10755-014-9313-4.

Mahmood, Saba. 2005. *Politics of Piety: The Islamic Revival and the Feminist Subject.* Princeton: Princeton University Press.

Mahmood, Saba. 2009. "Religious Reason and Secular Affect: An Incommensurable Divide?" *Critical Inquiry* 35: 836–62. doi:10.1086/599592.

Mahmood, Saba. 2006. "Secularism, Hermeneutics and Empire: The Politics of the Islamic Reformation." *Public Culture* 18 (2): 323–47. doi:10.1215/08992363-2006-006.

Mahmoud, Nahla. 2013. "Here Is Why Sharia Law Has No Place in Britain or Elsewhere." *National Secular Society.* February 6. Accessed June 2, 2022. https://www.secularism.org.uk/opinion/2013/02/here-is-why-sharia-law-has-no-place-in-britain-or-elsewhere.

Mahmoudi, Hoda. 2019. "Freedom and the Iranian Women's Movement." *Contexts* 18 (3): 14–19. doi:https://doi-org.ntu.idm.oclc.org/10.1177/1536504219864953.

Mamdani, Mahmood. 2004. *Good Muslim, Bad Muslim: America, the Cold War and the Roots of Terror.* New York: Pantheon Press.

Mandaville, Peter. 2007. *Global Political Islam.* New York: Routledge.

Mandaville, Peter. 2021. "Islam and Exceptionalism in the Western Policy Imagination." In *Overcoming Orientalism: Essays in Honor of John L. Esposito,* ed. Tamara Sonn, 293–314. New York: Online Oxford Academic. doi:10.1093/oso/9780190054151.003.0011.

Manji, Irshad. 2020. *Don't Label Me: How to Do Diversity Without Inflaming the Cultural Wars.* New York: St. Martin's Griffin.

Manji, Irshad. 2003. *The Trouble with Islam Today: A Wake-up Call for Honesty and Change.* Toronto: Random House.

Marchand, Marianne H. 2009. "The Future of Gender and Development after 9/11: Insights from Postcolonial Feminism and Transnationalism." *Third World Quarterly* 30 (5): 921–35. https://www.jstor.org/stable/40388159.

Maria, Sunaina. 2009. "'Good' and 'Bad' Muslim Citizens: Feminists, Terrorists, and U.S. Orientalism." *Feminist Studies* 35 (3): 631–56. http://www.jstor.org/stable/40608397.

Marsden, Chris, and Julie Hyland. 2006. "Britain: Jack Straw's Anti-Muslim Provocation." *World Socialisi Website.* October 7. Accessed June 6, 2024. https://www.wsws.org/en/articles/2006/10/ukin-o07.html.

Martin, Richard C. 2016. *Encyclopedia of Islam and the Muslim World.* New York: Macmillan Reference USA.

Mas, Ruth. 2006. "Compelling the Muslim Subject: Memory as Post-colonial Violence and the Public Performativity of 'secular and cultural Islam.'" *Muslim World* 96 (4): 585–616. doi:10.1111/j.1478-1913.2006.00149.x.

Massoumi, Narzanin. 2015. "'The Muslim Woman Activist': Solidarity across Difference in the Movement against the 'War on Terror.'" *Ethnicities* 15 (5): 715–41. doi:10.1177/1468796814567786.

Maumoon, Dunya. 1999. "Islamism and Gender Activism: Muslim Women's Quest for Autonomy." *Journal of Muslim Minority Affairs* 19 (2): 269–83. doi:10.1080/13602009908716442.

Maussen, Marcel, and Veit Bader. 2011. "Chapter 1: Introduction." In *Colonial and Postcolonial Governamce of Islam: Contnuities and Ruptures*, ed. Marcel Maussen, Veit Bader, and Annelies Moors, 9–26. Amsterdam: Amsterdam University Press.

McCurry, Steve. 1985. "Afghan Girl Revealed." *National Geographic*. Accessed June 6, 2024. https://www.nationalgeographic.com/magazine/article/afghan-girl-revealed.

McDonough, Richard. 2013. "Religious Fundamentalism: A Conceptual Critique." *Religious Studies* 49 (4): 561–79. https://www.jstor.org/stable/43659182.

McKenzie-Mohr, Suzanne, and Michelle N. Lafrance. 2014. "Women Counter-Storying Their Lives." In *Women Voicing Resistance: Discursive and Narrative Explorations*, ed. Suzanne McKenzie-Mohr and Michelle N. Lafrance, 1–15. New York: Routledge.

McMahon, Aine. 2015. "Activist Claims Trinity Speech on Apostasy and Islam Cancelled." *Irish Times*. March 22. Accessed June 6, 2024. https://www.irishtimes.com/news/politics/activist-claims-trinity-speech-on-apostasy-and-islam-cancelled-1.2149050.

Media Diversity Institute. 2010. "Re-programming British Muslims: A Study of the Islam Channel by Quilliam Foundation." *Media Diversity Institute*. April 1. Accessed June 6, 2024. https://www.media-diversity.org/re-programming-british-muslims-a-study-of-the-islam-channel-by-the-quilliam-foundation/.

Menoret, Pascal. 2014. *Joyriding in Riyadh: Oil, Urbanism, and Road Revolt*. Cambridge: Cambridge University Press.

Mernissi, Fatima. 1991. *The Veil and the Male Elite: A Feminist Interpretation of Women's Rights in Islam*. Cambridge: Perseus Books.

Mernissi, Fatima. 1996. *Women's Rebellion and Islamic Memory*. London: Zed Books.

Milani, Milad. 2014. "Cultural Muslims, Like Cultural Christians, Are a Silent Majority." *The Conversation*. September 29. Accessed June 6, 2024. https://theconversation.com/cultural-muslims-like-cultural-christians-are-a-silent-majority-32097.

Minces, Juliette. 1982. *The House of Obedience: Women in Arab Society*, trans. Michael Pallis. London: Zed Books.

Mir-Hosseini, Ziba. 2006. "Muslim Women's Quest for Equality: Between Islamic Law and Feminism." *Critical Inquiry* 32 (4): 629–45.

Mirza, Heidi Safia. 2009. "Plotting a History: Black and Postcolonial Feminisms in 'New Times.'" *Race Ethnicity and Education* 12 (1): 1–10. doi:10.1080/13613320802650899.

Moaddel, Mansoor. 2005. *Islamic Modernism, Nationalism, and Fundamentalism: Episode and Discourse*. Chicago: University of Chicago Press.

Moghadam, Valentine M. 2005. *Globalizing Women: Transnational Feminist Networks*. Baltimore, MD: Johns Hopkins University Press.

Moghadam, Valentine M. 2002. "Islamic Feminism and Its Discontents: Toward a Resolution of the Debate." *Signs: Journal of Women in Culture and Society* 27 (4): 1135–71.

Moghissi, Haideh. 1999. *Feminism and Islamic Fundamentalism: The Role of Postmodern Analysis*. London: Zed Books.

Moghissi, Haideh. 2011. "Islamic Feminism Revisited." *Comparative Studies of South Asia, Africa and the Middle East* 31 (1): 76–84. doi:10.1215/1089201X-2010-054.

Moghisis, Haideh. 1999. *Feminism and Islamic Fundamentalism: The Limits of Postmodern Analysis*. London: Zed Books.

Mohammadi, Narges. 2023. "The More They Lock Us Up, the Stronger We Become." *New York Times*. September 16. Accessed June 6, 2024. https://www.nytimes.com/2023/09/16/opinion/narges-mohammadi-iran-women.html.

Mohanty, Chandra Talpade. 2002. ""Under western eyes" Revisited: Feminist Slidarity through Anticapitalist Struggles." *Signs: Journal of Women in Culture and Society* 28 (1): 499–535. https://www.jstor.org/stable/10.1086/342914.

Mohanty, Chandra Talpade. 2003. *Feminism without Borders: Decolonizing Theory, Practicing*. New York: Duke University Press.

Mohanty, Chandra Talpade. 2013. "Transnational Feminist Crossings: On Neoliberalism and Radical Critique." *Signs* 38 (4, Intersectionality: Theorizing Power, Empowering Theory): 967–91. doi:10.1086/669576.

Mohanty, Chandra Talpade. 1984. "Under Western Eyes: Feminist Scholarship and Colonial Discourses." *Boundary 2* 12 (3): 333–58. doi:10.1057/fr.1988.42.

Mojab, Shahrzad, and Nadeen El-Kassem. 2011. "Cultural Relativism: Theoretical, Political and Ideological Debates." *Women Living under Muslim Law* Dossier 30–1 (The Struggle for Secularism in Europe and North America): 191–210.

Moore, Henrietta L. 1988. *Feminism and Anthropology*. Cambridge: Polity Press.

Moore, Henrietta L. 1998. *A Passion for Difference*. Cambridge: Polity Press.

Moore, Henrietta. 2007. *The Subject of Anthropology: Gender Symbolism and Psychoanalysis*. Cambridge: Polity Press.

Mouri, Leila, and Kristin Soraya Batmanghelichi. 2015. "Can the Secular Iranian Women's Activist Speak?: Caught between Political Power and the 'Islamic feminist.'" In *Gender and Sexuality in Muslim Cultures*, ed. Gul Ozyegin, 331–55. London: Routledge.

Muhanna, Aitemad. 2016. *Agency and Gender in Gaza: Masculinity, Femininity and Family during the Second Intifada*. London: Routledge.

Munro, Petra. 1998. *Subject to Fiction: Women Teachers' Life History Narratives and the Cultural Politics of Resistance*. Buckingham: Open University Press.

Nafisi, Azar. 2004. *Reading Lolita in Tehran: A Memoir in Books*. New York: Random House.

Naggar, Richa, and Amanda Lock Swarr. 2010. "Introduction: Theorizing Transnational Feminist Praxis." In *Critical Transnational Feminist Praxis*, ed. Amanda Lock Swarr and Richa Naggar, 1–20. New York: State University of New York Press.

Najjar, Fauzi M. 1996. "The Debate on Islam and Secularism in Egypt." *Arab Studies Quarterly* 18 (2): 1–21. https://www.jstor.org/stable/41858163.

Namazie, Mariam. 2019. "Mariam Namazie." In *Islamophobia: An Anthology of Concerns*, ed. Emma Webb, 75–80. London: Civitas.

Namazie, Mariam. 2010. "What Isn't Wrong with Sharia Law?" *The Guardian*. July 5. Accessed June 2, 2022. https://www.theguardian.com/law/2010/jul/05/sharia-law-religious-courts.

Namazie, Maryam. 2011. "Religion Is a Private Affair: One Law for All." *Journal of Women Living under Muslim Laws* Dossier 30–1 (The Struggle for Secularism in Europe and North America): 149–51.

Naples, Nancy, ed. 1998. *Community Activism and Feminist Politics*. New York: Routledge.

Narayan, Uma. 1997. *Dislocating Cultures: Identities, Traditions, and Third-World Feminism*. London: Routledge.

Nash, Jennifer Christine. 2019. *Black Feminism Reimagined: After Intersectionality*. Durham, NC: Duke University Press.

Nencel, Lorraine. 2014. "Situating Reflexivity: Voices, Positionalities and Representations in Feminist Ethnographic Texts." *Women's Studies International Forum* 23: 75–83.

New York Times. 2005. "Virgin Territory for Egypt as Paternity Suit Filed." *The Sunday Morning Herald*. January 29. Accessed June 6, 2024. https://www.smh.com.au/world/virgin-territory-for-egypt-as-paternity-suit-filed-20050129-gdkl6e.html.

Offenhauer, Priscilla. 2005. "Women in Islamic Societies: A Selected Review of Social Scientific Literature." A report prepared by the Federal research Division, Library of Congress under an Interagency Agreement with the Office of the Director of National Intelligence Council (ODNI/ADDNIA/NIC) and Central Intelligence Agency/Directorate of Science and technology. chrome-extension://efaidnbmnnnibpcajpcglclefindmkaj/https://www.justice.gov/sites/default/files/eoir/legacy/2013/11/08/Women%20-%20Islamic_Societies.pdf.

Olufami, Lola. 2020. *Feminism, Interrupted: Disrupting Power*. London: Pluto Press.

Omar, Manal. 2007. "Islamic Feminism." In *Encyclopedia of Activism and Social Justice*, ed. Gary L. Anderson and Kathryn G. Herr. London: Sage. doi:https://doi.org/10.4135/9781412956215.

Omer, Atalia. 2014. *Is "Docile Agency" Good for Women?* May 20. https://berkleycenter.georgetown.edu/posts/is-docile-agency-good-for-women.

Orenstein, Ziv, and Itzchak Weismann. 2016. "Neither Muslim nor Other: British Secualr Muslims." *Islam and Christian—Muslim Relations* 27 (4): 279–395. doi:10.1080/09596410.2016.1148892.

Osman, Tarek. 2010. *Egypt on the Brink: From Nasser to Mubarak*. New Haven, CT: Yale University Press.

Othman, Norani. 2006. "Muslim Women and the Challenge of Islamic Fundamentalism/Extremism: An Overview of Southeast Asian Muslim Women's Struggle for Human Rights and Gender Equality." *Women's Studies International Forum* 29: 339–53. doi:10.1016/j.wsif.2006.05.008.

Otto, Dianne. 2006. "Lost in Translation: Re-scripting the Sexed Subjects International Human Rights Law." In *International Law and Its Others*, ed. Anne Orford, 318–56. Cambridge: Cambridge University Press.

Ovais, Mehreen. 2014. "Feminism in Pakistan: A Brief History." *Express Tribune*. September 23. Accessed June 6, 2024. https://tribune.com.pk/story/764036/feminism-in-pakistan-a-brief-history.

Owen, Roger. 2005. "The Brismes Annual Lecture 2004: Biography and Empire: Lord Cromer (1841–1917) Then and Now." *British Journal of Middle Eastern Studies* 32 (1): 3–12. doi:10.1080/13530190500081519.

Ozyegin, Gul. 2015. *New Desires, New Selves: Sex, Love, and Piety among Turkish Youth*. New York: New York University Press.

Pacwa, Jessica. 2019. "War on Terror as a 'Fight for the Rights and Dignity of Women': A Discourse Analysis of the U.S. 'Liberation' Campaign for Afghan Women." Pepperdine University. https://digitalcommons.pepperdine.edu/etd/1101?utm_source=digitalcommons.pepperdine.edu%2Fetd%2F1101&utm_medium=PDF&utm_campaign=PDFCoverPages.

Patel, Pragna. 2019. "Pragna Patel." In *Islamophobia: An Anthology of Concerns*, ed. Emma Webb, 46–64. London: Civitas.

Patel, Pragna, and Uditi Sen. 2011. *Cohesion, Faith and Gender: A Report on the Impact of the Cohesion and Faith-Based Approach on Black and Minority Women in Ealing*. London: Southall Black Sisters.

Pearce, Emma. 2013. "'Gender Apartheid' Is Real in UK Universities. So Why Aren't More People Fighting It?" *The Telegraph*. December 11. Accessed June 6, 2024. https://www.telegraph.co.uk/women/womens-life/10510284/Gender-apartheid-segregation-is-real-in-UK-universities.-So-why-arent-more-people-fighting-it.html.

Pelham, Lipika. 2023. "Iran Frees Niloufar Hamedi and Elaheh Mohammadi, Jailed for Covering Mahsa Amini Death." *BBC*. January 14. Accessed June 6, 2024. https://www.bbc.co.uk/news/world-middle-east-67975811.

Pepicelli, Renata. 2017. "Rethinking Gender in Arab Nationalism: Women and the Politics of Modernity in the Making of Nation-States. Cases from Egypt, Tunisia and Algeria." *Oriente Moderno* 97 (1): 201–19.

Pew Research Center. 2017. *U.S. Muslims Concerned about Their Place in Society, but Continue to Believe in the American Dream*. PEW Research Center. https://www.pewresearch.org/wp-content/uploads/sites/20/2017/07/U.S.-MUSLIMS-FULL-REPORT-with-population-update-v2.pdf.

Pile, Steve. 1997. "Oppositions, Political Identities and Spaces of Resistance." In *Geographies of Resistance*, ed. Steve Pile and Michael Keith. London: Routledge.

Pojmann, Wendy. 2006. *Immigrant Women and Feminism in Italy*. Aldershot, VT: Ashgate Press.

Pojmann, Wendy. 2011. "Muslim Women's Organizing in France and Italy: Political Culture, Activism, and Performativity in the Public Sphere." *Feminist Formations* 23 (1): 229–51. https://www.jstor.org/stable/40980992.

Poletta, Francesca. 2006. *It Was Like a Fever: Storytelling in Protest and Politics*. London: University of Chicago Press.

Quayum, Mohammad. 2013. *The Essential Rokeya: Selected Works of Rokeya Sakhawat Hossain (1880–1932)*. Leiden: Brill.

Rabasa, Angel, Cheryl Benard, Lowell H. Schwartz, and Peter Sickle. 2007. *Secular Muslims: A Forgotten Dimension in the War of Ideas*. Santa Monica, CA: RAND: Center for Middle East Public Policy.

Raissiguier, Catherine. 2008. "Muslim Women in France: Impossible Subjects?" *Dark Matter: In the Ruins of Imperial Culture*. May 2. http://www.darkmatter101.org/site/2008/05/02/muslim-women-in-france-impossible-subjects/.

Rashid, Naaz. 2014. "Giving the Silent Majority a Stronger Voice? Initiatives to Empower Muslim Women as Part of the UK's War on Terror." *Ethnic and Racial Studies* 37 (4): 589–604. doi:10.1080/01419870.2013.816759.

Rashid, Naaz. 2016. *Veiled Threats: Representing the Muslim Woman in Public Policy Discourses*. Bristol: Policy Press.

Rathore, Aakash Singh. 2010. "Habermas's Post-secularism: The Penetration / Preservation of the (European) Political Public Sphere." In *Discoursing the Post-secular: Essays on the Habermasian Post-secular Turn*, ed. Aakash Singh Rathore and Peter Losonczi, 75–92. Wien: Lit Verlag. http://eprints.lse.ac.uk/42645/.

Razack, Sherene H. 2004. "Imperilled Muslim Women, Dangerous Muslim Men and Civilised Europeans: Legal and Social Responses to Forced Marriages." *Feminist Legal Studies* 12 (2): 129–74. doi:https://doi-org.ntu.idm.oclc.org/10.1023/B:FEST.0000043305.66172.92.

Reay, Diane. 2012. "Future Directions in Difference Research." In *The Handbook of Feminist Research: Theory and Praxis*, ed. Sharlene Nagy Hesse-Biber, 627–40. London: Sage.

Rectenwald, Michael, and Rochelle Almeida. 2015. "Introduction: Global Secularisms in a Post-secular Age." In *Global Secularism in a Post-secular Age*, vol. 2, ed. Michael Rectenwald, Rochelle Almeida, and George Levine, 1–24. Boston, MA: De Grutyer.

Reilly, Niamh. 2011. "Rethinking the Interplay of Feminism and Secularism in a Neo-secular Age." *Feminist Review* 97 (1): 5–31. doi:https://doi-org.ntu.idm.oclc.org/10.1057/fr.2010.35.

Rizvi, Ali A. 2016. *The Athiest Muslim: A Journey from Religion to Reason*. New York: St. Martin's Press.

Rosello, Mireille. 2005. *France and the Maghreb: Performative Encounters*. Florida: University Press of Florida.

Roy, Olivier. 2013. "Secularism and Islam: The Theological Predicament." *Italian Journal of International Affairs* 28 (1, Europe and Islam): 5–19. doi:10.1080/03932729.2013.759365.

Roy, Olivier. 2007. "Secularism Confronts Islam." *Open Democracy*. October 25. Accessed June 6, 2024. https://www.opendemocracy.net/en/34938/

Roy, Olivier. 2007. *Secularism Confronts Islam*. Trans. George Holoch. New York: Columbia University Press.

Sabbagh, Suha. 1997. *Arab Women: Between Defiance and Restraint*. New York: Olive Branch Press.

Sadeghi, Fatemeh. 2010. "Bypassing Islamism and Feminism: Women's Resistance and Rebellion in Post-revolutionary Iran." *REMMM: Revue des Mondes Muslimans et de la Mediteranee* 128: 209–28. doi:https://doi.org/10.4000/remmm.6936.

Sadr, Shadi, and Shadi Amin. 2012. *Crime and Impunity: Sexual Torture of Women in Islamic Republic Prisons*. Tehran: Azam Javadi Aida Orient Books.

Safi, Omid, ed. 2003. *Progressive Muslims: On Justice, Gender and Pluralism*. Oxford: One World.

Sahgal, Gita. 2000. "Secular Spaces: The Experience of Asian Women Organizing." In *Refusing Holly Orders: Women and Fundamentalism in Britain*, ed. Gita Sahgal and Nira Yuval-Davis. London: Women Living under Muslim Laws.

Sahgal, Gita. 2011. "'The Question Asked by Satan': Doubt, Dissent, Discrimination." *Journal of Women Living under Muslim Laws* Dossier 30–1 (The Struggle for Secularism in Europe and North America): 109–26.

Sahgal, Gita, and Nira Yuval-Davis. 2000. "Introduction: Fundamentalism, Multiculturalism and Women in Britain." In *Refusing Holly Orders: Women and Fundamentalism in Britain*, ed. Gita Sahgal and Nira Yuval-Davis, 7–31. London: Women Living under Muslim Laws.

Said, Edward. 1979. *Oreintalism*. New York: Vintage Books.

Said, Edward. 1985. "Oreintalism Reconsidered." *Race and Class* 27 (2): 1–15.

Said, Edward. 2001. *The Clash of Ignorance*. 4 October. Accessed February 1, 2017. https://www.thenation.com/article/archive/clash-ignorance/.

Said, Edward W. 1994. *Culture and Imperialism*. London: Vintage Books.

Salem, Sara. 2017. "On Transnational Solidarity: The Case of Angela Davis in Egypt." *Signs: Journal of Women and Culture in Society* 43 (2): 245–502.

Saliba, Therese. 2002. "Introduction: Gender, Politics and Islam." In *Gender, Politics and Islam*, ed. Theresa Saliba, Carolyn Allen, and Judith A. Howard, 1–13. Chicago: University of Chicago Press.

Salih, Mohammed A., and Marwan M. Kraidy. 2020. "Islamic State and Women: A Biopolitical Analysis." *International Journal of Communication* 14: 1933–50.

Sardar, Ziauddin. 1999. *Orientalism*. Buckingham: Open University Press.

Satterthwaite, Margaret L., and Jayne C. Huckerby. 2013. *Gender, National Security, and Counter-Terrorism: Human Rights Perspectives*. London: Routledge.

Schielke, Samuli. 2009. "Being Good in Ramadan: Ambivalence, Fragmentation, and the Moral Self in the Lives of Young Egyptians." *Journal of the Royal Anthropological Institute* 15 (s1: Special Issue: Islam, Politics, Anthropology: S24–S40. doi:https://doi-org.ntu.idm.oclc.org/10.1111/j.1467-9655.2009.01540.x.

Schott, Robin May. 2009. "The Politics of Piety and the Norms of Analysis." In *Pieties and Gender*, ed. Hilda Rømer Christensen and Lene Sjørup, 47–55. Leiden: Brill.

Scott, Joan Wallach. 2013. "Secularism and Gender Equality." In *Religion, the Secular, and the Politics of Sexual Difference*, ed. Linell E. Cady and Tracy Fessenden, 25–45. New York: Columbia University Press

Scott, Joan Wallach. 2017. *Sex and Secularism*. Princeton, NJ: Princeton University Press

Scott, Joan Wallach. 2011. *The Fantasy of Feminist History*. Duke: Duke University Press.

Scott, Joan Wallach. 2007. *The Politics of the Veil*. Oxford: Princeton University Press.

Seedat, Fatima. 2013. "When Islam and Feminism Converge." *Muslim World* (Hartford Seminary) 103 (3): 404–20. doi:10.1111/muwo.1202.

Sehlikoglu, Sertaç. 2016. "Exercising in Comfort: Islamicate Culture of Mahremiyet in Everyday Istanbul." *Journal of Middle East Women's Studies* 12 (2): 143–65.

Sehlikoglu, Sertaç. 2018. "Revisited: Muslim Women's Agency and Feminist Anthropology of the Middle East, *Contemporary Islam* 12 (2018): 73–92. https://doi.org/10.1007/s11562-017-0404-8

Serrano, Julia. 2016. "Prejudice, 'Political Correctness,' and the Normalization of Donald Trump." *Medium*. November 22. https://juliaserano.medium.com/prejudice-political-correctness-and-the-normalization-of-donald-trump-28c563154e48#.sypha7app.

Shaarawi, Huda. 1987. *Harem Years: The Memoirs of an Egyptian Feminist (1879–1924)*. New York: Feminist Press, City University of New York.

Shah, Bina. 2014. "The Fate of Feminism in Pakistan." *New York Times*. August 20. Accessed June 6, 2024. https://www.nytimes.com/2014/08/21/opinion/bina-shah-the-fate-of-feminism-in-pakistan.html#:~:text=A%20feminist%20movement%20can%20succeed,both%20Islamic%20and%20secular%20principles.

Shah, Saeeda. 2012. "Muslim Schools in Secular Societies: Persistence or Resistance!" *British Journal of Religious Education* 34 (1): 51–65. doi:10.1080/01416200.2011.601897.

Shaheed, Farida. 2017. "The Women's Movement in Pakistan: Challenges and Achievements." In *Women's Movements in the Global Era: The Power of Local Feminisms*, ed. Amrita Basu, 89–118. New York: Routledge.

Shaikh, Sa'diyyah. 2003. "Transforming Feminism: Islam, Women and Gender Justice." In *Progressive Muslims: On Justice, Gender and Pluralism*, ed. Omid Safi, 147–62. Oxford: One World.

Sharpe, Jenny. 1993. *Allegories of Empire: The Figure of Woman in the Colonial Text*. Minnesota: University of Minnesota Press.

Shohat, Ella, ed. 1998. *Talking Visions: Multicultural Feminism in a Transnational Age*. New York: MIT Press.

Siddique, Haroon. 2011. "Muslim Women: Beyond the Stereotype." *The Guardian*. April 29. Accessed June 6, 2024. https://www.theguardian.com/lifeandstyle/2011/apr/29/muslim-women-fighting-islamic-extremism.

Soares, Benjamin, and Filippo Osella. 2010. *Islam, Politics, Anthropology*. London: Royal Anthropological Institute of Great Britain and Ireland. doi:https://doi.org/10.1002/9781444324402.fmatter.

Sonn, Tamara. 1987. "Secularism and National Stability in Islam." *Arab Studies Quarterly* 9 (3): 284–305. https://www.jstor.org/stable/41857932.

Spivak, Gayatri Chakravorti. 1993. "Can the Subaltern Speak?" In *Colonial Discourse and Post-colonial Theory: A Reader*, ed. Patrick Williams and Laura Chrisman, 66–111. New York: Columbia University Press.

Starrett, Gregory. 1998. *Putting Islam to Work: Education, Politics, and Religious Transformation in Egypt*. Oakland, CA: California Scholarship Online.

Steinmetz-Jenkins, Daniel. 2017. "Do Secularism and Gender Equality Really Go Hand in Hand?" *The Guardian*. December 30. Accessed June 6, 2024. https://www.theguardian.com/commentisfree/2017/dec/30/secularism-gender-equality-joan-wallach-scott.

Suleri, Sara. 1992. "Woman Skin Deep: Feminism and the Postcolonial Condition." *Critical Inquiry* 18 (4): 756–69.

Surhan, Iris. 2021. "Secular and Islamic Feminism in Turkey: Polarized by Current Politics or Two Sides of the Same Coin?" Leiden: Universiteit Leiden. https://hdl.handle.net/1887/3192811.

Swaby, Nydia A. 2014. "'Disparate in Voice, Sympathetic in Direction': Gendered Political Blackness and the Politics of Solidarity." *Feminist Review* 108: 11–25. http://www.jstor.org/stable/24571917.

Swarr, Amanda Lock, and Richa Nagar. 2010. "Theorizing Transnational Feminist Praxis." In *Critical Transnational Feminist Praxis*, ed. Amanda Lock Swarr and Richa Nagar. New York: State University of New York Press.

Tadros, Mariz. 2008. "Egyptian Women Activists Without a Movement." *Carnegie Endowment for International Peace*. August 13. Accessed March 8, 2018. http://carnegieendowment.org/sada/?fa=20685.

Tadros, Mariz. 2021. "Stop Homogenising Us: Mixing and Matching Faith and Beliefs in India and Beyond." *Institute of Development Studies*. May 21. Accessed June 6, 2024. https://www.ids.ac.uk/opinions/stop-homogenising-us-mixing-and-matching-faith-and-beliefs-in-india-and-beyond/.

Tadros, Mariz. 2018. "The Pitfalls of Disentangling Women's Agency from Accountability for Gender Equality Outcomes." *Feminist Dissent* (3). doi:10.31273/fd.n3.2018.307.

Takhar, Shaminder. 2013. *Gender, Ethnicity, and Political Agency: South Asian Women Organizing*. London: Routledge.

Tarlo, Emma, and Annelies Moors. 2013. *Islamic Fashion and Anti-fashion: New Perspectives from Europe and North America*. London: Bloomsbury Academic.

Tatchell, Peter. 2019. "Peter Tatchell." In *Islamophobia: An Anthology of Concerns*, ed. Emma Webb, 20–1. London: Civitas.

Tatke, Sukhada. 2021. "'Not French Enough': What It Means to Be an Immigrant in France." *Aljazeera*. March 2. Accessed June 6, 2024. https://www.aljazeera.com/featu res/2021/3/2/not-french-enough-what-it-means-to-be-an-immigrant-in-france.

Taylor, Charles. 2007. *A Secular Age*. Cambridge, MA: Belknap Press of Harvard University Press.

Taylor, Charles. 2011. "Why We Need a Radical Redefinition of Secularism." In *The Power of Religion in the Public Sphere*, ed. Eduardo Mendieta and Jonathan Vanantwerpen, 34–59. New York: Columbia University Press.

Thapar, Suruchi. 1993. "Women as Activists; Women as Symbols: A study of the Indian Nationalist Movement." *Feminist Review* 44, Nationalism and National Identities: 81–96. doi:10.1057/fr.1993.22.

Tickner, J. Ann. 2001. *Gendering World Politics: Issues and Approaches in the Post-Cold War Era*. New York: Columbia University Press.

Tohidi, Nayera. 2023. "Iran in a Transformative Process by Woman, Life, Freedom." *Freedom of Thought Journal* (13): 29–57. doi:10.53895/ftj1314.

Tohidi, Nayera. 2017. "Women's Rights and Feminist Movements in Iran." In *Women's Movements in the Global Era: The Power of Local Feminisms*, ed. Amrita Basu, 75–89. New York: Routledge.

Tohidi, Nayereh. 1991. "Gender and Islamic Fundamentalism: Feminist Politics in Iran." In *Third World Women and the Politics of Feminism*, ed. Chandra Talpade Mohanty, Ann Russo, and Torres Lourdes, 251–67. Bloomington: Indiana University Press.

Valdez, Inés. 2016. "Nondomination or Practices of Freedom? French Muslim Women, Foucault, and the Full Veil Ban." *American Political Science Review* 110 (1): 18–30. doi:10.1017/S0003055415000647.

van den Brandt, Nella. 2015. "Feminist Practice and Solidarity in Secular Societies: Case Studies on Feminists Crossing Religious—Secular Divides in Politics and Practice in Antwerp, Belgium." *Social Movement Studies* 14 (4): 493–508. doi:10.1080/14742837 .2014.994094.

Vasilaki, Rosa. 2016. "The Politics of Postsecular Feminism." *Theory, Culture and Society* 33 (2): 103–23. doi:https://doi-org.ntu.idm.oclc.org/10.1177/0263276415590235.

Verghese, Namrata. 2021. "What Is Orientalism? A Stereotyped, Colonialist Vision of Asian Cultures." *Teen Vogue*. October 13. https://www.teenvogue.com/story/what-is-orientalism.

Vince, Natalya. 2010. "Transgressing Boundaries: Gender, Race, Religion, and 'French Muslims' during the Algerian War of Independence." *French Historical Studies* 33 (3): 445–74.

Vishwanathan, Kedar. 2010. "Aesthetics, Nationalism, and the Image of Woman in Modern Indian Art." *CLCWeb: Comparative Literature and Culture* 12 (2): 1–7. doi:10.7771/1481-4374.1594.

Wadud, Amina. 2006. *Inside the Gender Jihad: Women's Reform in Islam*. Oxford: One World.

Wadud, Amina. 1999. *Qur'an and Woman: Rereading the Sacred Text from a Woman's Perspective*. Oxford: Oxford University Press.

Wasserfall, Rahel R. 1997. "Reflexivity, Feminism and Difference." In *Reflexivity and Voice*, ed. Rosanna Hertz, 150–68. Thousand Oaks, CA: Sage.

Webb, Emma. 2019. "Emma Webb." In *Islamophobia: An Anthology of Concerns*, ed. by Emma Webb, 2–12. London: Civitas.

Werbner, Pnina. 2000. "Divided Loyalties, Empowered Citizenship? Muslims in Britain." *Citizenship Studies* 4 (3): 207–324. doi:10.1080/713658798.

Wickham, Carrie Rosefsky. 2015. *The Muslim Brotherhood: Evolution of an Islamist Movement*. Princeton: Princeton University Press.

Woodiwiss, Jo, Kate Smith, and Kelly Lockwood. 2017. *Feminist Narrative Research: Opportunities and Challenges*. London: Palgrave Macmillan.

Wright, Robin. 1991. "Islam's New Political Face." *Current History* (Periodicals Archive Online): 25–8.

Yazdani, Enayatollah. 2008. "US Policy towards the Islamic World." *Alternatives: Turkish Journal of International Relations* 7 (2–3): 1–10.

Yegenoglu, Meyda. 1998. *Colonial Fantasies: Toward a Feminist Reading of Oreintalism*. Cambridge: Cambridge University Press.

Youssef, Adham. 2017. "LGBT People in Egypt Targeted in Wave of Arrests and Violence." *The Guardian*. October 8. Accessed June 5, 2024. https://www.theguardian.com/world/2017/oct/08/lgbt-people-egypt-targeted-wave-arrests-violence.

Yuval-Davis, Nira. 2006. "Intersectionality and Feminist Politics." *European Journal of Women's Studies* 13 (3): 193–209. doi:10.1177/1350506806065752.

Zakaria, Rafia. 2021. *Against White Feminism*. London: Penguin.

Zarbighalehhammami, Shakib, and Fatemah Abbasi. 2023. "The Demand for Freedom and Equality in the Street below the Movement of Woman, Life, Freedom." *Journal of Advanced Research in Social Sciences* 6 (3): 122–4. doi:10.33422/jarss.v6i3.1048.

Zempi, Irene. 2016. "'It's a Part of Me, I feel Naked Without It': Choice, Agency and Identity for Muslim Women Who Wear the Niqab." *Ethnic and Racial Studies* 39 (10): 1738–54. doi:10.1080/01419870.2016.1159710.

Zia, Afia S. 2018. *Faith and Feminism in Pakistan: Religious Agency or Secular Autonomy*. Brighton: Sussex Academic Press.

Zimmerman, Danielle. 2015. "Young Arab Muslim Women's Agency Challenging Western Feminism." *Affilia* 30 (2): 145–57. doi:10.1177/0886109914546126.

Zine, Jasmin. 2006. "Between Orientalism and Fundamentalism: The Politics of Muslim Women's Feminist Engagement." *Muslim World Journal of Human Rights* 3 (1): 1–24. doi:10.2202/1554-4419.1080.

Zine, Jasmin, Lisa K. Taylor, and Hilary E. Davis. 2007. "Reading Muslim Women and Muslim Women Reading Back: Transnational Feminist Reading Practices, Pedagogy and Ethical Concerns." *Intercultural Education* 18 (4): 271–80. doi:10.1080/14675980701605139.

Index

Note: Entries for secular/secularize/secularism, Muslim/Islam/Islamism/Islamic Feminism, religion/religious/religiosity and feminist/feminism/women are too numerous to be indexed for any gain.

9/11 14, 26, 33, 77, 90
   post 5, 75, 81, 91, 95, 103, 104, 107
   pre 5
#WomenLifeFreedom 59, 154, 155
Abu-Lughod, Lila 69, 95
affective dissonance 177, 178
Afghanistan 63, 95, 97
   interventions in 77, 81, 91
   Taliban takeover of 16
   Taliban rule in 33, 151
   women of 91
Afghan Women 77, 91, 93
agency 17, 7, 14, 24, 26, 30, 33, 34, 35, 69, 74, 75, 77, 84, 94, 95, 107, 109, 110, 111, 112, 113, 115, 116, 117, 118, 121, 173, 174, 175
   docile 19, 110, 111, 114, 118, 119
   gendered 106, 119
   lack of 91
   limits of 6, 112
   political 108
   religious/pietist 2, 19, 73, 103, 104, 105, 112, 114, 118, 119, 120, 179
   and resistance 27, 94, 100, 159
   theorizing 105, 106, 120
   turn 107
   women's xv, 10, 66, 83, 97, 105, 106, 107, 111, 120, 183
agent(s) xvii, 5, 86, 90, 94, 115, 161, 183
   agential 117
   agentive 107
Ahmed, Leila 34, 53, 88
Akbar and Oza 7, 8
al-Ali, Nadje 5, 9, 40, 69, 71, 82
Alinejad, Masih 21, 22, 27, 34, 182, 183
al-Qaeda 74, 77, 131

Amini, Mahsa xvi, 151, 154, 155, 170, 173
anti-colonial 4
   movements 61, 86, 157
   resistance 94
   struggles 69, 87, 89, 100
anti-Muslim 96
   discourse 15
   hatred 166
   racism 44, 44
   rhetoric xv
   sentiment(s) 2, 8, 35, 91, 163, 179
   secularism 150
An-Na'im, Abdullahi Ahmed 142, 143, 147, 148
appropriation 27, 87, 89
   political 80
   re 24, 108
apologetic(s) 67, 71, 95, 166
   apologia(s) 162, 175
   apologism 163, 172
   apologist(s) 26, 42, 161
   unapologetic(ally) 2, 175
Arab Spring(s) xiv, 2, 13, 158
Arjomand, Homa 6, 40
Asad, Talal 106, 126, 127
authoritarian
   political projects 95
   regimes 74, 96, 161
   rule x
   settings 65
   systems 72, 124
authoritarianism 151
autonomy x, xi, 96, 97, 108, 109, 113, 116, 117, 129, 138, 145, 149, 154, 156, 168, 171, 173, 174, 175
   autonomous 25, 123, 126, 136

Badran, Margot 31, 53, 66, 69
Bayat, Asef 65, 117
Bhabha, Homi 148, 149, 182
binary 118, 121, 133, 134, 168, 177, 179, 183
  categorizations 82
  conceptions 104
  constructs xvii
  labels 133
  logic 83, 113
  narratives 47
  perspectives 113
  positions 94
  representations 69
  secular-religious 123
  view(s) 101, 133
Bouachrine, Ibtissam 31, 66
Brah, Avtar 83, 89, 90
Bush, George W. 77
Bush, Laura 77, 90, 91
Butler, Judith 106, 111

capitalism 57, 58, 85, 89,100, 114, 126
  western 81
capitalist(s) 88, 89, 100
  anti 15, 57
Chafiq, Chahla 6, 34, 39, 44, 45
Chatterjee, Partha 55, 86, 87
clash(es) of civilizations 1, 45,123, 125, 138
Cold War 126, 134, 137
collective action 20, 25, 26, 29, 59, 60, 108, 153,155, 169
colonial 1, 30, 40, 41, 79, 80, 81, 82, 89, 90, 91, 100, 124, 135, 136, 139, 161, 168
  agendas 78
  anti 4, 61, 69, 86, 88, 94, 100, 106, 107, 157
  contexts 94
  discourse 83
  domination 3
  encounters 18
  expansions 107
  influences/power(s) 4, 69, 83, 86, 144, 169
  legacies 77, 152
  narrative 101
  neo xviii, 58
  past 20
  reasoning 85
  rule 44, 86, 145
  surveillance 55
  undertones 4
colonialism 13, 19, 58, 77, 78, 79, 80, 86, 89, 94, 101, 129, 134
  historical contexts of 83
  impact of 49
  legacy(ies) of 77, 79, 81, 85, 89, 90, 168
  neo 49, 81
  post 82, 86
communism 126, 131, 137, 144
critical Islam 12, 13
cultural xv, xvii, xviii, 1, 2, 3, 9, 10, 28, 37, 57, 60, 61, 68, 69, 71, 82, 84, 92, 99, 100, 104, 108, 111, 117, 118, 120, 123, 129, 130, 139, 143, 144, 145, 149, 161, 181, 182
  appropriation 80
  assimilation 96
  baggage 13
  Christianity 35, 36, 38
  constraints 50
  diversity 29, 35
  essentialism 113, 159
  identity(ies) 7, 11, 20, 40, 72, 113, 132, 147
  influence 103
  Jew/Judaism 35, 38
  Muslim/Islam 14, 35, 37, 36, 38, 215
  narratives ix, 88
  norms 47, 87, 88, 95, 109, 110, 161
  relativism/relativist 18, 28, 32, 42, 43, 44, 45, 152, 164, 167, 168, 169, 170, 171, 172, 175
  turn 58

Dabashi, Hamid 3, 185, 188
Da'wa 108, 109, 115
Deeb, Lara 107, 116, 119
diversity xiv, 4, 5, 7, 9, 13, 16, 18, 20, 22, 23, 28, 29, 34, 36, 37, 39, 44, 45, 50, 60, 65, 72, 94, 103, 110, 118, 120, 128, 139, 145, 149, 150, 158, 162, 163, 164, 166, 170, 175, 178, 181
  cultural 35, 171, 172
  ideological xiv
  normative 13
  religious 128, 144

East(ern) ix, x, xii, 37, 78, 79, 80, 82, 85, 92, 118, 135, 136, 155
East/West binary 78, 79, 80, 82, 85, 90, 116, 135, 136
Egypt(ian) ix, x, xi, xii, xiii, xiv, 5, 32, 35, 45, 51, 54, 55, 60, 61, 64, 65, 71, 73, 79, 87, 104, 107, 109, 112, 119, 133, 139, 142, 157, 158
Egyptian feminist(s) xii, xvii, 2, 7, 52, 53, 62, 65, 69, 160
Eltahawy, Mona 2, 28, 31, 34, 37, 40
El Saadawi, Nawal xii, 6, 7, 33, 115, 160, 163
empowerment xiv, 6, 8, 11, 12, 50, 53, 54, 61, 70, 75, 87, 95, 96, 105, 111, 124, 137, 151, 155, 156, 175
enlightenment 12, 78, 86, 123, 125, 129, 182
  post 127
ethics 19, 42, 108, 110, 112, 124
essentialism 71, 82
  cultural 113, 159
Europe(an) xi, xii, xv, 2, 8, 12, 19, 20, 23, 33, 40, 43, 44, 54, 55, 66, 73, 78, 79, 80, 81, 84, 88, 91, 96, 106, 121, 125, 127, 130, 131, 137, 139, 141, 144, 152, 153, 163, 164, 168, 174, 179
everyday life 38, 107, 116, 118, 119, 146, 159
extremism 43, 165
  counter 14, 28
  ideological 4
  religious 7, 58, 97
  right-wing 166
  violent 14, 43

far-right 93, 96
  groups 91, 163
  organizations 8
  terrorism 171
female genital mutilation/FGM 11, 30, 43, 44, 56, 120, 161
Fernando, Mayanthi L. 73, 116
Foucault, Michel 99, 106, 124
France 17, 33, 34, 39, 40, 60, 70, 73, 90, 96, 97, 99, 126, 130, 132, 134, 135, 138, 146, 147, 171
France (French)-Algerian relations 98, 99

freedom(s) xiv, 13, 23, 24, 39, 40, 45, 47, 62, 84, 90, 91,107, 109, 113, 128, 130, 136, 138, 145, 146, 150, 154, 175
  of choice xi, 1, 34, 42, 63, 117, 134, 149, 182
  of expression 7, 46, 157, 173
  from 40, 108, 131
    negative 108
    positive 108
  to 40, 97, 131, 165
  of religion 2, 42, 108, 144, 182
  sexual 104, 137
  of speech x, 174; 22 -to 9
French 88, 99, 126, 130, 134, 164, 174
  academic landscape 78
  colonialism 86
  constitution 40
  Islam 7
  Muslim feminist 34
  orientalism 83
  Revolution 60
  secular model/secularism 39, 138
  secular feminist 56
  society 33, 73
fundamentalism 4, 90, 93
  Islamic/Muslim 38, 43, 44, 58, 73, 93, 97, 98, 164
  Jewish 164
  religious 6, 9, 21, 23, 24, 33, 132, 164, 172, 174, 179
fundamentalist(s) xi, xvi, xvii, 20, 21, 37, 39, 41, 46, 73, 90, 93, 142, 152, 161, 162, 163, 164, 165, 167, 180, 183
  absolutism 90
  activists 45
  agenda 92
  anti 42
  domination 100
  groups 44
  ideologies 63, 132
  Islam xv, 40, 63
  movements 1, 4, 19, 78, 90, 97, 127
  narratives 92

Gaza
  women in 119, 179, 180
gender(ed) 4, 15, 18, 27, 57, 58, 59, 60, 77, 83, 84, 85, 86, 89, 91, 95, 100, 104, 118, 134, 137, 174, 175, 179

agency 106
based violence 136, 157, 172
biases 92
consciousness 173
discrimination x, xii, 43
disparity(ies) 58, 61, 115, 138
division 34
discourse(s) 85
dynamics 27, 32, 70, 85, 87, 133
equality/inequality xi, xiv, 1, 2, 7, 8, 9, 10, 11, 19, 26, 31, 32, 44, 45, 46, 51, 56, 61, 65, 66, 67, 70, 73, 85, 91,96, 110, 123, 124, 125, 130, 133, 135, 136, 137, 138, 147, 149, 151, 155, 158, 164, 183
equity 70
gap 133
ideologies 64
issues 49, 63, 83
justice/injustice(s) 10, 11, 27, 60
minorities 157
narratives(s) 78, 87
norms 6, 96
oppression 30
orientalism 19, 78
performativity 111
policies 55, 156
politics/political discourse 4, 5, 31, 74
roles 70
relations 109, 137
research 54
scholarship/studies 16, 56, 83, 94, 107, 112
segregation 43, 45, 105, 165, 166
theory 134
globalization 16, 58, 97, 98, 100, 128, 175
Grewal, Kiran Kaur xviii, 5, 27, 40, 89, 168, 172, 176

Habermas, Jürgen 127, 128, 129, 140
headscarf 22, 24, 32, 34, 35, 38, 64
  affair/controversy 33, 136, 137, 138
  ban 130
Hélie-Lucas, Marieme 44, 56, 73, 74, 163, 167
hijab 21, 26, 32, 33, 34, 35, 94, 138, 151, 154, 170, 171, 173, 175
  anti 22
  ban 33, 174

Hirsi Ali, Ayaan 39, 40, 163
homogeneity 9, 36, 92, 137, 178
homogeneous 24, 85, 101, 113, 118, 138
homogenization 143, 163
Hudood Ordinances 64, 97, 156
human rights xi, xii, 6, 7, 8, 9, 11, 13, 18, 21, 25, 26, 30, 37, 38, 39, 42, 44, 46, 50, 56, 64, 77, 142, 150, 151, 152, 163, 164, 166, 167, 168, 171, 180
  abuse(s) 155, 160
  convention(s) 40
  discourse(s) 9
  frameworks 168, 172
  organizations xii, 158, 165, 166, 180, 182
  principles 1, 72
  violations/abuses 45, 71, 155, 157, 160, 168, 169, 172

identity xviii, 8, 14, 23, 29, 37, 39, 41,43, 67, 71, 74, 80, 94, 95, 99, 101, 108, 109, 111, 119, 127, 137, 165, 176, 183
  Christian 33, 130
  collective 86
  cultural 10, 11, 18, 40, 132, 147, 215
  ethnic 32
  false 37
  Jewish 37
  group/collective 25, 86, 177
  movements/ideologies 26, 44
  Muslim/Islamic 24, 31, 33, 36, 45, 64, 73, 106, 132, 134, 142, 161, 162, 165, 166
  politics 8, 23, 24, 26, 176, 182
  national 72, 85, 86, 87, 88, 99, 144
  religious 31, 45, 109, 118, 170
  women's 89, 106
immigrant(s) 33, 35, 39, 106
  communities 44
  Muslim 32, 39
  societies xvii, 95
  women 96, 135, 152
imperialism 10, 13, 60, 79, 80, 81, 82, 83, 85, 90, 97,100
  European 81
  French 86
  maternal 84
  neo xviii, 59, 84
  neo-liberal 159
  US 104, 115

western xvi, 57, 73, 104, 161, 169
imperialist(s) 17, 20, 25, 69, 74, 78, 89, 91, 93, 94, 97, 100, 104, 152, 159, 161, 168
  neo xviii
  western 3
India(n) 49, 51, 55, 60, 62, 78, 79, 83, 84, 86, 87, 88, 89, 90, 130, 144, 145, 146, 147, 148, 155
injustice(s) 26, 27, 59, 60, 77, 154, 178
Inspire UK 17, 28, 43, 45, 73, 165
instrumentalize/instrumentalization 2, 43, 45, 179
interpretation(s) xvi, 2, 9, 14, 17, 23, 24, 28, 36, 37, 39, 41, 57, 61, 68, 83, 92, 103, 108, 110, 119, 124, 129, 143, 147, 148, 150, 181
  cultural 170
  conservative xiii, 6
  fundamentalist 37, 45, 165
  liberal 12
  mis xi, 27, 67, 146
  misogynistic 66
  orientalist 117
  patriarchal 11, 36, 50, 67, 171
  re 1, 66, 99, 137, 139
  religious 139, 146, 179, 180, 182
  sexist 58
  western 140
intersectionality 15, 23, 25, 26, 30
Iran 7, 12, 21, 22, 45, 52, 60, 61, 62, 63, 64, 65, 72, 74, 139, 151, 153, 154, 155, 156, 159, 160, 170, 172, 173
Iranian 70
  feminists 63, 72, 182
  police xvi
  regime 22, 155
  revolution 63
  women 22, 59, 63, 65, 71, 153, 174
ISIS xiv, 4, 14, 43, 74, 131
  anti 73
Islamic Revolution 12, 61, 154
Islamist(s) xi, xiii, 1, 12, 13, 14, 32, 71, 82, 116, 117, 121, 139, 142, 143, 152, 158, 161, 165, 166, 174
  agenda(s) 2, 74, 166, 167, 170
  forces 65
  ideolog(ies) xii, 20, 52, 152
  groups 20, 77, 164

  influences 45
  movements 40, 43, 51, 64, 90, 118, 123
  narrative(s) 170
  organizations xiv
  politics 75, 104
  resurgence 34
  violence 45
  women 64, 72, 75
Islamophobia 4, 18, 21, 26, 33, 44, 45, 46, 94, 98, 104, 139, 164, 165, 166, 171, 174, 180
  gendered 92

justice xii, xiii, 25, 26, 45, 56, 65, 67, 151, 167, 172
  social xv, xvi, 4, 6, 7, 9, 11, 12, 58, 169, 172, 180, 182

Kandiyoti, Deniz x, 86, 114
Karam, Azza 9, 10, 42
Khan, Sara 28, 32, 34, 36, 37, 39, 41, 43, 44, 164, 167
Khan, Shāhnaz xv, xvi, 97, 161
Khalid, Maryam 78, 82, 84, 85, 89, 91
Khomeini, Ayatollah 139, 153

laïcité 39, 40, 126, 138
Liberal Islam 12, 13, 14
Lorde, Audre 26, 178

Mahmood, Saba 3, 19, 33, 104, 106, 107, 108, 109, 110, 111, 112, 113, 114, 115, 116, 117, 118, 119, 120, 179
Manji, Irshad 6, 22, 23, 37, 162
marginalization xi, xiv 10, 56, 74, 110, 134, 136, 140, 156, 159, 163, 173
Middle East(ern) ix, x, xii, xiii, xviii, 2, 28, 51, 64, 69, 85, 105, 106, 130, 158, 163, 179
migration 15, 42, 62, 128, 130, 149, 167
minority 4, 8, 19, 23, 25, 42, 44, 96, 124, 130, 134, 146, 147, 149, 159, 182
modernity 12, 14, 34, 51, 80, 85, 115, 116, 124, 125, 126, 128, 129, 130, 139, 142,144, 147, 182
Moghadam, Valentine 58, 68
Moghissi, Haideh 63, 66, 68, 71, 117
Mohammed, Yasmine 21, 22, 32

Mohanty, Chandra Talpade 15, 57, 69, 85, 90, 175, 177
mosque movement 104, 107, 108, 109, 110, 113, 115
Mouri and Batmanghelichi 71, 153, 159, 160
multiculturalism 23, 39, 43, 44, 162, 164
multicultural societies 19, 124, 145, 149, 182
Musawah 56, 67, 70
Muslimness 24, 38, 166

Namazie, Maryam 6, 24, 34, 40, 46, 163, 166
narrative(s) x, xv, xviii, xix, 16, 18, 24, 26, 27, 28, 39, 41, 47, 55, 59, 69, 72, 77, 80, 87, 88, 90, 91, 96, 97, 98, 99, 104, 115, 123, 124, 135, 137, 144, 149, 152, 153, 159, 160, 162, 163, 177, 179, 180, 181, 183
  academic 22
  autobiographical 6, 52
  binary 78
  civilizational 78
  colonizer's/colonial 86, 94, 101
  counter xvii, 17, 47, 48, 55
  cultural ix
  dominant xv, xvii, 47, 175, 176
  feminist 46
  fundamental(ist) 92, 93
  gendered 78
  historical 123, 133
  Islamic/Islamist 56, 170
  Islamophobic 73
  limiting 75, 93
  personal ix
  opposing 15
  oppressive xviii, 60
  orientalist xvii
  personal 73
  political 5
  prevailing 2, 5, 93, 124, 166
  religious 55
  rescue/savior narrative 19, 28, 78, 81, 93, 103
  secular 125
  self 17
  western 69, 77, 97, 116
narrative performance 48

narratives of liberation 92
nationalism 8, 41, 51, 55, 87, 88, 100
nationalist(s) 30, 41, 56, 61, 69
  agenda(s) xi, 87, 146, 157, 170
  approach 87
  discourses 71
  ideologies 87, 100
  movements 43, 55, 88, 89, 96
  project(s) 62, 86
  protests x
  sentiment(s) 23
National Secular Society 9, 45, 165
native informant ix, xvi, 2, 3, 20, 25, 72, 160, 161, 162, 163, 167
neoliberal(s) 96
  Capitalism 58
  economic strategies 97
  political agendas 96
neoliberalism 58, 114, 162
neo-orientalist 7, 73
niqāb 33, 171
nineteenth century 12, 52, 56, 60, 78, 84, 87, 126, 134, 153

One Million Signatures Campaign 154
oppression xi, xviii, 2, 6, 11,23, 26, 27, 30, 33, 50, 58, 59, 64, 66, 77, 86, 91, 92,94, 95, 103, 108, 115, 126, 143, 152, 153, 157, 159, 170, 171, 175, 177, 178, 180, 181
orient 78, 80, 81, 83
oriental 3, 80
orientalism xviii, 3, 19, 27, 78, 79, 80, 81, 83, 84, 85, 100
orientalist xvii, xviii, 4, 20, 27, 79
  discourse 91
  interpretations 117
  research 106
  stereotypes 92
Other xv, 30, 78, 79, 91, 93, 103, 113, 149, 163, 170
Othering xvii, 15, 86, 119
Otherness xv, xvi, 83

Pakistan 5, 32, 63, 64, 72, 75, 97, 103, 104, 155, 156, 157
Pakistani women 28, 83, 97, 157
patriarchal 2, 11, 27, 60, 67, 89, 91, 97, 98, 133, 139, 154, 158, 161, 170, 173, 179

bargain(s) x, 114
constraints x, 96, 117
cultures 78, 84, 96, 171
domination 88
ideologies 100, 120
interpretations 36, 50, 61, 171
norms 7, 58, 85, 109, 117, 118, 157
oppression 33
systems/structures 27, 28, 60,65, 70, 72, 109, 114, 115, 156, 163, 166
violence 167
patriarchy 3, 24, 33, 66, 68, 69, 74, 75, 85, 97, 89, 91, 94, 103, 114, 123, 133, 156, 170, 174
performative encounters 98, 99, 100
piety/pietist 19, 34, 104, 105, 107, 109, 111, 112, 114, 116, 117, 118, 119
positionality xvi, xvii, 18, 92
postcolonial 33, 41, 57, 58, 66, 68, 81, 86, 87, 88, 168, 175, 177
critique(s) 69, 105
feminism/feminists xvi, 2,3, 4, 5, 15, 27, 30, 31, 43, 55, 57, 69, 71, 73, 79, 81, 84, 86, 87, 88, 89, 94, 100, 135, 143, 161, 168, 183
feminist scholar(ship) xvii, xviii, 20, 57, 68, 73, 84, 85, 94, 107, 152
feminist studies 100
Muslim nations/states 55, 56, 85, 86, 87, 89, 100
subject xvi
theory 79, 106
postcolonialism 82, 86, 132
post-secular 103, 120, 145, 147
age 125
critique(s) 128
discourse 108
society 128
turn 19, 111
post-secularism 103, 128, 146
post-secularist scholarship/research 103, 104, 117
poststructuralism 115
poststructuralist feminist theory/feminism 108, 109, 113
Principled Distance 145

racialized xviii, 4, 58, 78, 81, 92, 95, 96, 137, 138

Rajeev Bhargava 144, 145, 147
reflexivity xviii, 16, 17
representation 17, 78, 79, 80, 83, 84, 94, 98
binary 69
mis 3, 27, 46, 58
under 135
research 15, 16, 17, 35, 36, 50, 54, 56, 66, 73, 79, 105, 106, 108, 109, 114, 117, 121, 133, 181
scarcity of 74
right-wing 146, 152
extremism 166
groups 152
ideologies 19
nationalist parties 96
politics 24
populism 23
Rosello, Mireille 98, 99, 100

Sadr, Shadi 7, 27, 160
Said, Edward 79, 80, 81, 82, 83, 84, 106
saving Muslim women 3, 19, 26, 69, 77, 78, 92, 95, 104
September 11 90, 130
Shaaraawi, Huda 53, 61
Shaikh, Sa'diyya 10, 26, 27, 29, 31, 58
Sharia xi, xii, 6, 24, 29, 34, 37, 38, 40, 45, 47, 61, 68, 140, 161, 166
social media 59, 60, 158
solidarit(ies) xvii, 4, 15, 16, 20, 25, 26, 40, 42, 57, 58, 60, 108, 149, 152, 153, 154, 155, 156, 160, 167, 169, 172, 173, 174, 175, 176, 177, 178, 179, 180, 182, 183
strategic 59
Southeast Asia 35, 51, 130
Southall Black Sisters 36, 45, 165
Soviet Union 126, 131
Spivak, Gayatri xv, 17, 72
subaltern 174
approaches 66
gendered agency 106
masses 55
secularism 42, 149, 182
woman 89
subjectivit(ies) 4, 92, 106, 107, 111, 112, 113, 114, 119, 120, 121, 175, 183

Taliban 16, 33, 77, 91, 93, 103, 151, 157
Tibi, Bassam 12, 13

Third world woman/women ix, 5, 15, 27, 30, 47, 77, 85, 89, 90, 94, 100
transnational 16, 31, 51, 57, 72, 177
  alliances 4
  approaches 16, 176
  communities 15
  connections 56, 58, 59
  feminism 15, 16, 30, 58, 60
  feminist methodologies 15
  feminist movements 60
  feminist networks 58
  feminist solidarity 175
  frameworks 16
  Muslim feminists 101
Turkey 33, 60, 61, 63, 64, 65, 72, 78, 97, 130, 133, 144
twentieth century 10, 12, 18, 31, 50, 51, 53, 54, 56, 74, 86, 90, 126, 130, 153, 157

universalizing 30, 129
universalism 15, 32, 152, 167, 168

voice(s) x, xvii, xviii, xix, 3, 6, 7, 11, 28, 30, 31, 49, 50, 54, 57, 58, 59, 60, 65, 66, 69, 73, 100, 101, 141, 152, 153, 158, 159, 161, 162, 163, 166, 169, 170, 172, 173, 174, 175, 176, 180, 183
  dominant 46
  feminist xix, 61, 74
  native 94
  women's 15, 23, 89
  secular 25, 164

Wadud, Amina 66, 67
Wallach Scott, Joan 115, 116, 125, 134
War on Terror 3, 8, 19, 22, 24, 26, 33, 45, 75, 77, 78, 81, 90, 91, 92, 93, 95, 101, 103, 104, 131
Westernized 23, 28, 63, 88
Women Living Under Muslim Laws 17, 56, 73

xenophobia 23, 90, 135, 174

Zia, Afia 5, 6, 13, 26, 31, 53, 55, 63, 66, 68, 70, 71, 75, 92, 103, 104, 118, 156, 159
Zina Laws xv, 97, 224
Zine, Jasmin 26, 55, 58, 92, 97, 162